Sidney Howard and Clare Eames

American Theater's Perfect Couple of the 1920s

ARTHUR GEWIRTZ

McFarland & Company, Inc., Publishers
Jefferson, North Carolina, and London

Materials from the Sidney Howard Collection are used with permission from the Bancroft Library at the University of California, Berkeley.

LIBRARY OF CONGRESS CATALOGUING-IN-PUBLICATION DATA

Gewirtz, Arthur.
    Sidney Howard and Clare Eames : American theater's perfect couple of the 1920s / Arthur Gewirtz.
        p.   cm.
    Includes bibliographical references and index.

    ISBN 0-7864-1751-X (softcover : 50# alkaline paper)

    1. Howard, Sidney Coe, 1891–1939. 2. Dramatists, American—20th century—Biography. 3. Theater—United States—History—20th century. 4. Authors' spouses—United States—Biography. 5. Married people—United States—Biography. 6. Actors—United States—Biography. 7. Eames, Clare, 1896–1930. I. Title.
PS3515.O847Z68   2004
812'.52—dc22   2003025330

British Library cataloguing data are available

©2004 Arthur Gewirtz. All rights reserved

No part of this book may be reproduced or transmitted in any form or by any means, electronic or mechanical, including photocopying or recording, or by any information storage and retrieval system, without permission in writing from the publisher.

Manufactured in the United States of America

Cover photograph: Steichen portrait of Clare Eames and Sidney Howard taken in early 1925 *(Courtesy of the Bancroft Library, University of California, Berkeley)*

McFarland & Company, Inc., Publishers
   Box 611, Jefferson, North Carolina 28640
       www.mcfarlandpub.com

In memory of my lovely wife, Dorothy, who from the beginning was with me in the adventure of this book and through its highs and lows provided help, fun, and love

Acknowledgments

First and foremost, I am indebted to Provost Herman Berliner of Hofstra University who had faith in this project and was instrumental in obtaining the leave of absence for me which permitted the work to get under way. I also thank the Board of Trustees of Hofstra University for granting the leave. I am grateful also to the Bancroft Library of the University of California, Berkeley, for permission to use materials from the Sidney Howard Collection.

A researcher must always rely on librarians. Here I thank particularly the librarians of Hofstra University; the Bancroft Library of the University of California, Berkeley; and the Library of Performing Arts of the New York Public Library for their unfailing kindness and courtesy.

The late Mrs. Jennifer Coleman, the daughter of Clare Eames and Sidney Howard, was able to read the first half of the manuscript before she died. Her enthusiasm for the book gave me deep pleasure and incentive to continue. Her cousins Mrs. Clare Le Corbeiller and Colonel Eames Yates provided me with materials and support for this project, for which I am grateful.

Many thanks to Meg McSweeney, who at the time I started this book was the assistant to the president of the American Academy of Dramatic Arts. She provided me with a good deal of information about the school and with the Jehlinger pamphlet quoted hereafter.

Professor James Kolb was an early reader of this manuscript and wisely offered a suggestion which changed its course. Naturally, no error can be attributed to him. Professor John DiGaetani read the manuscript twice and was enthusiastic each time. Professors Ruth Prigozy and Marion Ponsford were always supportive, as were my good friends Elaine Horn, Steve Krupa, and Gary Reisinger.

Special thanks go to Evelyn Johnson, without whom my life and my wife's could not have gone on. Matthew Sager knows how much I owe him. Daryl Johnson was also helpful, and of course my love always goes to my children, Elizabeth, Matthew, Joshua, and Rivka, for their constant love and support.

Contents

Acknowledgments vi
Preface 1
Introduction 5

1. Clare 9
2. *Annus Mirabilis* 1924: Clare 23
3. *Annus Mirabilis* 1924: Sidney 55
4. Sidney 65
5. Clare and Sidney 91
6. Clare in Hollywood: An Interlude 119
7. Consequences 149
8. Theatre Guild Year 176
9. Smash! 207
10. Divorce and Death 242
    Epilogue 274

Bibliography 283
Index 285

Preface

In the two decades following his death in 1939 Sidney Howard was very much alive in the worlds in which he had most recently worked, the theater and films. The third movie version of his 1924 play *They Knew What They Wanted* was released in 1940 starring Carole Lombard and Charles Laughton, directed by the latest boy genius, Garson Kanin. The same censorious hullabaloo that surrounded its first presentation on stage arose once more, this time provoking a change to the ending. The new ending stood a central Howard idea—that a sin need not be punished—on its head; in the film, punishment is indeed visited upon the adulterous heroine. Also in 1940 Howard received a posthumous Academy Award for the 1939 screenplay of *Gone with the Wind* even though several other writers had worked on the script. At the end of the decade *They Knew What They Wanted* again made theatrical news when Paul Muni, a major star of the period on stage and screen, revived it, taking the lead role. Between the book-ended presentations of the 1924 play came two other Howard dramas. Eva LeGallienne and Margaret Webster unsuccessfully attempted to resuscitate the flagging fortunes of their American Repertory Theater with *Yellow Jack*, Howard's 1934 adaptation of a chapter from Paul De Kruif's *Microbe Hunters*. The year 1946 brought the production of *Lute Song*, a collaborative update of a fourteenth-century Chinese play that Howard had completed in the late twenties with Will Irwin. Mary Martin and Yul Brynner played the top roles. Nevertheless, Robert Edmond Jones's set received more praise than the play; yet the drama compiled a run of 142 performances, a bit surprising for an exotic work completed some twenty years earlier and based on a play about five centuries old.

In the fifties Howard continued to hover over the theatrical landscape. Frank Loesser, showing again the rich dramatic vein of *They Knew What They Wanted*, transformed Howard's 1924 success into the musical hit *The Most Happy Fella*, which continued to be revived, not always successfully, into the 1990s. Also in the 1950s the Phoenix Theater opened its illustrious career by finally bringing to New York his posthumous fantasy, *Madam, Will You Walk?* a failure when tried out of town shortly after his death in 1939, with Jessica Tandy and Hume Cronyn in the leading roles. An engaging evening in the theater, it reminded audiences who could recall Howard's earlier work of what a thoughtful, provocative, delightful dramatist he could be. Finally, students in modern American drama courses knew of Sidney Howard because of his regular inclusion in their syllabi.

But in the tumultuous decades that commenced with the 1960s, theatrical fads and fashions altered. More influential than the maturely intelligent, sometimes over-subtle Sidney Howard, who worked in generally traditional forms, were the overt political preaching, proscenium-breaking "epic" dramas of Berthold Brecht, or the productions of the Living Theatre with audience participation occasionally veering into group grope. National and local government support of fringe and regional theaters allowed for a great variety of experimental forms and the growth of the performance artist who wrote and acted alone in his show. The theater had thus come a long way from that of Sidney Howard and of his contemporaries. When Howard together with S. N. Behrman, Robert E. Sherwood, Maxwell Anderson, and Elmer Rice formed the Playwrights Company in 1937–1938 to produce their own dramas, Laurence Langner of the Theatre Guild thought that they had thereby destroyed that group by robbing it of its most respected and popular dramatists. These men continued for a few years to produce successful plays. But their success did not continue for much beyond World War II; as far as posterity is concerned, Sidney Howard does not seem to have lost very much by dying early, for his colleagues' plays are revived almost as infrequently as his. Mounted, they are treated as musty work. Only Eugene O'Neill and George S. Kaufman seem to have survived the critical snubs accorded to that generation of playwrights.

Nevertheless these same social upheavals that separated Sidney Howard and his colleagues from the playwrights and their audiences in the latter part of the twentieth century made me think, after a while, of earlier American dramatists who had concentrated on relationships between the sexes and marriage and the family. I thought especially of Howard's most famous plays of the 1920s, *The Silver Cord* and *They Knew What They Wanted*, which, I believed, in appropriate courses could help students gain perspective on current attitudes toward the place of women in society and the concomitant position of the family. But little

literature was available to support the teaching of Howard's work; virtually nothing had been published about Howard since the early sixties except for Sidney Howard White's brief but trenchant survey of his career in the Twayne series (G. K. Hall, Boston, 1977).

It was in White's book that I found a reference to "the major depositary of Howard material in the Bancroft Library in the University of California at Berkeley." My interest piqued by this reference, I traveled to Berkeley to examine the material. I was not surprised to find Howard's letters lively, suffused with his energetic personality. Astonishing, however, were the letters of the virtually forgotten actress Clare Eames, his first wife, famous and respected in her time. Literate and literary, they were charged with her emotions, as though her pen were plugged into her soul.

Clare Eames and Sidney Howard were at the very heart of the movement to change the American theater from a mainly commercial enterprise to one that placed art at its center. Their letters told part of that movement's story from the point of view of two of its participants. I felt that a dual biography based on those letters would help illuminate and bring to vivid life the growth of the American theater in the pivotal decade of the 1920s. But there was more: Also unfolding in the letters was the tale of a passionate, glamorous, doomed romance. I found in Berkeley, then, the basis for a book that would recount in intimate detail the dramatic relationship of two individuals in love and at work.

My major research for the book was accomplished at the Bancroft Library and at Hofstra University, which possesses an extensive collection of theatrical materials going back to the early twentieth century. This volume relies mainly on these contemporary sources, partly by necessity and partly by choice. As I said earlier, there has been little commentary on either principal for several decades. More important, however, the letters and the crosscurrents of reports, drama reviews, observations, and gossip bring an immediacy both to the lives of these individuals and to the story of developing theater they influenced.

Sources are cited parenthetically within the text. Some names have been shortened or abbreviated as follows:

Sidney—Sidney Howard
Clare—Clare Eames
HH—Helen Howard, Sidney's mother
John—John Howard, Sidney's father

Jean—Mrs. Jean McDuffie, Sidney's sister
Elsie—Elizabeth Shepley Sergeant, Sidney's friend
HT—*The New York Herald Tribune*

Introduction

Clare Eames and Sidney Howard, actress and playwright, wife and husband, almost unknown today but prominent in the 1920s, significantly contributed to the American theater in the third decade of the previous century, when it seemed to burst forth into something rich and strange. Theater people arrived at the realization that in artistic productions resided the most interesting part of their profession and furthermore that such efforts could make money. Actually that change, or the general sense of it, came after some two decades of ferment from native and foreign influences and the intensely transforming experience of World War I.

Of course, the theater had always been commercial, thriving in the late nineteenth and early twentieth centuries on musicals, melodramas, light comedies, and farces. However, a variety of people, some critics, some professors, a handful of actors and actresses, a few newspapermen, some rich folk and many bohemians pushed art onto the stage. Their main vehicle, the small art theater, utilized as its staple the major European playwrights who developed in the late nineteenth and early twentieth centuries—Ibsen, Strindberg, Maeterlinck, for example—and the antirealistic New Stagecraft practiced by such men as the scenic designer Gordon Craig and the director Max Rheinhardt. The forces making for art in the theater became particularly intense in the second decade of the century only to be interrupted by World War I.

By its very nature, the art theater—its existence dependent on its resolve to bring onto the stage only plays that were beautiful and true—seemed created to lose money and to rely for its funding and sustenance on private support. After World War I, however, some art theaters determined to do battle with commercial producers. The Theatre Guild especially, transmuted more or less from the prewar Washington Square Players, flourished as an art theater on Broadway (although it sometimes approached the edge of extinction), successfully battling for the buck with commercial producers, thus proving that art could make money. Money-loving producers, perhaps following the lead of the Theatre Guild, perhaps sensing a fresh spirit in the air, increasingly moved into the presentation of artistic work, the new gravy train, although a bit cautiously. Actually, even before the twenties, some commercial producers, most prominently Arthur Hopkins, brought forth dramas with artistic aspirations.

Some began their post–World War I artistic experiments cautiously. John D. Williams, for example, originally presented Eugene O'Neill's first full-length Broadway play, *Beyond the Horizon*, early in 1920 for a series of special matinees. But no such timorousness prevented George C. Tyler from producing in 1921 and 1922 the first plays of George S. Kaufman and Marc Connelly, who though more attuned to the popular ear than, say, Eugene O'Neill, still showed a merry satiric sprit that might have frightened away both producers and widespread audiences just a short time before. Nor were the quintessentially commercial Shubert Brothers, the much-maligned William Brady, a firm called Stewart and French, Brock Pemberton, and Arthur Hopkins (who continued to show the courage of his high principles) afraid to produce the serious endeavors of Zona Gale, Elmer Rice, Sidney Howard, Rachel Crothers, Philip Barry, and Maxwell Anderson. Nor did the playwrights themselves have any intention of starving. Americans all, they wished to live the good life; no twenties version of Alphabet City for them. They desired to create a world of profit as well as of delight.

Sidney Howard, a Californian, came to the theater through George Pierce Baker's prestigious playwriting class at Harvard. At the university he met once again his fellow Bay area resident Samuel Hume, who in Italy had sat at the feet of Gordon Craig, a prophet of the New Stagecraft. Hume's views deeply influenced Howard, but their seeming preciousness also repelled him. Nevertheless, ideas from the New Stagecraft informed Howard's thinking about the theater for the rest of his career.

After obtaining his master's degree from Harvard in 1916, he joined the war as an ambulance driver, and then, after America entered the war, he distinguished himself as a heroic flying ace in France. Upon his arrival home he first gained fame as an investigative journalist, then achieved both fame and fortune as a playwright in 1924 with *They Knew What They Wanted* (the basis for Frank Loesser's musical *The Most Happy Fella*). Critics and the public thought it a breakthrough work, especially for its unusual view of the eternal love triangle. Against Maxwell Anderson and Laurence Stalling's *What Price Glory?* and Eugene O'Neill's

Desire under the Elms, it won the Pulitzer Prize. Two years later the Theatre Guild, criticized for its excessive attention to foreign plays, made Howard its "American" dramatist; for that company he wrote the successful *Ned McCobb's Daughter* and *The Silver Cord*. Less introspective and less of a loner than O'Neill, he became the voice of the American theater in its fight against the increasingly ugly face of censorship. Despite his high reputation as a dramatist and his leadership in the theatrical community, Howard for a variety of reasons has unfortunately faded into obscurity. Even many theater buffs have not heard of him.

If Howard is not much remembered today, his wife, Clare Eames, has virtually sunk into oblivion. An actress of a generation that produced some of the most accomplished and loved actresses in the history of the American stage, Eames was generally regarded as standing equally with Katherine Cornell, Helen Hayes, Lynn Fontanne and Eva Le Gallienne. Of these, only she and Le Gallienne had an idea of a great career for an actress. Only she, by 1925, before half the decade was over, played some of the major dramatic roles written for women. For her accomplishment in acting in new dramas as well as in old ones and for her intellect, the Theatre Guild awarded her the unique honor of serving on its board of directors and a top place in its newly formed repertory company, which included an array of the brightest young talents of the theater. But before long she fought with the guild, quit, acted in England, and died there at the age of 34 in 1930 while the other actresses mentioned above marched ahead to achieve fame and fortune in later decades.

Howard and Eames were a glamorous pair, an ideal couple, he a major dramatist, she a major star for whom he wrote plays. Even when his dramas were not intended for her, she worked on them with him. They were the perfect couple to everyone who knew them in the theatrical world of America and England. But the marriage split.

Their story, told in this book in large part through their letters, also includes some account of the theater in which they worked. Their tale is particularly of two highly talented people who loved each other, seemed perfectly suited for each other, were the admired couple in the theater, and yet broke apart to their mutual unhappiness.

Clare's death in 1930 brings the book to a conclusion. Sidney lived for another nine years, and his life and work changed considerably with the Great Depression, as did the American theater. But Clare Eames and Sidney Howard helped shape a decade in the theater that pivotally and decisively influenced its artistic aims and its idealism for the remainder of the twentieth century.

1

Clare

Clare Eames invited Margalo Gillmore, her fellow student at the American Academy of Dramatic Arts, to have coffee with her one Sunday noon in 1917. "When I arrived, Clare Eames was lying in bed, drinking her coffee, reading *The New York Times* and smoking a cigarette. Maybe my eyes widened at the cigarette; she put it out. 'I always like a little driggie-draggie with my coffee.' I sat mute before the world of sophistication." Clare informs Margalo that she read through *The New York Times* daily. The sophisticate continues, "Do you know my Auntie Emma? ... she's a bitch." Auntie Emma was Emma Eames, one of the great Metropolitan Opera sopranos of her day. But the epithet was not applied because Mme. Eames had done something harmful to Clare in a personal way; it was, rather, because Mme. Eames had always hated Mary Garden. She had told Clare "never to hear her sing as Garden was a poor artist." Clare then "swooned back on her pillow and clapped her hand to her face. For a moment I thought she had fainted but she sprang up." Clare had heard Garden on the previous night in *Pelleas and Melisande,* and she was "Great! Great! Great!" Clare shouted at the top of her lungs. "I could kill Auntie Emma, to rob me of all those wonderful performances. That's what I call a bitch."

After coffee Clare asked, "What are your plans for the theater?" Margalo, coming from a hardworking actor's family, thought that her main aim was only getting a job in the theater. But Clare, without waiting for a reply, continued, "I shall play Queen Elizabeth, Lady Macbeth and all of Ibsen. I see you as Rosalind, Ophelia and Juliet. There's no use in being an actress if you don't embrace the best it has to offer—even if you fall flat on your face" (Gillmore, 119–123).

Clare took Margalo to lunch at the Plaza, in return for which Margalo's mother asked Clare to Sunday dinner. Charles Jehlinger, known as Jelly to his students at the Academy, escorted Clare. Margalo was uncertain as to whether or not her family would like her friend, for the Gillmores were down-to-earth working people, actors though they were, and Clare was an exotic. At first Margalo's anxiety seemed to be justified, "for as Dad was carving, Clare turned to him and said, 'I expect you are familiar with the complete works of Lope de Vega and the golden age of Spanish literature.' This drew a complete blank from everyone." After a silent moment she discretely broached another subject, asking Gillmore to name his favorite Shakespearean role; Shakespeare being a subject dear to his heart, the air became considerably happier.

"After dinner Clare gave a description of some nun she had seen praying in Paris. She flung herself face down on the floor and crawled all over the carpet murmuring Latin prayers. I wondered how the family was taking it, but they seemed very interested. She told Mr. Gillmore how enthusiastic she was about the newly formed Equity (the actors' union) and added, 'It's been my lifelong dream to have the privilege of meeting the best in the theater—thank you.' And she made a low curtsy before my father. I was afraid she had gone too far, but Dad looked decidedly pleased as Clare swept down the hall, followed by Jelly, who was even going so far as to take her home in a taxi."

Exotic though she was, Clare was born in West Hartford, Connecticut, on August 5th, 1896, and at the age of eleven went to Cleveland when her family moved there. Clare later remembered that as a child she was "often sick abed, but I was happy because (my mother and father) were determined that I should be, whether sick or well. And they gave me things to make my mind grow." Like many children who are sickly, Clare seems to have become fond of that condition. She refers to the "rare occasions" when she is "exceedingly, grandly well." She "does her best work when she is just a little ill." Her parents' luxuriant attentions during her enforced times in bed undoubtedly encouraged recurrent illness and made that condition the customary, comfortable state for her. That special attention surely encouraged in her also a sense of her own uniqueness, perhaps even of grandeur. A childhood friend (who wished to remain anonymous) of Clare's sister Haydie recalls that as an adolescent Clare acted above the other children, as though she were a queen. Although one readily sees the spoiled child in Clare, the regal quality, which critics quickly noticed in her acting seems also to have been inbred early. She was already on the road to exoticism. Perhaps more significantly, her parents gave her "things to make my mind grow" (G.P., *HT,* January 10th, 1926). We do not know the exact nature of these objects, but books surely claimed a large place among them. In an age unmarred by television, without even the radio, books proved a prime source of distraction and comfort for the many children who seem to have been ill in the Victorian or post–Victorian eras. These periods of illness, with plenty of time for reading, were certainly a resource for the well-stocked mind that everyone was to observe in Clare. But beyond that, the many hours in which she was left alone surely helped to lead her to a life of the mind, that is, an examined life. With all her gaiety there was an essential seriousness of purpose about her life that formed its very texture. Although in her youth she was certainly self-absorbed, she was also engaged in the process of becoming an intelligent and thoughtful human being.

To that end and to the undoubtedly unintended end of making her an exotic, "a cuckoo" as she later termed herself, her solicitous parents sent Clare at the age of sixteen to Paris to complete her education and live with Emma Eames. She "there met the celebrities of the artistic, musical, literary, and social worlds" (*HT,* November 9th, 1930). In Emma Eames's memoir of her youth and her professional years, *Some Memories and Reflections,* the singer informs us that she had a (nonsexual) friendship with the Prince of Wales (later Edward VII), "which was one of the most deeply treasured of my life" (95), that Henry James took her to her first production of *Hedda Gabler* (77), and that one summer, when she was "unable to leave Paris," Salvini, the great Italian actor famous for his Othello, remembered her birthday and wrote her a note for the occasion (163).

Although these great personalities were no longer about during Clare's stay at her aunt's, similar figures certainly appeared in the rooms of Emma Eames, who was "adored in the Place de l'Opéra, and received in the most exclusive French salons." Much of Clare Eames's self-assurance undoubtedly stems from her having listened to and spoken with these social and artistic giants (*HT,* November 19th, 1930). Against the background of such conversations Emma Eames taught her niece to "appreciate beauty and historical association and the play of ideas." Artistic stirrings quickened during her stay in Paris. For a time she studied painting, but Mme. Eames insisted that Clare study for the stage.

When she returned to Cleveland, she must have been very different from the adolescent who left. She spoke French fluently and perhaps startled the natives when she interspersed her English conversation with French phrases. She had spoken with important men and women of her aunt's several worlds. She knew a good deal about music, painting, and acting—we may say *a good deal* because the character of her aunt suggests demanding supervision. Clare had been truly "finished" in Paris. That her aunt's supervision would seem demanding and that Mme. Eames might well have acted as a model for the Clare who was dedicated to her career shows in the singer's opening sentence of her memoir:

"Great fixity of purpose, absolute absorption in the task in hand, and a complete obsession concerning the duty to be accomplished, have been the fundamental laws governing my career and life."

From such an example of devotion to art and the "task in hand" Clare learned much. But she had to be ready to absorb the lessons.

We saw that Clare's parents encouraged her intellectual development, but they would have had to encourage as well her expectation and desire to work hard in life. Emma Eames writes in her book: "Brought up as I was in the most Puritanical surroundings and nourished on Bible texts that were impressed upon me by my Grandmother as being absolute working possibilities, my creed became: 'Whatever thy hand findeth to do, do it with all thy might'—the unyielding command of that grim old preacher, Ecclesiastes" (1).

Emma Eames was the younger sister of Clare's father, Hayden. Although the two children were separated for much of their youth, both were born in Shanghai, to which their family, originally from Maine, brought their New England morality. Surely Hayden as much as Emma met with similarly harsh teaching of puritan habits and brought them into the household he created with his wife.

The family was certainly highly respectable and carried with it a sense of its place in the community. Clare's mother, Clare Hamilton, like her husband, came from New England stock, but the family had moved south, where her father was to become governor of Maryland. Her husband, Hayden, seems to have led an exemplary life. He attended Annapolis, after which he spent sixteen years in the navy. During World War I he was "called to Washington to take charge of the manufacture of small arms and ammunition, and later of machine guns, for the Ordnance Department of the United States Army, whence his commissions as Colonel," a title by which he was known for the rest of his life (*Cleveland Press*, November 25th, 38). The couple had four children, two girls besides Clare, Haydie and Julia (who was retarded and died in 1926), and one son, Hamilton, known as Bud. Mrs. Eames seems to have been a devoted mother. After Clare's death she remained perhaps excessively loyal to Clare's memory. Clare's daughter, Jennifer Coleman, remembered that Mrs. Eames turned her Cleveland house into a kind of museum for Clare. When her granddaughter visited, the "fat old lady" led the little girl around from exhibit to exhibit. This may have been a ghoulish trial for the child, but it may well show the depth of healthy love that was once there.

Soon after Clare returned to Cleveland from Paris she appeared in the first live-performance production, on May 31st and June 1st 1916, at the newly founded Cleveland Play House. Organized by young Clevelanders (including the lawyer Ernest Angell, who was to play an important part in the lives of Clare Eames and Sidney Howard) interested in the theater but bored by the usual commercial fare, the play house was a manifestation of a spirit stirring in the United States, one of ten art houses established in various parts of the country in 1915 and 1916.

The founders of the Cleveland Theater, like their counterparts elsewhere, amateurs all, became the actors, set designers, costumers, builders of sets. However, although their experience made them amateurs, their thinking derived from professional sources. Raymond O'Neill, the drama and music critic for *The Cleveland Leader* and the Play House's first director, had been to Europe and fallen under the influence of Gordon Craig, another strong proponent of the New Stagecraft (Flory, 53ff).

Clare Eames, after her European experience, would certainly have found this atmosphere electric with the talk of new European ideas, attractive and familiar; so too the work of August Strindberg, a great favorite in American art theaters, well known in European literary and theatrical circles, and the author of the first play performed by the Play House. The drama, in which Clare played a lead, was called "Motherlove, an Act." Concerned with a mother's destructive effect on her daughter and the hatred of women for men with a touch of lesbianism thrown in, its emotions displayed the familiar Strindbergian concoction of fear, selfishness, jealousy, and hatred, strong stuff for Cleveland in 1916, but a success nevertheless. However, Clare never acted with the Cleveland Play House again although it went on to become one of the most successful and admired of the country's art theaters and the only one to exist from that period until this day.

Clare, of course, aimed higher than a regional theater. By the time she applied for admission to the American Academy of Dramatic Arts, she had already studied with Mrs. LeMoyne, a distinguished actress who had performed in serious works. Perhaps Clare now felt that she needed a more thorough training than Mrs. LeMoyne's and therefore auditioned with the Academy on December 16th, 1916.

Her auditioning form incorrectly gives her age as 22, her height as tall, her weight as 128, her coloring as "blondy." Next to "Proportions" the auditioner wrote, "like her aunt." All pictures of Clare show her to be slim as a reed except her early photographs, which suggest that in her youth she had some baby fat that disappeared with maturity. Her auditioning chart shows still another association with her aunt. Next to "Stage Presence" is written "Good" with an arrow pointing to "like her Aunt" and in parenthesis next to "good" is "Distinction." In the first years of her career Clare could barely be mentioned without a reference to her aunt.

For her audition she did a piece from the Oscar Wilde character Lady Windermere and another whose name is illegible. Her reading was "good mentally and forcefully," her spontaneity "fair," her distinction "good," her pantomime "fair," her dramatic instinct "fair," her intelligence "very good," and her imagination "good." Most interesting are the lower determination for "spontaneity" and the higher one for "intelligence."

Many critics in her early years regularly and negatively saw Clare as possessing a strong intellect that etched her interpretations, which were diminished in their effect by a lack of passion. Other critics saw instead a gleaming flame through the ice. These became the regular critical attack and defense. But now her audition report was labeled "acceptable."

Although Franklin Haven Sergeant was the head of the school, Charles Jehlinger was the director of instruction. He encouraged a method of preparation for a role that alumni thought to be similar to Stanislavsky's. Unlike Stanislavsky, Jehlinger never wrote a book developing his system, but Eleanor Cody Gould, one of Jehlinger's students in 1918 and 1919, transcribed verbatim notes in her student days and returned at various times to do the same. These were published as a pamphlet by the academy in 1968. Her last notes are from 1951. Although Jehlinger's view of acting does not seem to have changed a great deal over the years, we refer only to the notes from the early period because those are close enough to the dates of Clare's stay at the academy to be valid for her.

Because this pamphlet is not a systematized account of Jehlinger's teaching, we cannot be sure how close to Stanislavsky his teaching was, and certainly, since the interpretations of Stanislavsky, especially in the United States, have seethed with controversy, we cannot be sure of what Stanislavsky meant. Yet some ideas are clear in Stanislavsky, and Jehlinger's most important sayings seem indeed to imply similar thoughts about the preparation for a role.

For example, Jehlinger said, "Every character has a heart, brain, and soul. You are the servant of the character; the character is not your servant" (1); "Language is thoughts, not words" (7); "You do not *live* with your characters enough. You must live with them, study their attitude towards the various other characters in the play, their habit of thinking and living" (4); "Get the *fundamentals* of your character" (10); "Establish the age of your character, his nationality, profession, social standing, temperament; his physical, emotional and mental qualities" (11). All of these imply working through a character from the inside out, getting inside his skin, thinking from the character's point of view. Jehlinger's remarks seem very close to the Stanislavskian idea of finding the "spine" of a character, that is, the character's basic aim in terms of the drama.

Sometimes Jehlinger states his thoughts in especially strong terms, denouncing the understandable fear in allowing a character to overtake the actor's own personality. "The secret of the whole thing is this: Yield to the character and let it take control of affairs.... Above all, *do not direct your character*" (6). "It is better to be crude by overdoing than to be negative. Obey your impulses at any cost. Don't fear mistakes. Be fearless! Yield! Obey!" (7) Again, "Trying to avoid making mistakes is the biggest mistake you can make. Don't be afraid" (11).

Certain precepts are surely different from Stanislavsky's dictates: "You are much nicer as a woman than as an actor. Why do you make your character so unpleasant? Never get cross unless you are playing a silly child. Let emotions be beautifully expressed. Never let ugliness creep in unless it has to.... Your eyes are the windows of your soul. Keep your head up and your eyes open, don't pull down the shades so the audience can't look in" (8). "*As a rule, dress comedy in light colors*" (10). Despite Jehlinger's insistence that his students prepare their roles in an organic rather than mechanical fashion, these maxims seem to go by the numbers. But the general thrust of his teaching is clearly in the creation, from moment to moment, of a whole character that derives from a thorough study and understanding of its general and specific aims and habits.

Of course, we do not know exactly what Clare derived from Jehlinger. She took his teaching very seriously, seemed to be his favorite student at the time, and apparently followed his instructions more attentively than anyone in the school. Undoubtedly, Jehlinger enforced the character trait of fearlessness, which marked her career, her seeming indifference to making mistakes as she created a character. Like all great artists, she worked like a dog at her job, taking seriously Jehlinger's injunction, if she needed it at all: "The capacity to take infinite pains is the most intelligent definition of genius" (9).

But Margalo Gillmore talks of Clare's apparently innate ability. "I suppose in every acting school there is always one student who seems to be a born professional and never puts a foot wrong, who is free from the struggle and awkwardness that beset others. In our school it was Clare Eames" (118). Margalo then goes on to describe Clare's appearance: "Although she was only a little older than I, there was nothing young or even pretty about Clare. Her skin was taut on her delicate bones and her aquiline nose gave her face an austere appearance. It was her smile that softened it into warmth and charm" (119).

At graduation Clare asked her entire class, twenty-eight, and Margalo to a party. Each guest was to bring his favorite food so that all could share each other's "special tastes." Clare received her guests in a pale green Fortuny tea gown, the first that Margalo seen. Among the goodies were caviar (Clare's contribution), anchovy paste, maraschino cherries, sardines, ice cream fudge, pate de foie gras. Finally, Clare offered a toast—with ginger ale. "'To my class, and the rules of Jelly. May we never transgress them.'" Margalo adds, "The party would have been a glorious success if we hadn't all been taken violently ill" (123–24).

Margalo Gillmore shows Clare to be a woman with joyful high spirits, eager to taste of the goods of life, intellectual, emotional, even spiritual in her high aspiration. Pretentious she is, egotistical, self-dramatizing, eager to play the one-upmanship game. Yet her ambition seems true, her literary background real, and in Charles Jehlinger she appears to have found a mentor whose method gave her a way into roles. "She was the only one that Jelly never yelled at," writes Margalo, indicating certainly that Clare not only appreciated his method but was adept at it, surely because she worked hard to acquire its process (119).

Clare Eames's ambition loomed large. She started young, wanting to play major roles in dramatic literature. She may have been something of a show-off about it, but she truly aimed high. The other young actresses of her generation, the ones who like Clare rose in the twenties but who lived on to hit their peak in the thirties, seem to have stumbled into serious acting. That is, they became artists because the American theater was becoming serious, not because they were initially serious.

Lynn Fontanne, for example, was an immensely hardworking actress who almost accidentally came to the Theatre Guild, then later chose to be associated with the guild where she was paid less than she could get elsewhere because she could work in fine plays there. She acted in Shaw and in the work of such first-rate American dramatists as Robert Sherwood and Maxwell Anderson; she created the part of Nina Leeds in O'Neill's *Strange Interlude*. But she seems never to have had the desire to measure herself against the great actresses of the past in the major roles of dramatic literature. There was no Lady Macbeth, no Millamant in Congreve's *Way of the World*, no Rebecca West in Ibsen's *Rosmersholm*. The only Shakespearean heroine she ever played was Katherine in *The Taming of the Shrew* in the thirties. When Alfred Lunt, later in his career, was asked why the couple had not appeared more frequently in Shakespeare, he replied that American actors "should leave Shakespeare's tragedies to the British. Only they can do justice to him. We are good in the comedies, but not *yet* the tragedies" (Brown, 191–92). There are obvious flaws in that argument. But accepting the argument for the moment, the Lunts not only withheld their talents from Shakespearean tragedy, but they also failed to do every Shakespeare comedy but one, as well as other comic classics, with which English dramatic literature abounds. Not only does their comic career lack Shakespeare and Congreve but Sheridan and Wilde as well. Their interest seems simply to have been lacking. With all the grit and effort they put forth in their roles, a certain largeness of ambition escaped them.

We can say the same of Katharine Cornell and Helen Hayes. They played some memorable roles in the twenties. For instance, Hayes illuminated Kaufman and Connelly's second comedy, *To the Ladies*, and played a much-admired Maggie Wylie in James Barrie's *What Every Woman Knows*. Cornell, to much applause, acted the title role in Shaw's *Candida* (prompted to it by Clare Eames) and seemed to catch some of the spirit of the time as Iris March in Michael Arlen's *The Green Hat*. After they became reigning stars, they acted some of the great parts, but it seems they did them because the theater world now expected them to do so. They did not early in their careers evince great ambition to develop the prize roles in the history of dramatic literature. Although we now think of them as great actresses, and they were, they lacked a powerful drive to form a great career by playing the magnificent parts in the grand tradition of their art.

Only one other actress of Clare's age and status seems to have approached her profession in the same way as Clare: Eva Le Gallienne. In *With a Quiet Heart*, her second autobiographical work, she, like Clare, makes a list of parts she hoped to play in the course of her career: Hilda Wangel in *The Master Builder*, the title roles in *Hedda Gabler* and *Peter Pan*, Juliet in *Romeo and Juliet*, Marguerite Gautier in *Camille*, the Duc de Reichstadt in *L'Aiglon*, Hamlet in *Hamlet*. We do not know at what age Clare first made out her list. Eva Le Gallienne was sixteen, and she had just started working in the theater, but the idea was the same, to make acting a significant career, not simply a job, to make it expand the mind and the soul, to reach into the depths of the human spirit. Otherwise there was no point in being an actor. To play in all of Ibsen, as Clare wished to do, seems foolishly, ostentatiously vague. Le Gallienne in her specificity, though presenting a "by no means modest list," appears to be much more realistic. Yet Clare was as serious as Le Gallienne, and both went about their business of working out their plans, Le Gallienne more systematically by the founding of the Civic Repertory Theatre, where she could act all the roles she wished to play (103).

Clare less systematically nevertheless carried out her aims. Before she left for England in 1927 she had played Queen Elizabeth twice and Mary Queen of Scots as well, Lady Macbeth, and two major Ibsen roles. She did these parts because, though she may have been fearful of ridicule, she nevertheless followed her ostentatious little list. A few years after Clare's death at the age of thirty-four, Eva Le Gallienne, who acted with Clare in two matinees of a Maeterlinck play and saw her as Lady Macbeth and Hedda Gabler, wrote: "...[H]ad she lived I am convinced she would have been the greatest actress of our time. Her death was an irreparable loss to the American theater" (*At 33*, 152–53). Le Gallienne surely understood Clare's high aims as well as her achievements.

Perhaps she also had a good sense of what Clare might have accomplished.

At the academy Clare, for no known reason, did not act in any of the school's public performances except her class graduation play, "La Souveraine," a Belgian drama by Gustave Vanzype. The leading New York newspapers regularly reviewed such exercises, and in *The Leader* (undated) we find a kind of synthesis of the show's reviews:

> The closing performance by the American Academy of Dramatic Art took place at the Lyceum Theater Friday afternoon, when interest centered around Claire [sic] Eames, niece of the well-known American singer, Emma Eames. Tall, with the distinguished presence and classic features of her aunt, Miss Eames showed many qualities which should win for her a prominent position on the stage. She is to the manner born and has extraordinary poise and composure, so much indeed that at first she gave the impression of being cold. Miss Eames has, however, reserve force and a powerful inner fire which smoulders and bursts into brilliant flame, added to which is the splendid technical equipment she has gained at the institution from which she has just been graduated. This warmth of temperament is sufficient to protect her work from being marred by cold intellectuality. Gifted, as she is, she may become as dominating a figure in the theater as her aunt was in the operatic world.

With such applause ringing in her ears Clare Eames went out to fulfill her promise.

"When Clare Eames graduated from the Academy, she accepted her diploma with the cool assurance that she would walk from that platform to the stage door of a Broadway theater. Which she did" (Gillmore, 123). Not exactly. But within a month of her graduation she was indeed on a professional stage, that of the Greenwich Village Theater, and in three years she had the leading role in a major production on Broadway.

The Greenwich Village Theater, with 299 seats, located at Sheridan Square, housed the aptly named Greenwich Village Players. They opened on November 15th, 1917 with the aim, usual for an art theater, that it would not "be handicapped ... by traditions or customs, that it will be free to produce plays of any length and of any sort" (*New York Times*, November 16th, 1917, 9). The actors were a "company of professionals who are on the stage for the love of the stage" (*New York Times*, November 18th, 1917, VIII, 5) but they lasted for only a season. It was with them that Clare Eames made her professional debut.

In the usual fashion of art theaters the Greenwich Village Players opened with three one-acters, among which was "The Big Scene," by a favorite dramatist of these ambitious groups, the Austrian Arthur Schnitzler. Clare had an important part in "The Big Scene," and in her first professional "go" in New York, she managed to snag a favorable review from the prominent Heywood Broun in the *Tribune*: "It has never been our good fortune to be particularly sagacious in picking out the stars of future seasons, but we are willing to risk another prediction. Never before were we so sure. The name, you may remember, is Clare Eames" (November 18th, 1917).

Earlier in the review he wrote:

> [S]he gives a performance in the Schnitzler play which is delightful. She has no excessive charm, nor is she particularly personable, but she brings subtlety to the interpretation of her role, and the quality is so rare on the stage that it is not to be observed more than two or three times in a season.

Clare probably failed to be entirely entranced with all of Broun's remarks, but the critic tries to ameliorate his negative observations.

> If a young woman aims high it is well that she should not be too dazzling. Of the great ladies of the stage almost none are beautiful. One or two are downright homely. However, it would be misleading, as well as ungallant, to pursue this phase further.... Miss Eames can think, or, at any rate, give the impression that mental processes are going on, without knitting her brows or resting her chin in her hand or staring at the audience, or any of those things.

Clare seems to have learned Jehlinger's lesson early and well.

Although also noticed by Arthur Hornblow in *Theatre Magazine*—"The best acting was done by Clare Eames, a recent dramatic school graduate" (June 1918, 356)—these favorable reviews did not help her immediately to land a fat part. In the next season she was cast in a small unnoticed role, that of Queen Elizabeth, the first of her queens, in a patriotic pageant, *Freedom*. In the 1919–20 season she does better, for she is cast in a minor role in one of Ethel Barrymore's great triumphs, Zoe Akins's *Declassé*, and is reviewed briefly but favorably by both the *Times* and *Tribune* (November 17th, 1919).

But in the 1920–1921 season her career begins to assume important proportions. In November, as the Princess Elizabeth who will become the great monarch, she again supports a major star, William Faversham, in *The Prince and the Pauper*. Her vivid acting in that part inspired such a description as that by Arthur Hornblow in *Theatre Magazine*:

> The absurdity of the star system was never more strikingly demonstrated than on the first night of 'The Prince and the Pauper,' when Miss Clare Eames—seen only once before on Broadway, in a small part in 'Declassé'—won hands down the honors and applause which, by all laws and customs of the theatre, are reserved for the star.

Miss Eames has only a small part—that of the Princess Elizabeth, sister of Edward VI, but she played it with consummate artistry. Admirably 'made up,' with flaming red hair, and historically correct as to a costume and manner, she looked a Holbein canvas descended from its frame. The traditional mannerisms and traits of England's Virgin Queen—her shrewish irascibility, quick wit, strong imperious will, her flashes of passionate ardor, her ambition, hates, her regal bearing, gestures, intonations—all are sketched with such authority, *finesse* and sureness of touch, that I sat back and gasped: "There's an actress!" [January 1921, 31].

Playing of this sort clearly stimulated the producers of John Drinkwater's *Mary Stuart* to cast Clare in the title role, that of another Anglo-Saxon Renaissance queen, thus providing her big break.

John Drinkwater, a poet and a product of the Manchester Repertory, another art company, had written *Abraham Lincoln*, a critical success in Manchester, London, and New York. He now turned to one of the great romantic figures in British royal history, Mary Queen of Scots (Strauss, 142–47). Because of Drinkwater's previous success, his new drama was treated as an event. Thus, when Clare Eames received the lead, top-cast in a major production of a drama by a widely respected playwright, it was also a signal occasion in her career. She came through with colors mostly flying. Although she received some negative criticism, New York was aware that it now had a major new star.

Edmund Wilson's strikingly written review in *The New Republic* reflects the general critical attitude toward both the play and its leading actress:

> The great thing about John Drinkwater's Lincoln was that, unlike most historical plays, it dramatized an idea.... And the fiction inspired by Lincoln ... suffered especially from this deficiency: it had concerned itself mainly with the high hat, the homely manner and the kind deed. What Mr. Drinkwater dramatized for the first time was the idea of not taking vengeance on your enemies....
>
> The same thing is true of Mary Stuart, which has just been put on at the Ritz Theatre. In this case, the idea is that of the 'great lover,' the woman whose capacity for love is so great that she can love several men at a time and whose tragedy is that she finds about her no one worthy of her love; and Mr. Drinkwater has made of it an intelligent and interesting play. But it is not the great play it might be: the tragedy of a superwoman condemned to inferior men....
>
> Miss Clare Eames, as Mary Stuart, is, I am sure, one of the most convincing queens ever seen on any stage; she looks as if she had been painted by Holbein. She has the dignity and sculptural beauty of royalty, and not a little of its smooth coldness. She is perfect in all the scenes which require poise and authority..., but Mary Stuart, as described in the play, she certainly is not. In the first place, it is impossible to imagine that she has

lived a long time in France; there is nothing French about Miss Eames, she has very little lightness and gaiety. And she is never really passionate or bitter; she gives no sign of the smoldering emotions which are supposed to be consuming her; ... When she gives herself up to Bothwell's embrace, you feel that something shocking has happened, as if you were a schoolboy looking in at the Superintendent kissing Teacher [April 6th, 1921, 162–63].

Left to right: Charles Waldron, Clare Eames, Frank Reicher in John Drinkwater's *Mary Stuart*.

Except for Wilson's remark about Clare's inability to indicate Mary's French upbringing, the reviewer's attitude toward Clare in the role is very much that of most of his fellows: regal, she is, beautiful, Holbein like, but passionless. But Arthur Hornblow in *Theatre Magazine* supplies the standard response of Clare's defenders:

> Some reviewers have brought against this actress the grave charge that she is cold in the passionate scene with Bothwell, forgetting that a queen does not throw herself incontinently about like a wanton. There is, perhaps, a certain haughty reserve—her aunt, Emma Eames, has it in even greater degree—but it does not necessarily imply lack of temperament. Beware of smoldering fires! [April 6th, 1921, 46].

Whether or not she was ice or smoldering fire, she achieved great personal success. Alexander Woollcott's initial write-up in the *Times* reports that the author's "first audience ... stayed at the last to beat a few palms for Mr. Drinkwater, but more especially to boom a very hearty tribute of admiration for ... Clare Eames" (March 22nd, 1921, 15). In his Sunday article he tells us that "all the town is bowing prettily to the regal quality of the new Mary Stuart" (April 3rd, 1921, viii, 4). But he regales his readers with word of "an official biography of Miss Eames issued from the office of her manager and containing this pure gem: 'She steps out of the Social Register, if you please, for Miss Eames has genuine social position in Cleveland, her home city.' Dear, dear! Straight from Euclid Avenue to the throne." Clare has both an official biography and satiric thrust at it; not yet a star, she now has the trappings of one.

2

Annus Mirabilis 1924: Clare

In the summer of 1923, when Eugene O'Neill, the foremost young dramatist of the time, Robert Edmond Jones, the foremost young stage designer of the time, and Kenneth Macgowan, a leading avant-garde critic, were mulling over their ideas for an art theater to succeed the shuttered Provincetown Playhouse, O'Neill wrote to Macgowan that he had a "hunch for your Senate of this theatre.... Two actors, one actress, Clare Eames (?) (Don't know her or work. Take her on what I've heard—woman with brains and imagination)" (Bayer, 37–38).

These four personalities were to stimulate the American theater in this fertile decade of the twenties. In fact, they had already done so. O'Neill, developing as the Provincetown Playhouse developed, had also been an artistic success and influence on Broadway. Designer Robert Edmond Jones brought to the new little-theater enterprise a major commercial reputation. He had been to Europe to learn from Max Rheinhardt, one of the proponents of the arts-conscious New Stagecraft. Forming a kind of partnership with Arthur Hopkins, the Broadway producer and director, Jones had designed critically admired and sometimes commercially successful sets in the new manner for Sam Benelli's *The Jest*, Lionel Barrymore's *Macbeth*, John Barrymore's *Hamlet*, and Sidney Howard's first Broadway play, the poetic drama *Swords*. He had always been loosely associated with the Provincetown, in fact had arranged its very first sets, and was now back full time in its new incarnation with the power of artistic and commercial success at his command (Hopkins, 154–58, 167ff).

Of the three directors of the new theater, Macgowan turned out to be managerially the most important but the least experienced in practical theater. By 1923–1924 he was a critic of some stature and had written or cowritten three books that advocated the New Stagecraft. In these he proposed a theater that was to advance beyond that of Ibsen or Shaw. These writers, using primarily the medium of language, probed their characters psychologically and explored a variety of ideas new and old. But Macgowan, like Jones, with whom he had written one of his books, campaigned for the New Stagecraft, where language was not the key element but rather one of several theatrical elements—action, dance, song, costume, and sets—utilized equally to convey a production's meaning.

The fourth of the figures to be involved in the Experimental Theatre, Clare Eames, whose reputation for brains and imagination had impressed O'Neill even though he had never met her, had stepped onto the New York stage in the heady atmosphere of its newfound creativity. New art theatres were everywhere, new dramatists seemed more serious than those which preceded them, exciting ideas and playwrights from Europe filled the air. She had supported such stars as Ethel Barrymore and William Faversham, had played in art houses in New York and Cleveland, her hometown, and in 1921, at the age of 25, had attained the leads in *Mary Stuart*, by the highly regarded English dramatist John Drinkwater, and in Sidney Howard's poetic drama set in medieval times, *Swords*. O'Neill then was talking of a woman who had achieved stardom young and an important reputation as a formidable actress with brains and imagination.

These four and others were to join in the formation of a group to be called the Experimental Theatre, an art house to succeed the Provincetown Players, one of the many art houses founded in the United States in the years 1915–1916. The Provincetown was one of the most influential in large part because two major playwrights, Eugene O'Neill and Susan Glaspell, emerged from it. Organized by a group of New Yorkers summering in the Massachusetts town at the tip of Cape Cod in 1915, the theater quite naturally migrated to New York after two successful summers in its native habitat. The Provincetown worked right through World War I and into the twenties' extraordinarily creative theatrical activity. Indeed it contributed significantly to the heady theatrical doings, especially with the breathtaking productions of O'Neill's *Emperor Jones* (1920) and *The Hairy Ape* (1922) (Deutsch and Hanau, 96ff; Hapgood, 395ff).

By 1924 the original Provincetown Players had disappeared. Commencing as a group of amateurs, they had developed, largely through the expanding and highly praised achievements of Eugene O'Neill's dramas, into something of a professional organization (Deutsch and Hanau, 60ff; 86–88).

2. Annus Mirabilis *1924: Clare*

At the end of the disappointing and dispiriting 1921–1922 season, *The Hairy Ape* its only success, George Cram ("Jig") Cook, the inspiration and guiding force of the Provincetown, announced "a pause" and wrote, "We have received more plays this season than ever before and the survey of the material at hand was as large a factor as any in deciding us on a silent year" (92). The next Provincetown season he said would open on October 31st, 1923 (91).

But well before the fall of 1923, the date by which Cook was to have reopened the Provincetown, in fact in the spring of that year, O'Neill, Jones and Macgowan gave the Provincetown a second life. But it would be another life, another kind of organization than its forebear. No more would the amateur spirit of the old group, which prevailed despite the professionalism it had grudgingly acquired, dominate the new company (Deutsch and Hanau, 96ff). This would be instead a truly professional theater, and Macgowan would be its head. He would oversee all the practical details and coordinate the artistic endeavors. The new theatre was to be called the Experimental Theatre. Although the earlier organization had also emphasized experimental drama, here the weight was to go toward a fusion of all theatrical elements. If the earlier theater was the playwright's theater, this was theater for theater's sake but equally as serious as the playwright's theater. Although in a sense this enterprise was created for O'Neill, he wished to be the dramatist who would forge ahead in the forefront of the new theatre; he wished his plays to allow "opportunities for Bobby" (Robert Edmond Jones), and he wanted other plays that the organization chose to give Jones the same opportunity.

The year 1924, which began with great hope for the three founders of the Experimental Theatre, was to be a year of wonders for Clare Eames, the most intensive and intense year of her career so far and indeed of her entire short life. She undertook a series of roles in a variety of plays that would make the theatergoing public realize her apparent aim to be the best actress of her time. At least thus far none of her rivals had attempted the range and variety of the six roles she played in 1924 or the new part as director she took on early in 1925. In the latter capacity she entered a field that had become increasingly important in the international theater. There was no general agreement that she accomplished all that she had aimed for, but no one could deny the greatness of her ambition or the quality of her achievement.

Kenneth Macgowan did not require O'Neill's advice to bring Clare Eames into the new Provincetown company, for his reviews show that he admired her inordinately. Before she embarked to Hollywood for a film, he spoke to her and to the English actor Roland Young, who was to make his career in America, perhaps most famously as the character "Topper" in the movies. But in the conversation Macgowan was apparently unclear about how the new theatre would work. "If I could have got hold of Bobby," Clare wrote to her husband, Sidney Howard, from the Blackstone Hotel in Chicago, a stopover on her way west, "I could have got a more coherent idea of the whole Provincetown project—as it is I know as little as I did before. Roland Young took me to dinner at the Coffee House one night to talk about it and has promised to appear with them—engagements permitting. I have done the same. If nothing better turns up it stands a chance of being interesting anyway and certainly if R. Young can do it, I can." On October 7th, 1923, she writes to Kenneth Macgowan from Hollywood: "Do keep me posted on the developments of the—what?—theatre. (For Heaven's sake, don't call it the art theatre or anything like that....)" Whether or not the name, the Experimental Theatre, suited her, events show that she agreed to join their venture.

Clare, Young, and other actors turn out to be not a senate of the theater but "guest-players" who "will come wholly because they believe in the project"—thus the prospectus of the new organization, which continues: "We cannot ask them to sign in advance binding contracts for a few weeks in the midst of a long season. But we can accept their word—and add our own to it—that they will appear in the productions of this theater, Broadway contracts permitting." There was always the awareness that a star had to follow the money when it beckoned. The prospectus also contained a list of designers, among the most admired, who promised to work with the theater: Norman Bel-Geddes, Jones, Reginald Marsh, Herman Rosse, Lee Simonson, and Cleon Throckmorton.

Thus, when Clare returned from Hollywood in December, 1923, she must have plunged right into rehearsals of August Strindberg's *Spook Sonata*, for the play opened on January 3rd, 1924, to begin this extraordinarily active year.

But Sidney Howard as well as Clare committed himself to the Experimental Theatre. In the spring of 1923 O'Neill wrote to Macgowan, "Your scheme for the P.P. sounds fine to me." A note in the O'Neill book of letters to Macgowan tells us that the scheme was a proposal of plays for production that included "*The Brothers Karamazov*, *The Taming of the Shrew*, a play by Sidney Howard ... and an adaptation by O'Neill" (Bryer, 35).

Howard's interest in the Experimental Theatre grew intensely, without doubt as a result of the first visit to New York of the Moscow Art Theatre in the winter of 1923, which stirred excitement throughout the American theatrical world (and led a few years later to the formation of the Group Theatre). On November 23rd, 1923, Sidney Howard wrote to Norman Hapgood from Hollywood. Hapgood, now the editor of the Hearst *International*, was one of Howard's employers, but at the turn of the century he had been a thoughtful drama critic and an exponent of the advancement of serious drama in America. Howard wrote:

2. Annus Mirabilis *1924: Clare*

Clare Eames as Mummy in Strindberg's *Spook Sonata*, the triumvirate's first production, a failure. (Courtesy of the New York Public Library.)

> My present obsession is a Moscow Art Theatre in New York, for I am convinced we have the actors for it and can get them. The trouble is money, of course, because American actors cannot get over the idea that they are people and must be paid decent salaries if they are to be held together. And without holding them permanently together and binding them to exclusive services there is no good to be hoped for. But I know the actors and I have worked out a plan and I am resolved to try what can be done about collecting funds to float a permanent nucleus of ten players, a permanent director and scenic man and a permanent theatre to act good plays well and do one very little played English classic a season until a real repertory theatre can be evolved.

Howard is characteristically enterprising, forthright, and energetic. No sooner does he think of something that he regards as important than he puts it into action. Not yet a Broadway success, he nevertheless confidently bodies forth in a letter to Kenneth Macgowan written on November 10th, 1923, a detailed, pragmatic idea of a theater in a day before government and foundation funding for the arts. As far as the theater is concerned, this is still the time of the individual private donor, the patron:

> Read this letter through, and see if there is not something in it to catch the eye of a millionaire. Try it on your favorite millionaire. D[']abord a permanent company of ten actors and one designer of productions. That last, Bobby, no substitutes accepted. For the actors I submit the following: Eve LeGallienne, Mary Brandon [Robert Sherwood's wife, a puzzling choice since no one among the friends of Sidney Howard and Clare Eames seemed to think her a very good actress], Clare, Ernita Lacelles [a respected young actress who played in various artistic productions in the early part of the decade], Augusta Haviland [another young actress], Dudley Digges, Roland Young, Frank Conroy, Ivan Simpson [Sidney admired him but otherwise of no apparent importance], Edward G. Robinson [who was beginning to make a name for himself as a serious actor]. Each actor to be offered a year's contract at seven thousand five hundred per head, no difference to be made between any member of the company and any other, and each one of them to be assured a reasonable year's income. Then you have a permanent company which will stick together and may do some extremely good acting if given a few years.

Howard disagreed with O'Neill, Jones and Macgowan, generally known as the triumvirate, about the need for a permanent company, for they were content to rely on visiting stars who deigned to stop by when a more lucrative job failed to appear. Further, the pragmatic Howard insisted on a business manager who "knows what the word 'overhead' means ... a very important word." He wanted a literary director (Macgowan) who would consult with the permanent company about the choice of plays "as the cabinet consults with the president and has no more power to restricting his decision." A third manager would "have complete and dictatorial power in casting and in the direction of the actors."

Careful, solid thought with an "eye on finances" and company cohesion is to be at the heart of planning:

> I think that the first thing to draw up ... is a definite program of organization and the second thing is not to start until you are financially ready. I ... am not interested in a makeshift and I believe that if we get down to brass tacks with two or three men of financial experience and artistic interest and money to risk, that we can draw up a program which will work and attract money on your three names plus a sound financial plan.
> What you want is a Stanislavsky company.... The thing that I want to see is a group of able actors all of versatility who will stick together year in and year out and there isn't one on the list I named who wouldn't stick to God himself for seventy-five hundred, year in and year out....
> You ought, I really believe, to stick to this for a year or two if necessary until you have it properly shaped.

The directors declined to take Howard's advice to plan with thought and care and wait for the means to obtain financial stability. They started rehearsals for the new Provincetown in December. As a result Howard declined to save his new play, *They Knew What They Wanted*, for them. To avoid another unhappy Broadway production, he had been determined to give his new work to the Experimental Theatre. But when the Theatre Guild, an art theatre successful on Broadway, offered to buy it, Sidney sold the play to that group, writing to Macgowan: "I've had an offer from the Guild that I simply cannot turn down. That play has to be *acted* or its [sic] nothing. If things had got further advanced they might have been different. But, frankly, as they are, the Guild is still the best berth.... I hope there won't be any hard feelings" (undated letter, probably April 1924).

The triumvirate seemed to hold no grudges, for Sidney soon adapted two plays for them. But a letter to Sidney from Eugene O'Neill written April 23rd, 1924, indicates that there must have been some fear that Sidney would bad-mouth the company's management, thus hurting its prospects:

> Dear Sidney:
>
> Thank you for your ultimatum. We will talk it over when we meet— the things upon which we agree and disagree.
>
> I understand your disinclination to approach the vast stores of wealth at your command, under the circumstances. My only request is that you will not air your views except to Kenneth, Bobby, Clare and me. Let the outside world rest in ignorance and learn from their own experience. After all, the early stages of an idea have to be supported and the real test will come two or there years from now when something has crystallized which is now in solution.
>
> Altruistically yours,
> [signed] Gene

It did not take more than two years for something to crystallize, for this theatre which started with great hopes and some important successes petered out with a series of failures.

Clare Eames acted with the Experimental Theatre in their first two productions. In a January 21st, 1924, letter to Jean McDuffie, his sister, Howard wrote, "Clare has made a hit in a rank play by Strindberg which is being done by artists for art's sake for three weeks." She had opened on January 3rd in the initial production of the Experimental Theatre, *The Spook Sonata*, or, as Strindberg preferred to call it, *The Ghost Sonata*.

Given its aims, the triumvirate were altogether right in choosing this play as its first production. Certainly the venue was perfect, for *The Ghost Sonata* was written as one of four chamber plays to be presented in Stockholm in a store converted into a theater, matching well the Provincetown Theatre, which had been converted from a stable (Sprinchorn, Seaberg, and Peterson 8).

The directors of the Provincetown were aware of the parallelism between their theater and the Intimate Theatre, the name of Strindberg's playhouse. A note in the playbill reads:

> In a theatre oddly like the Provincetown Playhouse in conception, "The Spook Sonata" was first produced just sixteen years ago
>
> Under Strindberg's guidance the Intimate Theatre made interesting and daring theatrical experiments which link it logically with the experimental theatre of today. Strindberg ... simplified and standardized his scenery, working with interchangeable backgrounds and the fewest possible properties. Some of the plays were given entirely with draperies, which in pre-"little theatre" days, when box sets and realistic scenery were the rule, was radical indeed. Another innovation in one of the productions was the abolition of intermissions, which, according to Strindberg, were put in chiefly for the benefit of the liquor traffic.

In a separate article in the playbill Eugene O'Neill, as though sailing out into a brave new world, explains something of the nature of Strindbergean drama and of the kind of play his theater expected to produce:

> In creating a modern theatre which we hope will liberate for significant expression a fresh elation and joy in experimental production, it is the most apt symbol of our good intentions that we start with a play by August Strindberg; for Strindberg was the precursor of all modernity in our present theatre just as Ibsen, a lesser man as he himself surmised, was the father of the modernity of twenty years or so ago when it was believed that "A Doll's House" wasn't—just that.
>
> The old "naturalism"—or "realism" ... no longer applies.... [W]e have taken too many snap-shots of each other in every graceless position.... We are ashamed of having peeked through so many keyholes, squinting always at heavy, uninspired bodies—the fat facts—with not a nude spirit among them; we have been sick with appearances and are convalescing.
>
> Strindberg ... [foreshadowed] both in content and form the methods to come. All that is enduring in what we loosely call "Expressionism."

The Strindbergean experimental drama became and remains today the basis for much of avant-garde theatre. A modern scholar elaborates on its nature: "[A] chamber play was to be written like a piece of music and to require from an audience attention to theme and development rather than to plot and character...." The mood of a chamber play "must be imposed on the audience with such force that they will no more think of questioning what is happening than they would think of questioning what happens in their dreams." Strindberg "did not want the audience to reflect on the events of the play until the curtain had come down" (Sprinchorn, et al. xx). Strindberg wrote these plays drawing continuously on the unconscious, which for him was the "voice of God," and expected the audience to respond not with its rational mind but with its unconscious.

That the daily New York reviewers were unprepared for such a response is shown in their hostile and satiric reviews. John Corbin, for instance, in a piece which appeared in *The New York Times* on January 7th, wrote,

> The heroine's mother, who is played by Clare Eames, sits all day in a cabinet sealed against the light, which she cannot bear, and from time to time she utters raucous bird calls. The butler opens the door exhibiting her to a teatime caller, and to the audience. "She thinks she's a parrot," he says, "and maybe she is," whereupon "The Mummy," as the program calls her gibbers and squeaks [23].

In a Sunday article Corbin wrote: "[I]t is said to have been the one hope of the Provincetown management that the audience would not laugh—a hope that was rudely blighted" (January 13th, 1924, vii, 1).

But not all the reviewers were unsympathetic. In a remarkably insightful review that appeared in *The New Republic* of January 23rd, 1924, Stark Young showed that he understood how to approach the play:

> I have seen *The Spook Sonata* twice at the Provincetown Playhouse and on both occasions I have followed it not with a steady excitement but with a persistent and unflagging interest from start to finish. The audiences in both cases have listened, especially the audience after the first night, with an attention such as I have rarely seen in the theatre. I might easily say, then, that it does not matter what Strindberg's play means, we find it alive and absorbing. *The Spook Sonata* could be taken as a good illustration of how a work of art can be expressed only by itself ... in it they [the audience] have given themselves to something that was like the flux and confusion and urgent logic of dreams.

He continues a bit later:

> To convey this interpretation of the play masks are used on various characters, and there is a complete freedom in the use and dramatic variety of the lighting [231–32].

It is clear that the Experimental Theatre was commencing boldly with a play demanding a wildly different response from that usually expected in the theater, a play also that could orchestrate more than any realistic drama the variety of elements that go into a theatrical production.

The New York theater needed critics of Young's stature, but it had very few. It is true that audiences and critics had appreciated expressionistic and nearly expressionistic drama that had already appeared in New York: O'Neill's *Emperor Jones* and *The Hairy Ape*, Elmer Rice's *Adding Machine*, and John Howard Lawson's *Roger Bloomer*. But *The*

Spook Sonata more sternly demanded that the audience use its imagination freely, and audiences needed critics to encourage them to fearlessly dismiss their rational control as it witnessed the play. For other forms of literature readers were learning to understand such works as James Joyce's *Ulysses*, when they could get hold of a copy, and T. S. Eliot's "Wasteland." Maurice Valency reminds us that the play under discussion, when it was written, "had everything in common with the current trends in painting, sculpture, and music" (348–39). The arts, including drama, the most objective of forms, were becoming increasingly subjective, reflecting and projecting chaotic worlds.

When Stark Young turned to the acting in *The Spook Sonata* as contrasted to the production and to the play itself he hardly felt entranced. He found it "average and rather above the average. Our four weeks' system of rehearsing and the lack of any grounding in our actors cut down the chances of secure excellence in any but realistic plays."

Of all the actors he praised Clare the most:

> Miss Clare Eames as the Mummy did fine acting throughout; she gave to a fable and symbol a kind of reality dependent on nothing outside itself. She was able technically to render a numb and timeless suffering and long penance. And she drove what might easily have been ludicrous into a quality and power that was grotesque and dominating.

If Stark Young is to be believed, in Clare Eames there seems to have been an actress made for this new kind of theater. We have two pieces in which Clare comments on acting. One is from her days in Hollywood in 1923 in an undated letter to her husband in which she compares movie and stage acting. Of acting in the theater she says: "On the stage, you say a line over and over again, until, in the saying you evoke five dozen trains of thought and mental images each one of which leaves its trace on your inflection, until the precedent and subsequent pause, and the voice and look carry perfect conviction and seem to spring from that particular individual's history with absolute inevitability." That method—probably taught by her teacher at the American Academy of Dramatic Arts, Charles Jehlinger (and it might well have come from Stanislavsky if she had studied with him)—is a way of penetrating into a character by using one's own personality and one's constantly increasing knowledge of the character to give it complexity.

In her work, however, Clare seemed to be looking for something beyond the creation of merely a realistic character. In 1922 she appeared in a two-character play *The First Fifty Years*, by Henry Myers, in the course of which she "aged" a lifetime. One of her friends at the time, the writer Elizabeth Sergeant, in a letter to *The New York Times* on March 26th, 1922, maintained that Clare's character portrayal went beyond "photographic realism," that the actress showed not just a "certain unhappy wife, but woman of the ages in her relation to man of the ages; woman more constant, more suffering, more deeply involved in marriage, even when love ends, than man can ever be." Elizabeth Sergeant, then Clare's fast friend, perhaps understood her intentions in the role because Clare may have imparted them to her.

Moreover, that Clare as an actress sought to go beyond the character to serve as an instrument for the play's theme is explicit in notes for a letter to a Miss Coffin, who wrote to her for her observations about the problems of the modern actor. These notes bear no date, but a young woman writing for advice to Clare as an important actress in the United States would most likely have written somewhere between 1924 and 1927.

The problems of the modern actor are no different, Clare wrote, from those of the older actor:

> [T]he real problem that confronts us is the fundamental one of variation. During the course of a career we are called upon to interpret the works, the point of view, the Weltanschauung of ... these authors. We not only have justly to portray a particular character, but if we are honest people, we also must give it the very special attitude of the author. We have to understand not only the impulses which govern the personages of the play during its action but we must understand the impulses of the author when he wrote it. We act in innumerable plays for each play we must call on different reserves and facets and crochets of our temperament. We must be able to live a healthy character from a degenerate point of view, a degenerate character from a healthy point of view, an incident in a kitchen that implies the cosmos and a cosmic conflict reduced to terms of the kitchen.

If she conveyed such thoughts to Elsie Sergeant in 1922, she was in the midst of a good deal of thinking and discussion about the nature of acting, much of it attributable to the influence of European drama and the companies that were staging it, the call for the New Stagecraft and the new kinds of acting that would accompany it, and the heady desire for a serious American drama.

Especially interesting for us is Kenneth Macgowan's article on "The Art of Acting," written for *The Freeman* for October 11th, 1922. Macgowan, of course, was one of the triumvirate for the Experimental Theatre. Earlier in the same year he and Robert Edmond Jones, who would become another member of the Triumvirate, had published *Continental Stagecraft*, a view of theatrical doings on the European stage. By 1922 Macgowan was already an admirer of both Clare Eames and Sidney Howard. In his capacity as reviewer for *The Evening Globe* he had called Howard a "poetic dramatist with a fire and vigor of young manhood." In the same review he wrote of Clare that she was "the greatest talent developed upon the feminine side of our theatre in a generation" (September 11th, 1921).

His essay on the art of acting begins with the announcement that "the art of acting is a miscellaneous sort of art" because it is of several kinds, actually four. The first two are concerned with impersonation; either an actor is a "different character in every play, and never himself" or he is the "same character in every play and always himself." Both types of actor are "histrionic symptoms of the disease called realism." The third type of acting may be demonstrated by "Sarah Bernhardt, Giovanni Grasso [an acclaimed Italian actor], Margaret Anglin [a Canadian-American actress of classic roles], or Clare Eames." (Clare is the only young actor on the list.) An actor of this type uses his "own mask frankly for every part, achieving impersonation and emotion by their use of features and voice as instruments."

Macgowan continues a bit later:

> Such acting may be given—and usually is given—to the interpretation of realistic drama. It achieves the necessary resemblance through the inner truth of its art. But it never submits to submergence. It reaches out towards a kind of acting that we need to have and that we shall have again, while it meets the necessities of realism.
>
> This fourth kind of acting may be called presentational—a word that derives its present use from a distinction set up by Alexander Bakshy in his "The Path of the Russian Stage". Presentational acting, like presentational production, stands in opposition to representational. The distinction is clear enough in painting, where a piece of work that aims to report an anecdote, or to photograph objects, is representational, and a piece of work striving to show the relation of forms which may or may not be of the everyday world, is presentational.... The distinction applies to acting as well. A Broadway actor in a bald wig or an actor naturally bald who is trying to pretend that he is in a room in Budapest, and who refuses to admit that he knows it is all a sham, and that a thousand people are watching him, is a representational actor, or a realist. An actor who admits that he is an actor, and that he has an audience before him, and that it is his business to charm and move this audience by the brilliance of his art, is a presentational actor.

That kind of thinking must have influenced Clare's remarks to Miss Coffin. In 1922 Macgowan already saw Clare as reaching out to this fourth style of acting. The triumvirate must have seen her as an actress capable of carrying out its intentions to pursue a presentational type of production. According to Stark Young, she, more than any of her colleagues, understood the part she was to play. She made no suggestion of daily reality in her performance nor of character development. Instead she simply rendered a "numb and timeless suffering and long penance," giving a "fable and symbol a reality dependent on nothing outside itself." That is, symbol and emotion would seem to have risen from her subconscious and directed itself to that of the audience. The acting would have been entirely self-referential, alluding to nothing in the audience's immediate daily presence. If Young is correct, and there is little reason to doubt so fine an observer, Clare's was a remarkable accomplishment, bringing her boldly into a fresh field of acting. Although she never did this type of play again, it surely allowed her to unlock stores of psychic energy and technique which stood her in good stead in this year of amazingly various endeavor.

What Clare and her fellow actors were trying to do in *The Spook Sonata* was very new in the United States. Today, when most regional theaters present avant-garde drama with actors who have been trained in its techniques, what Clare did seems comparatively easy. But Clare, certainly with the aid of Jones and Macgowan—but surely in large part by herself—was one of the first American actresses to develop a method to deal effectively with the disjointed avant-garde play.

However, her next play for the Provincetown was a romp. *Fashion* "was an adaptation of Anna Cora Mowatt's comedy of manners, first presented in 1845; the acting version, with songs of the period, was arranged by Brian Hooker and Deems Taylor. Two-dimensional chairs and draperies painted on the wings, the view of the Battery on the back drop, the curtain which rolled down with a thud after each act to reveal Reginald Marsh's painting of a languorous lady surrounded by cupids and flowers, steered just the right course between authentic reproduction and travesty. The costumes, the songs, the acting, combined with the scenery to make, not an obvious burlesque, but a revival which nevertheless was touched with a gentle and indulgent laughter. New York was enchanted. Old-timers came to renew their youth and hear Mary Morris sing 'Come, Birdie, Come'; the Village, the Bronx, Park Avenue and Suburbia rubbed elbows in the little Provincetown lobby ... clapped accompaniments to Clare Eames as she sang 'Walking Down Broadway'" (Deutsch and Hanau, 102–3).

Sidney Howard wrote to his sister Jean on February 8th, 1924, "We are all considerably elated by Clare's tremendous success in "Fashion." ... The first three weeks were sold out the day after the opening and they are buckling down to what looks like a long run. Clare's comic song, 'The O.K. thing on Saturday is walking down Broadway' is one of the grand and thrilling surprises of the history of art...." Not every critic was as enamored of Clare as the proud husband, and some dared to prefer others in the cast—Percy Hammond liked Mary Morris better—but the show was generally a great success with highbrow and lowbrow reviewers alike. This phase of the Provincetown's sheer theatricality appealed to everyone.

"We are all in a frenzy,"—Howard again writing to his sister on March 20th, less than six weeks after the premier of *Fashion*. "Clare has again set New York by the ears with her Lady Macbeth and critics are fighting each other in hotel lobbies for what they have written about her.

She's rotten and superb and there's no middle ground. I know that she's superb...." Offered the part of Lady Macbeth opposite the well-known James Hackett in the Equity Players' production of the Scottish tragedy, Clare fearlessly left her personal success in *Fashion* to try a classic role.

Clare Eames (right) in the production of *Fashion*, 1924. Produced by the triumvirate consisting of Robert Edmond Jones, Kenneth Macgowan and Eugene O'Neill, a great success for the Experimental Theatre. (Courtesy of the New York Public Library.)

The production also gave James Hackett, Clare's costar, an apparently serious actor, an opportunity to present in New York his reframing of the title role. He had appeared as Macbeth seven years earlier, and restudied the part before his successful appearances in the play in London and Paris, where the French government had decorated him for his portrayal of the tragic Scotsman (*New York Times*, 18). But for all that, he seems to have been old fashioned in his approach with his Herculean frame, his organ voice, and his cutting the play to rags for his own purposes. As divided about him as about Clare, critics hardly rose to a fever pitch of emotion in their reviews of his performance. The final paragraph of Percy Hammond's piece sums up much of the attitude toward Hackett: "He is a prophet not without honor. Celebrated in London by the critics and populace, and decorated by the French Republic for his feats in Shakespeare, he can well afford to disdain the inappreciation, if any, of his native land. As Macbeth he has the god-given gift of mediocrity, which while highly valued on the other side may be underestimated by the drama lovers of the New World. It is said that the elder Guitry indulged in an unworthy sneer when he heard that Mr. Hackett's 'Macbeth' had been further ennobled by the Legion of Honor. 'They decorated him,' observed M. Guitry, 'because he played it only once!'" (*Herald Tribune*, March 17th, 1923, 8).

If indifference was the keynote of most of the critical response to Hackett, there was nothing like it, as Sidney indicated in his letter, in the reviewers' responses to Clare. Even those who disliked her usually praised some of her traits, her voice and diction, the seriousness of her enterprise. John Corbin in *The New York Times* wrote: "Like everything else this talented young woman attempts, it has a vigor of physical presence and a vocal authority that command attention and, for the most part, respect." But he goes on to say that "her performance seemed to lack psychology, to lack imagination—in short, to lack reality. It was lean and angular in spirit as well as corporeally; it was forced, self-conscious, uninspired. There were times when the gesture seemed not so much an expression of the mood and the moment as an excerpt from the daily dozen" (March 17th, 1924, 18). But another reviewer perceived it as a "wholly novel and original interpretation" (*Theatre Magazine*, May 1924, 15).

Clare's performance inspired some fine critical writing. Robert Gilbert Walsh wrote that the

> spell of this presentation is woven by Clare Eames as Lady Macbeth.... She is a neurasthenic woman in a primitive day where nerves were unknown....
>
> She shows the strength of an indomitable will shining through the frail physical woman and finally wrecking the physical life by the sheer force of her spiritual disaster. She is like a fine spring wound too tightly. Under ter-

rible strain, it must snap at last. Her final scene of Lady Macbeth wandering through an actual night with a dark spiritual night in her unseeing eyes is one of the keenest tragic notes ever expressed in the theatre.
... Miss Eames strikes at once the note of a spirit too big for its frail tenement, and to predicate at once the sense of impending disaster. She read the letter [from Macbeth announcing Duncan's impending arrival] with a cyclonic power and swept through this scene with an impetuous quality that never deserted her, even in the final scene, when her gusty sobs seemed to make her bend over double in her despair.

Clare has obviously expended vast physical, psychic, and intellectual resources on the part to make it an original, modern, and personal portrayal. The neurasthenic Lady Macbeth reflects the neurasthenic Clare and the neurasthenic modern woman often pictured in contemporary literature. Even her Lady Macbeth's inordinate ambition, too great for its physical and even psychic self, can be seen as an aspect of Clare and perhaps of other women of her generation. Knowing that she wishes to imply the author's view in her work, we can understand also the "sense of impending disaster" she imparts from her first entrance. Of course, we can never know without attending a performance whether or not we would have liked it, but Walsh's description makes one understand its vivid fascination.

Gilbert W. Gabriel of *The New York Sun* adds to our knowledge of Clare's characterization with his valuable and ambivalent metaphors:

Miss Eames is acting her first Shakespearean part and brings it a strange and virulent individuality. It is as if she had been persuaded to this neurosis theory. She has cut and scratched every inch of softness from the role; there is nothing on the bones of it but twitching blazing nerves. The graciousness it must occasionally show she makes abhorrently feline. One wonders, out of what stone thrown up from the red core of the earth this thin face has been carved. Nobility is graven on it like a malediction. Its eyes are of iron, and the brain behind them is a cold, sick thing that harries heart and body.
Yet out of this hatefulness incarnate, with its waspish exaggeration and meager, deliberate stateliness, Miss Eames succeeds in evolving the most actual performance of the evening. There's the art of it, of a sort—and of a fine sort, too. There is a remarkable knack of pose behind it, something that arrests the eye and holds it prisoner, however unwilling. Fortunate costuming helps. The ear is as quickly confronted. Her voice is an engine of clear, multi-colored diction [March 17th, 1924, 16].

In Gabriel we find the repugnance sometimes prompted by the unexpected and yet the realization that here was something not only new but monumental. His striking metaphors show him to be deeply affected. He is not altogether sure he likes it all—perhaps it is an art, in fact it is a fine sort of art.

We can see why other critics saw her as playing the role "in the pace of a Mack Sennett thriller" (Lawrence Stallings, *The New York World*, March 17th, 1921) or as though she were engaged in calisthenics. One reason may be that they thought her interpretation dead wrong. Almost certainly, the main reason is their failure to respond to a technique and interpretation galvanically different from any they had previously experienced.

The sensation she caused in *Macbeth* was not enough for Clare. Riding high, she went on to act another intense, neurotic woman who in the next play dominates the entire drama, Ibsen's *Hedda Gabler*. Howard writes to his sister Jean on May 9th: "Clare has a shot at 'HEDDA GABLER' ... and apt to be remarkable. Which makes her fourth role this season, not counting the picture (*Dorothy Vernon*). She is a sensational person these days in New York and very well under it and grand as ever."

Robert Edmond Jones, undoubtedly under Clare's persuasion, "tore himself away from the Provincetown Theatre" to create the setting and direct the production of *Hedda Gabler* for the Equity Players, now the Actors' Theatre. At the Provincetown Jones, who believed with many of the faithful of the New Stagecraft that a single hand should preside over an entire production, had moved into direction retaining, of course, his job as scenic and costume designer.

Mary Morris, who had acted with Clare in *Fashion*, partially directed by Jones, and in the next season went on to play the leading female role of Abbie in *Desire under the Elms*, wholly directed by him, appended an essay on Jones as director to Eugene Black's dissertation, "Robert Edmond Jones: Poetic Artist of the New Stagecraft." The essay is brief, about eight pages, but two or three items are particularly important to us.

Mary Morris writes: "Jones needed to work with trained and experienced actors who were technically equipped to carry out his enormously creative ideas. He had had no experience with and possessed no actual knowledge of the technical skills which the actor must have. He knew what these *should* be, but he knew nothing of *how* to arrive at them." That kind of director was fine for Clare because she felt secure in her technique. She needed someone who could appraise the result of her efforts or to locate the meaning of her character in the context of the drama as a whole. To do just that was the Jones method, for he was suggestive in his criticism to his actors rather than directive: "He could say the word that illumines, plant the seed that bears the fruit, and instill confidence in you." Again, "He never made you feel that anything critical he said was because of *him*. It was always *because of the thing itself*, the play, the part, the line." The actor therefore felt in himself an objectivity, a devotion to the thing at hand, on which, of course, Clare prided herself.

She had long admired "Bobby," and he clearly admired her; they had been friends at least since *Swords* in 1921. Jones's respect for her undoubtedly allowed her to go as far as she wished in working up a role. If he gave her criticism without her asking for it, given his obvious objectivity and his tact, she could easily accept it. Although they would seem to have been a perfect match as director and star, they never again worked together. Some of Clare's later problems in the New York theatre may have derived from her lack of such a director.

Clare's Hedda must have been immensely exciting because the reviewers not only were split among themselves, but critics sometimes seemed schizophrenic, beginning with apparently dire criticism but ending with positive superlatives. John Corbin, for example, in *The New York Times* writes that she is a central problem in the production, that she appears to be self-conscious, "archaic and angular" in her "attitudes." But the character "becomes convincing in proportion as it is played at a white heat." Clare Eames's failure to play the role in this way is a "great pity...." And then Corbin suddenly seems to change. "For," he says, "in its conception, and frequently also in effect, this is by far the most interesting since the electric performance of Mrs. Fiske ... [Mrs. Fiske acted Hedda in 1903.] In a word, the performance requires only to become evenly sustained to rank as a distinct and distinguished achievement" (May 17th, 1924, 18).

Corbin begins by finding Clare a "vitally placed" difficulty and ends, astonishingly, by declaring that the performance requires only a little more work to be a "distinguished achievement." Again apparently the unfamiliarity of technique and interpretation made him initially rear against the actress, but as the performance continued, and perhaps as he thought about it in writing his review, her aim became clearer to him, and he went from regarding it as the chief failure of the production to thinking of it as one that does not shy far from perfection. It looks as though Clare's daring experiments in technique and interpretation drove some critics to distraction but also to (sometimes grudging) admiration.

A fellow actress, however, may have put her finger on a major problem with Clare's performance. Margaret Webster informs us that Clare's "Hedda Gabler, according to Eva Le Gallienne, who probably knows more about Hedda than any other living actress, was still unfinished, but potentially the greatest Hedda of our time" (287). That is, Clare's Hedda was not totally worked through in either conception or execution. Yet enough was visible of that electric combination of idea manifested in performance that even critics who may have been initially antagonized somehow realized that an interpretive event was on stage.

Le Gallienne gives us another insight, ambiguous yet precious, into Clare's interpretation of Hedda. Le Gallienne and Clare were friends and spoke to each other regularly. Le Gallienne once told Jennifer Coleman, Clare's daughter, that Clare based one of her main images of Hedda on John Singer Sargent's portrait of Mme. X.

Mrs. Coleman writes that in light of the Sargent portrait Clare's Hedda must have been "profoundly seductive and feminine" (letter to author). Perhaps. But when we compare other Sargent portraits of women with that of Mme. X at the Metropolitan Museum of Art in New York City, we may notice a defiance in her sexuality emphasized by her grasping a table. Other women whose portraits by Sargent hang in the same room as that of Mme. X show them wearing their sexuality and strength easily, without the need of clutching a table. They stand tall and certain. By contrast, Mme. X, though strong in her defiance, yet requires a nervous, sharp hold of her strength.

Of course, again, at this distance it is hard to know what was in Clare's mind or what its effect in performance. So far as we are able to understand them, however, Clare seems to have created a complex modern, tense, neurotic woman whose straightforward emotions were sometimes obstructed, sublimated, rationalized, and self-dramatized.

In the winter and spring of 1924, Clare went at her career full tilt. Its object was not money; she was acting for the enhancement of her art and for artistic prestige. Because of illness and her Hollywood commitments, she had been away from the theater for a year and a-half, and as we all know, theatergoers have short memories. Surely one aim of her strenuous activities was to reestablish her reputation in the theater. But beyond that, she grasped the opportunity to become a great star, not merely financially, not only in popularity, but a star as Ellen Terry and Eleanora Duse were stars, loved and respected by all for her art.

Her aim if not her accomplishment seems to have been generally recognized. In an article titled "Who Is the Best American Actress?" in *Theatre Magazine*, December 1925 (9 and 56), Marc Goodrich, its author, lists six possibilities among the young leading ladies of the theatre: Clare Eames, Katharine Cornell, Leonora Ulric, Laurette Taylor, and Pauline Lord. He goes on:

> If the decision were to be made only from the somewhat statistical eminence of the greatest variety of parts played since the war and the successful application of distinguished interpretation to the greatest number of high-powered pieces of dramatic writing, then there would remain nothing to do but trumpet retreat and award the guerdon to Clare Eames. Her record runs a gamut from Ibsen's Hedda, through Elizabeth in Mark Twain's *Prince and the Pauper,* Sidney Howard's *Swords,* a comic matron in *Fashion, The First Fifty Years,* a fifty-year-old woman in Vajda's *Little Angel* [to be discussed later], an insane woman in Strindberg's *Spook Sonata,* and Prossie in Shaw's *Candida* to Shakespeare's *Macbeth,* through which ambush of ponderous misery, as Lady Macbeth, she swirled like a thin, vermillion vortex.

Clare Eames as Prossie in Bernard Shaw's *Candida*, in which she achieved an enormous success in a secondary role. (Courtesy of the New York Public Library.)

Despite Clare's achievements, which seem considerable to the ordinary reader, Goodrich finds her and three of the other ladies that he ranges beneath her "untainted by genius." Pauline Lord, because she is much less obviously an actress and yet accomplishes major effects for the advancement of the plays in which she is acting, gets the award of greatness. Nevertheless, even as he downgrades Clare, he recognizes from her importance in the theater that she has encompassed what no other actress of her youth has, that if greatness is absent, ambition and strong determination are present in large measure. And we may add that if greatness has not yet been accomplished, what may not ambition and determination bring?

After *Macbeth* Clare seems to have returned to *Fashion*, and her growing fame apparently brought her into the precincts of high society. In the same May 9th letter in which Howard tells his sister about Clare's forthcoming Hedda he writes: "At a soiree the other night, given by Mrs. Vanderbilt with Clare as hostess, was to be seen one of the most brilliant parties *ever* seen. It began with a special performance (the 100th) of Clare in 'FASHION' during which she recited Poe's The Bells in the manner of an elocutionist of the 40s and wound up with a state of supper in the old ballroom of the Hotel Brevoort (the room decorated still in honor of the Prince of Wales—Edward VII—when he came over in the 70s) and everybody in 1845 costume—hundreds of 'em and Clare as toastmistress which she did in elegant American French, for some reason, and all very funnily fashionable."

Life is rich, and the tired couple—for Howard has also had a busy year—head for Maine for rest and rejuvenation. And life becomes richer still. Clare, after a painful period which seemed to have derived from a failed pregnancy, at last becomes pregnant. Understandably, they tell no one until September, when Clare is in her third month.

On the nineteenth of that month, back in New York, Howard writes to his mother, "Clare opens next Saturday night ... in 'The Little Angel' by Vadja who wrote 'Fata Morgana.' [a hit of the previous season] ... and here is the real news—of a young Howard who is expected some time in March. I don't know how I can write that so calmly.... This is a very different pregnancy from her last—if indeed it was a pregnancy—one that she will bring to term and during which she will be working virtually to the end."

"The summer in Maine," according to Howard, was "ideal.... Sleep in the morning for Clare who is becoming fat and roseate while I write my first novel [at this point to be called *Spite House*] and don't get on so easily with it, either, novels being damned hard things. Then a large meal and then a long walk with the dogs. Then a large tea. Then conversation. Then supper touched up with mixtures out of our wine cellar. Then more conversation with Mrs. H. up the hill. Conversation about natives and art and wisdom and how the rain has spoiled the lilacs...." Later he says, "Clare also reads aloud and plays Beethoven sonatas on a nonagenarian square piano."

It all sounds as though creativity is germinating, getting ready to go into action. Clare, however, has had enough of vegetating. In a July 30th letter to his mother Howard writes, "Clare is fine but getting restless for work," and we learn that Clare "has been put in charge of Equity [Theatre] matinees" and plans to revive *Candida* "first with Kit Cornell instead of herself and she playing Prossie. Then she will do another Shaw play for herself with Kit in the second part. It's all great fun and a real theatre may come out of it yet." In an August 24th letter to his mother, Sid writes: "We are trying to rig things for another varied Clare season. First a play with Henry Hull in which she plays an East Side Jewish Streetwalker, then Beatrice [in *Much Ado about Nothing*], then the long awaited 'FEAR OF THE TIGER.' Next year, perhaps, a play by me about Queen Elizabeth or, if I decide to hold it, SAM MCCARVER. She's been enormously in demand for bad plays and she's got quite a lay out of good ones...." Of all the plays mentioned in these letters Clare does only one, *Candida*, in the forthcoming season, and in the fall of 1925, she will do *Lucky Sam McCarver*. In the usual show-business way, almost all plans are shot to pieces.

Sidney Howard spent two periods in Cleveland that summer for the tryout of *Bewitched*, a drama he had written with Edward Sheldon, who, beset with an immobilizing illness, could not attend to the play out of town. Clare's letters to Cleveland are full of domestic news and love for her husband, but we shall note some irritants that any married couple have, which, however, may acquire significance because of the couple's later separation and divorce.

Except one, the people named in the following letter are all neighbors in Wiscasset, Maine, and possess importance only in that they give a sense of the social life of the Howards there. The exception is "Margalo," the actress Margalo Gillmore, Clare's very good friend, who stayed with her during Howard's absence. All the letters are from 1924 and undated:

>My darling Sid—
>
>Your dear letter and telegram have come and I feel a little cheered, particularly by the news that *Bewitched* opens on Sunday. New York sounds too terrible; it has been hot here and thunder stormy but bearable. We went to Mary Raster's to tea, and found Helena Bellas and Mrs. White there, who helped to take the cuss off Mary. But every time we started to talk about anything interesting, she leant forward with an eager expression, and gave us contes rendires of articles in the *Atlantic*.... We dined alone and missed you terribly. Last night we went to the Haushalters and had a lovely time. To-night we are supposed to go to Cavanagh but I haven't heard from Mrs. Winslow yet whether she wants us without you. Probably not.... Tomorrow the Nashes are coming to supper.

But in the company of ordinary people Clare is "tongue tied," acquiescing to remarks with a "vacant smile." One can well imagine what these people said of her behind her back. She does not like ordinary people and enjoys the shoptalk with Howard, their small talk. Theater is meat and drink for her, indicated again later in the letter when she says that she is "bursting with curiosity" about *Bewitched*.

> The boys [their two dogs, one of them named Fizz] have been very naughty.... They have taken up the old Oscar Wilde and Douglas Game which is unsuited to Margalo's virgin eyes and I have to throw books at them to make them stop.
>
> I got a letter from Stark [Young] asking me again to play American Pigeons which I *will not* do. It's too boring. And I also heard from Kenneth [Macgowan] that Joseph Schildkraut [the actor who had made a great success in the Theatre Guild's production of Molnar's *Lilliom*] wants to join the troupe putting up a large sum of money as a guarantee of good conduct. He would be a draw and we are Jewish enough not to want to lose his money.

Poor Stark Young, who in his *New Republic* reviews had regularly admired Clare, could not convince her to act in his own play. Artistic consequence wins over gratitude.

> I love you and I wish I could go to Cleveland. But my dear I don't dare leave the dogs and I don't dare leave the maids and I don't dare leave the house and I can't shunt Margalo. I'd give *anything* to go. I want to see you and I'm bursting with curiosity about *Bewitched*. My love to my parents. And my dearest love to you, Sidney always.
>
> Clare

Howard was most uncertain of the outcome of *Bewitched* during rehearsals. Clare seems to think that Florence Eldridge, the play's female star, might save the piece, but despite Howard's initial appreciation of her work, he grew to dislike her as the tour continued, and indeed her reviews in New York were mixed.

Mary Brandon, Robert E. Sherwood's wife, mentioned in the second paragraph of the next letter, was the object of everyone's cordial aversion. The possibility of her acting the leading role in *They Knew What They Wanted* had already been discussed by Howard and the Theatre Guild. On May 8th of this year he wrote to Theresa Helpburn, the Guild's executive director: "About Mary Brandon, I am inclined to agree. I don't put her fault so much to youth as to physique. She has a well fed stolidity which doesn't wholly gibe. Also, she knows nothing about acting...." Further on he adds: "I don't want you to think that I am talking to actors. I'm not. Mary Brandon read the play through her husband who, as you probably know, is a pretty intimate playmate of mine and reads most of what I write pretty early in the game."

> My Sidney—
>
> Your dear scrawls have just come [among his friends Howard's handwriting was famously illegible], and I send this to Cleveland, in spite of the early opening, because I am sure you won't be able to get away. It sounds like the most awful muddle. What with Israel [Jose Rubin, one of the male stars of *Bewitched*, who was Jewish] and Fairyland [Glenn Anders, the other male star of the play, who was a homosexual] competing for the honours. If [John] Cromwell [the director of the drama] must have a mascot[?], why doesn't he choose a goat, or a bear cub, or something in the battleship tradition. But let's hope it all gets over in a Big Way. If Miss Eldridge makes a hit, it may save us. How does the play usually seem to you apart from the acting?
>
> In the Times this morning Mary Brandon is announced for *They Knew What They Wanted* "according to rumours," or, as Margalo says, "according to the lady herself, but not according to the management, the author, the author's wife, or the author's wife's friend." Isn't that just like Mary? The little shit.

In the letter's next paragraph Clare seems to have read aloud from *Hedda Gabler*, perhaps helped by Margalo, who had played Mrs. Elvstad to Clare's Hedda in New York:

> M. and I went to the Winstons Saturday night, and were thrilled particularly by Hedda who talked all evening about beautiful suicides. It made us proud of Henrick, you have no idea. Thank heaven, M. has been with me. We have laughed and laughed. But it is all hollow without you, my darling, and at breakfast and at night I miss you consciously and terribly.

In the first part of the letter's next paragraph Clare seems to be responding to a complaint in a letter from her husband that she had been insufficiently responsive to his sexual advances during the summer. But she clearly wishes to make light of it:

> Do come back soon, love. It does seem such a waste of time to be without you. Don't worry about my summer. It has not been passionate, truly, but that was because I have really seen so little of you. I wouldn't have minded had it been Spite House because I would have rejoiced in every moment you spent with that, but when I saw you so bored and harried by a silly piece of hack work I couldn't help being upset.

In giving the reason for her sexually distancing herself from Sidney during the summer, Clare seems to be guided by her strong artistic conscience which dictated that one follow one's star no matter what. Sidney, on the other hand, "bored and harried" though he may have been, nevertheless took a pragmatic view of his work. At this point in his life he has had no major success in either the theater or fiction; he has made an impact only in journalism, his only important source of income. Work

2. Annus Mirabilis *1924:* Clare 47

at journalism he therefore must. Yet despite her nettlesome behavior, they love each other too much for either to dwell now on such a problem. His apparent good sense follows Clare in letting it pass.

She takes up once again the matter of ordinary people boring her:

> The people here are no resource for me, in spite of their distinction and goodness, because they are so personally curious about me and épatés [flat] that they tire me. The only one who takes me at the foot of the letter [literal English translation for French idiom, *au pied de la lettre*] is Helena Bellas, who is something of a cuckoo herself. My natural gregariousness is thwarted by the absolute matter-of-fact domesticity of these people.... Had I had you, it would have been different, but I didn't. I could stand Detroit if you were with me.

These ordinary people would seem to be curious about her for two reasons. One, naturally, is her fame, and they have the usual curiosity of unknowns for those widely known. Perhaps more important is that she is a peculiar personality, a natural "cuckoo." She was almost always onstage, full of dramatic pretensions, insufferable perhaps to the everyday personality, but fun to those in the theater and to other creative types, who were often themselves outsized. Although she calls these people distinguished and good, she is very much bothered by their matter-of-fact domesticity, their flat personalities.

Clare continues in this letter:

> I have been working on *Much Ado.* What a job! And how grateful I am for the variorum. It is the most marvelous help in all sorts of ways. Love my darling Sidney. Come back soon or I shall cry—
>
> Love
Clare
>
> I am delighted about Bobby [Robert Edmond Jones].

The next letter requires no comment except to say that it is an interesting account of life in rural Maine in the '20s, Clare describing the ways of the locals, whom she finds odd:

> Wednesday
> Darling Sid—
>
> ...In the evening M. & I went to the Tabernacle and were thrilled. Nobody spoke to us or paid the slightest attention to us.... The audience was irreverent to a degree, restless and inclined to giggle, and sprawling in easy attitudes although they were obviously farmers and their families. The only group that was attentive or impressed was the saved (of whom Mrs. Cunningham was one) and who sat way down in front. Mr. Greenwood

got up and hoped that all would buy a copy of the Pocket Testament on sale after the service at 25 cents per, and then Mr. Rader, the pugnacious gospel Rotarian, told us that we would all be lost to eternal damnation unless we consulted the Bible at every juncture. There was not one single sentence in his speech, which was [not] interlarded with stampings and lurchings and the most atrocious puns and really mean cracks at college men, bishops, and well dressed women. The audience was skeptical. Two women sang a hymn to the concertina about

> You may have your pleasures
> Give me Je-e-e-esus!

The soprano had one of the most beautiful voices I have every heard, pure, even, with that floating instrumental quality that only *very* good singers have. The collection was taken up as the audience filed out. There was no ardour, no humility—only a sort of apathetic amusement from the audience, and veritable overacting from the performers.

Last night the Warlands dined here, and I had a lovely time, they are certainly nice people.

The boys have been good though perverted. Samivel [the second dog] is the worst offender.

I love you darling and I need you terribly. I am going to send you a desperate wire if you don't come home QUICK.

My dear
Clare

In the final letter of this series the "Bobby" referred to in this letter as in the earlier one is Robert Edmond Jones. The reason for his presence in Wiscasset becomes clear in the typically candid, straight-from-the-shoulder letter Sidney Howard writes to Kenneth Macgowan on July 26th:

> I don't know how much you know about cancer. I know a little. You and I have both been through tuberculosis and it's child's play next to the party Bobby has sustained this summer. You had better realize as much and get him out of New York and the heat and this damned theatre work before you are very much older ... if you will forgive my saying so, I have a distinct feeling that you and O'Niel [*sic*] could do better by your all but mortally ill raison d'etre than to leave him to sweat while you sojourn in the cool breezes. Frankly, I know enough about Bobby's case to tell you that if he is not cared for now there will be no reason for any one's bothering to do anything about the Provincetown theatre experiment next season because it won't have Bobby on duty and without him it won't be worth much of any trouble, now will it? So get busy and fire him away if you expect any cooperation from anybody in your future activities because Bobby is the candle that the game is worth and without him there isn't any game and he has been looking at death with a very slim chance of survival at best and any one who fails to do what he can to increase that chance is undertaking a very grave responsibility. Recoveries from cancer at Bobby's

age are almost unheard of ... if the Provincetown can't take respectable care of Bobby it won't get much of anything out of the Howard family which happens to be quite a lot interested in the case.

In the postscript he adds, "Consign him to Wiscasset or to New Hampshire without further delay." Jones's family home was in New Hampshire. So when Clare had said earlier that she was delighted about Bobby, she was delighted that he was coming to Wiscasset to be cared for by the Howard family. As it turns out, it seems to have been Clare mostly that took care of him because her husband was on the road a good deal.

In Clare's final letter to Sidney from Wiscasset, she indicates that there had been some doubt as to whether John Cromwell, an actor-director friend of Sidney, would give her the part of a lower-East Side prostitute. Now that he has, unusual for her—though understandably given her queenly persona in stage, screen, and life—she is uncertain about her ability to play the role of the Jewish streetwalker. However, as a serious actress, she means to expand and to show off her range, and she fearlessly picks up the challenge. The letter also implies that her accepting the part in the Cromwell play meant her unavailability for the Experimental Theatre season, for she is hesitant about telling Bobby about her new role.

> August 27th, 1924
> Darling Sid –
>
> We have been kept in the house for three days by a Northeaster; a gale and terrible rain so bad that I couldn't even get to the post-office. Mr. Haushalter brought up our mail in the Ford so that I have got your dear long letters and have felt like a Pig not answering and not daring to brave the Elements.... Last night the wind went round to the North West and to-day is a burning washed glory. And you in Cleveland. Bobby is in pain a good deal of the time—often very severe pain. But I notice that if he stays in bed all morning, and lies down for two hours in the afternoon—in other words, if he carefully avoids irritating it by the friction of movement he doesn't suffer nearly so much. I have made him get some soft white cotton socks a size too big, as I was afraid for the dye in the black socks with only a most unprofessional bandage to protect the wound. In the morning I go in and have my breakfast with him and share the coffee pot—and when I first go in the room fairly reeks of the faint sweet cancer smell. It is sickening and unmistakable. My own health is good. I have had one quite sleepless night, but I think it was because I miss you so and not because I am ill. The doctor's remedy for my insides has helped me a lot. Your telegram about Cromwell's decision cheered me to the skies. But now that I know I'm going to do it, I am prey to misgivings. *Can* I? Mr. Cromwell must help me at every step. The more I think of trying to impersonate—not imitate—a wanton young Jewess, the less capable I feel of doing it. Usually I am not given to morbid doubts of my own powers, and I suppose even

now they are silly and vain. For if I work and listen to what he says I can at least avoid disgracing myself. But the more I know of my profession the harder it is. Bobby doesn't know yet I'm going to do it. I thought I'd wait until you got back to tell him. [Jacob] Ben-Ami has left them [presumably the Experimental Theatre] in the lurch to go into vaudeville of all things. I do think he has behaved very badly as the scenery is all built and rehearsals were to start next week.

That's all our news, except that we have run out of cigarettes and everything. I have *never* missed you as much as I do this time, not even when you left London [in 1923, when he went to Geneva and she was about to return to Hollywood for the Pickford film]. Why is that, I wonder? I love you darling.

Clare

Shall I write to J. Cromwell?

Again I love you.

Clare withdrew from the Experimental Theatre because, she wrote to Macgowan, "in all probability I am about to have a baby." More likely she resigned because she wished to act in the Cromwell production, which however did not materialize. On September 19th, Howard writes to his mother: "Clare opens next Saturday as a pinch hitter in 'The Little Angel' by [Ernest] Vadja who wrote 'Fata Morgana,'" which had been a Theatre Guild success in the previous season. She had received a quick call for this "very amusing lowbrow farce" and did it "on six days of rehearsing," undoubtedly enjoying both the challenge and the money. In a letter to his mother on September 29th, Howard reports that Clare "made a great hit in the role, the lead as an old Hungarian lady, very amusing and eccentric. As which she is exquisite and very funny and very expert."

Not all the reviews were as appreciative as her husband's. Percy Hammond, on September 29th in *The Herald Tribune*, wryly observed: "Miss Clare Eames, who, I think, ought not to be required to impersonate anything less than empresses is imperial as Anita's strict aunt, wielding her flyswatter as if it was a royal scepter. Whenever the play lagged on Saturday night Miss Eames's commanding and spinster histrionism was at hand to give it force." Percy Hammond is his usual ambivalent self, but even faithful Stark Young, writing for this season in *The New York Times*, is uncharacteristically negative toward Clare's performance—not that he altogether lets her down. Her acting, he believes, is the best in a bad lot that is insensitive to the play's manner. "But even she often slurred the obvious intentions of the dramatist to make the parallels and artificialities by which comedy prospers...." Undoubtedly the short rehearsal time harmed her performance, a perhaps insensitive production did not help her, but despite Sidney's report, she does not come off as well as she might have.

An October 20th letter from Howard to his sister Jean informs us that Clare will leave "'The Little Angel' this week to fill a motion picture contract and, that done, revives HEDDA and then does Beatrice in 'MUCH ADO' [sic] which role is selected because the big renaissance skirts enable her to play until the very last weeks which, considering her very excellent health, she may just well do."

Clare does the film, perhaps *The Swan*, but instead of *Hedda Gabler* or *Much Ado*, she performs in *Candida*, which production will become famous because the title role develops into one of the great parts for Katharine Cornell for the rest of her career. But at the time the production was equally a triumph for Clare Eames in the secondary role of Prossie, the secretary to Morrell, Candida's husband, a handsome, vigorous, ostentatious preacher, with whom all women, including Prossie, fall in love.

Candida, directed by Dudley Digges, opened at a special matinee of the Actors' Theatre (formerly the Equity Players). Glancing at a few of the reviews, we sense the excitement the production generated and the hopes grown higher for the future of the art theater. Arthur Hornblow in *Theatre Magazine* is typical: "A play such as *Candida* and a production such as the Actors' Theatre has given it, shows what the theatre might become under ideal circumstances. Intelligence in the writing, in the acting and in the staging is a rare combination, and that this organization of players has been able to obtain it at these special matinees is a happy omen for the future."

But it was the acting, especially of the two leading female roles, that called forth the most praise. We first hear of Cornell. Arthur Hornblow wrote of the performance of the part of Candida: "The tenderness, the poetry, the supreme womanliness of Katharine Cornell's impersonation of the title part puts this actress a notch ahead of anything she has yet attempted..." (February 25th, 1924). Stark Young praised Cornell even more and gave more insight into her playing of the part: "Candida in the hands of Katharine Cornell was a deep revelation of the part. Her frail presence had something in it of the light of another world. She was strong, not with womanly aplomb and maternal astuteness, but with an exquisite power to feel and understand. Miss Cornell's playing of the last act was a thing so delicate and translucent and moving as we rarely see, more tender and practical than the dramatist himself perhaps quite imagined..." (December 13, 1924, 12). No actor could expect higher praise, nor any dramatist a finer understanding of one of his major parts. It is easy to understand why Cornell was to play the role for many years. But we must remember that it was Clare who saw that Cornell, who had not yet achieved success in a really serious play, who had doubts cast upon her ability to do so, could perhaps go beyond her usual range.

Clare emerges from the proceedings at least as well as Cornell. Percy Hammond reports in *The Herald Tribune* of December 13th: "This gathering ... wasn't abashed to think that the best thing in the play was Miss Clare Eames's humorous simulation of a drunken stenographer." He tells us later that as Clare "staggered from the scene she received the demonstration of the afternoon." Stark Young insightfully gives us the reason for the demonstration:

> Clare Eames as Proserpine Garnett, the secretary, in love, like all women, with Morell, played the role to the last capacity. All in all Miss Eames achieved the most complete performance that I have seen in her career. [Considering the extremes of praise he had previously heaped upon her, we can only wonder what goes beyond extremes.] What she did with the scene where Marchbanks pries out her secrets and her love for Morell was a profound revelation in comedy and pathos. Her comedy in the last act was as good as this wry gauche tragedy forty minutes before. And over her entire performance there shone from start to finish a kind of brittle, lustrous wit.

Theatre Arts gave Clare a full-page picture in her part of Prossie and a caption which justifies Kenneth Macgowan's description of her acting two years back and gives a sense of a new comic dimension of Clare's career: "Clare Eames's Prossy, in the Actors' Theatre revival of Candida, is one of the most adroit and completely satisfying comic performances of recent years. Practically without the uses of make-up, Miss Eames's regally modeled face—so suited to Queen Elizabeth and Mary Stuart—become a fine and pliant mask for comedy. Even without the amusing externalities which emphasize this impersonation, the lightning rapidity of Miss Eames's thoughts as they race across her face and take shape in amusing action would create a brilliant Prossy. It is a performance of exquisite intelligence, which, while it never forces a laugh, never misses one."

Clare seemed now set free from her stereotypes, the queens and the tense, modern neurotic women, and successfully loosed herself in the world of comedy. Never had she received such uniformly good reviews, and perhaps never had she been so pleased with her career.

On January 5th, 1925, Howard writes to Jean that Clare would be "writing you, no doubt, if it weren't for 'Candida' which has been such an enormous success that they have been forced to put it on evenings instead of just the special matinees for which we bargained. And that means, with the baby some eight weeks off, that Clare can do Prossie and not much besides."

But her husband did not count on Clare's drive and determination. On February 25th, 1925, there opened a production of Ibsen's *Wild Duck* by the Actors' Theatre, and listed as codirectors are Dudley Digges and

2. Annus Mirabilis *1924: Clare*

Clare Eames. *Candida* had closed its run on January 16, and in part to keep Clare's mind off the oncoming baby, "she directed most of the greatest artistic success of the current season" (Sidney to Jean and Duncan McDuffie, April 19th, 1925). Stark Young's *Times* review is headed "As Fine as 'Candida,'" and his appreciation reads:

> The sign "Wild Duck" glittering outside the Forty-eighth Street Theatre last night might have suggested to the general passer-by a lively evening's entertainment, something livelier than the Ibsen of the colleges and drama leagues could ever be. As a matter of fact "The Wild Duck" was entertaining from the first curtain to the last, a magnificent satirical tragedy moving straight to its end. Ibsen's power was always in evidence last night. "The Wild Duck" was devastating, stubbornly moving, exciting, provocative, unforgettable.... It was finely directed by Clare Eames and Dudley Digges, who in his third venture of the season, surpassed even his triumph [as director] in 'Candida'.

So we find Clare early in 1925, just before the birth of her baby, ending the busiest and so far the most brilliant phase of her career. She had acted six parts in one year in the theater and one in film. Only the film and "The Little Angel" were commercial endeavors. All her other work was for art theaters for the love of her craft and of drama; of course, it was for the prestige as well. And then, barred from further acting, she entered another field of theatrical work, learning from a respected, experienced director, readying herself for another kind of creative task and joy in the theater.

More significant was the expected birth of their child in March. On April 19th, 1925, Howard writes to Jean and her husband, Duncan McDuffie, that after the opening of *The Wild Duck* Clare heaved a sigh and said:

> I have a pain, and the doctor came and said: The baby is going to be born tonight, send for her mother. Which I did and the damned baby waited for three weeks. After Mrs. Eames had been here two of them, she could no more, and shipped Clare off to the hospital in a blind faith (which we all shared) that the presence of the hospital would somehow be communicated to the considerably inaccessible infantile instinct for being born. So Clare went to the hospital and waited for it another week during which we started by walking her up and down the corridors and ended by walking her twenty and thirty blocks at a stretch and dancing with her between walks. Then finally, on March 23rd, it being a peaceful Sunday, I went up to call as usual in the afternoon and found Clare feeling very badly indeed and scared to death. "Jetzt fangt es an" says I, German, to the German nurse and she answered: "Gewiss ist es shon angefangen" or words to that effect only more grammatical [Howard: Now it has begun. Nurse: Certainly it has already begun] and an aestheticians came and the obstetrician and a surgeon and the general practitioner by appointment and from six o'clock

until three in the morning Clare wrestled with the devils of mortal agony like a trapped Amazon on her way to her own hanging and I held her hand and didn't like it at all. What they can do, nowadays, for mothers in labor is amazing, most of all this gas anaestheticians which catches the beginnings and ends of the pains and keeps the mother all but entirely conscious except at the beginnings and ends. At three they took her up to the operating room and at three fifteen the doctors came down to announce a daughter as the result of what they considered an easy confinement albeit a bit surgical at the finish. As a matter of fact, had we not had a wizard of an obstetrician, we should have lost the baby who evinced a very whimsical and capricious humor about being born at all. So then they carried the baby down and we inspected. Mrs. Eames, having been through it five times herself and watched her younger daughter go through it a year since, took the doctor's word for Clare's condition and went into immediate raptures over the child. But I am here to say that thrills of paternal pride are all right for the Duke who sits in his study and doesn't much like his wife anyway and is told that the dukedom has an heir at last. But for me, I looked politely at the baby, saw that she was less red than most and considerably prettier than most and otherwise registered nothing. I went home at five, having waited for Clare's unconscious return to her bed, with the picture of her still face and figure, so exhausted, so flushed, so faintly breathing. I don't think that the birth of a child makes anybody feel very religious. The deity made a damned poor job of that process.

3

Annus Mirabilis 1924: Sidney

This was a year of wonders for Sidney Howard as it was for his wife. The most important event was the immense critical and commercial success of his comedy *They Knew What They Wanted*, but Sidney, as usual, had his irons in a number of fires.

For some years the main source of Sidney's income and renown had been the investigative journalism he had written for Hearst's *International* and *The New Republic* on such subjects as the illegal drug trade and Florida investment schemes. In the summer of 1924 he completed a series for *The New Republic* on super patriots, "finished at last and go[ing] off today or tomorrow and how they did bore me. I find, oddly, that I can write fiction or a play about four times as fast I can write journalism." And in fact he was busy writing fiction. Sidney frequently complained about his activities in the field of drama, that plays were insufficiently artistic, that they became part of a collaborative process demeaning for both the dramatist and the work. Before long, in 1926, he would assert in a preface to one of his plays that drama's main purpose was to give good parts to actors, an idea that must long have been germinating in his mind. He therefore turned little by little to fiction. In the summer of 1924 he was reading proofs for a book of short stories called *Three Flights Up*, which "look[s] firm and comforting and I am really getting on and pretty well through the first book of 'SPITE HOUSE' my Maine historical novel."

But he certainly was not giving up on drama. In the same letter quoted above we see a man of immense energy as he outlines the nervewracking but potentially happy prospect of the season ahead. "Whatever, this winter makes or breaks me as a playwright and there can be no mistake about that. 'BEWITCHED' [a collaboration with the playwright Edward Sheldon] opens in Cleveland on the 11th of August and I go out here for the opening. Then, in all probability, 'THEY KNEW WHAT THEY WANTED' and after that 'LUCKY SAM MCCARVER' and translations of 'LE DERNIER NUIT DE DON JUAN' [by Edmond Rostand] and 'MICHEL AUCLAIR' [by Charles Vildrac] on the side at the Provincetown and Greenwich Village Theatres. [The Greenwich Village Theatre was also run by the triumvirate.] It scares me a little. I have made everyone happy with 'LEXINGTON'" (a pageant for which he was commissioned in the previous year by the town of Lexington to celebrate the 150th anniversary of the Revolutionary War).

The most immediate of the upcoming dramas was *Bewitched*. His collaborator, Edward Sheldon, older than Sidney, had been a highly respected dramatist for more than a decade, having made famous Professor Baker's English 47 class in dramatic composition. While a student in that class he wrote *Salvation Nell*, produced to great acclaim by the prestigious Ibsen pioneering actress Minnie Maddern Fiske, known to theatergoers simply as Mrs. Fiske. As a result of the success of that drama and other "strong" plays bearing such titles as *Nigger* and *The Boss*, not only did Sheldon become famous but English 47 became the mecca for seriously aspiring dramatists. But Sheldon's career was confined mainly to collaborations when in the twenties an immobilizing illness prevented him from ever leaving his apartment; nevertheless his personality so sparkled, his taste and intelligence were so keen that the most interesting theater people flocked to his bedside (Ruff, 34–36; Kinne, 41–90).

Bewitched, Sheldon and Sidney Howard's joint effort, the tryouts for which Sheldon's illness prevented his attending, concerns an aviator's dream in a haunted castled near which he has crashed. Howard called this fantasy a "Freudian Fairy Tale" (Clark, 192), and at first it seemed to go well. In an August 20th letter to his mother he wrote of its "enormous success" in Cleveland, "one of those phenomenal successes with extra matinees and the whole run sold out the third day and chairs in the aisles and cops in the lobby ... the thing is very beautiful to look at [Lee Simonson executed the sets] and very well done, particularly by [Florence] Eldridge and [Glenn] Anders. Jose Ruben is good, too...."

Howard goes on to say that the play might turn out to be a success on the order of that commercial powerhouse *Rain*, and its Cleveland run, slated for a week, has now been extended to a month. But only four days later Sidney again writes to his mother that although the "play is still an enormous hit in Cleveland ... it is not yet right for New York. We've got to fix the 2nd act curtain which is horribly difficult to fix, and at present painfully ineffective. But Cromwell's [the director and producer of the play] hopes are high and, I dare say, mine ought to be. Only I'm so mortally afraid of theater hopes which have led me astray so often." Sidney's fears are substantiated, for the play turns out to be a flop in New York. Also failures are his two adaptations for the triumvirate's Experimental Theatre.

The main event then for Sidney was *They Knew What They Wanted*. He first intended the play for the Experimental Theatre, but when the triumvirate rejected his financial plan for the organization, Sidney, believing that their shaky finances would affect the group's artistic integrity, sold his play to the Theatre Guild. Since both Clare and Sidney were to be intensely involved with the guild for the next few years, it is important to describe the nature of the organization.

The Theatre Guild grew out of an art theater, the Washington Square Players, which gave its first performance in 1915. Many of the same forces that gave rise to the Provincetown were also at work in the founding of the Washington Square Players: a tendency to left-wing politics, bohemianism, and idealistic theatrical aspiration. But there were important differences between the Provincetown on the one hand and the Washington Square Players and the Theatre Guild on the other hand, the differences being especially marked as applied to the Theatre Guild (Langner 40 ff).

The guild came out of discussions soon after World War I among a nucleus from the Washington Square Players, some other theater folk and lay people passionately committed to the theater. The aims of this group were different from those of the "little theater" which preceded it or any other little theater. First, the company was not to be comprised of amateurs but rather it was to be an "expert theater." As Lawrence Langner, one of the founders of both the Washington Square Players and the Theatre Guild, points out, the guild would thus be "entirely different from the Provincetown Players." Langner is here referring to the first Provincetown group, not the Experimental Theatre, which succeeded it. Second, the guild would secure a house which seated a "considerable number of people, and certainly larger than the usual Little Theatre ... in some place where the rents were sufficiently low not to make rentals a burden." Third, the guild was to be governed by a committee while executive and administrative powers would be delegated to individual members of the committee. In the guild's insistence on its professionalism to be exercised in a house considerably larger than those of the little theaters, it veered strongly from other art theaters. The Theatre Guild, however, betrayed its origins in the little theater movement by its determination to be governed by committee (Langer, 116). However, it did create the post of executive director, filled by Theresa Helburn, who "conscientiously [carried] out the decisions of the Board" (Langner 125–26).

Almost certainly contributing to the success of the Theatre Guild—despite its share of failures—was the presence on the board of two businessmen. Lawrence Langner was a successful patents attorney. Without any apparent difficulty he carried on two full-time careers, that of a lawyer and that of a leader of the guild, working at the guild in the early morning and at night and in his money-making job during the regular work day. On the board also was Maurice Wertheim, a Wall Street banker, who "introduced the other members to such mysteries as double-entry bookkeeping, corporation reorganization, and other practical aspects of business gleaned from Wall Street" (Langer, 124).

Like the other art theaters, the Theatre Guild sought plays of high artistic merit but did not think it incumbent upon itself to look primarily for American plays. In its first and in subsequent seasons it served up a menu of mainly foreign plays. For such an emphasis it was frequently criticized, as a reading of contemporary theatrical pages in the newspapers and magazines would reveal. But the guild must have exerted additional energy in its search for American drama, for in the 1924-25 season, it staged Sidney Howard's *They Knew What They Wanted*, John Howard Lawson's *Processional*, and the musical review called *The Garrick Gaieties*, devised by Richard Rodgers and Lorenz Hart, making three out of seven productions American. Two seasons later the guild again produced three plays written by American dramatists, two of them by Sidney Howard. It looked now as though Howard might well become the guild's American playwright.

But it was 1924 that first saw the fruition of Sidney Howard's theatrical dreams. The success of *They Knew What They Wanted* was everything a dramatist could desire. On November 25th Sid telegraphed to his mother: "Play looks like unqualified success," and on the next day another telegram: "Press enthusiasm as remarkable ... as any I have ever seen." Sid had been trying for four years to achieve a major success on Broadway. Most of his work had been translations and adaptations. Only *Swords* was an original, and that had been based on a scenario by the classical actress Margaret Anglin. He therefore considered *They Knew What They Wanted* as his first original play. Although Sidney had never had a commercial success, he had already achieved a measure of critical respect. With the poetic drama *Swords* and such translations as Vildrac's internationally admired *S.S. Tenacity* to his credit, observers believed him to be tilling nobly in the fields of art. But with *They Knew What They Wanted* he at once jumped to the forefront of new American dramatists.

The play concerns Tony, a sixty-year-old Italian owner of a vineyard in California during Prohibition. Now making money for the first time, never having married because he wished to support a wife well, he has arranged, through the mail, to wed a waitress he had seen once in a San Francisco restaurant. The only trouble is that, when she had requested his picture, he had sent that of his handsome foreman. In fear and trembling on his wedding day as he thinks of confronting his prospective bride, Tony gets drunk, and in an automobile accident breaks both legs. Nevertheless he wishes the wedding to proceed. Amy, the waitress, despite her disappointment, unable to bear any longer the barrenness of her life, desiring a home of her own, consents. But in the aftermath, in her confusion and disappointment, she has a one-night affair with Joe, the handsome foreman, who, she had thought, was Tony. In nursing Tony, however, she learns to love him; she also learns that she is pregnant. Joe is willing to take her away, but Tony, after his first rage, forgives Amy, for he has learned to love her and will love as well his ready-made family. Joe, who is a wanderer, is glad to continue on his way. Now each of the trio has what he wanted: Tony his family, Amy her home, and Joe the open road.

Of the daily reviewers, one need only quote Percy Hammond to catch the general tone. Hammond is unusually forthright in his opinion. He begins, "The Theater Guild last evening produced Sidney Howard's 'They Knew What They Wanted,' and it turned out to be an excellent tale, told with a fine veracity by the authors, the actors and the director." He closes with: 'They Knew What They Wanted' is a mature and a sophisticated comedy. I hope and I feel sure that it will run for many months" (*HT,* November 25, 1924)

Intellectual critics also took the play seriously. We may see the weight they gave the drama from the review by Joseph Wood Krutch, a professor of English at Columbia University and at this time and for the next few decades drama critic of *The Nation.* Krutch writes that the situation just before Tony's forgiveness

> to the conventionally minded ... is hopeless, and so, too, is it hopeless to those who love to find the unsolvable dilemma; but surely if clear vision and thought untrammeled by prejudice or sentimentality is worth anything it is because, after uncovering life's chronic unwillingness to gratify our romantic desire, it teaches us somehow to make the best of what it will give, and it is exactly that which Mr. Howard, choosing a method even bolder than that of the unhappy end, has made his characters decide. The guilty youth wants his freedom, the girl wants her home, Tony wants her baby. Why then should not the man and wife remain together? For then all three will get what they want even if not exactly in the way they wanted it. Thus the art of life is shown to be the art of compromise [*The Nation,* December 10th, 1923, 62–63].

Krutch goes on a bit later to say that Amy "is one of the most significant figures which the current stage has to offer. Through her Mr.

Howard has succeeded in salvaging romance for an age suspicious of the idealization which romance seems to demand. He has made her as fallible and as limited as the strictest realism demands, but he has made her at the same time as appealing as any spotless heroine ever conceived by the most inveterate sentimentalist."

Sidney could not have received more sympathetic criticism, for it caught the very nature of his mind. Krutch understood Sidney's wry, active rationality, his desire always to make life negotiable, his willingness, his sometimes grim determination, to make it so even in the face of seemingly intractable difficulties. Sidney detested plays such as Strindberg's *Spook Sonata*, calling them "rank," for they give off only life's acrid odor. Recognizing the fetidness of life, Sidney, however, insisted on its variousness. He refused to succumb to the "dominant thesis of the realistic drama which swept down from the North ... that life's favorite game was ... the devising of dilemmas from which neither good-will nor intelligence provided any possible escape." He insisted on his daylight world. To those who tried hard to make life deeply pleasurable and morally fine, life could be rotten but it could also be good. This was Sidney's credo not only in drama but in his own life as well. In the darkest moments of his separation from Clare, when he missed her horribly, when he felt his career was falling in a shambles about him, he rarely surrendered to his darkness. "I am in a bad state of self-loathing or self-contempt or something along those lines" (letter to HH, June 29th, 1928), he writes to his mother in the midst of his troubles, but he had earlier written, "I am a fool to miss Clare and will certainly get over it" (letter to HH, June 17th, 1928), and in the course of time he mostly does get over it.

And in his modern, limited way, as Krutch indicated, he believed then, and continued to believe, in romance. In a letter to Barrett Clark, the critic, he wrote on December 16th, 1924, that what he liked best in his play was his showing at the beginning of the third act, when men are blustering about their principles, that they "are all worsted by the woman's knowledge of the day of the week." In *Swords* he had put women on their traditional romantic pedestal. But although life taught Sidney the foolishness of traditional romanticism, for him women had never fallen so far that they were not on a pedestal still, lower perhaps, a little grimy perhaps, but to be worshiped anyway for their mysterious knowledge of life, superior to man's any day.

We can perhaps best catch the temper of Sidney Howard's mind by contrasting it with Eugene O'Neill's, as it emerges in *Desire under the Elms*, which opened less than two weeks before *They Knew What They Wanted*. These two plays bear a strange resemblance to each other not often noticed and one worth investigating.

We know that Sidney originally intended *They Knew What They*

Wanted for the Experimental Theatre. Louis Sheaffer, in his biography of O'Neill, suggests the unintended consequence of Sidney's submitting his play to that group. "One day early in 1924 O'Neill, in an excited voice, told [Kenneth] Macgowan that for the first time in his life he had dreamed a play, one that he felt had great possibilities. As he outlined the projected work, Kenneth (though he never mentioned this to O'Neill) thought it a case of 'unconscious plagiarism,' for its story of an aged farmer, his young wife and her lover, by whom she has a child, resembled a new play he had lent Eugene a short time before, by Sidney Howard." Sheaffer might have added that both women marry the old men because they want the security of their own homes.

When the plays were produced, enough people noticed the similarity of the plots for Sidney to issue a denial of any similarity between the dramas in the preface to the printed version of *They Knew What They Wanted*: "[N]o two plays could possibly bear less resemblance to each other than this simple comedy of mine and his glorious tragedy of New England farmers and their Puritan philosophy." But more than the plot makes the two plays alike. For one thing the oedipal theme inheres in both. More important for our immediate purpose, however, is precisely the buried anti-puritan theme in Howard's play to which O'Neill perhaps responds in *Desire under the Elms*.

When Amy, in Howard's play, discovers that she is pregnant, she says, "If you go wrong, you're sure to get it sooner or later. I got it sooner." A bit later she adds, "I'm glad of it. It serves me right" (157). But the rest of the play proves her wrong. She does not have to pay. Tony forgives her, Joe leaves, and she stays to enjoy the security of home, husband, and family. This optimism, this sense that reason can function without much interference from the subconscious, Professor Krutch called "native and original," not only to Sidney Howard but to the American psyche. Stark Young criticized the speed of Tony's transition from rage to forgiveness but not the fact of that transition, and he praises the "kindly, glowing atmosphere and the sense of the children, of songs and the vine and the sun that Mr. Howard achieves in the characters" (*New Republic*, January 25th, 1924).

Sidney seems to have infused his play with his own stirring hopes for decent individuals and for America itself, thus reflecting not only his own temper but that of many Americans of the twenties. He also thus denied another aspect of the American temper, a long tradition of puritan insistence that sin must be punished and that the punishment will come in large part from within.

It is O'Neill who takes up the older tradition in *Desire under the Elms*. Eben, the young man in the play, speaking of his unconscious complicity in infanticide committed by the woman he loves, his father's young wife, says toward the end of the play, "I go t' pay fur my part o' the sin!" (107). In writing a line like that and in his general resolution of the drama in which the two young lovers are satisfied to be executed, O'Neill seems to be answering Sidney Howard. It is as though in his dream prompted by *They Knew What They Wanted*, O'Neill not only took the plot, which is after all quite old (Sidney Howard says he stole it from the story of Tristram and Yseult), but he reacted against one of its themes. Where Sidney Howard implicitly rejected the self-punishment for sin, Eugene O'Neill reverted to the puritanism that accepted it even when the individual had not committed the act. Eben desires punishment apparently for contributing to the state of mind that caused his lover to kill their child. It is the puritanism that punishes the self for merely thinking evil thoughts or unconsciously causing another to do so. It is a strain the very opposite of American optimism and as deeply ingrained. Whereas Sidney Howard insisted that with a rational approach life can work itself out pretty well, thus catching up the feelings of many Americans who wished to overthrow the tyranny of bleak puritanism, O'Neill dourly insisted that the static from our puritan heritage would always prevent us from living happily with our pleasurable desires.

Sidney loved *Desire under the Elms*, praising it publicly and privately. But the implied tension between the points of view expressed in these plays reflected a tension in American literature itself. Thus Howard and O'Neill take their place in the long march of American literature in which the battle between the two attitudes is joined usually in the work of a single writer. Hawthorne, for example, demonstrates it in Arthur Dimmesdale's ineffectual attempt to escape his part of Hester Prynne's guilt and punishment. Huck Finn at the end of the book named for him "lights out for the territories" because the corruption of "sivilization" is too much for him, as though he can ever really escape it. Henry James has his beasts in the jungle and ghosts wandering through children's nurseries—or Isabel Archer deciding to remain married to the greedy and cruel Gilbert Osmond, an act really inexplicable except in terms of the puritan tradition of the American novel. Between Mark Twain and Henry James stood William Dean Howells, friend to both but like neither of these dark geniuses, who was as determined as Sidney Howard later, to allow the dark work into his novels but well in his control. Contemporaneously, novelists such as Fitzgerald, Hemingway, and Faulkner were busy exploring the worlds of malignant fate, social corruption and man's ineffectual attempt to escape them.

For Sidney this clash between goodwill and rationality on the one hand and insistent attendance to the obscure and irrational forces within had its personal side. But for him good health, high spirits and life's joys usually held the demons at bay. But Clare's was another kind of personality. She seemed to be a child of the sun. Margalo Gillmore's descriptions of her behavior and her letters to her husband from Maine show her to have a boisterous sense of fun. Her portrayal of Prossie in *Candida* and her singing in *Fashion* demonstrate her keen comic sense. But even as Prossie she played a woman hopelessly devoted to a man who could never love her. Also, Stark Young noted the "wry, gauche tragedy" she made of the role, showing, as a great comic actor does, the pain beneath the emotion that causes laughter. The parts that she chose when she could choose, the parts that seemed to suit her most, were precisely those of women, such as Lady Macbeth and Hedda Gabler, driven by unknown forces within. Even in consenting to do *The Spook Sonata*, she decided on a play which was dreamlike in its method, exploiting painful subconscious forces. In an interview Clare said that she did her best work when she was ill and noted the difference between herself and her husband, who did his best work when he was well. That reliance on, and comfort with, illness and off-centeredness that apparently allowed her to listen to obscure forces within shows the temper of her mind, which seemed to be reflected in both her work and her life. Later in her life she will suffer great pangs of guilt for pain she brings to her husband and child. But even when she does wrong by conventional standards, she says, "Be true to the God within you, ... Listen to your own secret heart, and you can do no wrong." That may or may not be good morality, but it is the attitude that Clare Eames seems to have taken to her art and to her life, obviously an attitude that will cause sharp differences in her marriage to a man of very different temperament.

However, the open trouble was still a few years off. The couple was still basking in the delights of its individuals' successes. And they lived in a yeasty, creative theatrical world. *They Knew What They Wanted* and *Desire under the Elms* were not the only plays critics and audiences appreciated that season. In a letter of December 16th, 1924, Sidney expresses to Barrett Clark his appreciation of the critic's review of *They Knew What They Wanted*. He adds: "I'm delighted, too, at your review of 'DESIRE'. *There's* a fine play!" He then goes on: "There may not be any *great* ones—though Stallings and Anderson are pretty near—but there are four of them, doing big business and earning at least serious respect, and that's *not* bad." The play by Lawrence Stallings and Maxwell Anderson was of course *What Price Glory?* The fourth play to which Sidney refers is probably *The Show-Off*, a satire of American domestic and social life by George Kelly, which had opened the previous season but was still running in the fall of 1924. Suddenly it seemed as though American drama was really coming of age.

While no American dramatist except O'Neill had so far produced an impressive body of work, yet the accumulation of highly respected plays by a number of native dramatists, plays to which many serious theatergoers were willing to listen, seemed to indicate that there was perhaps a place for serious American drama. Elmer Rice, working in the style of German expressionists, highly admired by contemporary intellectuals, had in the previous year written the widely respected drama called *The Adding Machine*. John Howard Lawson, also in the previous year, had produced the controversially exciting *Roger Bloomer*, and in January, 1925, the month after Sidney's letter to Clark, the Theatre Guild was to present Lawson's *Processional*, as controversial as its predecessor. The Provincetown had discovered not only Eugene O'Neill but Susan Glaspell as well. While she did not have the far-reaching impact on audiences that O'Neill did, yet many then rightly admired her. (Unfortunately, her plays still go largely unappreciated and unrevived today.) George S. Kaufman and Marc Connelly had written a series of popular comedies such as *Dulcy* and *Merton of the Movies*, which made no pretenses to anything more than popularity, but they contained elements of genuine satire of American life. Early in the year 1924 the collaborators had gone a step further and in *Beggar on Horseback* had written a fantasy highly satirical of American business, which like their less pretentious comedies, was successful.

One morning in 1924 America awoke and realized that indeed there was an American drama. Among those writing it was Sidney Howard.

4

Sidney

On September 17th, 1918, Sidney Howard wrote to his friend the writer Elizabeth Sergeant:

> I am having the time of my life leading two raids into Germany and bombing. It is a hard grind—we are only just beginning to get onto the tricks of it. Training was never like this. I never felt such an ass in all my days as during my first hour "over." For all that things are very much O.K. ... and breaking well for me.

He had anticipated loving the challenges and the fighting of the battle in the air: "It's a sport and by God it's poetry—the sublime physical experience of it is the stunningest thing we can do today. It is the only man to man affair in this war and the skill and wits of the best aviator are bound to win his fight for him." The experience itself matched his expectations (letter to Jean, July 17th, 1917):

> I adore this—every bit of it. If I come out of it I shall look back on it as the only reality amidst all the pale mirages of experience I have known. There *is* no *experience* possible wherein man is not at grips with ultimate fate. The only contrast is the contrast of life and death and the only living making nothing of life. I seem unable to stay out of the air here. If I miss a raid I am wretched until my turn comes again. I don't seem to know myself. I am neither a hero nor a degenerate.... I am having (I suppose, literally) *the* time of my life. That is the final consolation to death in battle. It doesn't matter what happens once the climax comes. The men I saw go down in flames yesterday were friends of mine. I knew it. Even that didn't matter. It's the *damndest* thing.

Sidney seems charged with his own manhood derived from the age-old excitement of battle. However, this urge for glory seems more urgent with the apparent advancement of civilization. In American society especially the writer seems fearful of submerging his manhood in his sedentary occupation. David Leverenz describes such a fear, going back to James Fenimore Cooper, for whom "real learning—and implicitly, real manhood—comes through 'the jostlings of the world,' where a man who may be 'existing in a state of dreaming retrospection, lost in a maze of theories,' comes up against antagonists at every turn" (14). Later American writers, while not necessarily seeking one-to-one combat, yet sought the "jostlings of the world" in a variety of ways and places: Melville in the South Seas, Mark Twain in the West, Ambrose Bierce in Mexico, Stephen Crane among America's vagrants—their lives frequently in danger. Sidney Howard, among other contemporary writers—Ernest Hemingway and Robert Sherwood, for instance—believed that to become a manly writer rather than an aesthete, one had to be jostled in the world, especially when the world was at war.

In his air battles Sidney had jostlings enough, but he seemed to be living a charmed life. On his fifteenth bombing raid Sidney's plane is again riddled. He once more manages to land his plane behind his own lines, and again he is untouched. (Although in the previous encounter, his observer was killed.) For his bravery Sidney will get the Distinguished Service Cross.

Sidney's early life hardly seems to have prepared him for such challenge and adventure. Like Clare Eames, Sidney spent a sickly childhood. He therefore "never did well at sports. That's always given me a complex" (Clark, 211). But whereas Clare enjoyed her illness with its accompanying coddling, Sidney found it a hindrance. Clare's habit of illness lasted into her adulthood and became the condition in which she worked best. Sidney tried his utmost to end his series of illnesses, finally did, and worked best when he was in roaring good health in body and mind. And he intended to remain well. Always as part of his tumultuously busy days as an adult, he found time for strenuous exercise to make sure he kept physically fit, and as a man his body was immensely strong.

One reason for Clare's and Sidney's varying attitudes toward their respective illnesses derived from the illnesses themselves. There is no indication that Clare's were life threatening, nor is there evidence that Sidney's were thought to be fatal until his attack of tuberculosis at the age of nineteen. On October 15th of 1929 Sidney wrote to Arthur Hobson Quinn: "I did all the things that Western kids do. After a while, for no very good reason, I got tuberculosis and was shut out of life for nearly three years, partly in Davos Platz [Switzerland] and partly in California on one ranch after another." According to Sidney, then, his sickly childhood did not prognosticate the tuberculosis, but his hovering mother, at least as anxious about his tuberculosis as she had been about his series of childhood illnesses, might fret about him forever if he did not recover perfectly. So, hating disease, the possibility of death, and the hovering of his mother, he determined, successfully as it turned out, to remain in good health for the rest of his life.

Clare, then, enjoyed her illness. She drew upon it for her work, which seemed angular and fragmented, modernist in its appeal. Sidney, on the other hand, hated illness, which always seemed to be lurking in the shadows, ready to pounce once more. He wished for wholeness in body, mind, and work. Aware of the dark underside of his and others' lives—mental as well as physical—displaying its ugliness in his writing, he yet wished to contain it with health, love, and determination.

The extra attention which Sidney's mother lavished upon him was the result not only of his vulnerability to disease but also came from the peculiar structure of the Howard family.

John Howard, Sidney's father, a self-made, self-educated businessman, married twice. His first wife died, leaving him with four children, a girl and three boys (letter to Arthur Hobson Quinn, October 15th, 1929). At the time of his second marriage, in 1890, the oldest of the children, Jean, was ten (letter from HH to Sidney, January 28th, 1917). The three boys were John, Harry, and Charles, who was called Chet. When he married Helen Louise Coe, she was clearly meant to bring up his children, and that she was in effect their mother is shown by their always addressing her in their adulthood as "Mama." Helen gave birth to two children in her marriage. Sidney was born in 1891 and Bruce in 1897 (letter from HH to Sidney, January 28th, 1917). Sidney never refers to the elder group of children as anything but his brothers and sister; never is there any indication that they are his half-siblings, but among all the children Jean is clearly his favorite, his intimate all of his life. In fact, she seems to be his alternative mother.

Helen, however, seemed to have made a distinction felt by all the children. There were her two children, and then there were the others. That division, perhaps smoothed over while the father was alive, quickly became apparent after his death in 1914. On October 7th, 1916, Helen writes to Sidney: "... [T]he family seems friendly but the fact remains that father's death untied the knot and we have all fallen apart—and can never be the same again—since leaving the old home too that breaks another tie and California is really becoming dreadful to me—I seem to want to put away and forget it all."

At this distance we cannot know precisely the reasons for the separation of the two groups apparently tightly knit before. But we can understand the reasons in a general way. Helen favored her own children above those of her husband's former wife. No matter how subtle her preference, the older set of children must have felt it and inwardly resented it.

When the father died, they all maintained friendly relations, but the resentment of the older group, by this time married and in their own homes, must have emerged, and Helen reacted against it. Also, like Sidney, they seem to have found an alternative mother in Jean and therefore did not have to be totally reliant on Helen for maternal love. Helen and her stepchildren treated each other cordially enough, but relations had so cooled that Helen, repelled by the estrangement that had developed, wished to leave California altogether.

But even before the father's death Helen could let loose her full throttle of emotion toward Sidney without blame from anyone. His general state of poor health was an obvious reason. Another is that for six years he was her only child. That she was partial to him shows, for example, in her letters when she addresses him in adulthood as "boy," or "dear boy" or "blessed boy" (letters from HH to Sidney, April 25th, 1916; August 25th, 1906; August 12th, 1910; October 7th, 1916). But even after her second son was born, Sidney remained her favorite undoubtedly because he had been her favorite all of those years (Clark, 212).

Helen, having "earned her living as a professional, an organist and a piano teacher" before her marriage, shared her love of music with Sidney rather than with Bruce. The former "liked music better than anything and always raged because I wasn't able to get on with it [presumably the piano]" (Clark, 211). They attended operas and concerts together, and he learned to trace themes and motifs of various types of music in musical scores. Like Sid, she enjoyed the theater. She encouraged his career in writing, giving what she felt were insightful critiques of his work; sometimes like the best of loving critics, she was harsh. But the intimacy went even deeper than the shared pleasures of art and creativity. When he is in the sanitorium as she and Bruce are touring, she writes, "I really can't enjoy sightseeing while you are shut up in Davos" (November 26th, 1910). When he is a volunteer ambulance driver in World War I, she writes, "When you come back don't you want to take me to Yama Farms [upstate New York] for a little rest? We will even be sporty enough to motor it if you wish—I have seen so little of the Eastern country that I think I should love it—" addressing him as though he were her lover (August 9th, 1916). Perhaps aware that her embrace of him was too close, she writes in an earlier letter, trying to dissuade him from volunteering for the ambulance corps in World War I, "Boy, I can hand you over to some lovely girl with good grace—but it's too much for me to even think of risking your life and health—Just think how dear you are to me—Sid" (February 23rd, 1916). Two years later she writes, "I would love to see you married but you *must* have one tiny extra room in your home so I can come once in a while..." (letter from HH to Sidney, February 12th, 1918).

4. Sidney

Sidney did a great deal to escape his mother's iron clutch. Apparently using Jean as an alternative mother seems central to his effort, and they furnished their letters with the assumption that his mother was an impossible package to handle. He went east to Harvard graduate school, then spent more than two years abroad, first in the ambulance corps and later as a pilot in the American army. He did all this even as his mother begged him not to go or to return as his enlistments ended. Earlier, to his mother's continued pleas to resist his desire to join the ambulance corps, he replied in an undated letter from Harvard: "Your letters always make me feel like a skunk but I am one, so why not?" And his derring-do seems in part a very strong way of saying "No" to Mama. He appears to be very much aware of his strong bond and his need to cut it: "All boys hate their families for a while," he writes to Jean. "We Americans have too much family and too much home. It isn't good for us" (November 19th, 1917). A violent break seemed necessary.

But although his upbringing tied him close to his mother, it also apparently helped him assert his independence. He writes to Jean from abroad, "I don't think either Father or Mother ever denied to any one of us a right to judge things for ourselves—and that doctrine of laissez faire of Father's which you and I bewailed once or twice has come to seem a very wise way of life and I only hope that we are all men enough to justify it. And he had a lot more respect for us than he showed" (February 5th, 1917). While John Howard may have pointed the way to independence for his children, Helen, though she hangs on mightily, finally gives her grudging consent to his enlistment in the ambulance corps in a letter of April 25th (1916): "Why, boy, if you are so bent on going to France and so unhappy about it [not enlisting], don't you know that I am not going to stay in your way no matter how wretched it makes me?" That last phrase still pulls her to him, means to make his guilt work, but she lets him finally choose.

Even as he escaped his mother, however, he simultaneously drew her near him. The flippant remark—"Your letters always make me feel like a skunk but I am one, so why not?"—is unusual. He is generally careful of his mother's feelings, and in fact he explains the reasons for his wishing to go abroad. When he is overseas, he sends her long detailed letters of the sights he has seen, the people he met, and the adventures he has experienced. Some of these missives are as many as thirteen pages in length. From Harvard he had sent her accounts of his friends and acquaintances, the nature of his work, activities in which he has been engaged, all so that she can participate in his life. When a very good friend suggests that Sidney and he share an apartment in New York, Sidney refuses. He writes to his mother that he prefers to live with her after he receives his M.A., and she answers that she "should love to adopt your plans and live East with you..." (February 25th, 1916). From Europe he continues to express his desire to live with her, and in fact when he returns, they settle together in an apartment in New York. While there are sometimes great difficulties between them, he has been and he remains the very model of the concerned, caring, loving son. She can complain of Bruce while he is attending the University of California, Berkeley: "I think he has very little affection for me. He hasn't been out with me a single evening since you went out and although he sleeps at home a few nights every week, he never spends an evening with us" (February 23rd, 1916). She could never make such a complaint of Sidney, who wrote *The Silver Cord*, the most famous mother-bashing play of its day.

Sidney's strong tie to his mother conspicuously affected his life, but it did not cripple him. Not only did his father's "laissez faire" attitude help him, with which his mother reluctantly agreed, but family circumstances also alleviated her drive to bind him to her. Helen Howard was not one to shirk her duty toward the other children. Not only did she feel obligated to be their mother, but she gave them maternal care at least for the sake of her husband, whom she loved. In addition her husband required and received her attention. The relationship was essentially a happy one. Remembering her marriage three years after her husband's death, she writes to Sidney, "[S]uch wonderful years—ups and downs of course and cloud and sunshine—but sunshine predominated..." (January 28th, 1917). She also respected her husband. On October 7th, 1916 she writes to Sidney overseas: "Make a fine, clean man of yourself—a man with an ideal as high as father had—I want him to be proud of his boys—and I daily hope that wherever he is his influence may in some way help you both—how he loved you!"

And Sidney evidently loved and respected his father. We saw that in his appreciation of his father's laissez faire policies toward his children. But we also notice it as he writes to Barrett Clark: "My father was a self-educated man. There is a story, I think true, that he began his education working in a second-hand book shop after the hours he spent working on the wharves of the Philadelphia and Reading in Philadelphia. He was twelve then.... My father opened the first steamship line to Alaska" (*Intimate Portraits*, 211–212). John Howard, like his wife, was a "pretty fair" musician. "My father was a real Handel hound. We had to learn Handel choruses as kids and keep time." Like many self-educated men—as well as educated ones—Sidney's father was "a great reader." Like his father, Sidney loved books, in his adulthood often reading a book a night after a busy day. But the correct son, he rebelled against his father's taste. "Once he gave me an edition of Ibsen which I very much wanted and added that I was to wash the taste out with a good draught of Huxley." But all the family seem to have had literate minds, surely a tribute to both parents. Their letters are clear and straightforward. Jean and Sidney, like Sidney and his mother, often give each other books as gifts or recommend or lend books to each other.

But they were a family that loved vigorous play as well. Sidney writes that he "camped in the High Sierras and rode horses," these presumably being two of the things "that Western kids do" (Clark, 211). Jean and her husband, Duncan McDuffie, go camping, too. Sidney wishes to impart such pleasures to his daughter, Jennifer, determined that she have the "great spacious West in her childhood, so that she may see ... that the universe is greater than any one human" (letter to HH, June 28th, 1928). Living lustily in the wide West lends not only bodily health but spiritual health as well. A few days later he writes to his mother that he wishes for Jennifer that "unbroken childhood for which all of us Howards have such deep reason to be grateful." He adds, "All of this has been strengthened in me by my visit to California where I saw marvelous healthy and fine children [presumably his nieces and nephews] growing up in that same sound and unpretentious tradition" (June 12th, 1928). That is, he wishes for his daughter the same joyous, vigorous childhood which benefited him, his siblings, and their children.

Sidney attended the public schools of Oakland, apparently then a fine public school system. But his formal education was interrupted when at the age of twelve, in 1903–1904, he accompanied his mother and sister to Paris and Italy. He writes to his father descriptions of paintings and sculptures which show an unusual ability to observe in a twelve-year-old. For example, in a letter dated February 18th, 1904, he writes:

> The Farnese Bull is a glorious group and I do not remember ever having seen a larger one. Seven fine marble figures in perfect preservation (Michael Angelo). This was found in Caracalla's baths much damaged but they put Mike at it and he did it up beautifully. The two sons of Antiope are trying to hold a wild bull long enough to blind Dirce (who had treated thier [sic] mother cruelly) to it's [sic] back. At the foot of the bull is a hound and beside him a little faun. In the rear is Antiope pleading (like a fool) for the life of Dirce. She looks as if she was shaking hands with a friend her attitude is so poor [letter from Sidney to A. H. Quinn, October 15th, 1928].

Although the spelling is problematic, the description, the knowledge of some background, the light-handedness of the account betokened an ease with art which must have made a self-educated parent proud.

The trip gave dimension to Sidney's formal education. But his parents never relied on formal education alone for their children. Both the mother and father were grounded in music and trained their offspring in that discipline. Sidney's parents regularly attended concerts and operatic performances, and, we may presume, eventually took their children to them. Also, his parents treated Sidney, and presumably the other children as well, with intellectual respect as they discussed books, the father recommending in one letter a life of Cromwell, in another a book on Egypt, in another providing a two-page analysis of a new novel by the American author Winston Churchill. This European trip then was part of a rounded, thorough education in Western culture. It was on another European journey, in 1910, when he was nineteen, that he was afflicted with tuberculosis while traveling with his mother and Bruce; Jean, also in Europe, had her own apartment in Paris. Sidney entered treatment at Davos Platz in Switzerland, where he stayed for about three months. His father wanted the family home and felt that Sidney could receive as good treatment in the United States as in Europe. The recovery seemed painfully slow to him, especially because it delayed his entrance into the University of California at Berkeley.

In a letter to Arthur Hobson Quinn on October 15th, 1928, he writes, "I ... got very little out of it [college] except the normal undergraduate wine, women and song. They eclipsed the curriculum to such an extent that I was flunked out in my senior year but Charles Mills Gayley made the powers give me a degree." That statement is untrue; in the fashion of many modern American writers who like to see themselves as rough and formally uneducated, who sometimes even like to picture themselves as nonreaders, Sidney prefers to undervalue the effect of his undergraduate education. It is hard to believe that Gayley, an eminent scholar of his day, would have fought for Howard's degree, if indeed he did have to do it, if Sidney had managed only mediocre work. Nor does his transcript support the notion that he did badly. For while he did not achieve uniformly outstanding grades, he generally did very well, especially in English and history, subjects that interested him, and the transcript shows no failures. Further, he became a personal friend of the Gayley family and of other members of the faculty.

In addition to his schoolwork at Berkeley he wrote:

> Two plays as an undergraduate in collaboration with one Frederick Faust who, as "Max Brand" has since made a great name for himself writing Westerns. [Faust remained a lifelong friend.] I also wrote a blank verse tragedy about the Black Death in Avignon. I did that under Leonard Bacon the poet, then an instructor at California. [Bacon became a confidential lifelong friend.] He had a seminar in which the students wrote poetry. That tragedy was subsequently produced by the artists' colony at Carmel by the Sea, California. They changed the setting to Monterey and Laura and Petrarch to an Indian Maiden and a young monk.

All of this hardly seems to be the efforts of a young man embarked on a college career of wine, women, and song. At any rate this young man who benefited little from his undergraduate work was admitted to graduate school at both Harvard and Yale.

"I went to Harvard and [George Pierce] Baker, not because I cared anything about the theatre, but because I had always wanted to go to Harvard." This was also in the letter to Quinn. That statement, certainly as he puts it, is also untrue. He came east, undecided as to whether to attend Harvard or Yale. He first goes to New Haven, speaks to a couple of professors in the Department of English, "and was entranced." He is less impressed with Harvard, but "there is the experimental theatre here, there is a real class of hard competitive workers here, and there is Boston with the chances it holds out for publicity" (undated letter to Jean and Duncan McDuffie). So much for his indifference to the theater.

When Sidney entered George Pierce Baker's English 47 class in dramatic composition, he came to one of the centers, perhaps to the very heart, of the excitement about the possibilities for new American drama. Baker had been prescient about the arrival of this new day. Just before the turn of the century he had set down some notes:

> Is not this the beginning of an *Epoch*? Young men turning to the drama—the growing interest everywhere—the discussion of new plays. *What we need is the skilled portrayal of life from a close study of it*, plays good in characterization, in plot, in dialogue..." [Kinne, 69].

In a few years' time Baker would act pivotally in shaping this "growing interest" by founding English 47, his playwriting class, virtually the first such course in the country and the predecessor of the deluge of playwriting classes that followed on other college campuses. Although Baker's course was only one force that helped shape American drama, it was a powerful one not only because it garnered many imitators and led eventually to the creation of the Yale School of Drama by Baker himself, but also because of the future playwrights and other theater workers who passed through his hands. Such men as Sidney Howard, Eugene O'Neill, S. N. Behrman, and George Abbott carried forward Baker's idea of the essential seriousness of the theater.

Baker gained his great influence soon after he commenced teaching English 47. A member of the first class, Edward Sheldon responded to Baker's admonition to observe life closely by looking on for hours at the efforts of the Salvation Army women to aid derelicts. He turned those observations into the drama *Salvation Nell*, which he sold to Minnie Maddern Fiske, the highly respected actress who had helped bring Ibsen to the American stage. Produced in 1907, *Salvation Nell* became a great financial and critical success, assured English 47 of national fame, and made the course a magnet for aspiring dramatists. They believed it the key to commercial as well as artistic achievement.

George Abbott, the enormously successful director and playwright, recalled the atmosphere of Baker's class: "Edward Sheldon became my hero. I knew nothing about him except that he was a very young playwright who was very successful and he had taken Professor Baker's course at Harvard" (63) Nor did Baker discourage the attitude that commercial popularity was as desirable as artistic accomplishment. "He could see that the success of his work in teaching dramatic technique, which the French thought well worthwhile for its own sake, hung on the sheer chance of some manager or actor liking a student manuscript.... GPB decided to find the necessary liaison between English 47 and what could be described only by the vulgar phrase, "Broadway success." Vulgar the phrase may be, but it apparently described in part Baker's intention.

Critics then and now condemn Baker for teaching mainly the technique of the well-made play and for ignoring advanced playwrights and new movements in the theater. But Baker was aware of much of what was new and advanced in the theater of his day. In fact, he put Eugene O'Neill onto German expressionism when the future playwright attended Baker's class in 1914–1915, and he was a correspondent of Gordon Craig, one of the leaders of the New Stagecraft. But unlike such figures as Craig, he believed that the play alone was the key element in a theatrical production and that "theatre is an art which is relevant to the life and spirit of the people." Therefore for a variety of reasons he found a number of European dramatists unsuited to "America's needs" (Kinne, 181–82).

But there can be little doubt that Baker, though limited by his time, believed in the artistic seriousness of the drama. He encouraged students, as Eugene O'Neill asserted, "to write plays of life as one saw and felt it, instead of concocting the conventional drivel of the time" (Baker memorial, 20–21) and "to believe in the dawn of a new era in our theatre where he would have a chance to be heard." Finally, Baker believed and taught "that there is no one rigid rule or theory of treatment," that dramatists should keep "abreast with the changing times and conditions of their art [and] shall interpret them in their work."

Sidney Howard's attitude toward Baker's teaching may be summed up in his remarks in a 1915 letter from Cambridge to the McDuffies quoted above:

> Mr. Baker must have his plays made on his plan of inspiration, so to speak—well, it gets by, it's efficient, and it *is* definite.... His criticisms are purely on matters of technique. I think that where psychology does not conform to his laws of the drama he is very apt to fix psychology, which is an undemocratic thing after all and *needs* discipline. It is good for the young and growing hero of our tale [himself, of course] if he preserves his sense of humor.... Mr. Baker persists in recognizing: 'Where is that seven

million you stole from my father's bank yesterday?' as an appropriate introductory line to a serious play....

Although Sidney satirizes Baker's "laws of drama" (Abbot, 65) he will submit to the discipline of learning the technique because it is a usable technique. Baker admired the tightly built play with a clear, causal, linear development, with no mystery in any character or motivation (except that which was eventually revealed), no incident which failed to contribute to the drama's immediately apprehensible progress (Kinne, 107–8). He taught his students to write a scenario before they embarked on the drama itself (a method both Sidney Howard and Eugene O'Neill always utilized). Much as Sidney as a student criticized Baker, he came to think more of his teacher's precepts later. In 1928 he writes to Barrett Clark: "I didn't like that [47 Workshop course], in which I was wrong and I have since eaten my words against it."

Actually, Sidney Howard wrote only one play, *The Silver Cord*, that in any strict way may be regarded as a well-made play. Most of his plays are more loosely constructed than the model set up by Baker, and some are frankly experimental in form. Sidney seems to have derived from Baker's class a respect for *some* definite technique for each play and perhaps the notion that a theme and plot ought to derive from the characters' circumstances and motivations, with these arising out of a close observation of life.

Sidney, apparently hiding his ambivalence to Baker, made an active and successful attempt to become close to his teacher. In a letter to the McDuffies he writes: Baker remains a bear, but now I have him...." At the same time, however, he responded much more positively to another figure at Harvard. In 1928 he wrote to Barrett Clark: "I came very much under the influence of Sam Hume and his first New Stagecraft show" (Clark, 212) That statement conforms with Sidney's contemporary correspondence.

Samuel J. Hume came from the East Bay, the Berkeley area, as did Sidney, where the latter had previously met him. A big, burly, two-fisted Westerner, Sam sometimes became rough and tough, a physicality which must surely have endeared him to Sidney. In 1909 he had gone to Florence to study with Gordon Craig, a prophet of the New Stagecraft, the intention of which was to place on an equal level with the language of the play the various elements of the theater, such as scenery, costumes, music, dance, gesture. A fervent disciple of the New Stagecraft by the time he left Craig in 1912, Hume returned to his native land in Cambridge rather than Berkeley, completing his final year of undergraduate work at Harvard. He enrolled in Baker's English 47, but eventually his differences with Baker about the New Stagecraft led to his rancor-free resignation from the class in March of 1914 (Bolin).

That spring he began work on his New Stagecraft exhibition, to which Sidney referred in his letter to Barrett Clark. The exhibition was intended to show off the new method of stage design as practiced by Gordon Craig and others of his persuasion in Europe. Hume "designed and constructed his own modern settings, made sketches, models and photographs...." The show was a great success in Boston, and the New York Stage Society brought it to New York in 1915. That version, which included work of Robert Edmond Jones, launched that designer's career.

By the time Sidney renewed his friendship with Hume, the latter had already succeeded with his New Stagecraft exhibit in Boston and New York. But despite his new fame, he found time to be kind to his newly arrived hometown friend.

In a 1915 undated letter to the McDuffies Sidney writes:

> The Humes ... have been great. Sam is a real genius and Boston, which is a nifty town, recognizes him.... [T]hey have taken me about a great deal. She [Sam's wife, Maude] took me to call on all the big men of the faculty or had me to dine to meet them and that has been more valuable than you think. I am on a very comfortable footing in Cambridge in consequence.... I have been to the [William Allen] Nielsons' to dine [Nielson, an important Shakespearean, later became president of Smith College] and to tea at several houses.

Sidney may be starry eyed and puffed up in his first weeks at Cambridge, but the fact is that throughout his life he had an extraordinary power to attract accomplished men and women, as did Clare Eames.

But Sam Hume did not stop merely at introducing him to Harvard faculty.

> There is a very good paper in Boston of which you may have heard—The Transcript. It has the leading dramatic critic of the country, H.T. Parker, Known to the terrified managerial world as the venomous H.T.P. He has recently made himself famous by attacking Geraldine Farrar in terms about which there could be no mistake and which caused that lady to refuse to sing in Boston, which she expected to do very shortly. Well, he is a great friend of the Humes and Sam recommended me to him. I am a sort of auxiliary already. I did Keith's bill [he reviewed the vaudeville presentation at Keith's theater] for the Transcript this week, and he has commissioned me to write a full page Sunday article on the history and present significance of marionettes the same to be signed and paid for.

He soon explains about the marionettes:

> I am much interested, now, in marionettes. They have a big place in the art world of the Germans, especially in Munich and Vienna, and The Mask, Gordon Craig's magazine, publishes articles on them and plays by Maeterlinck, Yeats, etc. Well Sam and I are going to try a marionette the-

atre next summer and fall.... [W]e plan to do things in all the newest German manners. That is, where theatres in this forsaken country are dawdling with the Belasco-Kismet [literal and elaborate realism] sort of production, we will be putting on decorative marionette productions in which the very most modern lightings and appliances will be employed in miniature. Our skies will not be flat blue drops, but domes, real domes lit as only the Germans know how.

This is in 1915, and Sidney is full of the New Stagecraft as was surely Clare Eames because of her stay in Paris and her connection with the Cleveland Playhouse in 1915, which at its opening featured a stage for marionettes as well as a living theatre.

Sidney, in devising these schemes, in his work on *The Transcript*, and in his proud pursuit of social intercourse amazingly still had time for his graduate studies. In addition to Baker's playwriting course he takes Baker's "history of the drama to the closing of the [London] theatres [in 1642] which I like because I am very keen for the [medieval] mysteries [of which he read fifty-two within a short time of his arrival at Cambridge]" (undated 1915 letter to the McDuffies). He is enthusiastic about Nielson, "the most wonderful man in the department.... I take Bacon from him—Milton after Christmas—and the Romantic poets, a seminar in the criticism of poetry in which we write one long critical thesis (I write on Browning the dramatist) and criticize one that another student has written (I do Oscar Wilde)." For Baker's playwriting course he has already done two adaptations, "one of Galsworthy's 'The Voice of...!' and the other of Kipling's 'Mary Postgate.'" He is also to do an original one-act and a "long play which I think will be on birth control in which I am much interested at present."

But that is not the end of his activities.

> There is a friend of mine in Boston who is the minister at the Second Church who wants to put on a Christmas play in the chancel of his church ... a modern mystery. I thought about it, and on last Monday night got a hunch which I took to Sam. He said: "You go home get that into a scenario before you go to sleep." I finished it about four and Sam was around to the rooms around eight to drag me over to breakfast that he and Mrs. Hume might see. Sam says it's great, the best thing that ever came out of Harvard. Sam raves, I suppose [he adds modestly]. Anyway none of the verse is done yet.

It all seems a whirligig, perfect for Sidney, who never in his life seems to be doing less than at this moment at Harvard. Frenetic as these many endeavors must have made him, all of his grades were *A*.

His multitudinous activities at Harvard continue to the end of the academic year, including the writing of his M.A. thesis. One more piece of extracurricular writing which Sidney undertook during that M.A. year was *The Cranbrook Masque*. This came about also from Sam Hume's efforts. Hume's New Stagecraft exhibition was so popular that he took it around to various cities. In Detroit a George C. Booth had built on his estate, called Cranbrook, a Greek theater, which he wished to dedicate. He was so impressed with Sam Hume's work that he hired the young man to direct the entire affair. Sam Hume suggested that Sidney Howard be commissioned to write a masque for the occasion, and that became Howard's first professional assignment. The success of the occasion was so great that the Detroit Arts and Crafts Society decided to include a theater in its work, and its director became Sam Hume, who made it into an important art theater.

Howard's masque was presented again as *The Quest* in 1920 in Santa Barbara, California, again under the sponsorship of Sam Hume. Mary Morris gives a description of it for *Drama* (November 1920, 41–44):

> It is written in varying poetic forms and contains lines of unusual beauty as well as excellent dialogue and dramatic values. The masque is made up of five episodes with an epilogue and a prologue spoken by the Tragic Actor. Through these five episodes is depicted man's unending search for Romance, Beauty, Love. We are shown Ancient Greece, the Middle Ages, Elizabethan England, Renaissance Italy, a symbolic modern episode, and finally the dedication of the theatre to a renewed faith and endeavor toward all that is beautiful.

> Send forth from here new men to seek new goals;
> Strike here the heart of lust with bloody scars;
> Set poetry here a-singing in men's souls;
> Light in men's lives the splendour of thy stars.
> So let the incense here burn to fantasy,
> And prayer on prayer be given all reverently.

Sidney was obviously making use of the knowledge he had stored up in the course of the year. The poetry strains for high aesthetic effect as did much of the "educated" poetry of the late nineteenth and early twentieth centuries. But the use of the various elements of the theater, such as dancing, singing, costuming, lighting, sets, the combination of nature's and man's settings, were very much of the strivings toward art of the New Stagecraft in which Sam Hume and the other leaders of the movement were engaged. Sidney never saw the masque, however, for he sailed to Europe before it opened.

During the year at Harvard, when Sidney saw a production utilizing techniques of the New Stagecraft, he was entranced. In an undated letter from Cambridge he writes to his mother: "I saw the comedy of the Man Who married a dumb wife [*sic*] Wednesday followed by Androcles and the Lion in Granville Barker's production. I have never seen anything which delighted me as they first did. I say this quite calmly and I am going again to see it. It is flawlessly staged.... In the first place it is the best example on our stage of the new scenic idea...." He also sees *Sumurun*, Max Reinhardt's "wordless spectacle." He thought it "The best thing I have seen. I went the opening night with the Humes...." The set for "The Man Who Married a Dumb Wife" was by Robert Edmond Jones, hired for the occasion when Granville Barker saw Jones's work in Hume's New Stagecraft Exhibition. In 1913 Jones had studied with Reinhardt, who himself was a sort of disciple of Craig in the sense that he put Craig's theories to everyday, practical use.

Importantly, however, Sidney did not remain interested in the art theater for its own sake. Actually, even in the letter in which he praises the precious *Sumurun*, we see him enthusiastic about quite another kind of play, *On Trial*, Elmer Rice's first drama, which brought to the stage the movie technique of the flashback. Except for the technical novelty, the play is an ordinary melodrama. But Sidney enjoys it, thinks it has "terrific grip and a real plot, and one of the most extraordinary exposition scenes in literature...." It should be obvious by now that Sidney's enthusiasms run to extremes, but clearly he is impressed by the technique that rivets the audience, that is able to hold it with a strong plot. Never mind the New Stagecraft with its symbolism and aesthetics. What held Sidney then and throughout his career is a good story based on convincing characters observed from life. That sounds like Baker's influence, but if it was, Baker solidified a fundamental impulse in Sidney, for he held firmly to the notion, in the face of much opposition in the circles in which he moved, that only individuals as they fought through the conflicts of their lives give rise to important drama. In proclaiming such a thought he seems to differentiate it from what he is supposed to be learning from various quarters at Harvard.

In an undated letter to his mother from Cambridge, he exclaims: "No more academics. You and me living somewhere together finding out about this American business and what there is in it. Faust laughs at me. Merrill [Baker graduate who became a good friend of Sidney's] groans and tears his hair. Come to New York says he, and write plays about pathological women. Go to hell says Faust and write about sex. But I'm going to put *men* back on the stage and *feminist* women and men into novels—American men." Immediately he adds, "Stop ranting, Sidney." Sidney often pulls himself up short as he does here, laughing at his grandiosity.

More important, Sidney wishes to plunge into and record the clatter and tumult of American life. Although this seems to be much the same as Baker's injunction to write about the life around you, as Sidney puts it, the life he wishes to record is a long distance from safe Harvard yard. Further, his cry to dive into the midst of American life seems to be an explosion from inside rather than a desire introjected by Baker or other. He wishes to put men, underlined, onstage. And feminist women are true women. Sidney may have apprehended the notion of feminist women in part from Ibsen, from the Nora of *A Doll's House*, for example, but we suspect that it is the independent American women that he saw about him, his mother and sister, for example, and the new women he met in Boston and New York and California, declaring their freedom from tradition. As far as women go, Sidney kept to his word. Never did he create a clinging vine type. His independent women are usually admirable; his virulent women are those who misuse their independence. In one instance, *Half Gods*, the play written during his period of divorce from Clare Eames, he proposes keeping a woman under a man's thumb. Often his men are weak, insensitive, or bumbling. Admirably used strength is more frequently the hallmark of Sidney Howard's women than of his men.

But he desires to keep away from plays about pathological women, presumably from the Hedda Gablers and the Miss Julies. His interest lies in health, not pathology. Apparently, like Baker, he felt that concentrating on pathological women would be a far step from penetrating to the heart of American life. However, as it turns out, a couple of Sidney's dramas are about pathological women, but they are placed in context and kept from totally destroying the good around them.

The concentration on pathology and sex he apparently leaves to oddly disposed writers, often the same ones who like aesthetics and aesthetic theory for their own sake. We hear him again on the subject in a letter to his mother from Europe, written on January 28th, 1917: "I don't want to degenerate into an artist...." This antagonism toward "art" for art's sake holds him for most of his career. Sidney's theatrical experiments were made for the purpose of probing more validly than he could in a conventional drama into a play's inner truth rather than for the sake of experimentation alone.

Sidney also expresses a desire to write fiction. He continues to believe for a long time that truth may be more honestly put into fiction than into drama and that fiction was more truly the writer's medium than drama. He does indeed write some well-received short stories, and for a few years he worked on a long novel of early-nineteenth-century Maine life, which he never completed. Subsequently, he never tries fiction again.

However, amidst all his academic work and fascination with aesthetic theory at Harvard he has already thought about plunging himself into the midst of life, which to him was three thousand miles to the east in a Europe at war. He wishes to enter the ambulance corps upon completion of his M.A. at Harvard. Ever the good son, he carefully explains his reasons to his widowed mother (his father having died in 1914):

> You know perfectly well that this idea has been in my head for a long time.... [I]t came to full fruit out of a talk with [Leonard] Bacon [Sidney's poetry teacher at Berkeley] one day in Berkelly [sic], nearly a year and a half ago.... I know it is rather dangerous, but I feel very sure that this career of mine would be far more endangered by my staying away now. I can't get it out of my mind.... I dont [sic] know if the Coes [his mother's family] fought in the revolution or the civil war, but some of our stock did, and with my ideas about things I have got to do something in this riot.... [T]he problems of the world and of humanity are bigger than the problems of a nation.... [H]ere is a chance to do the obvious thing in a direct way, to see and take part in world strife older than Plato, on God's side. And it will be a developing experience at that and of no mean sort.
>
> The doctors have pronounced me fit to go and do anything sane.... I beg you to trust me to do this. What I want to do, is to get over there and have some part in [t]he building, to see the peasants readjusting themselves and absorb the real Europe which I have never so much as tasted. [undated letter from Cambridge]

Here is a blending of various motives, all of which are in the American grain, some receiving greater emphasis than they would now. Sidney feels a high idealism to fight on "God's side" against the evil Germans who would destroy civilization. Idealistically, too, he wishes to help in the rebuilding. He also invokes his ancestors who fought in one or another of the epoch-making American wars. With such idealism and pride in his American heritage, we cannot be surprised that he was to become an ardent Wilsonian.

But perhaps most important, however, are three other motives also inside the American grain. First, he feels it necessary to be very much part of the great events of his time; without that experience he would be "entirely a worse" man. Second, all that he has learned about art in his previous European trips are as nothing compared to his learning from this experience, "the present human things that matter." This goes along with his denunciation of "academics" and his desire to learn about American life from its very midst. Finally, if he is to achieve his ambition to be a writer, he must have experiences of which to write. We note here his distrust of art as a validly illuminating experience about life.

As we have seen, Sidney was to get more than his fill of war experience. But something perhaps more profound and personal than his war experiences was to tear at him. In the midst of all the fighting Sidney gets the following cablegram from his mother: "WE HAVE LOST BRUCE EDGEWOOD HOSPITAL OCT SIXTH [1918] PNEUMONIA I WAS WITH HIM HE DID NOT SUFFER HE WAS SO PROUD OF HIS LETTER TO HOM [?] JEAN IS COMING LOVE AND COURAGE IN YOUR WORK."

Bruce had quit college to join the army when the United States entered World War I. Upon the advice of faculty members of the University of California at Berkeley he went to work in a factory that produced war chemicals. There, a bit over a month before the armistice, he contracted pneumonia and died. The news numbed Sidney. To Jean he writes, on November 6th, 1918:

> I have certainly come to learn a good deal about life and death—and the relation of one to another—for I have seen more of both than I could have. So I have for Bruce only the sorrow that I shall not see him again whom, I suppose, of all men I should most have cared to live beside. I am glad—and very proud—that you should feel me to have been closest to him. More close, certainly, since I came to France than ever before in so far as I have, these two years, done things in which he had some interest. I haven't yet the heart to write or talk about him....

Sidney is obviously in shock, and he is bewildered about how to feel. Emotions usually well up in him from the incidents of his life, but here he is frozen and uncertain. He is not even sure that Bruce was the man he would most have liked to live beside. Jean has to tell him that he was the man who was closest to Bruce. Not only did he lack the heart to discuss his brother, but he did not know what to say because he did not yet know what he felt. His grief had not yet hit him, but of several choices facing him once the armistice is signed, he selected the early demobilization the government allowed him as the only son left to his mother.

While in France Sidney became friendly with Elizabeth Shepley Sergeant, a Bostonian, a family acquaintance, and a writer, and with her brother-in-law, Ernest Angell, who was to become Sidney's lawyer. Katherine and Ernest Angell had lived in Cleveland, were among the founders of the Cleveland Playhouse, and friends of Clare Eames. In fact, they were to introduce Clare and Sidney.

Sidney knew Elizabeth Sergeant (called Elsie by her friends) at Cambridge. In 1917 *The New Republic* sent her as a correspondent to France. Arriving in Paris, she wrote Sidney a "charming note" (letter to Jean, September 4th, 1917). In France Elsie was "very badly hurt in a stupid way. A woman souvenir hunter who went with her to see the Battlefield of the Marne, picked up what she thought to be a German gas mask which was, in reality, a hand grenade. It killed her—blew the arm off the lieutenant who was conducting the party—and broke both of Elsie's legs—one a bad wound a compound fracture. She is in the hospital for some months. It appeared, when I left Paris, that her leg was saved. There *had* been a question of an amputation" (letter to Jean, November 16th, 1918).

Elsie Sergeant turned her experience into a book called *Shadow-Shapes*, in which she gives Sidney Howard, who before her accident had become her very good friend, a prominent role in the guise of Rick. She thus offers us insight into Sidney's mental state just before and after the war's end.

The first time Elsie sees Sidney after he has been knocked out of the sky with his co-pilot dead in the back seat, she observes:

> Rick is changed. Not by dropping bombs, probably by his brother's death, and the decimating battle of a month ago. Grey and stern he looked as he stalked in. Scarcely a flicker of his happy young smile. Moving heavily instead of with his usual light ease.... He never admits his own bravery.... His mother has been splendid.... She says he is not to try to get released on her account. So he will go back to the front.... He has been more affected by the loss of his comrades than he admits [41–42].

Elsie pulls out of him that he cannot eat in the restaurants which he visited with his dead friends. "It seems that he does nothing but look up [their] families—or write to them..." (43).

Then the Armistice comes. "Rick is going home—very soon. They will release him on his mother's account. Offered him a job in Paris. What's the point, after the front?" (96) But she cannot get Rick out of her mind: "That boy haunts me. He is so completely out of a job and sees nothing ahead but moral responsibility—from which he shrinks as much as he courts physical danger" (99). That moral responsibility must entail in part his duty to his mother, especially now that Bruce is dead. Sidney writes to Elsie on December 13, 1918:

> Things are *bad* at home. Mother is always touchy on the subject of Jean. Keeps things, in her foolish feminine way, rather strained. She never had the point of the close relationship between Jean and her brothers, was always jealous of it.... And that is going on now and the boys in California aren't acting pretty. We Howards are a poor selfish lot. It would help if only I could knock their heads together at Christmas.

By comparison wartime relationships seem simple and strong. Elsie quotes him in her book: "'They say war is inhuman. *I* never knew what brotherhood was before. Never really got outside my class. War is human. It's more than that—it deifies human relations!'" (Sergeant, 151).

But in speaking of Rick's desire to avoid responsibility, Elsie Sergeant is thinking of something different from his duties to his family:

> Superficially, the world is his oyster. He takes daily life with delightful ease and buoyancy. He is having a "good time" now. Disporting himself—so far as a clean-minded, vigorous, Western American can.... For the conscious or unconscious purpose of ignoring and repressing his doubt of himself.
>
> The doubt that he may not make good in real life as he made good as

a flyer. At heart he knows the worth of his own stuff and mettle. Yet he is afraid that his vaulting ambition will peter out when no longer backed by the violent incentive of risking the neck.... And despite his zest for action he has a literary temperament. He never acts but he reacts on his action. On paper [99].

Later she observes: "The poor fellow is more and more tormented by the prowling and rapacious specters of future literary projects. He doesn't yet know whether he is going to swallow them or they him..." (151).

Elizabeth Sergeant recognizes a central fissure in Sidney Howard's personality. On the one hand the war proved to him that no experience seemed deeply authentic unless one's life was on the line. By contrast his chosen career as a writer appeared to be trivial, and the prospect of pursuing it produced a kind of lethargy in him. Yet he loved to observe and to commit his perceptions to paper. But if he were to write, his work would come from his "jostlings" in the midst of American life—at least that was related to the risk of one's life—rather than from tracing obscure movements in the psyche and the soul. He apparently did not wish to probe, or wished to avoid probing, into these recesses. In a letter to Elsie he wrote: "You are quite wrong—I have concluded this much after as long concentration as I am capable of—in calling me introspective. I can't think about human relationships. I can only enjoy it [sic]" (January 21st, 1920). That is an astonishing admission for a future writer, especially one who indeed did write some penetrating plays about human character, implying, of course, that there was a good deal of introspection on the author's part. But Sidney wrote these plays in the twenties, when he was married to Clare Eames. He later, after his divorce from Clare Eames and her death, created impassioned plays, experimental dramas, a couple of great successes, but he never again wrote a play that truly grappled with a character's soul.

Sidney's return to New York after the war was none too happy. "New York was bad, very difficult, horrid trying. I was not anything like acclimated and the heavy family stuff all but did me under. Mother was waiting for me, not at the dock, thank heaven, in her hotel. I couldn't break away with a clear conscience to go to Boston..." (letter to Elsie, January 25th, 1919). Instead he escapes to Berkeley, where he stays with Jean, intending only a brief visit, but he remains for about three months. He seems seriously depressed: "All that I felt and dreamed and cared for during the two months [in which he fought] which seem to me, from this angle, my whole life, came back to me with a rush which has left me flat and contemplative of suicide" (letter to Elsie, February 16th, 1919). Understandably accompanying his suicidal thoughts is resistance to his future as outlined by friends who knew him before the war:

> I find Sam Hume [now teaching at the University at Berkeley] and the old outfit of professors with great plans for my future. Poor things, they don't know. Sam read me some of the masque I did for him in Detroit just before I sailed.... It was very amusing and rather uncanny to hear that masque. I don't want to do anything like it again but it will be a weary grind before I get my head broken into anything like a piece of decent work [letter to Elsie, January 25th, 1919].

Despite his complaints, in less than two months he has written one short story as a potboiler, "an article on aviation to Collier's, an article on assimilation to The Atlantic" (letter to Elsie, March 17th, 1919) and "three one acts and about a dozen more stories, "either completed or partially completed. He has also been "monkeying with a masque ... to be produced in the Greek Theatre here by Sam Hume acted by super-marionettes ... cardboard figures twelve feet to twenty feet tall with antiphonal choruses and dances in the diazoma and insane music. The subject, vaguely, Bolshevism, or, Watch your step ye worthy of the world" (letter to Elsie, February 16th, 1919). So despite his swearing off masques and his earlier swearing off aestheticism, here he is, under the influence of Hume, becoming interested again. The subject sounds new, but the style and surely the energizing force are the aesthetics of old Gordon Craig. All of Sidney's activities hardly sound like a man who is seriously contemplating suicide.

Elsie Sergeant seems to have got it right. Sidney was deeply concerned about his future, uncertain as to whether he will succeed, especially since his experiences flying and fighting seemed more exciting than writing. He clearly was not sure how to integrate them with his former interests. He was also now twenty-seven years old, to be twenty-eight within a few months, and he had to make a living, to stop his dependency on his mother. On February 6th he writes to Elsie: "Before I went abroad my natural reflex was literary expression. I am surprised to find that literary expression is easier in the sense of executive faculty than ever. But it is no longer natural. I am much more inclined to keep my mouth shut.... But perhaps it is good for a man to admit that he is mortally bored and to recognize that, for a time at least, he was vitally interested...." Existential angst clearly oppresses Sidney, but equally his emotional and financial future frightened him. He goes about facing his problems, however, with characteristic energy and courage, waiting for the desire for life and pleasure to wash back in on him.

Back in New York by April 22nd, 1919, he writes to Elsie that he is looking for "some sort of job in an editorial way which would be at once an introduction and an experience with magazine publication. And which would not be so confining as to interfere with my work as an author. Not easy to find and with my characteristic luck I found it the first day I looked merely by walking into the office of Life and tripping over it. I get a hundred dollars a month for doing very little."

To Jean he writes on May 7th that he would have liked to run off with some army friends to Constantinople on relief work, but it was his "job to come home under the circumstances of Bruce's death...." Although he asserts that he seems "to have lost my so-called artistic conscience in the war," he now has two aims: "Write well, first, and second, about things and p[e]ople and places which interest me in my own experience, i.e. never to miss a trick wherever the cards are played in this world or the next." While the last phrase is obscure—are not all the cards that one is going to play in the next world determined by how one plays them in this world?—the program seems to have returned to that which he had devised in graduate school when he threw off his "artistry" and was determined to put on stage truly vital American men and women.

To that end, presumably, he works on a book about his experiences in the Balkans during the war, on short stories, and on a variety of articles. His first piece to break into print is "Baiting the Bolshevist" [January 10th, 1920], which is accepted by *Colliers* before the end of the year.

In the next few years Sidney writes a good deal of journalism, actually his main source of income. His most important work is in investigative reporting, which he called "muckraking," the articles appearing in *Hearst's International Magazine*, *The New Republic* as well as in *Colliers*. Typical subjects concerned the sale of drugs ("The Inside Story of Dope in This Country," *Hearst's International*, February–June 1925) and labor spying ("The Labor Spy," with Robert Dunn, *The New Republic*, February 16th, 1921). His usual attitude is that of the fair, open-minded citizen, which is to say, that of a political liberal. His style, true as well of his book reviews, is colloquial and full of punch. Two series of articles were turned into books (*The Labor Spy*, New York, 1924; *Professional Patriots*, ed. Norman Hapgood, New York, 1927). Before he became recognized as a successful dramatist, most people knew and admired Sidney Howard in his role as an investigative reporter.

But for all that he did not give up the theater. Barrett Clark tells us that his friend Billy Merrill, Sidney's great pal from Cambridge days, had talked continuously of "wonderful Sid Howard, one of the swellest men I've ever seen." Before the end of the war Sidney had a reunion with Merrill, who was then in the army, and he had promised to look up Clark. Unfortunately, Merrill was killed, but Sidney still carried out his promise.

> It was at this first meeting that Sidney shot at me one of those characteristic questions that was not so much a question but an outright statement:
> "Do you think there's a play in *The Rivet in Grandfather's Neck*? That was a novel of [James Branch] Cabell's.... What this Howard fellow really

meant, only I didn't know it at the time, was that he was sure there *was* a play in *The Rivet* and he was going to get it out. I said I'd think it over.

"Think quick," he said, "and let's lunch here again tomorrow. If the answer is 'Yes,' we'll write the play together" [Clark, 189].

They did collaborate on the play. Clark, who was to become a prominent critic and teacher, formed a close relationship with Sidney. *Rivet* was optioned but never performed. Despite Sidney's assertion to Jean in a letter written on August 13th, 1919, that "theatres and such mean little to young Howard," at election time of the next year we find (from an undated letter to his mother) that he has been deep in playwriting:

> Tomorrow lunch with [Margaret] Anglin on "PHAEDRA" [the version by Italian dramatist Gabrielle D'Annunzio] the translation commissioned by Sam Hume to be performed at the Greek Theatre [Berkeley], and dinner tomorrow night with [Frank] Conroy to whom THE RIVET [*sic*] is sold. I have the Kohler contract and am awaiting contract arrangements on the COCK HORSE. [Francine] Larrimore has it, also Alice Brady, Billie Burke, and Grace George and someone else whom I am too sleepy to remember. Rachel Crothers will produce.

Sidney, deep in playwriting, is involved with some of the most prominent and active people in the theatre. Margaret Anglin, for example, had played a leading role in the famous *Great Divide* (by William Vaughn Moody) and had established a reputation in Shakespearean and classical parts. Frank Conroy, we may remember, was a founder of the ill-fated Greenwich Village Players with which Clare Eames made her professional debut. His failure obviously did not discourage him from continuing his producing career. Alice Brady, Billie Burke, and Grace George were all important actresses of the day.

In the same undated letter to his mother he adds at the end: "Anglin is reported in a frenzy over 'PHAEDRA' but still able to take nourishment." And in a postscript he writes, "We must have a Sunday night party for Miss Anglin whom I love so much that it should worry you." He reports to his sister in 1920 in another undated letter that he is working on a "play to be called 'GODHEAD' on the tragedy of being a radical—a dramatic portrait...."

None of these plays was produced. But Sidney certainly got around, and many theatrical people liked his work. Margaret Anglin had enough faith in him, though she did not finally act in *Phaedra*, to request a play based on a scenario of her own. That play became *Swords*, his first-produced drama, in which she also did not perform; Clare Eames acted the leading role, and it was this work that brought Sidney and Clare together in marriage.

Sidney also began to move among important people in the worlds of literature and politics. At various times his letters refer to his meeting, among prominent others, Edith Wharton, Amy Lowell, Willa Cather, John Drinkwater, Lord Dunsany, Thomas Chamberlin, and Clarence Darrow. Sidney, with his energy, sheer pleasure in life's activities, his wholeness and his talent, always had the gift of attracting other creative and successful people, whether of the faculties of the two great universities he attended, his contemporaries, or the greats of the various worlds he inhabited. With all this Sidney was still able to maintain a certain modesty and good humor.

Amidst all the playwriting Sidney was doing his articles, a book on Salonkia, his short stories, his one-acters. He had also become an ardent internationalist, and in the 1920 campaign he was publicity director of Herbert Hoover's presidential primary effort in New York (undated letter to Jean).

All of this time in New York Sidney has been living with his mother at an apartment she has found for them. On August 13th, 1919, Sidney writes to Jean:

> The apartment is perfectly great. For a time mother was supremely happy in getting it ready. Then it was done and she slipped back into the depths once more. I was in despair when she pulled herself out (as she has a way of doing) by discovering a music teacher who is training her technique with funny gymnastics which only a rubber woman could possibly perform but which seem to delight her heart. As a result she is already playing like a drum major and coming back accordingly. I am tremendously lucky to have her here with me. You were right. New York is a lonely place for her. But she seems to be gathering up a lot of friends of Dr. Powers—musical ladies who work about the slums and do lots of things and yet seem to find time to come here and tea with her so that she has a party on almost [e]very afternoon....

At the age of 27 Sidney lived with his mother, both leading independent lives, yet each feeling responsible for the other and sympathy pains as well, a very strong bond.

In 1920 Sidney received a commission to do a series on labor spying, which was published in *The New Republic* in 1921. Although he did the writing, helping him in his investigation was one Robert Dunn, of whom Sidney writes to Elsie Sergeant on August 27th, 1920:

> Perhaps I am chiefly weary of radicals because I am so weary of Dunn. There is a glib inevitability about his point of view which irritates me to desperate restraint. I can admire his resolve and fortitude which lines him beside the proletariat. But I cannot stick the complacency of his attitude. Perhaps I am still a vigorous anti-conscientious objector, and he was one, which, for me, discounts much else that he is. The world was not made to be reformed. It was made for man to struggle in against despair and hope

together. The cock sure conceit of the humble revolutionist is *too* much. As I have said before, Communism has all my sympathies, but the best people are still, on the whole, conservative. Dunn's cooperation has made this job possible. But I am wiser than he though he may be more right than I. And I shall part from him with gratitude—and in enthusiasm to engage in radicalism apart from radicals.

Sidney's sympathetic attitude toward communism, the new government in Russia, typified that of many open-minded people in this country because it seemed to be trying to help the oppressed of Russia and the world. This was not yet the day of Stalin; many people did not perceive Lenin as a despot but as a leader courageously trying in fierce adversity to change social conditions quickly for the betterment of Russians and mankind. Among those adverse circumstances were the Allies' invasion of Russia with the help of the United States. Sidney's sympathy with communism was the standard, understandable liberal view of the day.

But while he sympathized with communism, he separated himself from it. He was not a communist, even as he appreciated its goals. One reason, certainly, was the "glib inevitability" in its attitude toward history, which he ascribes to Dunn. And that same self-assurance he sees in radicals, whom he finds to be intellectually arrogant and hypocritical ("The cock sure conceit of the humble revolutionist").

Sidney's sympathies are with the "best people," who "are still, on the whole, conservative." The term "best people" is, of course, snobbish. It shows a class consciousness in Sidney which belies his liberalism and shows him to be, like the radical whom he denigrates, also a hypocrite. This class consciousness comes out also in his regular denigration of Jews in his letters, which contain remarks ranging from the mildly contemptuous to the sneering. Sidney remained always a political liberal, open-minded to a variety of viewpoints, especially those which tended to the left. He was never politically anti–Semitic. But his sense that he belonged to a class which really understood what the world and life were all about never left him. This class knew the whys and wherefores of everyday existence and were possessed of a general, serviceable philosophy of life though its members could not always enunciate its principles; they merely displayed them in their code of personal behavior. This class knew it by instinct because its members had it shaped by the training, going back numerous generations, that their parents easily gave their children. For all of Sidney's forward-looking politics his sense of belonging to the class of the best people never left him even though his father had worked his way up. If Sidney thought about it at all, somehow, socially, his father belonged even before he had the financial means of living in the class. Sidney never believed only in aristocracy of the talented.

But most important for us who are interested in his drama is the implication that his wisdom leads to conservatism. The wisdom of which he speaks here is only slimly connected to his snobbism. It derives much more from his existential view that the "world was not made to be reformed. It was made to struggle in against despair and hope together." That is, indeed, a profoundly conservative point of view. While in Sidney's mind that conservatism is not necessarily against reform, it does not see reform as the panacea that Marxists understood it to be. Reform, to Sidney, might relieve some man-made injustice in the world, but it could never eradicate agony and injustice which were the inevitable concomitants of life. Man's part was to cope with the despair life's horrors would surely bring and to banish as well the false hope other moments might raise. For example, whatever hope elation might bring, man as killer cannot be eradicated: One cannot be a conscientious objector because fighting was sometimes necessary and, perhaps worse still, enjoyable, and even worse, the arena for the discovery of one's manhood.

Sidney's view was not made for the drama of reform; instead it could give rise to the grim consolation of tragedy or the comic sense of social compromise which acknowledges life's limitations. Although Sidney wrote some plays with bleak strains in them, his view was essentially comic.

5

Clare and Sidney

It remains a mystery as to how Clare snatched the leading role in Sidney Howard's *Swords* from Margaret Anglin, an established star whose idea for the play Sidney presumably dramatized for her, or why Clare was even considered for it. Yet there seemed to be a bloody battle for the part, as Sidney indicates in an undated letter to his mother from Europe in the summer of 1921: "Of course, I am on pins and needles for further news of 'SWORDS.' With Clare and Anglin rowing over it, it is likely enough to prove fatal to both of them." The last clause is also a mystery, but apparently the two women fought some sort of battle for the privilege of playing the role.

Clare won, whereupon with good-humored aplomb, but with respect for Sidney's wishes, she immediately undertakes the burden of finding a producer for the play. She writes him in Europe from Cleveland on May 19th, where she is visiting her parents for "five filial days":

> Dear Sidney—
>
> Although strikingly unlike Madame de Sevigne in all respects I shall emulate her example et je laisserais la plume trottes. My existence has been such a complication of politics since you sailed; no, more than politics, high diplomacy. I have earnestly and sincerely tried to do what you would want to have done with *Swords* and if I have guessed wrong or blundered in any respect I beg you to be quite frank and tell me so. It can truthfully be said that the production of the play has always been my first object, and that my impulses have been almost devoid of self-seeking. (I say almost because who can disentangle the threads of his own motives?)

Sidney had apparently left the manuscript with an indecisive producer from whom Clare manages to obtain a definite negative. She thereupon places it in the hands of the young and newly minted producer, Brock Pemberton,

> with the remark that I left the thing with him in the sprit of altruism, simply to give a man of taste and feeling a most agreeable hour. Whereupon I left for Hartford to stand godmother to a ten weeks old baby.... When I got back to New York I found a file of messages from Pemberton entreating me to telephone him at once.

Sidney had intended for his very good friend Rollo Peters, whose work he admired inordinately, to design the sets. Peters had been a member of the Washington Square Players and a founder of the Theatre Guild. Designer and a first-rate actor for both companies, he had been one of several managers of the guild that had wished to discard its guidance-by-committee system in favor of a single strong hand at the tiller. Peters and his group lost, quitting the guild board (Langner, 124–25). At that moment his professional hopes were intertwined with Sidney's. Clare would unhappily betray those hopes.

> Of course, the one aspect of the affair which was in no sense amusing and which cost me many hours of very real pain was Pete's side. If you had only been here! Friedman [sic] and I did all we possibly could without jeopardizing the production but it was a grief to me to find Pemberton so pig-headed on the subject of R.E.J. [Robert Edmond Jones] You can see, I am sure, in what a horribly difficult position I was placed. But, in a difficult and perilous position, I have found that the only thing to do is to decide resolutely what the issue is and then proceed, forgetting all personal ties and never for one moment stopping to consider the possible effect upon oneself of the approval or disapproval of others. It was not only for my sake and the play's that I wanted Pete for the designer but also (and more) for yours, as I knew that you could not be happy in the thought of a production with him left out. But, when I found Pemberton obdurate, I made myself forget, for the moment, your personal relations and thought only of your artistic ones. (I took and take the risk of having you hate me.) Of course, I could have made Pete's part of it a sine qua non but then the play might have been shelved for another year ... and Pete wouldn't have had a look-in. I went on the assumption that the first quality of an artist is that he has something to say which simply must be said, and a play must be said before an audience. As I wrote to Pete there are "mute, inglorious Miltons" simply because they are mute; but once let their voices be heard and the world stops to listen. So I went ahead with Pemberton and I shall try, humbly and devotedly, to make the beauty and pride and mysterious and shifting color of *Swords* intelligible and thus atone for any mistakes that I have or that R.E.J. may make. (I don't think he will make many—let us pray that he will not).

Having herself done the dastardly deed, Clare assumes the responsibility of revealing it to Peters:

> Breaking the news to Pete was the worst thing I have ever had to do. I was determined that he should receive the blow from affectionate and gentle hands so I sent for him and told him ... and gave him whiskey and soda ... strong enough to deaden any sensation whatever and took him to the train. I just let him talk and I was so sorry for him that only tears of blood would have eased my heart. Salt tears were not enough; I tried them. I have told you now what happened and how I felt and what I tried to do and I can only hope that you are not too disappointed and unhappy.

After some news of personal doings in Cleveland and elsewhere, including a forthcoming visit to "my beloved (but definite) Aunt E[mma]," she signs off, to "cher maitre," with love.

Whatever Sidney wrote to Clare, his response to Clare's accomplishments is not one of gratitude, at least as expressed in an undated letter from London to his mother. "Forebodings always come true, don't they? When Anglin failed me, my next hope was Clare and Pete with Pete's wonderful scenery and warmth of personality to carry Clare's perfect and arctic technique ... here is 'SWORDS' sold for Clare with Bobby Jones to set it and Howard in for another MACBETH" (Lionel Barrymore in the leading role of a major Jones-Hopkins effort, an unmitigated failure although some critics now regard the sets as some of Jones's best).

Sidney's remarks about Clare hardly sound like a man in love, and indeed he may not have been in love, for absent is Sidney's wild enthusiasm for anything about the object of his love or even for anyone who has garnered his strong affection. Of course, he may not have known Clare for very long, for we cannot pinpoint when they met. However, Sidney insists in a letter to his sister that "*Swords* had never been thought of when I first fell in love with Clare and she had not yet seen hair nor hide of it when she first fell in love with me..." (September 22nd, 1921). We would take that at face value if he weren't writing these remarks in defense against his mother, a "doubting Thomas" about Clare and Sidney's relationship. Sidney explains, "Nothing can alter her conviction that this is a theatrical match between star and author resulting from rehearsals and similar mutual trials bravely borne." Sidney in his defensiveness here might well be expanding the length of time of their love affair. However, they seem to be the perfect subject for romance. Both are young, handsome, talented, professionally promising, and in complementary parts of the same profession. Moreover, they had similar backgrounds in upper-middle-class, well-to-do families; both loved books, possessed a strong grounding in art and music, had traveled to Europe, a major source of their culture, spoke French fluently and casually mixed it into their conversation and letters.

Perhaps most important, they approached the theater seriously, the art-theater way. But beyond the art theater, Clare had a sense of the great dramatic literature of the past and of the challenging roles it offered, which alone made the theater worthwhile, and she had apparently learned a technique which would help her to develop these parts. Sidney, too, looked beyond the art theater. He wished to put onstage his experience of American life. With all their seriousness about art and life they were joyous and humorous. They seemed to be the perfect romantic pair.

Yet when Sidney left for Europe in the spring of 1921, he seemed depressed, hardly ready for romance, not to say marriage. His professional future had reached a point of crisis. It was uncertain who would star in *Swords* or who would produce it or indeed whether it would be produced. Yet he takes off.

No doubt he was exhausted from his hard work on drama in the past two years (he had recently been working on four plays—new dramas and adaptations) as well as his journalistic activities, which were causing a stir. His series on labor spying, he writes to Jean in an undated letter in the spring of 1921, "has created a great deal of comment.... Senator Borah of Idaho has sent for me. I am only scared now that the thing may attain such proportions as to prevent my going abroad. Which, as it looms nearer and nearer, seems very much the right idea." He seems determined to escape artistic and journalistic activity and their aftermath.

At the end of the war he had wanted to abjure responsibility and continue wandering. Instead he had given up a job in Paris immediately after the war and had not gone to Constantinople with his old buddies. He had returned to the United States and settled into the drudgery of a job and the hard, perhaps trivial, work of making good at his writing partially because his mother required his company, his emotional intimacy, and hope in his future. This had seemed a depressing prospect for him, and with only his journalism successful, an experience he undoubtedly enjoyed but did not much desire, his sense of the worthlessness of his endeavors seemed to return. He also believed his mother was one of his jobs, and he had done his job well, perhaps too well. Now she intended to go to Europe, too: "I want her to go ... but I cannot afford to give up my own trip to her kind of thing and that she and I should operate independently is to her, as you know, a kind of cruel incredibility. She is much better now. If only she would be a friend to some of her friends! Spiritual matrimony between parents and children is a damnably difficult situation" (undated letter to Jean). Surely one reason that his sharp desire to go to Europe was simply to escape from his mother's matrimonial care.

Sidney knows that he is being irresponsible in his attitude toward *Swords*. He writes to his mother in an undated letter from London: "I, of course, know that my presence in New York would settle matters, and it *is* a little hard to be sure, or to feel at least that, for me, so much hangs in the balance and I not there to lend a hand, and none the less I am glad to be here."

Perhaps Sidney ran away because in an obscure corner of his mind he saw this fight between Margaret Anglin, whom he had cited as a possible stand-in for his mother, and Clare, a welcome stranger in his heart, as one he preferred not to settle, at least for the moment. Whatever his immediate relations with Clare, in the same obscure corner of his mind, he may well have had thoughts of marrying Clare; thus since he had already committed spiritual matrimony with his mother, he would, in choosing Clare above Anglin for the leading role in *Swords* with the possibility of marrying Clare, be committing spiritual bigamy. Better to run away than choose between the two strong and determined actresses.

On her side Clare seems to be utterly in control of herself, enjoying the entire enterprise of getting the play produced and writing Sidney about it. Her style is literate, literary, humorous. This is the same Clare depicted by Margalo Gillmore, full of outrageous life. Nevertheless, she is intensely serious in her effort to snare the right producer, displaying energy, determination, even executive ability. For she shrewdly plucks the play from a producer she considers undesirable and inveigles the young Brock Pemberton into reading a play she may have flattered him into enjoying. She also courageously takes the chance of offending Sidney by compromising with Pemberton on the scene designer to ensure a production of *Swords* in the knowledge of the unalterable fact that an unproduced playwright is an unknown playwright. She is certainly doing herself a favor in getting the play on the boards, but just as surely she is helping Sidney. Remarkably, she is only twenty-four years old, and she has carried it off without any help from the one person who should have done it all himself.

Astonishingly, she bore no word of reproach to Sidney for blithely leaving everything in her hands. Her energy and high spirits perhaps made it easy to ignore Sidney's lapse, and she must certainly have gloried in her plucking the play from Anglin if that is what happened. But another dimension of her relationship with him may have allowed her to assume the burden that Sidney shrugged off. She admired him devoutly. "Cher maitre," she calls him, in the European tradition in which the writer is sanctified. Appropriate to that view, she will "try, humbly and devotedly" to "atone" for her sin in permitting Peters's exclusion from the play. She virtually abases herself before Sidney. "I have earnestly and sincerely tried to do what you would want to have done with *Swords* and if I have guessed wrong or blundered in any respect then I beg you to be quite frank and tell me so." The writer of beautiful dramas deserves self-abnegation from his admirers, and Sidney, incandescent, buoyant, and seemingly whole, is enough to turn any girl's head, especially one who surely looked for some kind of king for her queenly self.

With the production pending, Sidney still could not manage to return to New York. On July 10th he writes to Jean that, after his stay in London, he traveled about on the Continent with and without his mother, finally returning to "Paris again to sail. When the idea of Spain struck me and Dixie Fish [an army buddy] appeared as a companion. So I cancelled my passage and made ready to go. Whereupon Dix has a cable calling him home at once. He came with me for a week ... as good fun as I have ever had—and returned and I came on south alone." One would think that after Dix had canceled, Sidney, with his play awaiting rehearsals, would also have canceled, but instead he continues the trip alone. When he finally gets to New York, the play is already in rehearsal for a September 1st opening.

Once back, however, apparently banishing interim resistance, he swings into action. Never again will he be recalcitrant in the face of work or obligation; unhappy, yes, angry, disgusted, depressed but in necessity's face he marches on and does what he must.

To Jean he writes on a Sunday night in August, 1921, from the Harvard Club:

> Clare Eames plays the Madonna lady with a verve and magnificent energy of spirit which are simply overwhelming. The others are all admirable. Our hopes are very high for a sensational triumph. To be sure, one never knows. The play will be printed at once by Doran. It is all awfully and wonderfully exciting. I am in a new world—it is always new—of the theater. From Clare's electric magic (at 24) to the charm of the old character lady (of 65) who always comes drunk to rehearse the charwoman and said to me, yesterday: "Say kid, what kind of poppy seed was you eatin' when you wrote this?" It is tremendously exciting but *such* work.

George Pierce Baker came down from Harvard for the opening: "[T]hey sat together through what was painfully and obviously a failure ... after the final curtain, G.P.B. looked into Howard's tear-brimming eyes and began to chuckle, and the tears turned into laughter and they both laughed until they cried" (Kinne, 289) That is how Sidney, in 1935, remembered the opening.

Contemporaneously, however, but after the opening, Sidney thought he knew beforehand that the play would fail:

> We had a heck of a time getting the play on, opened cold in New York without so much as a dress rehearsal worthy of the name. I made my speech and was cheered and whistled at and it was very exciting, but I knew from the beginning of the last week of rehearsals that we were done for. I recognized two things. 1. Inherent weaknesses in the play which made the first two acts inevitably dull. 2. The fact that Brock Pemberton [this was his

first production] was in no wise equipped to cope with so elaborate a production ... but Clare, [Jose] Ruben [who played the leading male role] and Jones did magnificently and we were severely and mercilessly panned. Some people rose to raptures. Walter Lippmann [the highly respected political commentator], bless his heart, was among them..." [letter to Elsie, September 10th, 1921].

Later he quotes Walter Lippmann's letter to him:

> I didn't begin to tell you last night how fine both of us thought your play was. I have seen many first plays by my friends, but none in which everything necessary was there right away, not as a promise, merely, but in fact. It was beautiful, thrilling, and great, and there doesn't seem to be any piece in the orchestra that you don't know how to use. I wonder if you know how very, very, good it is ... how very rare it is that perfect virtue is perfectly entrancing. Clare Eames and Bobby were complete, but it was you who made that possible.

Sidney loved Lippmann's valuation of the play but knew it was false. Much more to the point, much more slashing, much more painful was Francis Hackett's review in *The New Republic*:

> Having read Mr. Sidney Howard on the tremendous drama of modern labor [the labor spy series which had appeared in *The New Republic* earlier in the year], I went with real respect to see his poetic drama called Swords, now playing at the National Theatre. That Swords was not realism seemed to me, on the whole, alluring. A "costume" play, as people call it (forgetting that even bedroom plays are frequently costumed) is, in itself, an excellent medium. By leaving the present a dramatist drops the harness of actuality and on that very account is often enabled to release his audience's imagination under circumstances which favor rather than distract the heart in its pursuit of unity and beauty....
> But [such a drama] is not self-acting. By flinging away the restraint of actuality, by taking on the picturesqueness of something not dulled by use and wont, a dramatist cannot thereby assume to succeed. He cannot do without intuition, without a knowledge of life and character, without dramatic surprise and imaginative sympathy. The picturesque is not in itself kinetic....
> This, I regret to say, seemed to me doubly true after seeing Swords. One renews one's acquaintance with the literary moon, the lily in the field of night. One learns again that in an exalted hour people's feet are "on the mountains." One is told of emotions that are like "seagulls dancing on the waves." Breasts, hair, swords, stars, the Virgin Mary and all sorts of other properties that go to make up romance according to the standards of the college English course—these one gathers are still in vogue among the more expressive and romantical. But of the poetry that inhere in men and women or even in ideal emotions personally and authentically conceived—there is nothing measurable. One finds oneself in the whispering gallery of other men's visions, passions and dreams.

Reading the play now, we can only agree with Hackett. The history, the art seems studied: the heroine, Fiamma, first appears only at the end of Act I, then says nothing until "She lifts her hand for silence, then in her low vibrant voice intones the Pater Noster in Latin" (*Swords*, 60). The poetry is pale neoromanticism:

> Will you come down to me?
> A sea bird, balanced on distended wings
> Might float into your reverent seclusion
> And, by comparison with your fair grace,
> Seem a distorted and obnoxious thing.
> Shall I, who am a graceless man,
> Bred in the rough adventure of the world,
> Who only, humbly sue the privilege
> Of a brief word, Madonna, desecrate
> the shrine your presence sanctifies [64].

No wonder that when the members of the Algonquin Round Table gave a satiric revue later that season, a curtain in a sketch held a sign that said "WORDS," but one could see that the first S had fallen halfway to the floor. Not merely wordiness was the problem, however. Sidney's pseudoromantic poetry failed to reflect the modern temper. In 1917 serious readers had already positively responded to:

> Let us go then, you and I,
> When the evening is spread out against the sky
> Like a patient etherized upon a table....

Working in America and England were, in addition to T. S. Eliot, Ezra Pound, Wallace Stevens, William Carlos Williams, and Marianne Moore.

But poetry in the theater does not require versification. In 1920 Eugene O'Neill had brought to Broadway two prose dramas that for a variety of reasons such as their spoken and unspoken rhythms, the power of their plots, and the insight of their characterizations were by general consent deemed poetic. In the season following *Swords* Elmer Rice in the expressionistic drama *The Adding Machine* suggested a kind of wry and ironic poetry both in its structure and language, the latter perhaps reminding readers of the new poetry to be found in some magazines. And before long Sidney Howard would offer audiences *They Knew What They Wanted*, a comedy, also in prose, which would possess its own magical glow.

Clare Eames received reviews which were typical for her early in her career. Critics complained that she lacked passion or they admired her artistic restraint. Alexander Woollcott in the *New York Times* wrote that the author "must have wondered how his play would have fared had its great central role fallen to an actress of first rank. Clare Eames always an interesting and an intelligent actress moves chill and prim through a tumult of a barbaric story far beyond her depth in a play which, when it is good at all, is made up of such robust passion and such mighty terror as needs a new Margaret Anglin to give it voice" (September 2nd, 1921). The last must have been a low blow because almost certainly Woollcott knew that the part was originally intended for Anglin.

One of Clare's defenders was Francis Hackett, who in the same review in which he had cut Sidney to ribbons, writes:

> Miss Clare Eames manages to give her part as Fiamma a degree of reality that is compelling. For some, I know, Miss Eames's restraint has no magic. She is described as chill and even prim. But on the occasion when I saw her ... her "primness" seemed to me to be that of a singularly expressive actress who declines to rant. She is an actress for tragedy, possibly, and possibly for parts in which there is a touch of wintriness or at least not the flashing fruitfulness of July. Her style in repose is sometimes still and formal, like a da Vinci painting. But there is in her the secret fire of imaginativeness, in this case the ability to convey a woman destined for high ends, cast in a noble mould. In Ibsen, I believe, one could properly measure the range and depth of her gifts, and I am certain those gifts are rare. At any rate, her icy splendor almost redeems Swords.

From the beginning of her career Clare was the kind of actress that interested critics, even when they did not like her. Those who appreciated her work wished to see her in better plays or in the great works. They found in her abilities depth and imagination. Some, like Hackett, in suggesting that Ibsen might be her métier perhaps realize the modernity of her personal style.

On September 10th, 1921, Sidney writes to Elsie:

> The play's poor reception had, however, a positive side. I am bitterly disappointed [by the drama's failure], of course, wiser in my business by many points. And, NOW COMES THE POINT, I have actually beaten life at its own game. Because, my very dear Elsie, out of all this mess, I have been pretty wildly in love with Clare for a long time and never thought to say anything concrete about it and, the other day, in the midst of a brawl and my own impertinent comments on the ways of the world and the production of my master work, it became suddenly evident to Clare and me that the real purpose of this play was to marry us. Which being the case the world can call SWORDS a failure and I can know it a triumph. Why this marvelous creature should care a whoop about me I don't know and can't understand. But there you have it, entirely unmotivated as the critics say, a flip remark from an angry youth in a taxi, a casual flash of sym-

pathy from his companion in misery and the lights are on for the rest of the time in his life and, he prays with all his might in hers too.

To Jean he expresses more certainty: "We are as confident as two people can be that we belong together. I may add that we are rather a pair.... In terms of successful marriages I know I believe that both man and woman should have jobs and work at them" (September 22nd, 1921). There is the man speaking who expected to create feminist women for the stage. With a strong woman as his mother, he seems unafraid of an intimate relationship with one. But something does seem to frighten him. "I am certain of my own happiness forever if I can only manage to make Clare happy."

His fear that he might make Clare unhappy may be at first ascribed to the feeling that some men have that in a way they are unworthy of the women they will marry. This seems to be true of Sidney but in a complicated fashion.

In a note which prefaces *Swords* he writes:

> FIAMMA is marvelously like the medieval concept of the Virgin Mary, the concept which inspired the cathedral of Chartes [sic], the hymns of Bernard of Clairvaux, and the Paradiso of Dante, the concept of an altogether human Empress, devoted to her servants, none too scrupulous, temperamental, exacting, very feminine, wholly glorious [10].

He clarifies this in writing to Jean, trying to understand the anger of some people against the play: "The nearest explanation I can make is that the very idea of writing a play around man's reverence for womankind, or, indeed, womankind as man's loftiest divinity ... that very idea simply won't go down the cynical throat which is today in the fashion" (September 22nd, 1921).

The problem is that Sidney, like Clare, had an ideal picture of his partner. He revered Clare, indeed any woman whom he would love. Clare, playing the Madonna of his imagination, surely became confused in Sidney's mind with his idea of the Virgin Mary, "womankind as man's loftiest divinity." He might well question his ability to make that kind of woman happy.

For Clare, Sidney embodied the incandescent spirit of the writer. Doubtless most couples in love idealize their partners, but if they remain long together, they learn to see each other more honestly. When they do, the consequences vary; sometimes they are more validly appreciative of their partners, sometimes they are totally disillusioned, with disastrous results.

Although Clare and Sid remain in a bubble of romance for a while, trouble in paradise comes fairly soon. While Sidney was out of town for a period in 1922, Clare had received a letter from Jean to which she had not yet replied by Sidney's return:

> When I came back we had that subject out. I was damned sore when I heard that she hadn't written you. She seems to be one of those people who is constitutionally unable to take pen in hand. It's more important in life to be grateful for qualities than to be pesky over weaknesses. I don't deny that she should have written sooner but I confess that I'm disposed to bless her heart that she did write eventually—and so will you, when you know her [April 22nd, 1922].

Sid, much like a parent toward a child, scolds Clare for neglect of her social duty, but when she repairs her failure, again acting much as the parent, is "disposed to bless her heart," categorizing her as the kind of person who cannot take pen in hand—even after all the letters at length she has written to him—as easily as can he and Jean, the adults. Sidney's attitude in this minor incident regarding himself as the adult and Clare as the child who must be controlled will spread and deepen in their marriage, this despite his tremendous regard for her as an actress and as an intellect. Oddly enough, patronizing her is the reverse side of his idolatry. On the one hand she is the Madonna, the source of all spiritual ecstasy and the balm of understanding. On the other hand, for precisely her perfect spiritual powers, she seems incapable of handling the tasks of daily life and must be looked after.

As Sidney recounts this little incident, Clare gave no reasons for her failure to write Jean, yet she had reasons enough. Before Sidney left town, she had acted in a couple of matinees, perhaps against his advice, in *Aglavain and Séylesette*, by that "dreary moron Maeterlinck," an art theater favorite (letter to Jean, January 23rd, 1922). As he is about to leave New York in early 1922, Clare was slated for a Eugene O'Neill play called *Made in Heaven*, according to Sidney, "very powerful and fine and an extraordinary comedy of modern marriage for two people in seven acts.... It's horrid but downright thrilling." As it turned out, *Made in Heaven* never reached the stage. (The play was finally produced as *Welded* on March 17th, 1924.) While Sidney was gone, she accepted yet another two-character play called *The First Fifty Years*, prepared the role and opened it on Broadway. Very busy Clare then had good enough reason to omit answering Jean's letter. If she did not make excuses for herself, perhaps she simply wished to please her self-confident, handsome, incandescent future husband, who in turn wished to please his adored sister.

Of course on the surface this incident did not cause a ripple in the course of their romance. Nor did Sid's engagement cause much of a furrow in his spiritual matrimony with his mother. On October 30th, 1921, he writes to Helen Howard "A before bedtime letter—just like the things you read to me every night out of the evening papers. Since you are not here I must write one for myself and send it to you." And he proceeds with the details of his personal and professional life. This is spiritual matrimony, indeed.

Now Sidney's marriages, that of the spirit with his mother and that of the flesh (and one hopes of the spirit as well) pending with Clare Eames, seem to be the cause of conflicts with Elizabeth Sergeant.

Elsie first comes into conflict with Helen Howard. On January 23, 1921, Sid writes to Jean:

> I have had a series of odd experiences with E.S.S. who is in town and of whom, now, I see as little as possible.... She started a fishwife's quarrel with Mother who says now that she can never darken the Howard doors and I confess I am on Mother's side. All things considered, she makes a psychological fool of herself and I told her so which she interpreted strangely. She is a curious person. I think I could do her in a story, and a good one.

We do not know the cause of the quarrel, but considering the closeness that Sid claimed for him and Elsie and his intimacy with his mother, we might well surmise that the hidden cause was Elsie's jealousy of Helen Howard, that Sid intuited that to be the underlying motive of her quarrel with his mother, that he told her so and that she understandably reacted against him in some negative fashion.

However, Sid decides that his bond with Elsie has been too important to him. On his way to Europe in the spring of 1921 he writes to Jean in an undated letter:

> I dislike being baffled by relationships. Wherefore—and because the old friendship with E.S.S. had always been valuable, I know, to her and to me, I opened old wounds again about a month since and have left things on a happy and calm basis. I have learned a good many things in life. In all seriousness, I am often deeply impressed by my wisdom! I know that things can be very difficult for men and women, I am deeply fond of Elise and ashamed of my own impatience. I buried Mother's hatchet first and then my own. I am sorry that I told you—or anyone, of course—so much of the story and so little of its significance. Not sporting of me. Well—

Despite Sidney's apparent success in performing a surgical procedure by opening up old wounds (and uncharacteristically—although perhaps partially joking about it—preening himself about it), Elsie erupts once more, but this time with Clare. On January 23rd, 1922, sometime after the resumption of his close relationship with Elsie, he writes to Jean: Clare "and Elsie have struck up a friendship now and are going strong and inseparable." But then something terrible happened between them while Sidney was away on a trip in the late winter and early spring of 1922—a cruise to California given to Sidney, Robert E. Sherwood, "my best man to be and managing editor of LIFE," and Ralph Barton, "the Saturday Evening Post illustrator. We three to lend tone or something to the cruise" (letter to Jean, February 9th, 1922).

After his return, he writes Jean that "Clare went through complete hell while I was away at Elsie's hands ... she did everything in her power to break Clare's love for me ... she provided evidence to prove every thing from my jealousy of Clare's work to the names and addresses of mistresses and went on to other and worse charges..." (April 12th, 1922). Is that because the "old wounds" on which he performed a surgical procedure predate Elsie's fishwife quarrel with Helen Howard? Did they involve some sort of rejection of Elsie by Sid? It is idle to speculate further. Clear, however, is that she was so shaken by her emotional involvement with Sidney and Clare, so obviously irrational that her own brother-in-law, with whom she was very friendly during the war in France, threatened to institutionalize her.

On the other hand, Clare handled this demoralizing situation with firmness, dispatch and intelligence. By going immediately to the person, Ernest Angell, now a successful New York lawyer, who could most efficiently and impressively handle the situation, she obtained written retractions from Elsie and kept her at a distance. In a time fraught with terrifying emotion Clare acted with admirably thoughtful, steadfast independence.

With all this the careers of Sid and Clare are bumping along but without great progress. Sid had one more play on Broadway for the season. On January 23rd, 1922, he wrote to Jean: "My affairs prosper. The 'S.S. TENACITY' is a success and a distinct feather in my cap, as translator. We are landing frenzied reviews in the weeklies now and it's as beautiful a play as ever was and as true. I call it the most important thing of recent years in New York. I wish you could see it, admirably done as it is. I turned it into out and out American and managed to keep it absolutely French. And I had only two days to do the job." The pleasure with which Sidney accomplished his work blinded him to its faults. The play, quiet and ironic, without the fireworks of the French well-made play or thesis drama, was one that serious theatergoers enjoyed then and continued to enjoy in years to come. But the production was not the success that Sidney thought he had nor was the translation always greatly admired. Kenneth Macgowan as critic wrote that it "has been one of the genuine successes, artistic and financial, of Copeau's post-war season at the Vieux Colombier. There, of course, it was acted within the conventionalized setting of a permanent and almost naked stage.... In New York Robert Edmond Jones has given it realistic scenery tempered by lines and tones that suggest mood in addition to the place" (*Theatre Arts*, April 2nd, 1922, 96–110). Nevertheless Macgowan is not very enthusiastic about the play, which he sees as an exercise in "discreet realism," which he does not believe is the "true fare of the theater." Stark Young in *The New Republic* is sympathetic to the production but thinks "even such a fine performance ... [is] un-French after all" (January 25th, 1922, 251). But it was the critics like Arthur Hornblow who gave the production its coup de grace: "What charm the S.S. Tenacity may have originally possessed has been lost through translation and adaptation. As presented at the Belmont Theatre, it is but a hackneyed story, tenuous and slow, stretched cruelly to make a full evening's performance" (*Theatre Magazine*, March 1922, 166–67)

Clare's season fared better than Sid's. In early January she did *Aglavaine and Sélysette* by "that moron Maeterlinck," to quote Sid again. Maeterlinck was an art-theater favorite, but more important, this production, meant to be the first of several matinee presentations, shows the continuing intention of serious theater folk on and off Broadway to bring before audiences what they considered to be important drama. Unfortunately, this production was no great success, and the project for matinee performances ceased when it closed. Still, it did not halt the idea of afternoon productions of serious drama.

Alexander Woolcott in *The New York Times* gives the kind of critical reaction that doomed the entire program (January 4th, 1922, 11):

> The vaguely identified persons responsible for the performance of "Aglavaine and Sylesette" [*sic*] at Miss [Maxine] Elliot's playhouse yesterday provided us with an interesting afternoon in the theater. It was interesting because of the speculations it provoked. Speculation, for instance, as to how such able and adult players as Clare Eames and Eva Le Gallienne could be persuaded to participate in so palpable a bit of near-poetry, near imagination and near-drama as this old piece by Maurice Maeterlinck. Yet the audience was awfully nice about it.
>
> Doubtless the lack of demonstration was maintained out of respect for the players. Of these Miss Eames has a true magnificence, which, with her unusual voice and her plastic grace and her knack for effective posturing, equip her for playing Maeterlinck as he should be played, if at all.

Of course, Woollcott could not bestow praise on Clare without also slapping "her knack for effective posturing." Nevertheless, his review was distinctly positive and, as we shall see, apparently accurate in its criticism.

This review contains a line which has become a classic if it indeed originated here:

> But after all the matinee was best summed up by the beautiful lady in the back row, who said: "There is less in this than meets the eye."

Unusually enough, we have the testimony of the two leading actresses about this presentation. Le Gallienne and Clare, two actresses with similar ambitions, probably the only two young actresses on Broadway with such goals, unfortunately never again worked together although they remained friends. In *At 33* Le Gallienne writes:

> I was much interested in Clare Eames. At first I couldn't make out whether she was one of the worst actresses I'd ever seen or whether she was a genius; her work was bewilderingly uneven; the intensity and even violence of her temperament made moderation impossible; there was no middle path; in one scene she would be unbelievably bad and in the next superb. She was an indefatigable worker and one of the most uncompromising artists I've ever known. Later years proved her unmistakable genius; had she lived I am convinced she would have been the greatest actress of our time; her death was a shocking and irreparable loss to the American Theatre [152–53].

Le Gallienne is only one of many witnesses to Clare in her uncompromising attitude toward her work in the theater, taking Jehlinger's advice, if she needed it, that she be fearless in trying things out though she may make mistakes. She disregarded any possible low opinion Le Gallienne, who had made a great success in the Theatre Guild production of *Liliom*, or any of her other fellow players, might derive from her working methods. These rehearsal habits, although they doubtless became less uneven as her experience grew, certainly remained the same throughout her career.

As Le Gallienne looked back at the performance of the Maeterlinck drama some eleven years later she thought that it "was not a good one. I was completely out of my depth, and played in an indefinite, colorless manner. Where Clare Eamnes *over*stressed, I *under*stressed; there was no cohesion in our work together; we had started at different ends of the scale."

We possess a few pages of a diary Clare kept at the time of *Aglavaine and Sélysette*. Whether any more of the diary ever existed we do not know. The pages we have are headed January 19th, 1922.

Among the items are the following:

> A performance of Aglavaine and Sylesette [*sic*] in the afternoon. About four hundred dollars in the house and it went well. New curtains of purple—much better. Eva good but appeared absent minded.

Clare's contemporary assessment of Le Gallienne's performance coincides with Le Gallienne's own, "absent minded" being very much of a piece with an "indefinite, colorless manner." Her assessment of her own performance, deadly honest, "showy but empty," agrees with Woolcott's in the writer's reference to Clare's "knack for effective posturing." Also, it again indicates the Jehlinger influence in her belief that a performance is worthless unless the character is built from the inside out.

She tells us, too, that she had lunch with Sid, who spoke of a coalminers' union convention, and in the evening she had been at a dinner attended by a number of old-time theatrical people such as Daniel Frohman, Dorothy Donnelly, and Cosmo Hamilton. Frohman was the international producer who owned the Empire Theatre, a distinguished house across the street from the old Metropolitan Opera House. On the boards of the Empire had trod such shining lights as Billie Burke, John Drew, and Maude Adams. Dorothy Donnelly was New York's first professional Candida but more importantly an author of some of the Schuberts' most successful musicals. Cosmo Hamilton was a British author of musical and straight plays popular both in England and in the United States.

Of course, they talked of the theater all night, mainly pragmatically, nostalgically, and sentimentally. "Sardou [a French proponent of the well-made play, the butt of Shaw's coinage 'Sardoudalism'] was also discussed as a great dramatist. Cosmo Hamilton said that nothing would be easier than to modernize La Tosca. 'Why,' he said, 'I could modernize the Merchant of Venice and make a ripping good play of it.' This in perfect seriousness and with a naiveté that was quite touching. He also thought very little of the works of 'Macneill—Macneill—What's-his-name?' I gathered that he was referring to Eugene O'Neill." They discussed "plays rescued from dire failure by some daring coup of advertisement or brilliant sleight-of-hand in the cast usually brought off by the story-teller himself. I thought of the Tenacity and said nothing. Bobby and Sidney don't know the point of view of such people." They and she, of course, were pure artists of the future, and in fact they tried very hard to be.

With O'Neill's *Made in Heaven* canceled as well as several other prospects, Clare finally opened on March 13th in a play by Henry Myers called *The First Fifty Years*. Sidney writes to Jean on April 12th, 1922: "Clare's play is a success of kinds—a personal triumph for her. What she does is pretty extraordinary in acting and in supplying a really blazing vitality to a sordid and shoddy piece of writing." Sidney was in no mood to look kindly on a piece which takes an acrid view of marriage. He thought very much the same of the content of the O'Neill play, we may remember, although he thought the drama itself thrilling, but then O'Neill was O'Neill and his friend and his rival.

The critics disagreed with Sidney about the play and joined him in his opinion about Clare. *The First Fifty Years* is a two-character play that covers a bitter fifty-year marriage. The most indifferent opinion of the play came from Kenneth Macgowan in *Theatre Arts Magazine*, who found it only "mildly interesting" ("Broadway at Spring," July 22nd, 1922, 190). Stark Young in *The New Republic*, more positive, thought it "deft enough ... not without profound feeling at times" (March 19th, 1922, 137). Arthur Hornblow, however, is enthusiastic, calling the author "a keen observer of life, a tried student of applied psychology, and a dramatic technician of daring and achievement" (*Theatre Magazine*, June, 1922, 373) The *New York Times* called the drama's story "authentic" sustaining "it and you throughout a crowded evening" (November 2nd, 1922).

Clare's reviews were much more interesting than the playwright's. All were favorable, but for some critics there was a problem in Clare's playing domestic roles. The *Times* article, after praising Clare, spells out the problem: "It is true, too, that it is a little difficult to subdue the magnificent Miss Eames into the accent and look of an ornery Harlem cottage. She trails something of the Medea ... into the most homespun surroundings and succeeds along about 1887 in taking on something of the austere mystery of a Wilkie Collins melodrama."

The most trenchant reply to this view of Clare's acting comes in a letter to the *Times* by Elizabeth Sergeant obviously written before the break in the relations between Clare and her. She admires the play and the fascinated audience reaction, its "excessively heated arguments as to whose fault it is, anyhow, the man's or the woman's..." (March 22nd, 1922, 1: 4). She praises the work of Tom Powers, Clare's partner in the drama, and allows that he has

> brought to his Harlem clerk-husband a much more photographic realism than Miss Eames to her Harlem domestic drudge. But it must be said that Anne Wells, as interpreted by Miss Eames, has undertones and echoes which Martin Wells lacks. Those undertones make Anne not just a certain unhappy wife, but woman of the ages in her relation to man of the ages; woman more constant, more suffering, more deeply involved in marriage even when love ends, than man can ever be, and more frank and courageous to face the depth of her loss and failure and know it irretrievable. There are unforgettably beautiful moments in Miss Eames's acting.

It is difficult to take on the surface a letter from a friend, especially a letter whose author, we may suspect, is in love with the subject. But not all descriptions prompted by personal feelings are necessarily invalid, and the insight here has a persuasive ring. It may be true, as the *Times* critic suggests, that Clare is constitutionally unable to play a small character. Given that, however, she tries for something that places the character in the larger scheme of things. The *Times* reviewer sees her as trailing Medea behind her, but Elsie Sergeant, with perhaps greater understanding, sees the generalizations Clare tries for in terms of the specifics of the play. Even if Elsie knew from Clare the nature of the latter's intention, that Clare should have had such an intention, even if she was unsuccessful in the execution, indicates her reach. But as we saw from Clare's comment on her playing *Aglavaine and Séylesette*, that an empty but showy performance was not enough. Her attempt then was to work in two directions, from the inside out, from the deep emotionality of the character, and from the character to the contexts of the drama, intellectually lending the play a significance perhaps even beyond the author's clear intention.

Despite their preoccupation with their careers and the disturbing elements in their lives in the months just before and after their marriage, the couple is joyous. Sidney expresses to Jean and his mother his heady feeling of love for Clare; Clare, in writing to Sidney, shows her unmistakable feelings. Yet as we shall soon see, as we read through Clare's letters, beneath them there also seems to be a certain ambivalence toward the marriage.

Occupying much of their time during the preparations for their marriage and afterward is Sidney's adaptation of Melchior Lengyal's *World of Sancho Panza*, on which he had been working, at the commission of Emilie Hapgood, who owned the rights, at least since early 1921.

Emilie Hapgood had been interested in the theater for a long time. She had been head of the New York Stage Society when it presented Sam Hume's New Stagecraft Exhibition and Granville Barker's production of "Androcles and the Lion" and "The Man Who Married a Dumb Wife," this last production bringing to the New York theater the New Stagecraft in the form of Robert Edmond Jones's set design. Her work in the theater was respectable. Less so was her personal reputation. Her former husband, Norman Hapgood, never mentions her in his autobiography (Marcaccio, 84). His brother, Hutchins, does talk of her in his autobiography. His characterization of her there may help explain why Norman does not. Hutchins calls Emilie "largely selfish and egotistic" and pictures her "often lying in a chaise lounge looking picturesque and impressive" (Hapgood, 128, 146). A few lines from Sidney's "bedtime" letter to his mother suggest another reason for Norman not mentioning Emilie in his autobiography:

> E[milie] H[apgood] (I shouldn't tell you this but it's funny) asked me to (marry her) or (live with her). I can't make out which and think either one would have done for her. Poor mad woman! I wrote her a note and told her with brutal honesty what was what and that I am engaged, not naming Clare, of course.... I hope to god she doesn't "speak or forever hold her peace" at my wedding.

We infer that Sidney had an affair with Emilie, perhaps in London, where she oversaw his work on *Sancho* in the spring of 1921, as Clare was plotting to sell *Swords*. More important in his immediate future is his attempt to take away the rights to *Sancho* from Mrs. Hapgood. "Now I learn that "SANCHO" isn't hers unless she can pay $500 more on Nov. 15 and I'm damned sure she can't. So Lengyal and I can sell it together and I pay back my $500 that she gave me and that's that" (letter to Jean, July 10th, 1921).

About this time, between the closing of *Swords* and the opening of *Aglavaine and Séylesette*, Clare visited Cleveland whence she writes in an undated letter to Sidney in the full flush of her feeling for him but without the ability to express it. She also has Emilie Hapgood on her mind.

> Sidney dear—
>
> I am a pig not to have written to you. It was not because I didn't want to but because I was overpowered by the most ridiculous shyness. There are so many things I wanted to say to you and I didn't have the nerve to do it. And except that, I had nothing to say. Do you understand? I can tell you, however, that I have had many moments of "tranquil understanding." Emilie Hapgood is a bore and a devil. Let us hope that you can get *Sancho* away from her somehow because really to think of your having wasted all that time and energy and thought is too exasperating. She may hold onto it just to annoy you, you know. Hell knows no fury etc. Cleveland isn't bad. I am now the Great Educational Power. All the schools have been after me to read from the classics to the young idlers [?] It is rather amusing and tomorrow I am going to talk to the students of the Ohio State Dramatic School. And I am going to tell them a few home truths. Any illusions about the stage are going to be shattered, so that when they finally go on they may possibly be agreeably disappointed. Always paint any job worse than it is to one who is about to undertake it. I fail to understand *why* your sister did not get my immediate answer to her letter. I am humiliated. A horrible suspicion has occurred to me that I addressed it to the Turnpike but even then it ought to have reached her. And then again I may not have. New York will see me on Tuesday morning. Always my love dear Sidney.
>
> Clare

The letter from Jean which Clare refers to earlier is the one causing the minor imbroglio on Sidney's return from the West Coast, and indeed, that being the second unanswered letter from Jean may have caused Sid's sharp reaction to her failure to respond. If Clare failed to answer this letter as well as the next, she would seem reluctant to reach out to the sister whom Sidney loved, distrustful of her as she undoubtedly was of his mother. At any rate, whatever antipathy she may have worked up against Jean vanishes when she finally knows her.

Clare refers to Emilie as a woman scorned, and we may well wonder how much she knows about the extent of Sid's relationship to Emilie if indeed the inference about it is correct. Whatever she knows, her attitude seems to be sophisticated, her main interest being in Emilie Hapgood's attempt unfairly to hold on to *Sancho*, which she seems reluctant to produce quickly. Also, Clare seems to enjoy her role as Eminent Personality in Cleveland, one who had already made good on Broadway and can use her charms to entertain the local schoolchildren and to tell tales of the wilds to student actors. She is an actress to the bone.

Seemingly also from Cleveland at the same time she writes Sidney in an undated letter, probably in response to words of discouragement about *Sancho*, which bring out the depth of her adulation for him:

> Sidney dear
>
> How you could possibly have thought *Sancho* was anything but magnificent I cannot imagine. It really can only be explained by saying that like William Shakespeare you don't know a good play when you see one. Here you have taken Lengyel's original tract and scalded [?] it with the reckless fire of your imagination; and you have made something that reduced your affianced bride to tears. Moreover, the actual writing is so simple and manly, the cumulative effect of your perfectly unadorned and downright sentences is a romance that has its roots in candour and pity and merriment instead of satiety and then the magic of your extraordinary imagination rubs up everything you touch into a most dazzling splendor. What I really ought to do is learn to enter your presence without getting off a long string of complimentary epithets, as in the Arabian Knights [*sic*]. Sort of Protector of the Poor stuff. And to think that this beguiling, humorous, sturdy, touching play should be in the hands of someone who probably thinks of Dapple [Sancho's donkey] as a symbol. Oh god.
>
> Thank you my darling
> Your
> Clare

After a number of delays the June 1st date for the wedding is set, and Clare goes out to Cleveland to prepare for the occasion. Clare and Sid have been hunting for an apartment, and apartments "are expensive. Dreadfully expensive. We cannot do six rooms under 3000 a year [250 a month!] in any possible part of town with light and air enough to preserve health" (undated letter to Jean). Both Sid and Clare have had a bad season financially, and they cannot afford even that. Sid's mother has offered them her apartment while she is abroad, but Sidney has been reluctant to take advantage of his mother's generosity. When Clare reaches Cleveland for the wedding, she has some time to think over the matter.

> Darling
>
> The first thing I did on my arrival was to smash my finger in the front door hinge. It didn't hurt very much but it shocked me and mother put me to bed where I stayed for two days meditating. I finally, like the Indians, came to the conclusion which prompted the telegram I sent you last

night. Now, darling, the final step of course is up to you, as the one who holds the purse-strings is naturally the one who has to decide. But it seems to me that it would be cheaper to take your mother's apartment for one year at the end of which we would know exactly where we stood. At the annual expenditures of only a hundred dollars more we should save many hundreds on the initial cost of moving into a new place. I absolutely share with you a desire to start out fresh to-gether in a way that would bind us to no associations except the ones we would make ourselves and which I know would be happy ones. At the same time, I cannot bear the thought of your being over burdened with financial worry as well as all the other excitements that, in our professions, we shall never be free from. I love you, my own dearest, and I say this because I want you to be ultimately perfectly happy and as for me I am marrying you and not a house or a pair of Aberdeen terriers (however charming). Still as Mrs. Wilson says, it is as you say, R.W., not as I do. You may agir comme bon tu amble. I shall be equally happy in either place, if I share it with you. I know you will be glad to hear that my two days of rest have made me much calmer and altogether less given to chimeras.

> I love you, darling Sidney.
> Your
> Clare [undated letter]

This odd accident may well have been a way for Clare to take to her bed to meditate. Whether it was to meditate over the problem of the apartment is another question. It hardly takes two days for her to figure out her solution to the apartment problem, which makes sense, and her reasoning shows her once again to be pragmatic as well as loving and concerned for his welfare.

But the main reason for her finding a way into her bed away from the clatter of wedding preparations must have been to become "much calmer and altogether less given to chimeras." We can imagine perhaps the nature of those chimeras: a fear of marrying Sidney, who innocently wished to rob her of some independence she has had since she came to New York while shaping a successful career and a way of life for herself. The fear of that prospect may well have summoned up the chimeras that aroused what seemed to be undue excitement. Another chimera may have been the fear of other women.

Very near the time of the wedding she writes a charming (undated) letter:

> Dearest Sidney—
>
> This is the last time I shall write to you under the name of Eames –
>
> Clare Howard

What do you think of that? I am very pleased about the honeymoon, and in fact about everything including some of the presents. Some are loathsome. Jimmy Lee sent us very handsome breakfast cups—but you will see them when you come....

She goes on to list events leading up to the wedding and ends: "Keep your courage up, my paragon, and remember that I love you and that I am *not* a myth." After her signature she adds, "I think Emilie Hapgood is what Richard Bennet called Mrs. Burnett [Frances Hodgson Burnett, a popular novelist]." We can well imagine what that was.

The couple had hoped to go to Europe on their honeymoon but for lack of funds stayed in the United States, visiting various parts of the Eastern Seaboard, mainly as house guests of several friends and one important relative, Emma Eames, who "made a regal pilgrimage to New York to inspect the man whom she calls 'her new nephew.' Being a nephew to Emma Eames isn't the snap it sounds. But Clare says I am doing nicely" (letter to Jean, February 9th, 1922). Clare and Sid visit her during their honeymoon summer.

Sidney decides to take Clare's advice about their living in his mother's apartment, but in a June 27th letter to Jean, he seems more concerned about his emotional relationship to his mother than about starting a new life with Clare:

> It was a hard week for Mother—between our return to town and her departure. She lost a son and a home at once—or so she felt although the son is well enough and the home at her disposal. I think I had never known how close Mother and I are until I put her on the train for Quebec and went home with Clare, happy as a lark—for so I was, by heck—and devastated by such an inundation of loneliness as I have never known. Which Clare, brick that she is, understood and, even, liked. The changes we made in the house, replacing Mother's treasures she would not leave with Clare's very handsome presents, were fun. Even Mother found amusement in that.

It is difficult to believe that Sidney "had never known how close Mother and I are." He had already written to Jean about their "spiritual matrimony." We had seen him write that "bedtime" letter to her. He wrote to her details of his career and seemed to confess at least some intimate details of his personal life. That he would then resist understanding the depth of his feeling for his mother would seem to show its true depth and to confirm what he had once said to Elsie, that he was not introspective. At least he did not now hide from himself the extent of his attachment.

Clare on her part seems to be handling Sid's difficulty with a great deal of tact. She is a "brick," who understood and, even, "liked" his emotion. Helen Howard, however, was not a brick. She plainly showed her unhappiness at having lost a home and, especially, we may believe, a son.

5. Clare and Sidney

Clare and Sidney's behavior in the previous weeks indicates that both were ambivalent about their marriage. However, many happy marriages as well as unhappy marriages begin with ambivalences for both members of the couple. But Clare and Sidney's looked as though it would turn into one of the happiest. They merrily visit friends in the summer following their marriage (letter to HH, June 30th, 1922). During a summer visit with the redoubtable Aunt Emma in Maine, they fall in love with an old house, look forward to buying it and remodeling it when they have the cash. Clare appears to enjoy the role of the traditional frugal wife: "Clare is an astounding housewife. Her daily remark is: 'Did you enjoy your dinner? It cost $1.92'" (letter to HH, July 22nd, 1922).

On July 14th Sid writes his mother: "Clare is fine and here is the news. Though I can hardly call it news yet. There is, according to the docs, every symptom of an heir, though the docs will guarantee nothing. We are petrified with fright, of course. Don't say that it is ill-advised. Clare wants a child far more than a play this winter. I want one far more than anything else on this earth. Even if it means grinding a bit to meet expenses, it is worth it to not be too much older than one's offspring. I have weighed everything and I hope with all my heart that it may be true. We shall know, of course, very soon."

They do not learn anything definite for some time, "and this damned uncertainty about an offspring makes Clare's plans too difficult.... I am so damned happy about it that I can't worry over finances or anything except that it may *not* be true" (letter to HH, July 24th, 1922).

But Clare was not as straightforward with Sidney about the possible arrival of a child. "There is a scheme afoot to open a new repertory in October, each play to go for four weeks, the stars to be Clare, Eva Le Gallienne and Ben Ami and Robert Ames. There is a great deal of money behind it and I can see the possibility of a child causes some conflict in Clare. But, wonderful person that she is, she manifests no more than occasional bursts of wanting to act and spends much more of her time hoping and planning for herself. I know that a fallow year of acting which brings her to motherhood can only help her work afterward and I want a youngster myself so much that I'm very happy even if it means a certain amount of hac[k] work to keep things from worry" (letter to HH, August 18th, 1922).

But on September 13th he writes his mother:

> We have been having rather an unfortunate time lately. Clare and Rob Woods and I all went up to Stockbridge in the car to John Marquand's wedding and the evening of our arrival she fell quite ill. She rose for the wedding the next day and came back to New York in fair order only to cave completely upon her arrival here. Some kind of a germ infection, very

much inside and quite painful with two docs and a trained nurse. Though it isn't serious and doesn't mean an operation, it is disheartening now because the doc's [sic] are afraid that what they had previously diagnosed as pregnancy is only this inflammation. So both of us are a little discouraged and disappointed. However, if it isn't the youngster we hoped to have, he (or she) will come later when we have more money.

Later he adds: "Fortunately Clare can go into HAMLET with John Barrymore if she wants and that will quite easily fill her winter." Perhaps Clare did not want to become a cast member of what turns out to be the most memorable Shakespearean production of the decade. But ultimately, whether or not she wished to act in it did not matter, for she seems to have fallen ill again. At first she appears to improve:

She is better, but the hope of a child is for the moment beside the point which has been pretty hard on her for she takes things hard and would, naturally, have taken that harder than anything. Whether it was something wrong or merely an inflammation we can't tell. There was terrible pain for two weeks and high fever and much consultation and now she is almost herself again. There isn't much doubt that our hopes were well founded but things went wrong with a vengeance as they often do in the first weeks and there you are. So that your check for the rent came in more opportunely tha[n] even you had imagined [letter to HH, October 2nd, 1922].

But the misery continues. Sidney writes again in an undated letter to his mother: "I left without breakfast what with hysterical appointments and Clare ill again. Poor child, she is having a rotten time. A play has come her way which she wants to do and God knows whether she can risk it or not. There seems to be no way of finding out what the trouble is, no signs of a child and all the misery. I have never seen the like and I do wish that some of the damnable and costly consultations would draw some conclusions."

Sidney, in financial stress, accepts a job of investigative reporting paying one hundred dollars a week during the probe itself and five hundred dollars per article (undated letter to HH, probably August 1922). The assignment is from Norman Hapgood, Emilie's former husband and now editor of *Hearst's International Magazine*. But the work will take him away from Clare. Clare, in a series of undated letters, wrote Sidney out of her misery, longingly but with humor and spunk. We sense the depth of their feeling for each other. We also get the context of their lives, their up-and-coming and already-arrived young friends, their keeping up with the literary world around them, their close relations with their families. Despite her illness, she is highly responsive to the world around her.

5. Clare and Sidney   115

Darling—

La. Marsh [apparently the nurse] says I can get up for a minute and write to you. I must feel that you are somewhere in this dark world and wide. Everything is so grim without you to witness it.

...Fizz [their dog] has decorated the rugs until I feel that stilts are the only safe means of locomotion and he is taken out regularly—I am better, although I still run a temperature. I have no pain—or at least so little that it doesn't count.

I miss you and need you—really. *Don't* stay away any longer than you can help, Sidney dear—

Your
Clare

My darling Sidney –

Your Monday letter has just arrived, bringing two blows. First, about a possible War. That I can't get through my head. If it must be, it must be but lets [sic] pray for the English. The thought of you going is like the thought of fatal illness—one of those things you must be brave about. Just now, any public disgrace seems preferable to that private loss. Sidney and Sidney. To find my life and lose it. And the second blow is about my Howard letters of thanks which were written from *Cleveland* in *May*. With the sole and sordid intent of ingratiating myself with your family I thanked them at once and effusively. It really seems too bad. When I really am in the wrong I sulk but when I am put there unwillingly I am crushed. However, I shall write again at once if you think it best. But your letter is a wonderful one ... Fizz was so naughty in the house that I had to send him to Elaine Ralis's in the country until I am strong enough to drag him around the streets. Both Stetten and Hendel [her doctors] said that any strain on my abdominal muscles such as lifting or pulling was out of the question. But nevertheless I am going to get him back this week. I miss the little devil so.... I wish to-day were Thursday so that I could see you. I love you.

Your
Clare

At the top of the letter just quoted Clare adds a superscription which shows that she has the same anti–Semitism as Sidney. Still referring to the possible war, she writes:

Moreover I refuse to stand up for a pack of half-bred Jews and venal time-serving journalists. I am going to stick by the race that gave us Cromwell and Latimer and the elder Pitt and Washington. The far seeing political consciousness of modern times. This is terrible.

Your
Clare

Sidney Dear—

...My real news is that Stetten returns to-night which means that our troubles are at an end. He will *know* absolutely, and I shall let you hear what he says at once. John Farrar came to see me and told me that Magaret Severn is a nymphomaniac, that [Robert] Milton was ill and Kaufman and Connelly are going to do his play.... Hardly any temperature to-night, my dear. What has become of my wedding-present money? Couldn't I use some of that for two days at Washington? After all, it would be the same as a present....

The next few sentences have to do with Robert E. Sherwood, one of the Howards' closest friends, still working for the old *Life*. Clare's remarks become clear if we quote a letter from Sidney to his mother written at about this time:

> Sherwood's wedding and another grief. He is to marry a girl named Mary Brandon, a cutie ingénue, on October 9th. I don't approve at all. She is a frivolous little girl who plans a life of cabarets and theater parties and no maid except to make the beds and lots of drink and no youngsters and all meals in restaurants except breakfasts so that there will be no household cares and "none of this home business." And poor Bob is torn between misery and infatuation and I see where Bob goes the way of all others who marry girls who don't like their husbands' friends. And I see how lucky I am [October 1st, 1922].

In her letter Clare writes: "Never have I seen anyone so unhappy as Bob. Mary said she likes children but was afraid to have them and would have to get used to the idea. We mustn't let him suffer. Although you and I were pretty unhappy, my response to the children idea kind of cleared the atmosphere. My love to you darling always. I hate having anyone but the Great Lout in your room."

The Great Lout, of course, is Sidney, and Elaine, who has either brought back Fitz or is about to take him to the country, must be sleeping in Sid's room. The line about "you and I were pretty unhappy" is unclear. Perhaps it means, although Sid's letter points to the opposite, that the first reaction of Sid and Clare to the news of a possible child was negative for financial and career reasons. If that is the case, then it was Clare's positive response to a child, which later did not always remain positive, that brought them out of their funk and sent them up to the stratosphere.

> My darling Sidney—
>
> Your letter did my heart good although I hate to think of the difficulties you have to surmount in the cause of William Randolph Hearst when you might be writing something as good and as unsuccessful as the S. S. Tenacity. It makes me feel very conscience stricken. California and New Orleans sound like the Antipodes but wouldn't it be swell if I could go with you. Inasmuch as Stetten says there is no extra-uterine formation (he examined me this afternoon) but only a local inflammation, and that in case I

am pregnant traveling won't hurt me. I could make it, granting the cash. If the cash isn't forthcoming I shall take the second woman in the fifth company of Hearts of Gold coast-to-coast tour and hope to play these cities while you are there. My temperature continues but I am sure it will subside with the pain which decreases daily. Mother arrived this morning for a few days—as I suspected she might—and sends you love with the message that she was glad to find me as well as she did. Yesterday Bob came to see me, very down in the mouth but had to leave to make way for Stetten, who, however, did not examine me until to-day. Roland Young and Monty came, bearing flowers. And John Farrar sent me the galleys of Heywood Broun's novel which is really distinguished and delightful except for one small slip which I shall tell you about *next week-end*. Can I bear it. I rather think not. Oh my very dear, do come. I love you more than anything or anybody in the world, and I shall execute your commissions for you.

Darling, it is awful not to have you—
Clare

My darling—

[O]f course the cocaine-hashish-heroin story is too frightful and the bare idea of such a horror is unbearable. Imagine. Your letter was a joy— and thank you for the cheque which paid for the Marsh (who left today) and for the picture of the Flowers.... Bob and Mary came to see me this afternoon, Mary amiable and excited and Bob rather down-hearted. But he has set the date for the 25th of December. Stetten also came and hedged on his diagnosis. That is to say, he is not yet sure whether I am going to have a baby, on account of the inflammation. I am going to be examined again on the 8th of October. Mother spent the morning looking on 9th Avenue for cheap grocery stores and she found them so that our bills can come down by half. I *hated* the thought of burdening you with my extravagance and carelessness. As to what you say of journalism, you are no doubt right; but I want you to be happy and to do what you want to do. Although if the investigation goes well you will enjoy it, of course. I am so thrilled at the thought of seeing you again, my dear dear Sidney, that I can't possibly write sense. This absence has taught me that we are each other's always. I love you so much that I can't bear it.

Your
Clare

Despite what must have been a terrible strain on the marriage resulting from Clare's illnesses and Sid's absences, their feeling for each other seems to have survived strongly. But the effect of the strain comes through in the final letter of this group, painful because of the blame and burden Clare takes upon herself. But the thought in this letter may have resulted from Clare's attempt to conform to Sidney's idea of the nature and context of his marriage. She calls herself an egoist and blames herself for hasty words and a "cantankerous" personality. But that she lacked any particular idea of a marriage, as she says in the letter, may have shown that she was not ready for this or any marriage, that an independent single state was her true desire, and that she was swept into marriage by Sidney and the general social ideal of the station a woman should assume in her life. This also may have been in her mind, consciously or otherwise, in those two meditative days in Cleveland after she smashed her finger.

>My darling Sidney—
>
>...My dear, two people who love each other as we do *must* be happy. And I know that our happiness is in my hands. You have a picture of married life which includes sports and dogs and the country and amiable companions and a faithful attractive wife and babies. I have no picture of married life at all, as such. I have merely an ideal of life with you. So you see it is up to me to supply you with your picture. But my dear you must be patient with me. If you only knew how I have prayed that I night never be led into a hasty word or a selfish act or an unjust thought. And if you only knew that blighting consciousness of failure that comes over me sometimes. It is hard for an egoist and empiricist suddenly to become generous and united. The only thing I hope is that some day my prayers will begin to bear fruit and that the lesser cantankerous sensational part of me will be dead forever. I beg you not to think bitterly of me and to realize that when I have behaved particularly badly I am nevertheless in an obscure and feeble corner of my mind reproaching myself and trying to do better. I feel now as a Christian might if he had betrayed his god. Help me to be strong darling. You are the only person who can. And remember always that I love you so that I would do literally anything to clarify and steady our life together. My dearest dearest Sidney.
>
>   *Clare*

6

Clare in Hollywood: An Interlude

Clare accepted an offer from the (Mary) Pickford studio in Hollywood for several reasons. One was her continuing poor health. On January 6th, 1923, Sidney wires his mother that "Clare has been ill again with infected glands" and on the fifteenth that "Clare [is] still miserable." Her persistent vulnerability to illness undoubtedly prevented her from taking a stage assignment, which would have required stiff rehearsals and repetitions eight times a week after the show opened. It seemed easier to work in films. Certainly the California weather was a factor in Sid and Clare's decision. Sid's telegram to his mother on the sixth says that if the "California scheme is definitely off I will send her [to] Florida or Bermuda for sunshine and rest." The couple's expectation then was that the movie assignment would keep her acting without the strenuous effort required by the theater while it provided the needed sunshine.

Probably a factor just as important in motivating Clare's trek west was the salary. She would receive $625 per week, an amount she could never make in the theatre for a comparatively short period of seemingly easy work in a supporting role. The money, a boon at this time of the couple's lives when they had nothing toward a nest egg, might also partly be used to purchase the house with which they had fallen in love while visiting Aunt Emma in Maine during their honeymoon summer. It all seemed simple and benign, a pleasant interlude, for her true work was in the theater.

But life, as usual, provided a major drawback. Sid, because of his various assignments, could not accompany Clare. Such a separation, onerous for any newly married couple, was doubly hard on Clare and Sid. Her illnesses and his work assignments had already brought painful separations that prevented the occasions as well as the physical intimacies that help resolve inevitable problems of the early stages of marriage. Further, their feverish desire for a child placed its many-faceted strain upon the marriage, part of which derived from Clare's creeping ambivalence about wanting one at all and yet surely her guilt for her failure to conceive it; she was also fearful of the birth process itself. Living in Mrs. Howard's apartment, a wrong decision on their part, added to their difficulties, for Sidney's mother proved to be officious. Nevertheless, Sidney and Clare remained strongly bound to each other when she went west. While their separation still prevented them from resolving their earlier matrimonial difficulties, when she left Hollywood in 1923 for a summer abroad with her husband, clearly they loved each other still.

One cause of their problems disappeared before Clare left for Hollywood. Helen Howard returned to New York from her trips to Europe and Berkeley. Clare and Sidney, vacating her apartment on January 15th, moved to 969 Lexington Avenue, where Alfred Lunt and Lynn Fontanne also lived.

On the very day of their move Sid wires his mother: "CLARE'S [California plans] ENTIRELY ABANDONED AND PAID IN FULL DUE PICKFORDS CHANGE PLANS." Mary Pickford, having been a grown woman for some time, had decided that now was the moment for her to surrender the child roles that had made her famous and grow up on the screen as she had in life. *Dorothy Vernon of Haddon Hall* was to be her vehicle. To ease her transition she imported the highly admired German director Ernst Lubitsch. Lubitsch had apparently approved the script when he read it in Germany, but once in Hollywood he refused to do it because, he believed, the conflict between Elizabeth, the role to be played by Clare, and her rival, Mary, Queen of Scots, detracted from the central character of Dorothy Vernon. Pickford was forced to shelve the film for the time being. But since she was paying Lubitsch, she found another project for him, which turned out to be *Rosita*, "the worst picture, bar none, that I ever made" (Pickford, 252–53).

As with Lubitsch, so with Clare. Since she too was being paid, and since *Rosita* also contained a queen, albeit a Spanish queen, why not assign her to play a Spanish queen? But apparently the studio failed to tell her of the change, for in her first letter to Sidney on her way west Clare writes, "I am scared to death of Queen Elizabeth," obviously still believing that she would play Elizabeth. The Pickford failure to inform Clare of its change of plans proved to be only the first of many disillusionments that aroused Clare's ire against the Pickford studio and against Hollywood generally.

6. Clare in Hollywood: An Interlude

Clare's first letter from Hollywood, one of twenty-five surviving letters (almost all undated) from, as it turned out, their two periods of separation in 1923, tells of her unhappy arrival in Los Angeles irritated by the studio's expectation of her helplessness.

Clare Eames as Elizabeth I in Mary Pickford's *Dorothy Vernon of Hadden Hall*. (Courtesy of the New York Public Library.)

> I arrived this afternoon, only 40 minutes late, which is doing well; and I don't think that in my life I have ever felt more forlorn. Mary Pickford had sent a car to meet me, presumably with outriders from the way she talked about it, but as I didn't stand and look helplessly around but went and got in a taxi immediately, I was evidently taken for a native. The Ambassador was full, but they had reserved rooms for me here [the Beverly Hills Hotel and Bungalows]. It was all very bewildering and depressing notwithstanding the vegetation, and had it not been for the fact that I had to keep Annie [her maid] cheered up, I should have wilted in earnest....
>
> As far as I can see I shall have 3 or 4 days in which to get settled. The Pick studio has told me that a suite (cheap) has been reserved for me at the Laurel Inn, Hollywood, and that I should not be needed for a day at least. We all know what that means. If they put me off too long I shall leave them flat.

But she is not so unhappy as to be unappreciative of her entering upon an interesting new professional enterprise or of the amazing country she has crossed for the first time.

> Don't get the idea that I am absolutely wretched. I am not—only excited and uncertain and very very disoriented. And besides, I have no one to talk to about the marvelous impression of this extraordinary country which is at once so sublimely beautiful and so despairingly merely ugly. What you said is true—the hand of man has uglified it.

Remembering her beautiful trip west does not keep Clare calm very long. The studio's attitude toward her payment schedule angers her, outraging her sense of justice, more so than it might have otherwise because she has apparently all along distrusted the "Pickford bunch." She is further offended as she watches the studio's handling of the payment of one of its foreign employees. Clare's contempt for the organization is not lessened by its place as one of the premier studios in Hollywood, where she was thus starting at the top.

Edward Knoblock, the author of the screenplay of *Rosita* mentioned in the following letter, was a well-known dramatist whose play *Kismet* had been an extraordinary success in both England and America, where it had starred the popular actor Otis Skinner. Holbrook Blinn, a highly respected stage star, had acted one of the leading roles with Mrs. Fiske in Edward Sheldon's *Salvation Nell* in 1908. Blinn was slated to play the Spanish king opposite Clare's queen:

> But my fears about the Pickford bunch have certainly been justified. Wait. You are going to hear about the baseness, the deformity, of criminal lunatics. I have to keep my mind very firmly fixed on Marcus Aurelius, Abraham Lincoln and yourself to remember that there are, after all, decent people in the world. My telegrams have shown you what they tried to do. They are not going to use me until Blinn's arrival, April 1st, and they had every intention of starting to pay me on that date. The worst thing though, that they have done, was not done to me, but to Lubitsch's secretary. He is a poor, cowering, gentle little German boy, about nineteen or twenty, totally without English, except a few slang phrases such as make it snappy and I'll tell the world. Kerrigan, the business manager and Chief Robber, told me the following story with pride. When he asked Fritz or Heinrich or whatever his name is what his salary is, F. or H. said 100 marks a week and Kerrigan said that would be fine, and pays him with an eye on the exchange. Now whether the story is true or not, whether or not he actually did it, the fact that he boasted of such an exploit where another might boast of having upheld his convictions against odds, is enough. Some day I am going to avenge that German boy and in the still watches of the night I plan. Kerrigan is doomed. I formally in writing demanded my salary, after his verbal refusal, and he called me up to say that I would get it to-day. Fortunately, [William] Faversham [whom she had supported in *The Prince and the Pauper*] by a great stroke of luck has been here and has been most kind, and has told the Pickfords in no uncertain terms who and what I am. He also has introduced me to a dear old gentleman and his wife Mr. and Mrs. Stearns from Detroit who have been sweet to me. It is with them that I went to the concert. It is hard to judge their social status because all Detroit people are so queer, but I should think they belong to the army of the Quiet Rich, who do good work and who don't, as they say, mix, except on hospital boards.

Clare obviously absorbed from her family background a strong strain of social-class puritanism which came into play in Hollywood. Whereas others were content to take Hollywood gold and enjoy its easy life (as they scoffed at its mores), she found intolerable the waste of time, energy, and money as well as the lack of artistic seriousness at the studios:

6. Clare in Hollywood: An Interlude 123

> Edward Knoblock and I had a long talk the other day and he told me his tale of woe. He says he is a nervous wreck, the disorder is so dreadful. $260,000.00 have been wasted already this season. Not a thing, except, apparently, myself, to show for it. The scenery isn't even built. Occasionally you hear the sound of a tack hammer but on investigating you find that it is only a table being made for the publicity man to write on. Annie says that they are trash and is very haughty with them.
>
> The Goldwyns want Pickford to lend me to them. Well, I don't care who pays me.

Clare's mood now changes to despair because the Pickfords plan to shoot *Dorothy Vernon* immediately after *Rosita*, which would keep her in Hollywood past the summer, causing Clare and Sid to miss their planned trip to Europe.

Robert (Bob) Milton, mentioned below, a theatrical producer and director, occasionally wrote shows tending toward art, sometimes artiness.

> The most appalling news. My letters must seem like wails of despair. But to-day at the studio I asked them about engaging passage on the Rochambeau [apparently the ship on which she and Sid planned to sail to Europe] and they said that this picture could hardly be finished before the middle of July and that after they intend to do *Dorothy Vernon*! Which means October. Now, what I want to know is how far am I bound by contract to do Elizabeth? I didn't think it wise to make them suspect for a moment that I am unwilling to do anything they ask of me (except play for nothing) and I didn't dare to say a word. But I *can't* be separated from you like that. It is asking too much, and moreover it puts my dander up....
>
> Toledo, the scene of our picture ... is nearly built, looking as unlike El Greco's idea of the place as possible—in fact, looking like a group of California bungalows. It may be all right in a photograph. I don't mean to be sour—but when Bob Sherwood says these are nice people or intelligent people, or even decent people, he must be mad. D'abord, they are so disorderly that Bob Milton would be in his element with them et enseinte they, quite amiably, have no taste and no convictions. Not even convictions about money. [Charles] Brabin, of the Goldwyn, is a remarkable man; a Cockney but most interesting and with amazing powers of observation. Some day I shall tell you what he has told me about acting in pictures. Illusion acting. Tomorrow he is going to take me over to his picture to see just how the whole thing works. I can find out nothing at my own Studio because they put heavy screens around the set where they are "shooting" to hide Pickford from the vulgar gaze.

Clare now moves with her usual speed and determination to secure her European trip. Her love for Sidney may be the initial cause of her action, but her native independence and strength drive her:

> In a mood of desperation, I consulted Mr. Goodwin, Mr. Stearns's lawyer, about the validity of my contract to play Elizabeth [in *Dorothy Ver-*

non]. And he said they cannot possibly hold me to it, and that their persistent misrepresentation of what I came out here to do absolves me from all duty to them. So that, the instant this is over, back I go where I belong, with you, my darling, unless you come out here for *Sancho*, in which case I shall stay here to be with you, but shall not act. *Rosita* may not be finished by that time anyway....

This idle foolish life gives me too much time to think. There is no question of creative impulse nor of work (except physical work, once it begins) connected with it. Every effort I make to study the script or to learn something about my job is discouraged, not rudely, but as if I were a fool to bother about such things. As I told you I went to the Goldwyn studio to see the thing in action, and learned nothing. And it is corrosive to draw over $600.00 a week for doing literally nothing. I am awakened at eight and think about you. I breakfast at 8:30 and at 10:30 report at the Studio. After lunch (alone—all my meals are alone) I lie down and try to sleep and usually succeed. Faversham told me to do this, as he said nervous fatigue shows more than anything else on screen. At seven I dine alone, and after thinking about you for a couple of hours I go to bed. The people in the hotel have been nice to me but it is the niceness of curiosity. The Stearns have been really nice. I am grateful to them. I am staying on here because after exhaustive investigation I find that it is cheaper. Although the rents are low here, everything else is horribly dear. There were no flats possible, and the bungalow I looked [at] which was all right (and the only one that was) necessitated a man for the lawn and someone for the house. And the servants demand from $35.00 to $40.00 a week! Here, the management has made me good rates $8.00 a day food included, and that, with the car for $20.00 a week, are all my expenses barring toothpaste and make-up. This place is utterly divorced from the motion picture atmosphere which is a blessing. I can't bear them. Never again. I wish I had the nerve to go back now. As far as that's concerned, I have the nerve, but I haven't the heart. I *can't* go off and leave them in the lurch even if they have treated me shamefully. But a weak-kneed desire to never be in the wrong is not going to prevent my throwing over Elizabeth.

Clare's next letter shows her returning to her mood of outrage at the studio's "immoral" behavior in its handling of money matters. She also tells the story of the great epic *Rosita*.

This last week was too awful. To feel that your employers are doing their best to intimidate and exploit your hatred of suspicion is beastly. I simply loathed dictating the formal request for my salary. It was sent down to them by messenger and in about an hour they called up (that is, Kerrigan did) sweet as peaches and said the money was mine. Oh Lord. The picture has been started and I am having my clothes made. I am not, alas, a Velasquez infanta, but a Queen of Spain, name unknown, about 1800. Holbrook Blinn is the King, also nameless. Mary is Rosita, a little streetsinger, of whom Holbrook becomes enamored, and whom he tries to win to a life of shame. But I see through him and thwart him by bringing Mary and her sweetheart (a Grandee) to-gether after various reprieved executions, listenings-at-doors, catchings-with the goods etc. etc. I am the one

6. Clare in Hollywood: An Interlude 125

who carries the reprieve to the block itself, which is a great moment. If possible I shall look as much like Aunt E. in Tosca as possible. Fortunately I brought my *First Fifty Years* wig with me so that I don't need to worry about my coiffure.

Clare now fights with the costume designers about her gown:

> But they have as little sense of line as Sundelius, and when I say that the Queen ought to look so
>
> [drawing]
>
> instead of so
>
> [drawing]
>
> they won't believe me.

Finally, the production of the movie is beginning to move along, and Clare's social life, much to her regret, becomes a little livelier as she attends a Hollywood party:

> I start work on Friday. My dress, after numberless fights, is lovely, jade green and silver and really first Empire, with long heavy earrings and a bunch of short pseudo-classic curls on the back of my head. It will probably look nice. My costume in the street (that is, my un-clothes) are so Inglische [?] that you would die. The light hurts my eyes so that I have to wear dark glasses *and* a brown chiffon veil which, with my suit and the yellow hat, is really too ridiculous. But its [sic] the right get-up for this place. I put on an evening dress to go to a dinner at Robert Hughes', into which I was roped, and the men, except Mr. Knoblock, got fresh. It was too uncomfortable and from now on I shall be too ill to go anywhere. When I see you I shall tell you some of the things one man, the Vice President of the Goldwyn Corporation, said to me. I have to remember the Civil War and General Johnston getting a chill at General Sherman's funeral, very hard indeed, at moments.

Clare's social life is therefore brought to a standstill. Even the respectable Stearnses she finds intolerable because ordinary people have always bored her, and her puritanism, in high dudgeon prevents any sort of gregiousness:

> Social intercourse is out of the question. For a while I thought I could talk to Brabin [of the Goldwyn studio] with pleasure and profit but alas! I found that my beaux Yeux and not my ideas are what he likes. He is a servant. The Stearns are kind but inconceivably dull. And the other decent people in Beverly *will not* call on or be seen with a motion picture actress. Did you know that *nooone* [sic] connected with the movies, even if armed with credentials from people of distinction elsewhere, can show their face

at the Country Club? So that I either have to flock alone or with these animals, these bedizened laundresses, these drug-addicts, pimps, adulteresses and degenerates. I assure you I am not overstating the case. They all make a great fuss of me and ask me to their parties; most of them being in this hotel (the parties I mean) I have to stay in my rooms in order not to be seen dining alone in my corner. There is no use in offending them. If it is known that you are in the movies you cannot have an account at any shop. The very cab drivers look at you askance. Never did I think the day would come when I would be classified with a group of criminals, or that the tendencies of any kind of people would be so generally recognized that no exceptions are made in favour of an individual. Fortunately, I can be alone, day in and day out without going mad, but I can imagine some people in my situation who would blow their brains out.

At last she begins work.

Yesterday I worked for the first time. I was called to be made up and dressed at 9 o'clock in the morning. At nine o'clock I was made up. At eleven the camera man came to pass on my make up. At one, my dress was ready, all but the shoes, which finally came at four and were miles too big. At quarter to five, in full court dress, with diadem and brown brogues, I entered the set, walked down a short flight of stairs, crossed the stage and looked out of a window. (all of this at three-quarter distance on account of the brogues.) Soft music played to Golondrina while I was doing this in a blinding glare of light with the camera sounding like a sewing-machine in the darkness beyond. Then someone called out "All right" and I went back to my dressing-room, my hard day's work over. Mary Pickford was there when I did it, and as I was waiting my turn I heard her say to a young woman near her (presumably a reporter) that if the time ever comes for her to retire from public life she was sure she would never look for amusement and interest while she has her birds and her flowers.

It's a crime to take $625.00 a week for such trash.

But her contempt for the mores of the studios did not prevent her from thinking seriously about the technique of movie acting. Not all of her thought is comprehensible:

Not that it's not a difficult bodily technique, but you can only improve from picture to picture and not from moment to moment as you can on the stage [why?]... in this business you change, if at all, so completely that you would not recognize the two photographs as being photographs of the same scene.

However, here one can understand her more easily: "It is not boring because an elaborate and artificial dance is not boring to the dancer." But thoughts other than movie acting now impinge on her mind, supplying further reason for her to be angry at the Pickford studio. Sidney's sister Jean had invited Clare to her home in Carmel, but Clare's request to go away for a weekend is turned down causing Clare to fume yet again:

6. Clare in Hollywood: An Interlude

> I am in a pet and this is just a note to blow off steam. I asked permission at the studio to go to Carmel and without a word of excuse it was refused. But I am going anyway. What people! I shall leave here Saturday the 24th spend Sunday and come back Sunday night. If you knew what slights have been put upon me. I haven't told you of them but it seems strange that I should have been brought from New York only to be treated with studied rudeness. Everyone else shows me the greatest respect and even awe. But the Pickfords are embarked on a policy of morale-breaking.

As a result of such treatment and because her playing Elizabeth I in *Dorothy Vernon* would prevent her from spending her planned summer in Europe with Sid, Clare is determined to refuse to play the part in it. Sidney had apparently disagreed with her, fearing that her reputation would be damaged by such a walk-out.

Violet Kemble Cooper, to whom Clare refers in the following letter, although a member of a famous acting family and apparently an actress with the talent to become a star, never reached star status and ended as a supporting player to the likes of such greats as Laurette Taylor and Ethel Barrymore because, according to Clare, she lacked the courage to be independent.

Clare contrasts her own behavior in supporting Ethel Barrymore with that of Kemble Cooper's in her support of Barrymore and others. Presumably the situation to which Clare refers was her throwing over Barrymore in *Declasse* to play Princess Elizabeth in Faversham's *Prince and the Pauper*.

> I know your [Sidney's] motive perfectly well in telling me to think over the Elizabeth business. It is like you, my dearest dear, not to want to stand in the way of my career. But throwing Pickford over won't hurt it in the slightest, anymore than it hurt it to throw over Ethel Barrymore. A performance with a star of the same sex is the thin edge of the wedge, and should *never* be indulged in twice, except in an all-star cast. Violet Kemble Cooper has ruined herself by sticking to Laurettes and Ethels etc. when she might be almost anywhere. No, my dear. Not only do I not want to stay in this misbegotten atmosphere, but it would be most impolitic even if I did want to. Gol[d]wyn are ready to receive me with open arms—next Fall, if I felt like it. So you see that I would be sacrificing nothing if I left. Frankly, my beloved Sidney, I should have done the same in any case, but luckily, the right thing coincides with the business thing in these circumstances.

Clare acted on her own advice independent of Sidney. There is now more news about the possible date of the movie's completion:

> This evening at the Studio the Strumpet [?] told me they are taking about 15 scenes a day really it may not be so long. It doesn't do to count on it. Nemesis is always watching people who count on things. But oh Sid darling when I think that our love has to take itself out in patience—

Clare never completed the picture. Irene Rich, a movie actress, took the part. But Clare did return to play Elizabeth.

Clare's troubles with her management in the spring of 1923 were matched by Sidney's with his for the production of *The Kingdom of Sancho Panza*, which came to be known simply as *Sancho Panza*, by the Hungarian dramatist Melchior Lengyel. The sponsor of the production was Emilie Hapgood, who perhaps had been Sidney's lover.

Sidney had been working on the play for at least two years, probably three, a prospective London production had been cancelled, and at this point he became fearful that after all of his work, Emilie would never put the play on the stage. After she rejected Sidney's suggestion of Holbrook Blinn as star and producer, she chose a producer whom Sidney abhorred. From Shreveport, Louisiana, where he is on assignment, Sidney writes to Lengyel on March 8th, 1923, that he is "seriously disappointed and very angry" at Emilie Hapgood for her rejection of Holbrook Blinn as sponsor of, and chief actor in, the play. Blinn, says Sidney, "an actor of great charm and ability and prestige wants to do the play. His managers made what seemed to me an excellent offer. A production was to be undertaken in California where many of the best plays are first produced during the summer. I should have been there to work with the directors." Instead Mrs. Hapgood "has allied herself with a manager [Russell Janney] who is famous only for his failure to pay either actors' salaries or authors' royalties. He has wasted a year trying to raise money enough for the production of *Sancho*."

Later Sidney adds, "My power under my contract is considerable and I can make it virtually impossible for her to make any production of which I do not approve. I believe that her contract expires in July unless she again renews her option. I will do my utmost to keep Mr. Blinn's interest warm; and, when July comes, I will try to arrange that he makes an offer to you for a new contract."

Because Blinn was to play opposite Clare in *Rosita*, it was in large part up to her to keep Blinn's interest warm. "Blinn gets here on the 26th," writes Clare, "and I shall do my best to sell him on *Sancho*. But if Emilie persists in her illegal and unreasonable attitude, why don't you cable Lengyel for instructions to Alice Kauser [a well-known New York agent, obviously acting in that capacity for Lengyel] to take the play away from Janney. What's Emilie to do with it, anyway?"

In another letter we find Clare suspecting a personal motive for Emilie:

> As to Emilie Hapgood, she should be sent to Coventry (that is the worst punishment I can think of for anyone) what got into her? Do you think it was a game to bring you to her side? I shouldn't be surprised; but if it was, it was a darned stupid one. She always counts on the mean

motive—counts on supplication rather than gratitude. If I'd been in her place I should have given you full permission to do as you liked with the play and then have cut your acquaintance—gently and with an heroic assumption of delicacy and dislike of a false position. But then, of course her gains have to be tangible. (I can think of one tangible gain I should like—I should like you here, Darling I love you). But if Janney is her lover that explains it fully. The idea of your acting as a medium for Emilie['s] latest! It makes me choke to think of it. Could a personal appeal from Blinn do no good?

Eventually Sidney became so disgusted with the production that, before the New York opening, he ordered Harold Freedman, his agent, to have his name removed as adaptor: "I have enough sins of my own to live down without assuming those committed by Emilie and her boy friend" (letter to Howard Friedman, November 21st, 1923).

However, despite Sidney's and Clare's disdain for Emilie and her producer, the script of *Sancho Panza*, as it stands in the Sidney Howard collection at Berkeley, has a good deal of charm and point. Apparently, those responsible for putting on the play tampered with the text, but Arthur Hornblow's summary in his review of the play in *Theatre Magazine* (February 24th, 1923, 16) accords with the script we now possess. Further, the intentions of the producers seem to have been serious. They hired Otis Skinner to play Sancho. Skinner, a beloved and admired actor, had helped make *Kismet* a smashing success in the early part of this century. After he was hired, even Clare writes, "Perhaps Otis Skinner is the best person for it. Since I saw Blinn in Pickford's picture I realize that he was not the perfect choice. Who would be barring Sancho himself?" In addition, they engaged as director Richard Boleslavsky, who had been a member of the Moscow Art Theatre and went on to develop a distinguished career in this country not only as a theater director but also as a film director and teacher.

The producers' efforts seem not to have gone for naught. Everything about the production was praised but the play itself, which Arthur Hornblow, speaking for many critics, called a "well-written comic opera libretto with the music left out." Sidney smelled failure even in rehearsals, for he wrote to Jean sometime in October that they were the "orfullest mess I have EVER seen." The production ran only forty performances in New York, but it provided Otis Skinner with a successful road tour and Sidney, we may presume, with some income.

But keeping Holbrook Blinn warm for *Sancho* was not Clare's only assignment for Sidney. She hoped to bring about some resolution of the deep divide between Sidney and his elder brothers and sister. "After all that is really what I came for..." she wrote Sidney from Hollywood. To understand Clare's part in the action, however, necessitates first traversing a good deal of Howard family history.

After the death of John Howard dissension between the children by his first wife and Helen Howard developed such bitterness that she no longer wished to stay on the West Coast. In a diary entry of November 26th, 1915, she writes: "I shall try to do right by John' children though they are making it very difficult," and she registers her ultimate disillusionment in her diary three days later, "it's hard after so many years to be *only* a step-mother." No matter how much she favored her own children—and she must have done it subtly, for there is no record that John Howard ever complained—she clearly thought that she was treating all the children equally, that she was truly their mother. In fact, they could hardly have known any other. Yet many years of resentment showed only now, and to this Helen Howard responded.

On August 26th, 1916, she records in her diary: "saw Olney [the Howard family lawyer] & talked to him about will—Decided to put everything in trust Income to be divided in 7 parts & Bruce & Sidney $200 each *anyway*—if income does not yield that—to be taken from the other children's parts or even from principal—estate to be divided when Bruce is 25 years old—if Sid or Bruce dies—the other is to inherit his share—if both—the shares are to be given to charities."

Bruce's death caused the conflict now, for it activated the clause which gave Sidney Bruce's inheritance. In 1922 Bruce would have been 25. Helen Howard first transferred the dividends to Sidney and in 1923 transferred the actual stocks to him. There seemed to be no question about the legality of the matter, but John Howard's older children kicked up a fuss about the fairness of it. They believed that Bruce's inheritance should have returned to John's estate and become part of the overall division of the property. Sidney had already accepted Bruce's inheritance, thereby making him an object of his siblings' three-year-old bitterness, which probably had touched him anyway as the recipient of Helen's special favor.

The controversy came to the surface in a letter from Jean to Sidney written on January 24th, 1923, before Clare's departure for Hollywood and after Helen Howard's annual visit to Berkeley. We quote the letter at length for several reasons. First, its initial discussion shows difficulties between the newly married couple and Helen Howard when Sid and Clare lived in Helen's apartment. Second, it gives an excellent description of the relationship of Sid and his mother from one who saw it firsthand and loved Sid, filling in information lacking before and validating assessments gained from other sources. Third, the letter gives an account of the controversy from the previously unseen perspective of the older children. Perhaps most important, we get a sense of Jean as a person. She was a major figure in Sid's life, a kind of mother substitute. This letter gives us an opportunity to see why Sid loved her generous, frank, direct, humane, wise spirit. Clare also came to love her, and because she

6. Clare in Hollywood: An Interlude

trusted Jean immensely, one of the main sore points in the divorce procedure between Sidney and Clare could be eased.

The first part of Jean's letter concerns the couple's relationship to Helen Howard. A strain had developed between them, and Sid had asked Jean, while his mother was visiting her, to help him out in easing it. The second part of the letter has to do with the controversy about Bruce's inheritance.

> I wrote you that I would do all I could to help you and Clare—and Mama—for whom you know I have a real affection—and I have done my best, but it was more difficult than I expected, because she insisted that she has been over-careful not to do any of the things that I know of course she has done—
>
> The root of everything is not so much jealousy of Clare, whom she likes and admires, but fear that any wife & any change, will separate you from her. Ever since you were born you have been her obsession, in a way, just as she was an obsession with her mother, and she does not maintain a true balance when anything touching you, your health, happiness, prosperity, work, or your nearness to her, is in question—and her way of holding on is by showering THINGS on you. It has always been so. It was so with me in a very *much* lesser degree as I was growing up, and I've watched it with you for years. Presents are wonderful, but reluctant acceptance of obligations saps one's feelings of independence and makes one lose the savour of the gift, and often turn upon the giver. I could give you 1000 cases, but the apt. [apartment] is so perfect an example that that suffices. You 2 ought to have had your chance to begin alone, not to see her before she left for Europe except under your own roof, and should have begun your housekeeping in your own way, making the inevitable mistakes in money & in comfort that are part of beginning, and that really help a lot in the end. Instead of that the apt. is pressed upon you (with of course the most generous kind of motives) and you take it against your better judgment because there is no visible reason for not doing so, and you & C. dont [sic] like it, & resent the whole thing, you[re] probably put out with yourself for ever getting into the mess.
>
> But that is her way, and has always been—she is a most unselfish and self sacrificing, but with a queer little twist that usually keeps a string on the gift. With all her splendid qualities, there is one she has not, and that is the sense of straight *Justice*—she will give too much, and she will withhold too much, dictated to by feeling—but just the plain just course that is thought out and held to despite everything is seemingly impossible to her. At least, I have held that judgment for so many years, that I cannot remember not knowing that one thing—
>
> I never had so pleasant a visit with mama. She seemed to enjoy herself. She was un-nervous, not nearly as restless as always before, and she seemed happy except for some hurts—such as no Christmas present, no letters from you or Clare, a feeling that easy familiarity in your home had not been started (I am showing her side, which is only fair) a feeling that at present at least there is no particular place for her in your life & in Clare's—I feel deeply sorry for her, as for any woman, who knows such a day is inevitable, & who lays up no interests of her own against it....

> I think your own course you will work out for yourselves—of course I think that you should make every effort to think of her happiness and to preserve every friendly relation—always considering that you and C. are one—but remembering too, that the observances of every courtesy and politeness between relatives is the first rule of peaceful family relations. It doesn't take much time or thought to do little things, and they often make big differences impossible—

Jean then goes on to say what advice she had given Helen Howard about her relationship with the newly married couple: to take her mind off them because it makes them self-conscious about her; not to sympathize with Sidney apart from Clare; to keep "hands off" them for a while, not to attack Sidney's "pride & ... independence by insisting on your accepting a golden doll from her, where you would rather have a rag doll you make yourself and like."

In the second part of the letter Jean discusses the friction between Sidney and his half siblings. Of course, Helen Howard is still at the heart of the matter:

> Curiously, Chet's letter of last night bears directly on this—Do you remember, when I was in N.Y. you told me that Mama wanted you to have Bruces [sic] estate, and that you did not think it fair and were not going to let her? I did not comment then, being proud of your decision alone, but took it for granted that that ended it, & have not thought of it since I believe, except in remembering our conversations—But since the matter has come up again I shall tell you exactly how I feel and why—
>
> Chet says that when he dined with us last Friday Mama took him into her room, and told him she wanted him, as co-trustee, to sign over Bruce's shares in the Howard Estate to you—Chet did not say much more in an. [answer] but it seems that she had written him before to pay all Howard Co dividends to you—I was very much surprised at the letter which came last night ... because Mama has never said a word of this to me ... of course Mama is the indisputed heir of Bruce's estate—and that income she should dispose of exactly as she pleases—no one wants to know what she does with it—but the principal has a different standing.
>
> I understand perfectly how and why she feels about increasing your capital—why should she not try by every means to do so But Sid, if Mama has but one child, Father has five, and those five were equal in his sight. The very fact that every bit of Mama's property comes from Father should bid her pause, and further, that Father left everything to her in his will, accompanying it with a letter that at her death she should hold the estate untouched, & should divide it then between the children—shows that he had no thought of this very thing possibly happening—
>
> ... [Bruce's] capital should justly remain a part of Mama's to be divided with the rest, or should be divided now in exactly the same way as the original—to Mama,—equally proportioned among the remaining children.... I cannot tell you how distasteful it is to me to discuss money—& especially family money—with you in this way, but I must say my thought now, when you have the right to know it....

6. Clare in Hollywood: An Interlude

Perhaps you will only have to say that you think it best to leave the principal in her possession (taking the interest—dividends as they come).... Perhaps she will say that if you wont [sic] take it she will deed it elsewhere rather than have it revert to us, but I dont [sic] think she will feel that way....

Jean is wrong. Helen confided in her diary that she would have deeded the money to charity if both Sid and Bruce were dead at the point of division.

It was a little later in the year, when Clare goes out West, that she enters the picture apparently in the belief that, because she is a neutral party, she could ameliorate the controversy which by this time had become acrimonious. Characteristically, she plunged right in: "I wrote to Jean the day I arrived but so far have not heard from her. It was a weight off my mind to hear that Olney agrees with us, because above all we want to do the right thing, and, not less important, we do not want to admit any Trojan horses into the peace of 696 [Lexington Avenue, the location of Sid and Clare's new apartment]."

Central to Clare's thinking is rightness and justice and the peace of mind that comes therefrom. Such moral apprehension moves Clare as it does Jean, a common trait that perhaps helped develop their mutual trust. Actually, Jean and Clare had not yet met, for Jean was unable to attend the couple's wedding because her husband, Duncan McDuffie, was very ill.

A letter from Clare written a few days after the one just quoted indicates the depth of the division within the family: "Jean I have not heard from yet, but I shall probably in a day or so. She may be in a difficult position about receiving me if her brothers are bitter about the money. If so, I should hate to make her uncomfortable, but I am going to see her if I throw gravel at her window and bring her downstairs to a midnight interview. You never mention your mother."

Clare finally hears from Jean: "A note from Jean has just come. It is very affectionate and cordial and eager to see me. She says that Duncan is very ill again. But I think in spite of that I shall go to San Francisco and stay at a hotel if necessary and see her, if only for a day. After all that is really what I came for and I won't be balked. Leave it to me, my dearest Sidney, and if it is humanly possible any misunderstanding will be cleared up. Really."

Duncan McDuffie was a member of an old East Bay real estate firm that still bears his family name. In addition to their house in Berkeley, Jean and Duncan owned a place in Carmel, a beautiful artsy resort about 150 miles down the coast from San Francisco. Clare writes: "A telegram has just come from Jean asking me to Carmel for the 21st to stay as long as I can. Praised be the Lord! I shall go if I have to break my contract and will wire you the result. I shall need your prayers. Don't tell your mother I am going. I have my own reason for this which some day I shall tell you." We never find out precisely what her reason was for wishing to withhold knowledge of her meeting with Jean from Helen Howard.

Before Clare goes to Carmel, she writes to Sid with shrewd insight into the whole situation, an understanding that proves itself in the meeting with Jean: "I still think that no matter what Olney tells you that there would have [been] no row had they perfectly trusted your mother. You can see that it stands to reason. We submit to the decision of people we believe in."

Clare, deeply impressed by the beauty of Carmel, writes to Sid that it is "without doubt, the loveliest spot on Earth. You are right. It is the place where Demeter was born" But she gets right down to the critical matter:

> Jean and I got on famously. She is a beautiful thing, so generous and so involuntarily good that she sheds a sort of balmy light about her, quite unlike the radiance produced by people who succeed in bringing good against odds. And she corroborated what I have always believed: That there is no ethical or clear-cut legal stand in this row about money. (She brought up the subject) The argument about whose money it is and does it belong to your Father's memory and did Bruce will it to you are nothing but arguments after the fact, the fact being that your Mother's connection with the affair utterly discredits it in her eyes. (Not that she said so in so many words, but she brushed aside or hastily conned over the verbal arguments, like a lesson, and then reverted to the main emotional theme—Mamma's lies, Mamma's obsession, Mamma's jealousy of her, her tactlessness etc. etc. etc.) She bears you not the slightest ill will for taking the money, she loves you as only a great person can love another, but she looks on you much as one of the gods might have looked on a Trojan caught in the act of welcoming the horse. I did not commit myself beyond saying that you would decide as you thought right and adducing the arguments in favor of accepting. To all of which, as I say, she simply didn't listen, but returned to the Raw Deal that your Mother is putting over on you. She says the other boys don't mind your taking the money at all, but resent your Mother's deceitful way of going about it. I don't know what they mean by that, unless it is the way she sprang it on Chet solus and never told Jean anything of her intentions although J. gave her the opportunity to do so. You see, all these things are very little and probably, in this case, innocent—it is the years and years of counterfeit money that makes one suspect even a good dollar bill. And that's the whole case. Jean adores you, no one wishes you anything but the best of luck. Everyone is a little sorry for you and that's that. Jean is probably mistaken in her reading of this particular case, but she *loves you* and she would *die* before she would let anything come between you. That's so and I beg you to believe it no matter what anyone may say.

In Jean's meeting with Clare, Jean she is not as reasonable as she is in the letter to Sidney, where she undoubtedly held in her emotions.

6. Clare in Hollywood: An Interlude

Clearly what emerged in her conversations with Clare is what Clare had foreseen, a sense of years of betrayal and the resultant deep-seated anger. Clare realized that the rational arguments adduced by Jean were merely camouflage for strongly felt emotions, and it is these to which Clara undoubtedly addressed herself in their conversation. Jean's readily revealing herself to Clara implies that mutual trust quickly grew between the two women in the course of their meeting, a trust that through Jean certainly transferred itself to the brothers, who like their sister, although not to the same degree, probably did not have a taste for the controversy.

Sidney found a solution to the problem which seems to have resolved the matter to everyone's satisfaction. We can understand Sid's view if we realize that he had his mother as well as his siblings to consider. On June 6th he wrote to Jean:

> I should have written you long ago about the final decision to which I came in reference to Bruce's property. It is simply this. I am in a position where I cannot decide either way without seriously offending somebody. Therefore I am going to leave everything as it now stands until Mother's death. If I die before her, both Bruce's share and mine will go to Clare. If I survive Mother we can then decide together and quite amicably and it will be a simple matter to make a complete restitution of income to the estate. I came to this decision after writing Olney and without saying anything to Mother. She does not know that I have not definitely decided to keep everything for myself. I cannot decide that and I cannot, either, turn the thing back and there you are.

Clare's deep involvement in Sidney's affairs shows the intimacy that has developed between them despite the difficulties of the early months of their marriage, an intimacy and a dependence that we noted in her letters from California.

But another letter suggests the complexity of their relationship:

> My darling darling Sid—
>
> How could I possibly forget you? When I read your letter and thought of all our happy times to-gether and the futility of life without you, although I was standing on the lot, I nearly broke down. The only other time that I nearly wept (only this time I really did, a little) was at a concert yesterday during the last movement of the Pathetique, and I thought of your dear hand, with mine in it, and that feeling we always have at beautiful music. And I have learned that I can't sleep without you. I don't dare to imagine that you are there, beside me, but I can't banish the knowledge that you aren't; and sleep is so insecure without the essential bulwark of yourself— now don't say this is patronizing, for Heaven's sake. And then I think of all the times that I have allowed my hyperaesthesia to get the better of me. And of all the times that I have been horrid to you, my very dear. But in extenuation, I can only say that in addition to not being very intelligent,

I'm also always afraid of everything and perceive terrors where there are none. In fact, my aquiline nose belies me altogether.

Clearly, she blames herself for the pain she had brought to her marriage because of her hyper-aesthesia, that is, her "morbidly increased sensibility," apparently the "terrors where there are none." Further, despite her immense love for him, she at times has been nasty to him. Undoubtedly most important, however, is his fear, apparently expressed in a letter to Clare, that she might forget him while she is in Hollywood. It is that which makes her almost weep because seemingly it comes from deep inside him, betraying some sense of masculine inferiority. Further, when calling him her bulwark might make him scoff that she is patronizing him, she indicates once more his sense of sexual insecurity.

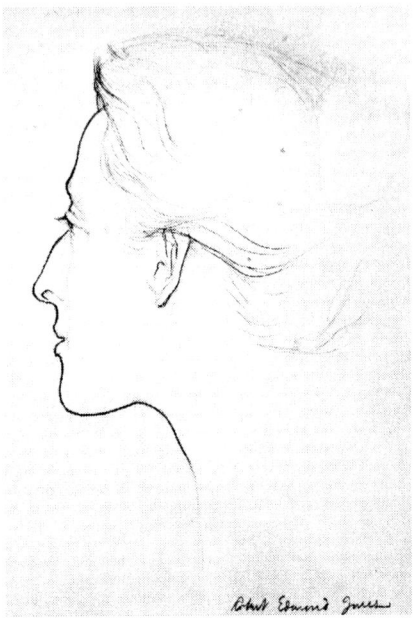

Profile sketch of Clare Eames by Robert Edmond Jones. (From a photograph by Peter A. Jeley and Son, New York City.)

However, the main burden lies in her sense of helplessness. She is really asking him to be her protector because of his moral and emotional superiority and because of his sexual ability. Yet evidence in the Howard collection at Berkeley indicates that at the beginning of their relationship a sexual problem may have existed resulting perhaps from his own sense of inadequacy.

With miscellaneous papers at Berkeley, dated 1924, may be found a fragment of notes for a story. One page begins with "Clare's dream," words that apparently conclude a sentence beginning on the missing previous page. Sidney's notes continue:

> Tell it literally as though it actually happened but keep all the dream quality. She is in Auburn riding about in a black and yellow taxi. The driver is Dionysus, almost nude, very tough in the way he looks back at passing drivers, wearing a high and very elaborate eastern headdress like a Bakst drawing for the Russian ballet. He has marked sex attraction. Wears a necklace.
> She is looking for a hotel in which to lodge herself, her husband and the baby while they hunt for a house. They have just inherited a great deal

6. Clare in Hollywood: An Interlude   137

of money, and her husband being an invalid, they have chosen Auburn as an abiding place. She, the strong one of the family, has come to make arrangements. She can't find a hotel or any place to take them in. Dream quality strong here. Dionysus takes her to a house. Describe Phippsburg. Or lay the whole story in Phippsburg [the Phippsburg location of their dream house which they saw in the previous year, during their honeymoon summer, while visiting Aunt Emma in Maine].

The house is completely furnished. The table laid, the beds made, the soap in the bathrooms.

She can't understand it. He tells her that it is a deserted house. She'll understand why later.

Finish the story by reuniting the wife and the husband. As things go better Dionysus comes to look more like the husband or the husband looks more like Dionysus. At last the quarrel (one might have that as a basis) is made up and Dionysus ceases to be in any way attractive to her. She sees him merely as a healthy country boy who drives a taxi from the station.

The sentence fragment "Clare's Dream" suggests that the story is based on a dream which Clare had. But we cannot know exactly which parts are literally from Clare's dream or even if the dream is actual. But the story idea is surely something that Sidney imaginatively evolved from their marriage. The location of the fragment in the Howard collection indicates that the notes were written in 1924; possibly they were written after their baby was born in 1925. Also, since the story apparently would end contemporaneously with the writing of the notes, that is, in 1924 or 1925, the main part of the story would refer to the beginning of their marriage, that is, from the time of their marriage through 1923, perhaps 1924. The notion that the story is most likely set in 1922–1924 is strengthened by its taking place in Phippsburg, where the couple were seriously considering buying a house at that time.

It is important to notice that the husband is sick, the wife well, the husband weak, the wife strong. If not Clare, Sid certainly, on some subconscious level at least, saw himself as ill and sexually inept. For the wife seems attracted to the naked Dionysus, who is perhaps a stand-in for the glittering movie stars who Sidney thought would make Clare forget him. Or perhaps Dionysus is a substitute for others who had interested Clare. But eventually Dionysus and the husband merge, suggesting that whatever sexual problems Sidney had were wonderfully resolved and that Clare and he now satisfied each other. Less likely, however, this may be wish fulfillment on Sidney's part, an atypical way of solving Sidney's handling any problem, especially since the problem seems to have been resolved in the summer of 1923.

Curiously, the framework of their real-life marriage did not prevent the reversal of illness and weakness of their relationship in the story. But in his subconscious mind Sid, after his childhood illnesses and his comparatively short recent bout with tuberculosis as well as some injuries he sustained in the war, could see himself as still with a fragility that might have caused his feeling sexually inadequate. If we carry this thought further, then Clare would be sexually adequate and searching for a more exciting partner. But in addition to her being sexually potent, where he is not, Clare's strength in the story in addition to being sexually able might derive from her ability to handle her movie problems where he failed to protect himself in his *Sancho* difficulties and even required her help along the way. The picture of Clare in the dream story is very different from her own characterization of herself as terrified of life and "insecure without the essential bulwark of yourself."

Yet Clare's portraying herself as "always afraid of everything" also seems to have a basis in actuality. For illumination we turn again to a story idea Sid called "Fear of Young Love" found in notes written after the couple's separation:

> A long short story which might afterward be made into a picture for Murneau [F.W. Murnau, a German director working in Hollywood in the late twenties] is in a young wife like Clare who is afraid of life. It begins with her first fear after marriage of sexual intercourse. It goes on through her terrors of housekeeping, of not living up to what her husband expects of her, of not appearing at her best in his eyes. It culminates in her fear of childbirth. She is certain her child will cure her of it, but the child only gives a new set of fears. She finally runs away from both husband and child to her father and we see that it is his influence that has made a coward of her.... I dont [sic] quite see the ending or her husband's attitude.

Sidney identifies the heroine of this story as Clare, but such an observation does not necessarily imply the truth of his observations. This is still a story, with the thoughts proceeding through the tumult of his imagination. But we may nevertheless examine the list of fears he attributes to Clare for verification from what we know of her life. There is no evidence that she had fear of sexual intercourse. In fact the notes for the previous story and her letters suggest the opposite. Perhaps there was some fear at the beginning but seemingly none later. Yet she concludes the last letter we have been discussing, echoing Sidney:

> My darling Sidney *Don't forget me*. I love you. I really love you.
> Your more-than-oriental
> Clare

We can, however, find evidence of more than the usual fear of childbirth. After Sidney paid the bill for the birth of their baby in 1925, Clare's doctor wrote him a note which reads in part: "Mrs. Howard ought to do very well now. I regret that, considering her psychological make up, we had to make so much fuss over the whole thing, but she was rather difficult as a case." We may interpret the physician's remarks to mean that whatever physical problems the doctor may have anticipated in Clare in the process of childbirth, her fears—her hyperaesthesia—made worse. Further, more ambivalent in her desire for a child than she would care to admit, Clare may have anticipated that her career, as a result of the birth and its aftermath, would come to another temporary and perhaps damaging halt, and this may have subconsciously exacerbated her fear of childbirth. To Clare, Sidney, and the doctor this may have looked like the fear of life to which Sidney refers in his notes for the story.

Clare's "Terrors of housekeeping, of not living up to what her husband expects of her, of not appearing at her best in his eyes" we have already seen confirmed by Sid's and Clare's letters and are part of what he considers her fear of life.

This Steichen portrait of Clare Eames and Sidney Howard must have been taken in early 1925, because it shows the actress very much pregnant. (Courtesy of the Bancroft Library, University of California, Berkeley)

Sidney blames Clare's father for such, presumably because he overprotected her, since she runs away to him for shelter from her anxieties with husband and child. We do not know enough to make a judgment here. But the statement hardly seems true because Clare's mother was supposedly the dominant one in the household.

Perhaps most revealing in Sidney's remarks is the clause, "I don't quite see ... her husband's attitude." Perhaps Sidney failed to see the husband's attitude because he did not wish to discern that he was really the father who, as he protected her from her fears, thus really encouraged them. That is why, according to her, he was her bulwark; he protected her from those very fears. She accepted that relationship because fears possessed her as she possessed her strength. Her fears were undoubtedly deepened by Sidney's readiness to protect her, by his competence, his radiance, his poetry. Yet she was obviously able to take care of herself in an uncertain theatrical world and when necessary to aid Sidney.

Their relationship then was a tangle of interdependence, individual uncertainty, and a striving for fearless action. They were two strong, talented, ambitious, intelligent, terribly vulnerable adults who loved and admired each other and tried to make their way together in a thorny field of endeavor.

Despite Clare's subconscious ambivalence about having a child and with all her intellectual, cultural, and business interests, the hopes for a child, to whom Sid and Clare referred as David, were constantly on her mind: "My dearest dear, will David never be? I have almost begun to believe that I would have to abandon the picture, for reasons connected with my silhouette, when the blow fell. Never mind. Love love him (or her) even if he (or she) isn't yet. Love love each other. My dear. I could go on telling you I love you forever—..."

The melody in all of the letters from Hollywood, as it is in the following, sings the tale of love: "Darling Sidney tell me over and over again that you love me. Our romance has been so sadly interrupted and we have so much of it. Never mind. Venice is ahead of us. But it is hard now. All the beauty and the fun and the eagerness and all love is with you, my Sidney, and there is none anywhere else."

But inevitably such a painful separation as theirs brings the problem of jealousy. She is jealous of him, and she tries to make him jealous of her. Clare also becomes ill, a usual thing with her, especially when she is under stress:

> I am going to scold you a little. Not that you deserve it, my dear (you may not), but that I must get [it] off my chest and not let it rankle when I am at such a long distance from you. In the last fortnight I have had *two letters* from you, one in which you lightly referred to an "ailment" which however does not appear to have prevented your going to several plays and enjoying them but which did prevent your writing to me, and another which you wired me to destroy unread which of course I did. Now, dear Sidney, you know I am not exacting. But I know that I am childish, and I have a child's ability to forget whatever is not directly under my nose. When you neglect me it is not you I fear for, because I absolutely trust you and believe in you and love you, but it is myself. Do you remember, my husband, a conversation we had on the davenport when you begged me not to let the motion picture industry take your place? And I swore I wouldn't. But just as great cities are too abstract for man to really swear for, so are silent lovers. I may be doing you a terrible injustice, Sidney dear, and if I am I know you forgive me; after all at this distance I can only judge by what happens to my own heart and soul. The scolding is nearly over now. It only needs the words I love you dear dear Sid to finish it off in style.
>
> I am sitting up in bed writing this, with the telephone book on my knee. The room is full of flowers, the several gifts of my swains at the Pickford Studio. It really is funny how a law of nature works in precisely the same manner always. And it seems to be a law of nature that all the men in any theatrical company I ever join (from the time I was in the mob) congregate in my dressing room and vie with each other to make my path easy.

6. Clare in Hollywood: An Interlude 141

> Since the men have discovered me my life at the Studio has been a beau feast. My dressing room is quite small and, from the moment of my arrival in the morning it is a seething mob. And yet Bob Milton says I have no sex appeal.

Perhaps it was the growing anxiety on both their parts, perhaps the possibility that the picture could not be finished before they could take their European trip or any one of a number of or combination of reasons, but the letters soon stop. She walks out of the picture, perhaps by mutual agreement. They have their summer in Europe.

In prospect the summer looked a little rocky financially but possible. Sid writes to Jean on June 6th:

> The present American Period draws slowly to a close. Clare and I sail for Genoa on the Conte Verde on June 30th to spend four weeks in Venice and two in London and possibly two knocking about Italy or the Tyrol. She has various plans for next season—Cordelia in King Lear and a French play—and it looks now as though there were considerable hope of her being well enough to see them through. I don't quite know how we shall get back for them. We have saved up a total of [six] hundred and fifty dollars all but twenty of which went for passage. She has fifteen hundred left from her movie days. I put that in my account as backing for a letter of credit and then write against it. [Norman] Hapgood pays me for the articles and the theory is that we shall make out somehow and that Clare will have her fifteen hundred back next fall to buy her winter clothes with.
>
> But Clare has been in the hospital since her return having some sort of an operation to the exciting end of stimulating or facilitating or something an offspring ... some youngsters and a Connecticut or Maine farm are our two obsessions. I'm pretty desperately weary of this city business ... she and I are quite happy as any two people ever have been since the beginning.

Sidney's prospects for the fall are two adaptations. One, *Casanova*, from the Spanish of Lorenzo de Azertis, which Sidney predicts (wrongly) "will probably be a hit of the most noisome sort." The other is the ever present *Sancho Panza*, which Sidney predicts (again incorrectly) "will undoubtedly fall as flat as *Swords* if not flatter."

But Sidney's letters that summer are full of his financial difficulties. Two managers did not pay him the money they owed him, and Sidney had to borrow money from his mother and his friend Dick Myers, who lived in Paris, all of which made him, as he did and continues to do many times, swear off the theater. To his lawyer, Ernest Angell, he writes: "[I]f I ever waste another ten minutes on the theatre in my life, I am willing to eat any carload of manure you may select" (August 10th, 1923). But with all their economic troubles Clare, whose health has improved immensely buys clothes in Italy at Fortuny, and they purchase dining room curtains, "two painted yellow chairs upholstered in divine yellow silk brocade, ... divine damask upholstery for those two arm chairs in our dining room" (letter to HH, August 8th, 1923).

We catch a glimpse of Clare and Sid in Venice in the first volume of Margaret Webster's autobiography, *The Same, Only Different*. Ben Webster, Margaret's father, May Whitty, her mother, and she were invited to visit Harrison Rhodes, who went to Venice every summer. "He took the whole penthouse apartment in the Grand Hotel, facing the Canal. He had his own gondola and gondolier, and an encyclopedic knowledge of the city, gained at leisure over many years" (285).

Rhodes was a good friend of Sidney, and at a gondola festival on the lagoon, Margaret is placed in a gondola with Sidney and Clare. She had already been impressed with another American theater personage she met that summer, Robert Edmond Jones, who was tagging along in Emilie Hapgood's entourage. Margaret had previously met Clare, whom she found to be "by turns fastidious and remote; generously partisan; mocking, scornful, raffishly amusing; never anything by halves, never less than passionate" (286).

Margaret was "exceedingly shy" with these two whom she thought of as among the "nobility" of the theater world, but they set her at ease, "lured me on to talk and pretty soon I began to feel that I really could do what I wanted to do, be what I set my mind to be.... Sydney [*sic*] and Clare, like Robert Edmond Jones, were life enhancers; this seems to me the most important of all things to be" (286–87).

Margaret Webster a bit later: "The New York critics were apt to apply to [Clare's] work the word 'cold.' A sillier adjective it would be hard to imagine. It was probably due to her bone structure—she looked irretrievably intellectual—and partly because she was never sentimental or mushy; she was stripped of the unnecessary flesh. But if she was cold, it was the coldness of the metal which burns your hand." She finishes these pages on Clare thus: "I wish, even now, that she had lived. So few people ever saw her, and she was a great actress" (288).

In some ways Clare and Sidney's summer was wondrous. Max Reinhardt invited them to his "rococo palace" in Salzburg to see a production of *Le Malade Imaginaire* "so perfect and beautiful in setting and acting that I shall never forget the living thrill of it" (undated letter to HH). Sidney himself is "well and rested and Clare has never been in such good shape.... I have written most of a very nice comedy," which turns out to be *They Knew What They Wanted*. Nevertheless financial reality obtrudes. Clare, who has had doubts as to whether she would act in *Dorothy Vernon*, in view of their financial difficulties, runs off to Hollywood, and Sid follows his journalistic nose in Europe. They are separated again.

When Sidney finally goes home at the end of September, he is

6. Clare in Hollywood: An Interlude

This portrait of Sidney and Clare may have been taken in London in 1926 during their European trip, or for the London production of *The Silver Cord* in 1927. (Photograph by Lemarc.)

aboard the *Scythia*, which crashes into another ship midocean, scaring his family half to death. To his mother in an undated letter he writes: "You must have known, however, that there was no cause for concern. There never was, even at the moment of the collision, for the sea was a pond. It was shear [sic] terrifying though (I saw it all, thank heaven) to watch the huge shape loom out of the fog and know that she couldn't possibly miss us. We put back here to Liverpool and sail now on the Majestic from Southampton."

We learn from an October letter to Sidney that Clare was sure that she had an extrasensory perception of the *Scythia*'s accident:

> I have just received from the Pickford Studio two telegrams from Harold [Freedman, Sidney's agent]—one, saying that the *Scythia* has been turned back to Liverpool disabled but that you thank God are all right and another that you have got passage on the *Majestic* due on the 9th. And now I shall tell you a proof of the clairvoyance of love, which you can believe or not at your choice. Last night I didn't sleep until about 4 in the morning. And what do you suppose kept me awake? A conviction that an acci-

dent had befallen the *Scythia*! It didn't worry me, because I thought it was only another of my morbid ideas but it prevented me from sleeping just as a mosquito does. I tried to reason myself out of it and every time I would curl myself up in as comfortable position back it would come to torment me. And then when the Studio called up to say they were sending over the telegrams *I knew what was in them* although I didn't know that you were safe. *Thank god, and I say it reverently,* you are. Of course I have no idea what happened, beyond what Harold said. I simply cannot, without disgracing myself and looking like a fool describe what I went through before I opened those telegrams. And then to see *Scythia* the first word in the first one was so startling and yet at the same time so inevitable that I came as near to fainting from shock I suppose as I shall ever come. You will think that I am mad with my psychic experiences. But I am sure that Harold's message, or part of it, got to me without the benefit of Western Union. Perhaps the very reason I wasn't alarmed at the recurrence of this rather alarming idea was because the announcement of your safety got through as well as that of the accident. Perhaps if you hadn't been safe I should have been wildly agitated instead of simply wakeful" [October 5th, 1923].

But Clare did not feel secure about Sid's safety until he was back on shore. She writes to him on October 11th:

I was in such a state of shaking happiness at the bare thought of your being once more on American soil that I haven't been able to write for the last two or three days. And it was so marvelous to hear your voice last night. Even if I, from excitement, dried up and didn't say what I wanted to say. Moreover, the voice of the man in the room next door was perfectly audible when he telephoned and I didn't want him to hear any remarks about Popes [?] which are for your ears only. But imagine. Two letters from you at dinner (with clippings from *The New Statesman* which were most interesting) and then the sound of your voice at eleven. The only thing was, it gave me a frenzied desire to obliterate space and return to the normal ½ inch.

Perhaps the same love and desire for Sidney which prompted what she calls her psychic experiences also incited her jealous warning in the "welcome home" letter she left in their apartment before her departure for Hollywood:

Do, do, Sidney, I implore you to come to California as soon as you can. I flatter myself that you want to come as much as I want to have you come—but don't, don't let casual bright objects distract you.
It is so terribly important, my dearest, and I feel that so very much hangs in the balance now, at a critical period of our common life. My dream is to keep growing nearer and nearer to you as I have in the past six months—so near that you are almost another me—and if we keep on going as we have done we shall one day be really indistinguishable. Don't let's go on the rock that other people go on. We're both worth more than

6. Clare in Hollywood: An Interlude 145

> that and I think we both know that the impalpable and fecund treasures and eternal vigilance. [sic] I have failed, what with my temper and my vagueness, many times but never I hope enough to make you feel that I held us or anything to do with us lightly.

The "critical period" to which she says they have now arrived is clearly the result of their last six months, crucially the European trip. During this time they had the kind of peace to which Sidney referred in his letter to Jean. They were able to iron out whatever problems afflicted them and grow together as two people do who experience life joyfully. She is now frightened, however, of what this new separation might bring. Perhaps in their previous separation Sidney had been so lonely or strained by the difficulties of his marriage that he did allow the casual bright objects to distract him. She may have guessed correctly that the paucity of his letters at one point meant that he was entertaining himself as he did in his bachelor days. Perhaps that was what caused her to give up *Rosita*. At any rate, having just been separated from him, knowing the temptations of the theater, especially as he is about to go out on the road with *Sancho* and she about to journey to Hollywood, she is concerned for the newly fused relationship. But this new group of letters, while they show her pain in being without him, do not have the same anxiety and grief of those written in the spring. Undoubtedly, the summer's growth of their relationship gave her a greater sense of security than she previously had.

Clare however, need not have worried about Sid—if she ever had to worry about him. In an October letter to Jean he writes:

> My slogan is "California and Claire, how long, Oh, Lord, how long?" I am trying to get copy in and money out to square myself with the bank for slight extravagances this summer which I don't mind because it was the best ever and the bank should really take the liberal view and say, that's all right, old man, don't bother. And just between whiles I have to charge about the rehearsal of *Sancho* which is the orfullest mess I have EVER seen.... I got off the boat with my 5.08 and my duty was 5.10 and the inspector had to make up the 2 cents out of the goodness of his heart and I have lived for three days on a borrowed ten dollars. But the checks will be rolling in presently pray God and I shall pay the milk man and buy that westward bound upper....

Not much of a check could have come in from Sidney's adaptation of *Casanova*, by Lorenzo de Azertis, which had already opened before his return to the United States, but Clare saw it previous to her departure for Hollywood. The play did not fare very well. John Corbin in *The New York Times* enjoyed the production but voiced the general critical opinion that "there was no play, not really" (September 27th, 1923).

Stark Young, like his colleagues, appreciated Katharine Cornell, who, he found, "has in the very lines of her head a singular and beautiful resemblance to the carnival masks of Venice. And she acts the part of Henriette at the same time both artificially and poignantly, as she ought to do, like a sad, impetuous, delicately passionate lady in an overpolished, thin day" (October 10th, 1923, 180) Of Lowell Sherman as Casanova he has less laudable things to say: "[H]e has no imagination, style, wit, speed or variety. And his ideas of sex in such a man as this Venetian libertine and the genius of the eighteenth century are completely naïve, Broadway" Clare, who saw the production before her departure for California, raffishly agreed with the critical consensus on Lowell Sherman but disagreed about Cornell, who of course was one of her major rivals among the upcoming young actresses: "I have seen *Casanova*. Terrible. Lowell Sherman is an effeminate bartender giving an imitation of Jack Barrymore on an off night. Kit is lovely to look at but not—oh not—good. Slow and artificial."

Although Clare may not have been right—or may have been—about Katharine Cornell, Sidney depended on Clare as both a critic of his work and indeed as a provider for ideas for his literary efforts. While she was in Hollywood, he sent her the manuscript of a story called "Such Women as Ellen Steele," which ultimately appeared in *Scribner's Magazine* in January 1925. It was about a man who, marrying an actress, makes her give up her career. The actress dies, but in turn the man cannot stop himself from applauding to give the actress the appreciation she craved and without which she died. The story may be a reflection of a battle Sidney subconsciously fought out with himself the past summer and resolved. However, that is not the point we wish to make here.

When Clare received the manuscript, she wrote Sidney the kind of sympathetic detailed criticism that any author craves and appreciates. Of course, she likes the story: "It gives the impression of being literally true as if it had really happened and that you had disguised the names of the characters for publication" (undated letter). That, incidentally, is a valid description of the story's effect. She cites specific places and suggests changes: "[A]at the top of page 9 you say 'they are defenseless women, I think quite like flowers.' It is lovely and true but it occurred to me that somewhere in that description of her you could perhaps generalize in a phrase, the passive fanaticism of the actress type—the type that permits itself to be obsessed more perhaps than any other, I mean. Obsessed by single minded emotion apart from any creative impulse. I may be wrong about this but it seems to me that you need to strengthen the impression of an apparently docile person storing up an immense amount of energy." Not only does she suggest the general direction of a change, she actually sometimes supplied a wording. That is to say,

6. Clare in Hollywood: An Interlude 147

Sidney in his literary efforts relied heavily on Claire's critical and even creative acumen.

But Clare was in Hollywood not for the leisure to criticize Sidney's literary effusions but to make a movie. This stay in Hollywood lacks the anxiety of the spring visit, one reason being that the manners and habits of the people she previously excoriated no longer surprise her, another being that since the natives know her and are more at ease with her, she can now take them all with some equanimity. At first, she still refuses to have anything to do with its inhabitants:

> Not a word have I spoken to anyone, barring servants, for almost a week and my voice is rapidly sinking to a whisper as they say the voices of old prisoners do. Of course, the instant I arrived Pickford and the rest went off to San Francisco to take mob scenes—why San Francisco and why mob scenes I don't profess to know. And I am left here to cool my heels and experiment with make-up and look out of the window on this withered, ignominious country. Not even my costumes have been started. But I don't dare say too much or I shall get so angry I shall be fit for nothing. The whole atmosphere of the studio is less hectic than it was the last time but is more unhappy and seems to be a hot-bed of animosities and petty spite. There is something very wrong with the emotional atmosphere—Ma Pickford glowering—Mary nervously fishing for compliments, the most bitter looks darting back and forth between subordinates. Rather for me life in the Beverly Hills Hotel (which is almost entirely empty) than any association which would make me the sympathetic ear....
>
> I will say, though, that everyone has been very kind about welcoming me back. Little Raymond, the hunchback chauffer, ... was so excited he could hardly drive [October 5th, 1923].

But it was not her familiarity with Hollywood ways and mores and Hollywood's familiarity with her that made this separation easier for Clare. She understood what was probably a key factor in her modified attitude. After describing a series of the usual events and nonevents, she says: "It is all disheartening, but my summer has given me a sort of patience and coolness (or reserve of obstinacy) that I didn't have last spring. You have never had a bread and butter letter from me, my beloved. I am not going to write one now, but some day you will know what our honeymoon did for me and for us both. Wasn't it wonderful?" (October 12th, 1923).

So the security in her marriage which she lacked in the spring gave her the ability then to withstand the waste and vulgarity against which her puritan spirit revolted. Of course she is still terribly lonely, reads continually, recommending with great enthusiasm Cather's *Lost Lady* (October 15th, 1923) and enjoying tremendously Trevelyan's *American Revolution* (October 12th, 1923), and Jean visits her for ten days (October 26th, 1923). But she grows less unbending about the company she keeps and the work.

On October 25th she writes Sidney that she had "one evening tete a tete with Theda Bara." In the same letter she says, "I must say that this is a good picture, like Chaplin's, but a well thought-out, exciting story well acted. (At least, all the others are good except the Mary Stuart who indignantly asked the costume designer how he expected her to vamp any body without a string of beads.) Altogether I am enjoying it more than I thought possible, perhaps because of the influence of the amazing woman, Elizabeth of England." Perhaps it is because she has less reason now to sneer at the citizens and their work.

Sidney finally arrives in Hollywood in early November. They are both working hard, he on articles and his play *They Knew What They Wanted*, she in the film. There now seems to be a reconciliation between the puritanical and artistically aspiring stage actress and Hollywood natives, whose morals she despised and whose work habits she deplored. She receives the mantle of approval from one of Hollywood's kings whose work we know she admired but whose morals she could hardly have condoned. Yet as Sidney reports the following scene in a letter to Norman Hapgood (November 22nd, 1923), there is not a trace of demurral from the approval Clare received: "It was rather exciting the other night when Charlie Chaplin, who always comes to watch her work, led applause with all the stage hands joining in, for a scene in which the w.[ell] k.[nown] virgin queen has giggles over a merry quip of Leicester's, she sitting on the throne of England the while…," undoubtedly accepting Chaplin's homage.

7

Consequences

When Clare and Sidney returned from California, their year of wonders began. She starred in a series of classical and modern roles that stamped her as the most daring if not always most admired young actress in New York, although no one denied her huge talent. At the end of this period, in the spring of 1925, she entered a new theatrical field with her codirection of the successful *Wild Duck*. For Sidney the culmination of his efforts to write a critically respected smash play came with the production in September 1924, of *They Knew What They Wanted* and its winning for that season the Pulitzer Prize over such respected and popularly acclaimed competitors as *Desire Under the Elms* and *What Price Glory?* For both Clare and Sidney the wondrous year was topped off with the birth of their daughter, Jennifer, on March 23rd, 1925.

Public success such as theirs of course has a variety of consequences, not all of them desireable. One desired consequence was Sidney's new earnings. In 1924 he paid taxes—about four percent of his income—on something over $15,000, but when in 1925 he realized the full economic benefit of his success with *They Knew What They Wanted*, he paid four percent of well over $47,000; his income had more than tripled. Not only was his family more comfortable, but now he could cease from his journalistic labors and devote himself entirely to art—the dramas he wished to write and, perhaps closest to his heart, the fiction on which he wished to expend an increasing amount of time. He was in the midst of a long novel of Maine sailing days that had been called *Spite House*, now *Godhead*, and eventually would be called *Jacob Ely*. It was to be edited by the legendary Maxwell Perkins at Scribner's, who would soon begin shaping the novels of Thomas Wolfe.

Sidney's larger income also increased the time he could spend with

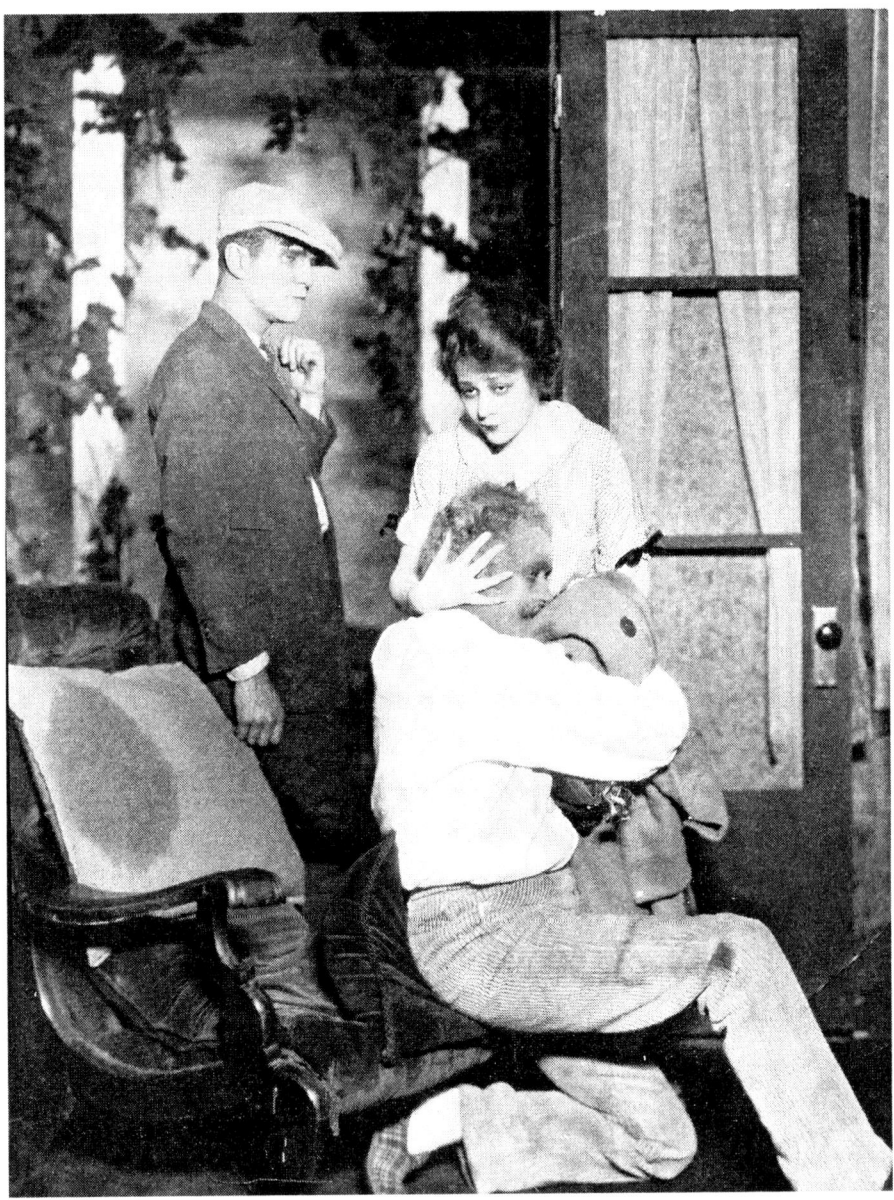

Glen Anders, Pauline Lord and Richard Bennett in Sidney Howard's *They Knew What They Wanted*, 1924. Some critics believed that Pauline Lord was the greatest young actress of her day. (Courtesy of the New York Public Library.)

his family, more important now that he and Clare were a real family with the child they so desperately desired. Surely one reason for the smoothness of Sid and Clare's emotional relationship was the presence of the baby, which removed the anxiety about conceiving and giving birth to a child and made as well for a tender loving common bond. Significant also was the reduction of the number of their separations, giving them time to further deepen their intimacy.

Perhaps unexpectedly came the alteration of their public lives. They evolved into pillars of the theatrical community, Sidney, for example, designated as a spokesman for "The Theater" in its fight against government censorship, Clare appointed to the board of directors of the Theatre Guild, its first new member since its founding in 1919. Now they were not merely playwright and actress trying hard to succeed: They were at the heart of a thriving theatrical community that was reshaping the theater itself.

This new theater was now under attack. Those fearful that traditional morality was losing its hold on society saw in the stage, as in all the arts, an instrument prying loose the glue holding society together. Undoubtedly they were correct, but more precisely, the arts were a reflection of a society many of whose members believed decreasingly in old-fashioned virtues. The Jig Cooks, the Susan Glaspells, the John Reeds, those who were radical in politics, culture and the arts, before World War I had already been living lives sharply different from those of the majority of men and women in the United States. World War I furthered the movement toward an untraditional way of life, but another event, the Russian Revolution, the frightened saw as undermining their system in which, they believed, morality and economics were inextricably intertwined.

Analyzing such a reaction, a shrewd contemporary observer in *The Freeman* wrote:

> The system has lately had a tremendous shaking; and we have seen how frantically and insistently the politicians of our race have had to invoke a specious morality to bolster their efforts to uphold it. Morality, idealism, righteousness, religion, have all been thrown like a smokescreen or like a distorting mist around the startling nakedness of this economic system.... Hence we had everywhere an irruption of the insane passion for regulation. The morality-mongers, sociologists, uplifters, reformers, editors, preachers, lecturers, forthwith began to make a great fuss about drinking; a great fuss about obscenity in art and letters, a great fuss about "irregularities" in sex relations; a great fuss about dress, dancing, moving pictures and the like....

Although there had been a great fuss about the theater before 1925, that year brought a veritable explosion of activity on the censorship front when the actress Helen MacKellar declared that she wished to be relieved of her role in *The Good Bad Woman*. *The New York Times* in its brief opening-night review had called the play an "involved, crude, tiresome work" (February 14th, 1925, 21). But Miss MacKellar's sudden—after all, she had rehearsed the play for some weeks—particular objection was to one word which occurred seven times in her part. But she continued to play the role when the word was blue-penciled in four lines but allowed to remain in three. For her original condemnation she was credited with starting the "crusade to make the stage better" (*New York Times*, February 19th, 1925, 13).

District Attorney Joab Banton now entered the scene. He had a difficult problem. On the one hand he wished to be counted as a fearless leader in the fight for a clean stage. On the other hand, since the theater was a major moneymaker for New York with slightly risqué plays adding coins to the box-office coffers, he did not wish to kill the famous golden-egged goose. So when the proposal was made that a citizen-jury system, which in a previous upshot of civic virtue had been devised but never utilized, now be revived as a way of calming outraged virtue, he and many in the theater acceded to it (*New York Times*, February 23rd, 1925, 5). Thus it came about that two of the season's most respected plays, *Desire under the Elms* and *They Knew What They Wanted*, came under the suspicion of moral culpability, were submitted to a citizen jury, and subsequently acquitted.

Ultimately, however, the play-jury system failed. The juries found almost no play under its inspection guilty of indecency, causing Banton early in 1927 to abolish the play juries (*New York Times*, February 5th, 1927, 1). Finally New York state law permitted the municipal government to revoke a license for a theater and to refuse to issue another license for a year if any part of a play acted there was found guilty of indecency or if its subject matter concerned "sex degeneracy or perversion" (*New York Times*, April 8th, 1927)

Sidney Howard was very much at the heart of the controversy. When police came to observe *They Knew What They Wanted* because it was under suspicion of badness, the guild fearfully cut some of the supposedly offensive lines. Sidney immediately wrote to the executive director, "I think you ought to restore the lines to my play at once (indeed, I want them restored) and invite the police to come and see the play as it has been..." (letter to Theresa Helpburn, February 18th, 1925).

When the censorship legislation came up in 1927, Sidney served as spokesman for the Authors' League and the Association of American Dramatists, which joined other elements of the theater in their fight against the legislation (*New York Times*, March 10th, 1927). Some days later, a still deeply troubled Sidney gave a stirring address to the graduates of the American Academy of Dramatic Arts:

7. Consequences

> You are coming into the theatre at a time when in many ways it is freer and more living than it has ever been before ... we have built it up here ... an amazing freedom of scope in every kind of subject matter ... it does seem as though from now on the theatre ought to be more than ever a kind of clearing house of the world's reaction to life. Because you are going into the theatre at this time, you are to be congratulated, but alas! you are going into the theatre at a moment when a great group of American citizens who consider themselves their brothers' keepers, are seeking to lay very, very strict and terrible laws and a very heavy hand upon this living, breathing, institution of which this country should be so very proud.
>
> You are undertaking a responsibility which should not be put upon you. You are going to have to defend the theatre from the greatest enemy any art can have in the world; that is the enemy of organized stupidity, of organized hate ... this censorship is founded, as I have said, upon such ideas as brothers-keepers are able to turn over in their minds and roll over their tongues and spout and comfort themselves with—people who hate life, people who fear talent, people who distrust any innovation, any liberty, any freedom ... the theatre looks to you the enlightened forward-looking theatre, to join in this hard fight and this, I am afraid, long fight.... It looks to you to help us pull our theatre to its rightful place at the head of all the theatres in the world [*New York Times*, March 10th, 1927, VIII, 4].

Sidney correctly understood that the censors meant to suppress not only those who exploited sex for merely economic gain. Acting Mayor McKee insisted, "Salaciousness cloaked as art is doomed as a box office proposition and pathological problems will not in the future be safe offerings with a stage for a dissecting room." The acting mayor "attributed what he called the steady degradation of the American stage to a determination to acquire European theatrical taste" (*New York Times*, April 7th, 1927, 27, 1). The censors, represented by the acting mayor, clearly intended to rid the New York stage of dramas that seriously explored political, psychological, and sexual issues in forms that possessed aesthetic integrity. That tension between creators of art and the likes of McKee remained a battle (with exploiters of sleaze always trying to hustle in) for another forty years. As long as Sidney lived, he remained on the side of unfettered free speech.

But Sidney had censorship problems closer to home. Because *They Knew What They Wanted* had come under the baleful eye of moral guardians, Sidney was having a tough time with the sale of the play to films:

> The movies were a bitter pill and may prove a famous one. We got bidding on the rights to my play up so that I would have pocketed some thirty thousand dollars when Hays stopped it. Hays—that is Will Hays is the [film] censor. We now think that we can prove movie-censorship to be in violation of the restraint of trade laws and we are about ready to sue the Hays organization a quarter of a million. There is good grounds for the belief that they are acting to depreciate the value of plays by censoring them. It is significant that the censorship of my play is probably illegal for

any group of corporations to make up a list of interdicted properties and that Mr. Hays does. If we do sue and happen to win we shall succeed in splitting the picture industry wide open and in putting Hays on the rocks for good [letter to Jean, August 6th, 1925].

But in time the desire for profits triumphed over "morality." *They Knew What They Wanted*, though attenuated, was eventually filmed three times.

Another "chief woe" in that summer of 1925 concerns attempts to censor the pageant *Lexington*. In 1923, at the instance of Sam Hume, Sidney signed to write an outdoor pageant for the 150th anniversary of the Battle of Lexington. The work is a kind of collage of various writings about the nature of freedom in this country. In the same letter just quoted he explains the problem with *Lexington*.

> A year ago, I wrote, for *The New Republic*, a series of articles called "Our Professional Patriots" about the menace manufacturers. At the same time, I undertook to write a pageant play [actually he agreed to do it the previous year] for the 150th anniversary of the battle of Lexington. I wrote, or rather, compiled the play and it was produced in June with sensational success. Whereat the patriots, unable to stand my intrusion upon their territory, began howling that I really wrote subversive propaganda and put it over on the innocent people of Lexington. I don't mind saying, in passing, that my play was on the magnificent side. I can say that without conceit because I used all the grand things that anybody has ever said about this country, anybody from Carlyle and Burke to Whitman and Sandburg and including Washington and Lincoln. They accuse me of making fun of our national heroes by quoting their most trite remarks. I asked them what portions of the Gettysburg Address or Washington's Farewell Address seemed trite to them and they refused to answer but just go on yelling: Sidney Howard's a Communist! Sidney Howard's a Communist in the pay of Moscow!

The attacks on *Lexington* by the professional patriots troubled Sidney for a while, but they do not seem to have affected his work, which in various ways turns out to be daring and exciting.

Still another unwelcome outcome of fame and fortune came in the form of a plagiarism suit on *They Knew What They Wanted*. It was not unique for successful plays to be the object of such a suit, nor was this the only time that Sidney was thus taken to court. These cases were more than irritants because, although Sidney won both in which he was involved, they cost time and money and seemed never ending. The suit against *They Knew What They Wanted* was settled only after two more years; the other, against *The Silver Cord*, took three years.

In Sidney's winning these cases, Clare's testimony played a vital part because Clare vitally influenced Sidney's work. The day after Clare's court appearance about *They Knew What They Wanted*, *The New York Times* wrote: "Mr. Howard's wife, who is known on the stage as Clare Eames, testified that her husband conceived the idea of the play in the Summer of 1922, and that she had assisted him in writing it..." (April 26th, 1927). About the exact degree of Clare's helping Sidney to write the play *The Times* is not explicit, perhaps as little (or as much) as she was concerned in criticizing the short story "Such Women as Ellen Steele," which Sidney sent her in Hollywood.

Clare's testimony for *The Silver Cord* clearly shows her to have been more closely involved with that work than with *They Knew What They Wanted*. In a deposition given in London for the trial to be held in New York she said in part:

> In the summer of 1922 we were staying with my Aunt, Madame Emma Eames, at her house in Bath, Maine.... I ... told him [Sidney] the story of some relations of mine—my great-aunt Mrs. Thomas Hyde and her sons Arthur and John—a story which almost exactly coincides with that of the "Silver Cord" ... it was not till the summer of 1924, while we were at our country house, Wiscasset, Maine, that he began serious work on "The Silver Cord." For a considerable time he was occupied on the scenario for the play. I think some 12 or 13 drafts were written, and I remember the principal difficulty was, that the fate of my cousins, Arthur and John, were so terrible, that had we adhered to it, the play, though true, would, in our opinion, have been unbearable to an average audience.
> ...David, Robin, Hester and Mrs. Phelps, all had their prototypes in real life; the only imaginary character was Christina.
> A great many notes and drafts of the play were written at various times but I am absolutely certain that my husband never departed from our original conception. There can be no question of Mr. Howard having at any time consulted any play, book, or other source other than my memory [Testimony taken November 1st, 1930, at the Picadilly branch of the National Provincial Bank, LTD.].

Clare then was invaluably involved in Sidney's work. She presented him with stories, she was the recipient of his ideas and the respondent to them, she aided in the conception of his plays, she acted as his critic and his rewrite woman. As we shall see, she also helped him with the pragmatics of a play on the stage. Her efforts involved themselves as a necessary part of every phase of his work in the theater.

Their closest collaboration came on *Lucky Sam McCarver*, Sidney's major effort for 1925. The Howards spent the summer of that year in Wiscasset in a house they learned to love and on which in the following year they took a long-term lease, expecting to occupy it every summer for the rest of their lives. There in the summer of 1925 Sidney was putting the finishing touches on *Lucky Sam McCarver* (and continuing his wok on the novel *Godhead*). He corresponded at length with John Cromwell,

Clare Eames as Carlotta Ashe and John Cromwell in the title role of *Lucky Sam McCarver* look fixedly at each other in the midst of a crisis. (Courtesy of the New York Public Library.)

who was to be one of the producers of the play, about the acquisition of a director, scenic designer, and cast.

One of the problems with *Lucky Sam* was finding an actor for the difficult title role. Sidney and John Cromwell finally decided that Cromwell himself, a noted actor, would play the part. But that meant that Cromwell would have to be replaced in his capacity as director. Clare's part in the search for a director now becomes exceptionally important because—she is now reporting Harold Freedman's remarks in a conversation she had with him—"the ideal combination for a director would be someone whom I could prompt, like Dudley [Digges]," with whom she had codirected *The Wild Duck*. Freedman obviously thought that Clare in a sense should be the play's codirector, and it is with that belief that she continues her search for a director, with the apparent approval of the others involved in the choice. "Have you ever thought of Marc Connelly?" she goes on in the letter just quoted. "Don't faint. I believe and know he could do it" (letters to Cromwell July 2nd–July 24th, 1925). Connelly, with George S. Kaufman, the author of highly successful comedies very different from *Lucky Sam*, had never yet, so far as the record shows, directed any play. Perhaps for that reason Clare thought that she could also coach Connelly into successfully guiding the show to its first night. At any rate, Connelly, duly contacted, turns out to be too busy.

Originally, Sidney, Clare, and Cromwell had wanted Robert Edmond Jones as both scenic designer and director, but Jones rejected the assignment because "he is nearly out of his mind with other work." However, Clare continues, "he is going to launch our rehearsals if we will let him." Permitting Jones to begin the rehearsals, if indeed he did, undoubtedly came with the decision that Sidney, whom Clare surely could prompt, would direct the show. No director except the inexperienced and uncertain Sidney would permit another to begin rehearsals which he would then take over. Whether or not Jones was indeed the initial director we do not know, but he did look in on them. In an undated note to Sidney he writes: "I thought the whole thing was very fine except the lighting which seemed to me atrocious. You leave [?] it to Clare to get that right immediately." Here again Clare is central to the production. Incidentally, out of Clare's discussion with Jones also came the designation of the scene designer, Jones's former apprentice, Jo Mielziner. Clare, involved with every phase of the production, had as well overall script approval: "I put my final pre-rehearsal touches on the manuscript this morning and it goes off to the stenographer as soon as Clare has finished reading it."

The Howards were as much in love as ever and loved their life together. On her way down from Wiscasset to New York, where Clare was to act in another movie after an impressive appearance in *Dorothy Vernon*, she writes to Sidney, missing him as much as she did when she boarded the train for California, "I sobbed when I gave my tickets to the conductor and he was sweet and gave me a lower. I shed tears into my plate in the diner; and the steward offered to show me the kitchen and pantries apparently to cheer me up" (undated letter). Obviously, her unhappiness does not seem to have wiped out Clare's sense of humor. Undoubtedly an aid to its retention was her compensation for acting in the film. Sidney informs his mother, "She pulls down the biggest salary she has ever been paid and it is only a step or so to star terms for her in the pictures from now on" (letter to Helen Howard, July 29th, 1925). Clare ends her letter from the train to New York thus: "I miss you so that I stayed awake until 4 o'clock this morning in a drench of misery." She also misses her new daughter. "And my P.[earl] of G.[reat] P.[rice] my darling Girl-Pearly O." Clare seems to have nicknamed her child after Hester Prynne's baby. Unlike Hester Prynne's Pearl of Great Price, so called because her mother was branded by the scarlet letter *A* as a result of the child's birth, Clare's baby seems to have been so named because of the pain Clare endured at her child's birth. The very last sentence of the letter, however, returns to Sidney: "And you, my delight, I love you sweetly, madly—." Then there is a postscript: "You will never know how absolutely indispensable you are to me, my own love." She ends another letter with "And tell me, every time, you miss me as I do you."

On top of one of Clare's letters from New York dated "July 29, 1925" she says, "I miss you more every minute and I have to drink cocoa at night to make me sleep. Otherwise I am well. But I do get so outdone with loneliness. It's awful to be so entirely dependent on you. But I don't care...." The old puritan idea of emotional self-reliance makes it bad to be dependent, but Clare tosses aside the puritan admonition. For one thing, the individuals of this couple clearly lean on each other, and Sidney's dependence on Clare undoubtedly redeemed her residual self-doubt about which both Sidney and she have written. To erase that self-doubt must have been an unconscious goal in her life as she sought greater emotional and artistic freedom.

In Clare's letters there is plenty of talk of their child, to whom she sometimes refers as "Magirl." The child's given name is the same as Clare's, Clare Jeness, but Clare's middle name "offers the inestimable advantage of being corruptible into Jennifer which is Welsh for Guinevere" (letter to Jean, April 19th, 1925), and Jennifer is how she would be known to all.

But the play Sidney finished that summer, *Lucky Sam McCarver*, turned out to be a failure. The 1925 comedy was very different from it predecessor. *They Knew What They Wanted* takes place in sunny California while *Lucky Sam* inhabits mostly the cold precincts of New York. *They Knew What They Wanted* portrays simple characters whose impulses of love and lust, quicker than their tongues, strive to articulate their warmth and compassion; *Lucky Sam*'s characters speak sharply, if laconically, lack love, control their lust in a "play of mind on mind," as both Clare and Sidney refer to it. The characters of the previous play live on a ranch whose owner, an illegal wine producer, is nothing but kind and understanding to his wife and friends; the figures of the new play meet on grounds where gangsters and high society coalesce and whose eponymous character is ready to sweep aside wife and friends for his ambition. *They Knew What They Wanted*, simple and straightforward, makes for a stark contrast with the jazzy *Lucky Sam*, which is nevertheless a network of hidden thought and emotion.

Sam McCarver has risen from "rustlin' drinks an' pickin' up towels for a Turkish bath" (78) to his present eminence as the proprietor of one of the most popular clubs in Prohibition New York, paying off and thus controlling both local and federal officers. Ambitious to rise further both financially and socially, he marries Carlotta Ashe, a multidivorced, high-stepping member of an old New York family whom he has saved from publicity in connection with a murder; out of gratitude she agrees to marry him. Although early in their marriage love seems to have welled up in both, the differences in their character and breeding separate them. They end living apart, she penniless, refusing to take his offer of money because it is proffered from a mean sense of duty rather than from love. She dies; he goes off to a profitable business and social engagement.

The drama is subtitled "Four Episodes in the Rise of a New Yorker." Each episode is in a different location, the first in Sam's place, the Club Tuileries, the second in the McCarvers' apartment, the third in Venice, the fourth in a Washington Heights apartment occupied by Carlotta. In the preface to the play Sidney tells us that he arranged the drama in a pattern that showed "first, the man in his world, with her comment upon it; second, the pair of them together; third, the woman in her world, with his comment upon it; and last of the pair of them forever separate" (ix). The "slight story" of the play the author works out "wholly by implication and never with any directness or technical proficiency" (iii). Taking a slap at his main rival, Eugene O'Neill, and a theater world that admired him, Sidney continues: "I might go so far as to call this an experimental play if I thought for a moment that any one would believe me. No one would believe me, because it was not produced in an art theatre and none of the actors wore masks."

In this play Sidney seems to have been affected most by Chekhov, having in his mind the recent New York appearances of the Moscow Art Theatre. "We should stick religiously to our Moscow Art Theatre Slogan and ... we should suspect any conventional or obvious theatrical type" (letter to Cromwell, July 20th, 1925).

That Sidney's tough, staccato New York drama requires a production similar to Chekhov's ironic, emotional plays is less surprising than it seems at first when we understand that Sidney's play, like Chekhov's, works mainly by implication. The characters do not always wish to state, occasionally do not know how to state, their own motives, and as in Chekhov these turn out to be fairly complicated and the main point of the play. The audience is therefore left to infer the major action, the "play of mind on mind." Further, as with Chekhov, the characters may be sharply etched individuals but they are also symbolic of phases in the country's social life. In Sidney's play they represent "the two most spectacular extremes of the American social pendulum as it swings, in all its shoddiness of standard and philosophy, across the handsome horizon of the handsome city of New York" (vii).

The subject matter of *Lucky Sam McCarver* is contemporary and immediate, and as such it is reminiscent of another work, *The Great Gatsby*, published in the same year that Sidney's play was produced.

Sam, like Gatsby, a gangster, also reflects Fitzgerald's character in that he regularly recreates himself. He tells the appalled Carlotta:

> You ain't never been but only one thing in your life. You ain't got nothin' on your mind to forget. Well, I got plenty and I been so damn' many different things, if I couldn't ha' kept each one separate and wiped the slate clean every time, where 'ud I ha' got to. I'd like to know? All mixed up an' getting' nowheres, that's what! [120].

That is, both characters, Sam and Gatsby, regularly wipe out their pasts and regularly make themselves anew; in Fitzgerald's terms, they are their own fathers. Both Gatsby and Sam pursue women of the upper class, but while Gatsby pines for the seemingly pure Daisy Buchanan, Sam marries the obviously flawed Carlotta Ashe. But herein we see something of the difference between the two authors. In rendering a rather similar sleazy and disappointing America in the fast-living 1920s, both authors mourn a lost promise of a new world. But Gatsby possesses an ideal which he does not fail whereas Sam never develops an ideal. He is and remains at the end of the play ambitiously materialistic. Further, no character in the drama is admirable; Carlotta's integrity at the end of the play in refusing Sam's support is a very thin reed on which to hang a desire for renewal of the human spirit. What hope for a communal spiritual life the drama projects lies not in its action but in the ebullience of Sidney's accomplishment, his sheer joy in orchestrating the rhythms of the jazz age, in the creation of his characters and the form within which they move. The audience can leave the play with some of the deep pleasure of creation because the only way it can understand the drama is by joining the author in the act of its creation.

The Great Gatsby went on to become an American classic whereas *Lucky Sam McCarver* lies unread and unperformed. Both are subtly executed works, but exactly therein lies one reason for the play's neglect. A reader can ponder a novel's difficulties, but few will read a drama that is not acted, and *Lucky Sam*'s huge and difficult subtext guarantees that it will be rarely performed. Indeed, as we read the second act, Sidney's favorite, it is hard to know how the audience can intuit all the author intended, its complex motivation, its "social pendulum as it swings in all its shoddiness of standard and philosophy, across the handsome horizon of the handsome city of New York."

But the play's largest problem is its third act. Sidney asserts that in it we are supposed to see Carlotta in her world with Sam's comment on it. But the playwright here peoples his world with grotesques. "I feel that everybody in the third act, except Sam, ought to be either too fat (a little) or too thin..." (letter to Cromwell, July 2nd, 1925). Sidney creates cartoon characters as though he was more interested in satirizing them than in telling Sam's story. Further, he changes the mode of presentation: "Sam is life in a nightmare like the ancient mariner at sea with the dead men. We must ... not stoop to any expressionistic easy way out." Although he has not "stooped" to expressionism, yet the feel is, as Sidney intended, expressionistic, for the audience inexplicably so. The accomplished fourth act, set back in New York, is reduced in its effect both because of the return now to strict realism and because of the unaccountable change of location in the third act. (Couldn't Sidney show Sam and Carlotta in her milieu in New York?) Therefore, the play as a whole strikes us today as brilliant but not wholly successful.

The respectful but negative reviews seem to reflect directly or indirectly our observations of the play. The anonymous *New York Times* reviewer, although finding the drama "worthy of the most recent Pulitzer Prize winner" (October 22nd, 1925, 22), yet believed that the second and third acts "seem more arbitrary" than the first. He perhaps meant that he could not understand the difficult-to-intuit motivations in the second act and that he had no idea why on earth the author shifted the scene to Venice and the mode of its presentation in the third. Even Barrett Clark, Sidney's good friend, erstwhile collaborator, and frequent defender, criticized the play, writing that Sam's "full-length portrait" was "obscured in order that other matters might be treated which have little or nothing to do with Sam" (*Drama*, December 1925, 95). That also perhaps points to the odd third act and perhaps to a scene performed on stage but omitted from the printed text because it "side-track[ed] the line of the play" (Preface, xxvii).

Sidney did receive one unreservedly positive review, written by John Anderson of *The New York Evening Post*, with whose analysis he altogether agreed:

> Since Mr. Howard hid in the alley of the Playhouse last night when a clamorous audience waited ten minutes to tell him how much they liked "Lucky Sam McCarver," he may not know yet in case he is still hiding, that he has written the most fascinating play in town.
> If any one could have imagined in either hot or cold blood the results of a collaboration between Jimmy Gleason and Noel Coward or George Abbott and Ronald Firbank, the he-chested and the decadent, they might have guessed what "Lucky Sam McCarver" would be like....
> Here is more than the tragedy of individuals, for though he has wrought two notable characters, Mr. Howard seems to have embodied in them two social orders and to have been unhumanly just to both."

Sidney was especially fond of Anderson's insight into the play. He writes to his mother a few days after the play's opening that the drama is "an experiment in dramatic biography and as the Post says ... it is inhumanly just to both sides and I don't yet know how much the public likes inhuman justice..." (October 26th, 1925).

Lucky Sam McCarver closed after just thirty performances, but strangely enough for a play that seemed to have sunk into the depths soon after its opening, it received a revival, obscure but prominently reviewed. The Equity Community Theatre, which performed dramas in the auditoriums of local New York City libraries, revived *Lucky Sam McCarver* in the Bronx. Two of New York's most important critics traveled all the way to that outer borough and reported their responses. Brooks Atkinson of *The Times*, who may well have been that newspaper's anonymous reviewer in 1925, in 1950 said that "it is still a pithy and absorbing drama" (April 15th, X, 1). Richard Watts Jr. of the *New York Post* wrote:

> It has faults as a play and it is something less of a masterpiece I had rather suspected it of being. But it is a drama of rare intelligence, subtlety and insight that studies two unusually complex characters with remarkable objectivity and lack of sentimentality....
> So objective was Mr. Howard that it is almost impossible to tell you just where his sympathies lay in his study of the child man with the gift of success and the weary, slightly decadent aristocrat with the pall of destruction hanging over her. I suspect that the author was rather on her side, because she has grace in defeat where he lacks it in victory [April 15th].

Sidney surely would have appreciated the nature of the praise the critic lavished on the drama.

But the quick closing of *Lucky Sam McCarver* did not diminish Sidney's fighting spirit. In pugnacious Shavian style, Sidney wrote a widely discussed preface to the play, published in 1926, in which he "whacks a head wherever he sees one." Concerned mainly with defending his drama and discussing the centrality of acting in the theater, Sidney in passing strikes out at the art theater and the New Stagecraft. He thus helps us to understand his notion of how a play should develop its form.

Sidney grew up in the art theater and with the New Stagecraft as a kind of ideal. Sam Hume, a prophet of the New Stagecraft, remained a kind of mentor almost to the very moment of his writing the preface, for it was he that recommended Sidney for the job of composing *Lexington*, the collagelike design which he describes at one point as expressionistic, a term which he now thinks of as pejorative. Even while at Harvard Sidney expressed ambivalence about the New Stagecraft and the art theater; nevertheless at the beginning of his career he continued to work in their manner. *Swords*, though on Broadway, was in its writing and presentation an art theater production, as we can infer from Sidney's insistence that Clare Eames's arctic technique required the warmth of Rollo Peters's sets. Even *They Knew What They Wanted*, although realistic in method, relies on a meandering plot construction as well as a kind of colorful theatricalism that ran counter to the tightly plotted commercial play.

But now more self-assured, he differentiates himself from playwrights in the art theater movement. Recent experiences must surely have helped his self-definition. Sidney, very serious about his work, hated the amateurism with which the art theater movement was pervaded. His skirmish with the founders of the Experimental Theatre showed him that even such professionals as O'Neill, Jones, and Macgowan, when starting an art theater, could be infected with the eager idealism that indulges amateurism.

Sidney also hits out at one of the art theater's chief tenets, that the setting was as important as the play: "To my mind, it was a sad day when [the scenic designer] Gordon Craig invented the New Stage Craft..." (xi). This attitude precisely contradicts Eugene O'Neill's, who wrote to Macgowan as they formed the Experimental Theatre, that he wished to give Bobby Jones plenty of opportunities. Sidney shows that he understood the centrality of Jones to the Experimental Theatre when he implied in a letter to Macgowan that if Jones died of cancer the Experimental Theatre would also die.

Still, there was something more than the rejection of the New Stagecraft. Sidney also tilts at what he thinks of as the art theater's arbitrariness in thinking of only one type of play, the expressionistic drama, as belonging in the avant-garde. *Lucky Sam McCarver*, he says, is a story told "wholly by implication and never with any directness or technical proficiency. I might go so far as to call this an experimental play if I thought for a moment that any one would believe me. No one would believe me, because it was not produced in an art theatre and none of the actors wore masks." Sidney complains that the externals, that is, an arbitrarily chosen expressionistic form, and the venue and the new, rather than its singular organic growth, make art theater patrons call a play experimental.

The positive side of Sidney's view he expressed earlier in an interview published in the September 1925 issue of *Theatre Magazine*. Sidney says there,

> I am rabid where impressionism is concerned. I am more interested in people than in anything else in the world. I would much rather have written one novel of Conrad's than the entire works of Kant. People are more interesting than philosophical ideas. When a playwright or a producer, even as notable as Strindberg and Bobbie Jones, put[s] actors on a stage and tell[s] them to be ideas instead of people, I am annoyed, because I feel that they are more interesting as people. Ideas must come out of people in the final analysis.

Conforming to that notion, he refers in the preface first to his mentor and then to Clare's:

> I went to school, once upon a time, to George Pierce Baker, at Harvard, in the 47 Workshop, and learned from him what little I have ever

learned about the craft of writing plays. "Write what you know to be true about your characters," he used to say, "and write nothing that you do not know to be true." That other great teacher in the American theatre, Charles Jehlinger, of the American Academy of Dramatic Art, who has developed nearly all the younger acting talents of our time, tells his students much the same thing. It is sound teaching [xxvi].

Sidney has totally reversed himself since his days at Harvard when he wrote disdainfully to Jean about Baker's views of playwriting.

Sidney now could not tolerate a preconceived idea of what should happen on the stage. Neither the use of masks nor the expressionistic form in a drama shows its author necessarily to be a deep thinker nor will they transform him into one who can penetrate the human soul.

Further, Sidney attacks the obscurity of language sometimes found in art theaters' productions, the very obscurity indicating for many members of the audience that an experimental play with profound insights into the human condition was onstage. Countering that notion, Sidney writes in his preface that, although the meaning of his play "escaped a good many people ... I understood every word myself, and I could have explained every word, and that would be unworthy, I know, of an experimental dramatist...." (ii). The implication is that while an O'Neill keeps searching for new forms, sometimes perhaps for their own sake, other dramatists, working more validly, found the form of a drama in the characters and their relationship to each other. If these dictate a form never previously or rarely used, then the author is an experimental dramatist.

"My two favorite plays of the past season are *What Price Glory* and *The Show-Off*," Sidney told *Theatre Magazine* in the article quoted above. "In both of these plays is novel form artistically accomplished, and without conscious effort. In *What Price Glory* characters are real and the incidents are developed and unfolded in a logical [way]....

"I think *The Show-Off* is a deeply and profoundly poetic play. Yet the author of it did not strive for form...."

That is, these dramatists created a form suggested by the characters and their relationship as they moved through the (perhaps sketchy) plot. A new form might emerge with the development of the action, not as a preconceived element. Although in the *Theatre Magazine* interview Sidney calls himself "an artistic conservative," it would seem that he would not necessarily eliminate masks and expressionism if the play dictated them although their present association with arty drama certainly made him "rabid" against them. Yet he was artistically conservative in the sense that he did not explore, as O'Neill and Strindberg did, those felt but barely expressible movements of the soul that sent them searching for new forms.

Still, *Lucky Sam McCarver* can be called an experimental play, for there is pioneering originality in it. Not only is the form of four fragments torn from a man's life unusual, but nowhere in modern drama does an author absolutely refuse to render anything more than the coruscating surface of his vulgar, jazzy society together with the shoddy lives of the main characters and at the same time insist that the audience must intuit the significant meaning beneath this surface. The author does not altogether succeed, but his work remains a fascinating experiment.

Perhaps the most widely discussed portion of Sidney's preface, however, concerned the relative importance of the playwright and the actor in the theater. Sidney calls the dramatist a "vicarious actor" (xvi) rather than a writer of literature.

"A great writer of stories normally dislikes plays, I think, because they do not allow him the space he requires to write as fully as he wants to write." The playwright, on the other hand, does not require that space, for his job

> is to serve actors. ... No matter how beautiful the writing of the play may be, no matter how profound or original or true an idea it may contain, it cannot be a good play (let alone a great one) unless it allows actors to give an audience a satisfactory exhibition of their art. The word "vehicle" has got to be a term for a bad play with an effective part in it. The best that any dramatist can hope is that his play may prove to be a worthy vehicle... [xvii].

Sidney's notions put the actor first and the dramatist second in the theater. In fact, he downgrades every other theatrical craftsman. "The scene-designer is a painter turned interior decorator of make-believe rooms.... To call him, as he calls himself, 'the artist of the Theatre' is so much good clean fun. The costumer is a bastard dressmaker who copies his designs out of picture-books...." Only the actor is essential to the theater. One might quote the old saw that the theater requires only two boards and a passion.

One might speculate that Sidney arrived at these thoughts because he was married to a strong-minded actress who thought highly of her profession. Actually, as we know, she saw the actor as a servant of the dramatist. Still, her strenuous efforts in her roles and the demands that she must have made on Sidney, such as any actor makes on a living dramatist—only here the dramatist was her adoring husband—may well have convinced him that the playwright must be at the beck and call of the actor. But it is probably no accident that the preface to *Lucky Sam* expresses these notions. That play with its demanding subtext really required *acting* (to use the italics he applied to the word in his letter withdrawing *They Knew What They Wanted* from the Experimental Theatre), and that knowledge must have crystallized his thought.

However, Sidney is saying something more than that all drama requires excellent acting and that some drama requires it even more. "The drama does not spring from a literary impulse but from a love of the brave, ephemeral, beautiful art of acting." Dramatic literature is in essence an accident. When the love of acting "becomes the obsession of genius, then great plays are written and great dramatists appear, as Ibsen, Shakespear [sic] and Chekhov.

"When the dramatist also writes such divine poetry as Shakespeare and Ibsen wrote, when he sees life with the understanding of godhead as Ibsen and Chekhov saw it, then he cannot escape literature..." (xvi, xvii).

Sidney's thought seems arbitrary. If it is true that a dramatist writes because he loves acting, does it mean that he necessarily excludes great literature as his aim or that he loves literature less than acting? May he not have both impulses equally or the impulse toward literature first and the impulse to acting a strong second? Perhaps an author prefers an immediate response to his work rather than the slow one that comes from fiction. Also the notion that a playwright need have less of an artistic vision than a novelist seems manifestly false as is the notion that great art is any more accidental in drama than in other kinds of literature.

But surely Sidney was driven to these thoughts not only by his love for Clare and her acting. A playwright's job is obviously only one part of the work in the theater. It may be the most important part because he supplies the words without which the actor cannot appear onstage. Yet lacking the other skillful craftsmen of the theater, whose work Sidney really appreciates when he is not racketing around the block, a modern production is lost. To a serious dramatist, working, say, for eighteen months as Sidney did on *Lucky Sam*—and even longer on some plays— then to rely on others for a realization of his hard-won words and of his vision must impart a terrible sense of loss and failure. To compensate for that, perhaps, he insists that in writing plays, he is not writing literature, really, that he writes for the actor alone. Only when engaging in fiction is he creating literature. That is undoubtedly the reason for Sidney's regularly swearing off the drama—he is usually then in a fit of temper about the undependability of theater people—and for his hard work on fiction at this time.

If Sidney's career was at a kind of standstill with the failure of *Lucky Sam*, so was Clare's for that and for other work afterward: "[H]ere she is, poor darling," writes Sidney to Jean, "with critical roasts for her perfect impersonation of Carlotta in my play, a semi-success in 'Androcles' and 'The Man of Destiny' and this Eyolf thing piled up in swift succession..." (letter to Jean, February 10th, 1926).

Actually, Clare's reviews for *Lucky Sam* were not as bad as Sidney suggests. John Anderson, who loved the play, also loved Clare. The play was an "amazingly rich and penetrating drama, finely, and in the case of Clare Eames, superbly acted." Woolcott, who did not like the play very much, was more positive about Clare than about the play: "Miss Eames brings that fine suggestion of a fretted thoroughbred which the play needs more than it needs anything else." But his praise was not total: "It seemed to me that Miss Eames was struggling to bridge over certain ellipses— doubtless deliberate ellipses—in the writing...." With one small cavil *The Times* reviewer dealt Clare lavish praise in his opening night review. Although, he says, Clare lacks the glamour for the role, "the indefinable, bizarre temper of the performance is in no small measure the effect of her electric personality. Her acting in this play has depth as well as vibrancy. The simplicity of the death scene at the end is a discriminating moment characteristic of her individual art...." But by the time he wrote his Sunday article, his emphasis had shifted. "'Lucky Sam McCarver,'" he writes, "enjoys the privileges of her genius.... Nevertheless ... she seems badly cast in this role. By many signs it calls for something much more worldly than her exotic beauty, something that appeals more frankly to the type of men Carlotta attracts in the play. And the result through all four episodes is a touch of factitiousness that all the splendor of her acting cannot quite remedy."

"Clare's career goes on uninterrupted," wrote Sidney to Jean on November 7th, 1925. "We close our play a week from today and a week from the Monday after that, she opens with my beloved Theatre Guild playing both the Lady in 'The Man of Destiny' and Lavinia in 'Androcles and the Lion.'" Sidney was right in his letter to Jean in which, summarizing Clare's season, he called these productions a semisuccess for her. John Mason Brown gives the general tenor of the reviews in the January 1926 *Theatre Arts Monthly*:

> *The Man of Destiny*, which preceded ["Androcles"] as a curtain raiser, found Clare Eames pitifully miscast as the Lady and Tom Powers [who had been her costar in the two-character *The First Fifty Years*] falling far short of Napoleon. Given an unsteady performance the defects of the play leaped into prominence and made one wonder why anything at all was needed to fill out an evening when *Androcles*, one of the most irrepressible of Shavian satires, was on the bill.... From the ranks of the huddled Christians Clare Eames' Lavinia, Henry Travers' Androcles, and Orville Caldwell's militant Ferrovius stand forth, to be met by Tom Powers' Captain and Edward Robinson's sleek Caesar [9].

But Clare simply could not act in one production at a time. She turned to Ibsen's *Little Eyolf*, a very difficult play, for a series of matinee performances. The rehearsals turned into a shambles:

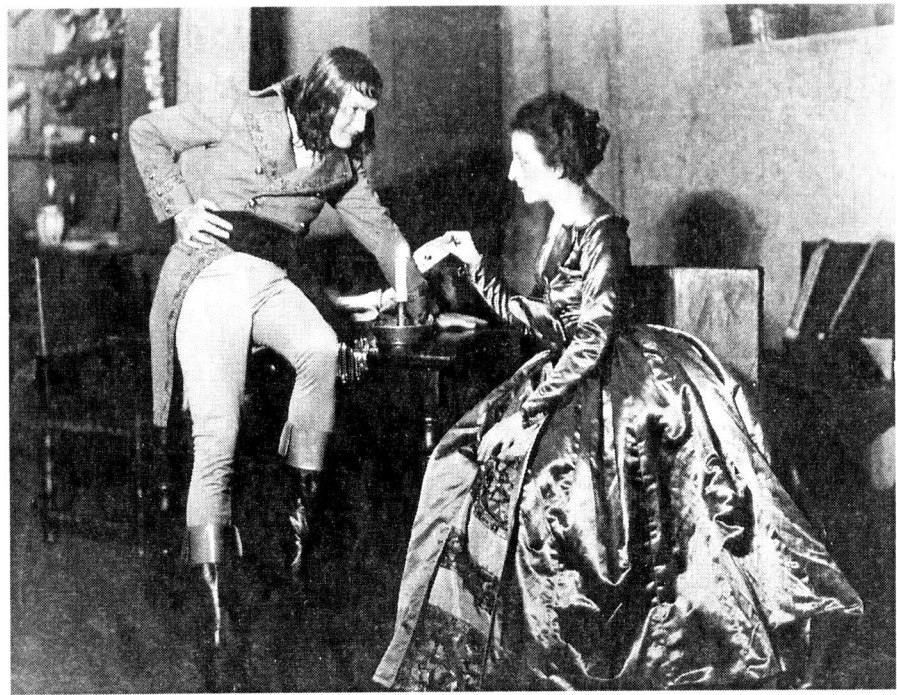

Tom Powers and Clare Eames in the Theatre Guild production of Bernard Shaw's "Man of Destiny." The critics were less than enthusiastic about the actors. (Courtesy of the New York Public Library.)

> DARLING SIDNEY [who was staying with Harrison Rhodes in Florida] HAVE NOT WIRED YOU BEFORE OWING TO CHAOTIC CONDITION OF LITTLE AYOL[f] [sic] STOP AFTER INCREDIBLY PAINFUL SCENE FINALLY CONVINCED MANAGEMENT THAT JOHN WOULD BE UNABLE TO PLAY PART STOP ROLAND AFTER GROSSLY INSULTING ME WAS ASKED TO RETIRE IN MY STEAD SO THAT WE CONTINUE PRODUCTION BUT WITH NEW ALLMERS HAS YET UNFOUND STOP THIS HAS ALL BEEN TOO TERRIBLE AND I HAVE MISSED YOU MOST AWFULLY STOP WHEN ARE YOU COMING HOME FOND LOVE ALWAYS FROM YOUR DEVOTED
>
> CLARE [January 20th, 1926]

The telegram's "Roland" was Roland Young, who had been her Judge Brack in *Hedda* and who had been a good friend when they were both interested in working at the Experimental Theatre. Young was a very successful actor, and his forced resignation must have resulted from a very gross insult indeed, for in the theater gross insults are tossed about and forgotten with amazing rapidity.

"John" is not so easy to identify. John Cromwell played an important role when the play opened, and whether Clare wished originally to expel both Cromwell and Young from the cast, we cannot know. In any case chaos reigned in the production, which in part may have been caused by the fact that Jo Mielziner, perhaps trying to imitate his master, Robert Edmond Jones, both designed the settings and directed the show. He may not have had Jones's ability at general control of the actors or of Clare.

The results were not gratifying. Reginald Owens, who replaced Young as Allmers, received less than rave notices. John Cromwell received good notices. But Clare's work, according to at least some critics, was problematical. Stark Young, however, in his usual role, chimed in as an exception, lavish with his praise of Clare: "Clare Eames brought to the part of Rita Allmers great intelligence and force.... She is especially admirable in the closeness and the vividness with which she follows her character throughout a whole gamut of moral phases..." (*New Republic*, February 17, 1925, 356). But even this critic found fault in the second part of the drama; he blamed Ibsen, however, who "seems to supply the actress with very few theatrical weapons with which to strike home her points." Brooks Atkinson in *The Times* still danced to the tune of Clare's excessive cerebral quality: "Miss Eames does not express the consuming passion that in a way is the foundation of the entire play.... She is a cerebral actress in whom the quick matching of wits, of mind against mind, comes off to fine advantage. But as this performance and previous ones appear to indicate, she does not impersonate sensuality..." (February 3rd, 1926, 22).

Despite her sometimes uncertain work in the 1925–1926 season, critics and the theater community commonly recognized her force as an actress, a personality, an intellect, even a genius, all flawed perhaps but alive. The Theatre Guild now gave its imprimatur to this general idea of her. "I don't know if you have heard what singular fortune has befallen her," wrote Sid to Jean on March 12th, 1926. "She has been made a member of the permanent company of the Theatre Guild and, more than that, has been added to the board of the Theatre with a considerable salary and a great deal of power. It's a unique thing for a child of her age and can only be explained on the grounds of her talents. If the job works out as she hopes, she will very soon be the leading figure in the English speaking theatre."

Although Sidney may have been too sanguine about Clare's becoming the leading figure in the English-speaking theater, yet he was right that this ratified her unique place among the young stars of her generation. Sidney was right to emphasize Clare's selection for the board of the Theatre Guild, for it was not only the guild's faith in her acting ability but its faith as well in her theatrical discernment, her intellectual attainments, and perhaps its belief too in her future as a director. None of Clare's rivals, Helen Hayes or Katharine Cornell or Lynn Fontanne, who was now in her second season with the guild and in the new acting company as well, had shown Clare's variety, accomplishment, or grasp of the various arts of the theater. Lynn Fontanne, for example, had just started on the great series of creations for which she was to become justly famous. To this point she had acted in only one of her famous roles for the guild, that in Molnar's *Guardsman*. Clare, however, in a brief eight years since her New York debut, had run through a variety of classic and modern roles, generating an unusual excitement and respect, and projected as well an intellectual power which in itself gave her aura a special glow.

That it was the Theatre Guild that gave Clare its stamp of approval had a certain cachet. Arriving on the New York scene at about the same time that Clare made her professional debut, the guild became and remained for many years the only continuous art theater on Broadway. Bringing to the grounds of the commercial theater such serious writers as Strindberg, Tolstoy, Shaw, Ibsen, Molnar, and Werfel, it became an amazing success. Not all of its productions made money, but enough of them did, and enough of them made a great deal of money to show that a sizable public now existed for works of dramatic art. By 1926 it was ready to go out on the road to many parts of the United States (Langner, 221).

The guild accomplished all of this on an economically viable basis. It asked free money of no one. Managed in a hard-nosed, hard-eyed fashion, the guild made art pay. Yet it pulled no artistic punches. It had presented over the course of three evenings Shaw's huge *Back to Methusalah* as well as his *Heartbreak House*, which other managements disdained. It brought to the stage Tolstoy's grisly *Power of Darkness*, the futuristic *R.U.R.* by the Czechoslovakian Karl Tapek, the expressionistic German drama by Georg Kaiser, *From Morn to Midnight*. None of them was certifiably successful before their production; on some, like the immense Shaw opus, they were sure to lose money. The Theatre Guild was doing the work of the art theatre but doing it on Broadway (Langner, 124).

Now the guild reached the culmination of its efforts, two goals of all ambitious art theaters. First in 1925, after years in the old cramped Garrick Theatre, it opened its own playhouse. President Calvin Coolidge pulled the switch in Washington that turned on the lights in the new theatre, which was built by the sale of bonds that returned to its investors "every penny of interest due" on them (Langner, 211, 12). Then, early in 1926, it announced that in the following season it would start a repertory program with its own acting company. Actually, it would not be a repertory company in the traditional sense in which a company each season at a single theater performed nightly from a staple of plays, with no performance of any one play receiving a run, a system still followed by most resident opera companies. Instead, the guild used two theaters in which each play in its repertory would be performed a week at a time. But it was close enough to the old repertory idea and gave the public variety in its dramatic fare and the actors variety in their work and a year-round salary. Besides Clare, the company included Alfred Lunt and Lynn Fontanne, Helen Westley, Dudley Digges, Margalo Gillmore, Henry Travers, Earle Larrimore, and Edward G. Robinson, all actors who were now recognized in their profession and all who continued to be individually important in their theatrical efforts.

Actually, the Theatre Guild's arrangement was similar to the one recommended by Sidney for the Experimental Theatre. It had two of Sidney's main features—a sound financial base and a permanent acting company that would be paid a living wage. But it had this difference from Sidney's plan: Where he had recommended three persons, each absolutely directing three separate aspects of the theater's governance, the guild was still run by committee with Theresa Helburn as executive director to carry out the wishes of the board.

Besides Helburn, on the board were Lawrence Langner, a patents attorney; Maurice Wertheim, a financier; Philip Moeller, a playwright and director; Lee Simonson, a designer; and Helen Westley, an actress; it was a mixture of figures with financial and artistic backgrounds. The board, originally larger, had early shaken down to these six, and there were no changes until it added Clare.

Langner, in his autobiography, says that Clare

> descended on the New York theatre from Cleveland like a hurricane blowing from the Great Lakes, and swept us all off our feet, with her brilliant acting, directing and sheer joy of living. We made her a transient member of the Guild Board and her enthusiasms often carried us along when we began to feel tired and bedraggled. "He wasted a precious hour of my valuable time," she said to me once, speaking of a person who bored her; and indeed her hours were precious and her time valuable, for she died far too young for a theatre that needed her fresh vital artistry.

Only one thing seems incorrect in that passage. No available contemporary source indicates that Clare was hired as a transient member of the board. Nor can we imagine she would assent to such an arrangement, certainly not the Clare that Langner describes. The passage suggests, rather than the likelihood of Clare's accepting a transient membership on the board, Langner's attempt to escape the difficult discussion of why Clare finally quit.

But the guild was not the only theater to establish a repertory company. Indeed, the year 1926 appeared giddy with art theaters and repertory. The Neighborhood Playhouse also announced that it would begin a repertory system with its own permanent acting company. That was the art theater located amidst the slums of Grand Street in New York's lower East Side. In his description of it while at Harvard, Sidney had been impressed with its seriousness. Financed in part by Irene and Alice Lewisohn to the tune of $40,000 a year, it had long owned its own small theatre. Thus the Neighborhood Playhouse "was an art theatre from the beginning," and now it also would have its repertory system and its permanent company. It had greater variety than the guild, for in the art theater tradition, it presented dance programs as well as plays, and its drama, as in its great success of the current season, S. Ansky's *Dybbuk*, prominently synthesized dance, song, and language (*New York Times*, January 31st, 1926, IV, 13; *New York Times*, March 12th, 1926, IV, 26; *New York Times*, May 2nd, 1926, IV, VIII, 2).

Eva Le Gallienne's Civic Repertory, traditional in its operational procedure, would, like the guild's new system, begin functioning in the fall of 1926. Le Gallienne announced that "she would sponsor a people's repertory theatre whose seats would be priced from 50 cents to $1.50 at nights and from 35 cents to $1 at matinees" (*New York Times*, May 27th, 1926, 23). The actress could now realize her ambitions to play the parts she had longed to act since she was an adolescent. Like many in the art theater world, she coupled the hopes for herself with the desire to bring dramatic masterpieces within range of the ordinary person.

Le Gallienne established her playhouse outside the theatre district, down at Fourteenth Street, and there she lived on the top floor. In a passage from her autobiography she describes a life rich with the joy of a busy daily routine:

> Each morning at nine o'clock Santelli [her fencing master] arrived and we fenced for half an hour. I then had breakfast. After that I gradually descended from one floor to the next, stopping on the way at the various departments that needed my attention, until at noon I found myself at the stage level, ready for the rehearsal. We rehearsed every day from noon to five or five-thirty, either on the current new production or on some of the old ones that needed tuning up. Immediately after rehearsal I had dinner, and slept for an hour before going down to play. After the performance I usually had a few people up to supper for informal conferences—actors, authors, or scenic-designers. These sessions usually lasted till around two A.M.

She adds,

> [L]ooking back on it, I can understand why people called me 'tireless,' for I don't remember ever really being tired. I was too interested, too deeply

absorbed...." As well as administering the theater and acting in it, Le Gallienne also directed some of the dramas.

Looking at Le Gallienne's life at the Civic, we wonder about Clare. Le Gallienne's father was a famous English poet. Brought up by a Scandinavian mother, she was given a continental upbringing and culture that suggested to her an independence and freedom of choice that did not seem possible to Clare despite her year in Paris with Emma Eames, who herself might have been a model of female independence. Clare's Midwestern roots, her puritan background, the excessive protectiveness in her home suggested that she would mature in the context of husband and family. Despite Lawrence Langner's description of her unbridled joy of life and possessing the effect of a hurricane, her fear of independence prevented her from early breaking out on her own and perhaps living the kind of rich theatrical life that was Le Gallienne's. We can well imagine that Clare, given her impulses but a quite different background, might have bravely gone her own way directing and acting in a theater of her own. As it was, the joyful hurricane manifested itself with the support of a husband, family, and a life that looked as normal as it can for a hardworking actress.

Everyone seemed to be struck by the arrival of repertory. *The New York Times* even wrote editorials about it, and a spate of articles appeared in the appropriate publications. But, of course, all this could happen because the United States was booming financially. The public was able to buy bonds for the new Guild Theatre because some part of the theatergoing public could afford to make the investment. The Lewisohn sisters could partially support the Neighborhood Playhouse because they could dispense with $40,000 a year. Of the three repertory companies that started in 1926, the Civic lasted longest as a repertory company. The Theatre Guild remained much longer as a producing institution, but it gave up the repertory system in 1928 with the production of *Strange Interlude*, which because of its six-hour length, including a dinner break, could not easily fit into a repertory system. The Neighborhood Playhouse folded in 1927 because with rising costs the Lewisohn sisters could no longer support it. The Civic, giving its last New York season in 1933, was ultimately destroyed by the Great Depression, when money dried up.

In their personal lives Sidney and Clare made a major decision. "The year begins pleasantly enough," writes Sid to Jean on New Year's Day, 1926,

> with the discovery of a house for us to live in the balance of our lives if no one builds an apartment behind it to cut off the sun.... It's a funny thing that the instinct for making and having a permanent home—and

owning it—should survive.... This house is on 81st Street, between Lexington and Third Avenues, very near Third, in fact the slums begin with a tenement next door. But the sun pours in the windows at the back, there is a place for a pretty garden, the rooms are twenty feet wide and charmingly Victorian. So there we go, I suppose, when we come back next fall from Maine.

Clare's problematical acting season seems to have had an ill effect upon her health. "I'm worried about her" writes Sid to Jean on February 10th, 1926. "So off we go (doctor's orders, too) cutting Ibsen [*Little Eyolf*] off in his prime.... It's to be Sicily and Rome. Then Paris and London for a few days each."

The trip to Europe turns out to be a great success. At their return, Sidney writes to Jean:

> Clare has this evening gone to Cleveland to see the baby and the baby's grandparents and I'm left to my own resources for the first time in three months. I find that I am badly demoralized. My only impulse is to walk about this blasted empty flat and kick the furniture. And I have stayed behind to do some work enough to sink a battleship. It has been an incredibly perfect three months. We have seen spring in Madeira, spring in Algiers, spring in Sicily and Rome and Umbria and the country of the Hill Towns, as they are called, and the general strike in London and, on the very last night before we sailed on the Olympic, they opened "THEY KNEW WHAT THEY WANTED" in London to the tune of a real triumph, both for the acting and the play, and we came away—packing from the close of the party after the performance until breakfast and train time—with darling London cheers still ringing in our ears and hearts. It is being done, now, in California, by the way—as well as in Prague, Boston, Baltimore and Vienna.

Britain's general strike of 1926, in which the British general public resisted the chaos that would have been brought about by the strike's success, brings out Sid's anglophilia as it surely did Clare's:

> As to the general strike, there is no describing the awful, human, brave wonder of it. We have no real need to fear for the well being of the world, because, no matter what the Methodists or Communists may do, civilization is still in British hands. I'm afraid that I have to add, alas, that sporting human good behavior seems to be rather a British monopoly. We saw civilization tried and saved without a shot fired. I saw trains, run by peers of the realm who had well passed the grand climacteric, start on their journeys to the friendly cheers of hundreds of strikers....

So much for Sidney's grand sympathy with labor.

The main reason for the trip seemed to have been accomplished, but in the following summer Sid writes to his mother:

7. Consequences

> We go tonight to New York and tomorrow Clare goes into the Lenox Hill Hospital for that general repairs operation which so many young mothers have to undergo, Williams performing it. It is discouraging and makes me just a little bit angry at him. Because it does seem to me that if it is necessary now, it must have been necessary last February when, had it been done, she would have had full rather than only partial benefit from our tour abroad. She has not been well. The excitement and strain of our three weeks in London pulled down all the good she got out of Italy. When she got up here [Wiscasset] she kept pretty well for a spell and then got pretty sick and lately has lost control of certain very essential muscles so that there is no postponing the operation any longer. Williams assures me that it is not serious, but I do wish that it might have come earlier with a longer respite between leaving the hospital and commencing the season of acting and general hard labor. Well, Williams may whistle awhile for his money if he wants much [August 3rd, 1926].

Of course, the prediction that this would be an easy operation proved wrong: "[S]he did suffer a great deal of very bad pain for some ten days after the operation and will be in the hospital for some week or eight days more and that, in itself, is bad, in New York, at the very crisis of the summer's appalling heat..." (August 14th, 1926). The early part of her season is threatened by the operation and its consequences, but in fact she is able to play.

8

Theatre Guild Year

The 1926–1927 season started with high hopes but ended in bitter disappointment for both Sid and Clare. Both cast their lots with the Theatre Guild believing they would find professional fulfillment with that artistically ambitious, pragmatic, successful company, and both ended in acrimonious withdrawal. Yet despite Sidney's debilitating battles with the guild, this year marked a great advance in his career. *Ned McCobb's Daughter*, his first guild play of the season, was a resounding box office success, and *The Silver Cord*, his second guild play, received great critical and box office acclaim. On notification that the guild would produce *The Silver Cord*, Sidney wrote to Theresa Helburn on September 3rd, 1926: "I don't at all know how to tell you how pleased I am that the Guild has taken the play. Clare is pleased, too, and the baby should be. I do like working for the Guild." But a note to his agent, Harold Freedman, only ten days later indicates trouble: "I don't believe in standing out too hard on cast, but I cannot face the play in hand without Clare as Christina. The clarity of her acting is the only thing that will ever keep me straight about it."

The guild was also producing in this season *The Brothers Karamazov*, written and directed by the eminent French theatrical figure Jacques Copeau (Langner, 216)—In its collective wisdom the Guild decided that it wanted Clare for *Karamazov* rather than as Christina in *The Silver Cord*, the part that Sidney had written for her. Sidney at first tried sweet reason in a letter to Theresa Helburn on September 14th:

> The three years I've been puttering and working over the play, I've identified Christina with Clare. That may be because she told me the story in the first place. At any rate, she and the character became one while I was writing and remain one for me now....

Clare Eames and Lynn Fontanne face up to each other in Jacques Copeau's production of *The Brothers Karamazov*, produced by the Theatre Guild during its first repertory season. (Courtesy of the New York Public Library.)

    What I see in Christina is a middle western, free-thinking scientist of considerable ability, rare womanliness (as distinguished from mere femininity), honesty, a keen and perceptive intelligence and immense courage. I made Christina a middle westerner because of the middle western thing that Clare is herself—how she would hate me if she knew that! The play asks Christina to top an emotional scene with a more exciting presentation of an idea, or series of ideas, which must also be both clear and absolutely convincing. It's Clare's cool and impersonal clarity that I want in the play quite as much as her emotional power and charm. She has a gift for infecting people with intellectual excitement. Apart from my admiration for her acting, I should say that every line of the part falls naturally from her lips and that she is quite the perfect type physically.

Toward the end he adds, "So do let Clare play Christina even if she doesn't much want to—which I think she may from the way she read it to me."

Even though Sid and Clare view her as filled with terrors, the Clare

Alfred Lunt and Clare Eames in Sidney Howard's *Ned McCobb's Daughter*, a successful production in the Theatre Guild's first repertory season. (Courtesy of the New York Public Library.)

he paints in *The Silver Cord*, strong, independent, insightful, intelligent, and fearless, is much more like the picture of her in the short story about Clare's dream he had planned at about the same time as he was working on this play.

Sidney's charming letter apparently at first proved persuasive, but then the guild changed its mind. On October 14th Sidney writes to Harold Freedman:

Laura Hope Crews and Margalo Gillmore in Sidney Howard's *The Silver Cord*, another success of the Theatre Guild's first repertory season. (Courtesy of the New York Public Library.)

>Clare has shown me the light. If I try to force the Guild to cast her as Christina I will succeed only in making her position on the board a difficult one....
>
>The Guild in refusing Clare the part in spite of the assurances they gave me two weeks ago upsets all my visions of three years standing on the play. In insisting on [Philip] Moeller's direction, furthermore, they let

me in for a kind of irritation which I cannot undertake under the circumstances....

Therefore I ask you to make it quite clear to them that I cannot participate in any portion of the production of "The Silver Cord" and to take back the scripts of "Ned McCobb's Daughter" and to send them to Hopkins for Miss [Laurette] Taylor....

Don't think this is a pet. I am looking for the outfit that will cause me the least trouble ... and, in the case of "Ned McCobb's Daughter" I won't buy a pig in a poke again.

No hard feelings. I'm tired and bored to death, that's all....

Sidney liked his business dealings to be straightforward and snareless, but in this case, as in many others, he hit nothing but a maze. Things became so bad that he unsuccessfully tried to buy back *The Silver Cord* from the guild. He concludes a letter to Maurice Wertheim, a member of the Theatre Guild board, with the remark: "The lesson of *The Silver Cord*, however, persuades me that there is small probability of the Guild's agreeing with me on any of the more ambitious ventures I now have in my mind" (November 18th, 1926).

Amazingly, on November 22nd he received from Warren P. Munsell, business manager of the guild, a letter of agreement to give the guild "first reading option on the first three plays you write after NED MCCOBB'S DAUGHTER...." Further the letter adds,

> It is understood that in the event of a collaboration, the Guild agrees to meet any reasonable special terms that may be demanded by the collaborator. It is also understood in the event that Mr. Howard does not wish any of the above mentioned plays on which he is giving the option to be included in the repertory system, the Guild either agrees that they will produce the play outside of repertoire in the usual consecutive manner or else will release their option on the play.

Sidney signed the agreement. Although we have no direct evidence to show it, this astonishing outcome undoubtedly had Clare as its cause. As in the case of his agreeing to cast another actress as Christina in *The Silver Cord*, Clare probably showed him the light. To help persuade him she surely used her influence with the board to have John Cromwell, Sidney's preference, replace Philip Moeller as director of *The Silver Cord*. What she gained was the prestige of retaining for the guild an already accomplished American dramatist.

The argument Sidney used to himself for signing with the guild may be found in an entry in a diary he had just started. The date of the entry is January 29th, 1927, after the double success of *Ned McCobb's Daughter* and *The Silver Cord*. Although he talks himself into signing with the guild, yet the idea of continuing to work with the group sticks in his craw:

> I try to look squarely at my resentment of the Guild. There is no doubt that the Guild subscribers saved "Ned McCobb's Daughter" from the fate to which the critics consigned it. ... I should not resent the Guild except for Helburn's shiftiness and Moeller's stupidity. They are the best of a bad lot as I have always said and I should be foolish to break with them however much I may dislike them. House dramatist to the Guild will do more for me than I can do for myself. The position is in the best tradition....

Clare's traces can be seen in those words, with their pragmatism mixed with a sense of tradition. But by March 5th, after returning from Nassau, undoubtedly for health reasons, he is ready to break with the guild. But by this time Clare herself has decided to cut her ties to the guild.

> I am reopening the subject of the Guild's option on my future plays. Now that I am home from Nassau and find Clare severing her connection with the Guild, I feel the discomfort of the Guild's option more than ever. As Maurice Wertheim said to you and me on the day we signed the option: "We want to make you our author." That ought to be a fine position in the best of the old theatric tradition of Shakespeare and Co. Unfortunately personal reasons make it a very unhappy position for me. I am not saying that I would not gladly work my head off for most of the Guild directors, but not for those with whom I come most into contact [the diary entry indicates that these are Helburn and Moeller] and, if I am to have a boss, I must have one I can respect. Nor can I undertake work permanently in an organization which is maintained in such a consistently unhappy state of mind as the Guild's permanent company. I am tired of acting as a clearing house for complaints against the management, complaints made by actors and stage hands alike with the most boring and vituperative frequency.... I am projecting things a good deal more ambitious and subtle than any I have tried so far and I've got to have peace of mind.... You know that I have had it in my mind ever since I began to think out "AMERICANS IN ROME" and the expressionistic religious play. I daresay that my feelings, like Clare's experience, arise less from any immediate act of the Guild's than from the very nature of the Guild's organization and spirit.... You must also tell her [Helburn] that I don't want to break with the Guild and that I hope to bring them many more plays for their permanent company and even for repertory.... I took my chances as brave as they took theirs this year and they will have no cause for hard feelings. I haven't so much talent that I can work in the Guild atmosphere or risk a repetition of this season.... I trust you to explain it to Terry. I had much not see her myself. The Guild office gives me such heebeejeebies that one visit there suffices to wreck my work for days [letter to Harold Freedman].

The Theatre Guild refused to release him from his contract, dejecting him still further. Despite his double success the season has so far been so deep an emotional trial for Sidney that it caused an edginess and uncertainty equaled only by that which he felt when he had returned from the war. His letters continued to show him dispirited and disillusioned with the theater even though his theatrical imagination remained rich and fertile, as indicated by his reference to the two ambitious plays further down the line. Even now he is working on *Salvation*, a collaboration with Charles MacArthur, and *Yellow Jack*, which supposedly is a collaboration with Paul de Kruif based on a chapter from the latter's *Microbe Hunters* but in fact is a play he is writing entirely on his own. He also started a drama for Clare, which eventually becomes, in 1933, *Alien Corn*, produced by and starring Katharine Cornell (letters to Harold Freedman, March 5th 1927; HH, March 15th, 1927; John Cromwell, April 22nd, 1927). Yet he continues unhappy and restless in the theater.

On June 12th, 1927 he writes to his mother:

> I am continually beset by the idea that my career as a dramatist is ended and I haven't much notion of what comes next. It isn't that I feel any loss of power, but a decided loss of impulse toward the theatre. I am beginning to believe, too, that the interesting place to be, from this time forward, is not the theatre but the motion pictures. All of this may be the outcome of this year's experience with the Theatre Guild, with all its unpleasant coloration. Still, I should like the theatre to see me through this year and then to release me for some less arduous and vexatious form of writing. I owe Clare one more part, having promised it, but I don't know.

He seems to be prophetic about his writing for films, for the next year he goes to Hollywood to become one of the early and most eagerly sought-after writers for the talkies. But now he faces the immediate future. Although several possibilities present themselves, he and Clare decide upon a London production of *The Silver Cord*, where she can play the part of Christina that had been written for her and thus introduce herself to London theatergoers. For anglophiles like Clare and Sidney, this looked like a great year for both if the play is successful. On June 20th Sidney writes of his plans to his mother:

> We sail on the first [of August] and go right to Eddie Knoblock's charming house in Montague Place, which he rents us, with cook and butler, for $40.00 a week, heat included. It is situated, for the baby's particular benefit, two minutes from Regent's Park.... If it [the play] does go, we spend the winter in London. I expect to return to this town [New York] immediately "The Silver Cord" opens to produce "Yellow Jack" and if things go rightly, "Salvation."

Sidney then looked forward to a 1927–1928 winter in London with only a short foray into New York for the production of perhaps two plays.

Sidney would arrive in London with clouds of glory trailing him. Although his relationship with the guild was strained for almost the entire season, his two plays for the company helped fill its coffers and his own. *Ned McCobb's Daughter* has a modern theme, plunking down a New

York lower–East-side bootlegger in the midst of native Mainers and richly develops the contrast in character and morals between the two types but eventually finds its way to melodrama and sentimentality. John Mason Brown in his *Theatre Arts Monthly* review recognizes the drama's major problem as well as its virtues:

> The pitfall for this genre lies not in its nearness to reality, however, but in its nearness to the crude devices of the domestic melodramas and rural comedies from which it has sprung. In *Ned McCobb's Daughter*, for example, Sidney Howard is often more than perilously close to the oldest tricks of the Down-East melodramas. He has his half mad old Sea-Dog, who murmurs snatches from chanties and dies of a stroke at the end of the first act. He has the city guy and the country girl and the local constabulary, too. But he manages, by the pungency and honesty of his characterization, to rise above these reminiscent dramatic means. If the play is disappointing as a play, and it undoubtedly is, it is because Mr. Howard, who can write with the best of them in our theatre, is much more concerned with making a "show" out of it than a play. It has stretches of such good and salty writing that it is doubly exasperating to find that all of its realism is but the preamble to another one of those silly little fairy tales which choke our stages. Its skillful contrast of New England cupidity and conscience, with the unctuous crookedness of the East Side is wasted, and almost out of place, in such hokum [February 1927th, 96].

The praise that John Mason Brown mixes with the blame was typical of virtually all of the reviewers, who showed great respect for Sidney's ability at characterization and dialogue. According to a letter to Arthur Hobson Quinn, Sidney thought the play the "best I have done" (December 8th, 1926). To his friend and former teacher, the poet Leonard Bacon, he wrote, "The play, I am glad to say, seems a success, though the intellectuals don't care for it. Some of them say it is a tragedy and others that it is a melodrama. I don't mind. I meant it to be a vehicle for Clare and by God it is that and no mistake" (December 1st, 1926).

The Silver Cord was much more than a vehicle for an actress, albeit the wife of the author. It took away the breath of audiences and critics alike with its bold Freudian, dramaturgically sound treatment of an Oedipal situation. Its characterizations and language were pointed and direct, its illustrative situations filled with tension and, interestingly, with humor, his portrait of the mother drawn with compassion as well as with acid.

"Howard wrote at least part of his autobiography in his masterpiece, *The Silver Cord*...," wrote Lawrence Langner (218), and Brian Aherne confirms this when he remarks, "Howard derived the play from his own experience...." Both observers speak with some authority because Langner, of course, was at the very center of Theatre Guild operations and Aherne was to become Clare Eames's lover (156).

But neither of these men could possibly have believed *The Silver*

Cord to be literal autobiography. Mrs. Howard was no Mrs. Phelps. Whereas Mrs. Phelps was married briefly and disappointingly, Mrs. Howard loved her husband and had a fulfilled married life for over twenty years. So far as we know, she did not try to prevent Sidney's marriage nor did she try to break it up, certainly not consciously. Even before Sidney was married, she tried to live a life of her own, taking the Dalcroze exercises, working away at her piano, and having women in to tea. After Sidney's wedding she very much lived a life of her own. Even though she wished to keep an eye on Sidney and Clare, still it had to be at a distance, for she traveled a good deal of the time.

Nor was Sidney a David Phelps, the son who marries a woman research biologist. Where David wavers, wondering whether his loyalty belongs to Christina, his wife, or to his mother, Sidney was unswervingly devoted to Clare. Further, Sidney had a long history of breaking away from his mother, leaving Berkeley by going to Harvard, afterward entering first the ambulance corps and then the air corps against his mother's wishes. Sidney also had in Jean an alternative mother.

Still, a very strong bond attached the mother and son. While they shared an apartment in New York, he writes her a "bedtime" letter in her absence, detailing his various activities as though recounting them for her before retiring for the night. In the first days of his marriage he is unexpectedly "devastated by ... an inundation of loneliness" for his mother. Jean's 1923 letter to Sidney about the disposal of Bruce's inheritance shows Sidney to have been the object of his mother's constant favoritism.

That the play had a deeply psychological and emotional impact for him is shown when he says in a letter to Jean, written on June 30th, 1926, that he "had to get it [the play] off my chest where it has been causing me considerable discomfort since Clare put the germ of it into my system on the train between Innsbruck and Salzburg back in 1923."

Sidney describes the play to his mother in the following fashion:

> The story being drawn, as I think I told you, from Clare's family connections, the Hydes of Bath. Briefly, Mrs. Phelps, a woman of 50 to 55, finds herself unable to face the marriage of her two sons, David and Robert. David is already married and Robert is engaged. Both of them have picked charming girls. David's wife is a research biologist by profession. Robert's fiancée, a sweet, human young thing. Mrs. Phelps' trouble is that she was unhappily married and lost her husband five years after her marriage and has turned for romance to her sons with rather disastrous results for them. David, a strong person, has managed to keep a kind of balance but Robert is just about a Douglas Soule [?, presumably a person totally dependent on his mother]. The play is the story of how the mother breaks up her sons [*sic*] marriages and is the study of a woman who, having given all her life

to her children, has absolutely no resource within herself except to demand her children give up their lives to her (August 14th, 1926).

While Helen Howard, so far as we know, made no attempt to break up her son's marriage, she also did little to maintain harmony between herself on the one hand and Clare and Sidney on the other. At first trouble does not seem to be altogether her fault. Apparently Clare and Sidney, perhaps to keep her at a distance, did not send her a Christmas card in 1922, the first year of their marriage. It seems incredible that they did not, Jean cautions Sidney against such behavior, and we can understand Mrs. Howard's chagrin. More important was her sense of discomfort in their house. Although she had been on the easiest terms with her son, and he had come and gone as he pleased, it was her house. Now she had to face her son in his own house, which was also his wife's. The adjustment could not have been easy, especially since he was now her only son.

In her desire for friendly relations she continues to try to be their patron, thus using, according to Jean's 1923 letter, her old ways of entrapment. She offered to drive them around Europe during their 1923 sojourn, and Sidney resorted to lying to her so that he and Clare could go be by themselves. They did visit her in Paris, and Clare seems to be the soul of courtesy to her mother-in-law. When she gets the sudden call back to Hollywood for *Dorothy Vernon*, she writes from London:

> Dear Mrs. Howard,
>
> I hate having to trundle off to America like this without having seen you again. We had planned to come to London by way of Paris from Prague, but found that the trains were suspended owing to the occupation of the Ruhr. And then I was summoned to Hollywood—post-haste and sail the day after to-morrow. Your summer has, I know, been beautiful—and may you continue to enjoy yourself as you have done.
>
> Love to you, dear Mrs. Howard, and again regrets that I have to go without seeing you from
>
> Yours affectionately
Clare

Later that same year when Helen Howard went to visit Clare and Sidney in Hollywood, Clare writes again:

> Dear Mrs. Howard—
>
> Welcome! When you are quite ready, I hope you will come right to my rooms—where I have to stay most of the time.
>
> Love
Clare

But Sidney's New Year's Day letter to Jean in 1926 shows the basic antagonisms at work:

> Mother stayed east in order to spend Christmas with us and wanted us at her house, but we have a lot of nice, homeless youths who always come to us and she wouldn't come. First she said she would and then she said she wouldn't and then she said she would and then, after all, she didn't and thus cast the proverbial pall of family happiness over all present by making Clare and me feel that we had somehow failed to realize how nearsighted she is.... She does let people know the unpleasant truth of her feelings. That is called candor in some circles. As her telling Clare that Sam would have succeeded if some one else had played the part. Only less frankly and more brutally phrased than that.... Mother made me furious with the way she talked about Clare and Sam, which had just closed.... Your letters always kid me about "in-laws". If you knew what a saint Clare is and what she puts up with and how it spoils everything from which Mother cannot be excluded and how tragic it is for Mother and how unnecessary. But there you are and she doesn't belong here and there's nothing to be done about it because the one thing about which nothing ever can be done is people. Love and happy New Year.

Sidney adds a handwritten postscript: "What a depressing letter!"

Mrs. Howard must have thought hard about the disastrous Christmas, for Sidney writes to Jean on February 10th: "Mother seems very well. She came here to dine the other night, ate hearty and stayed late. In fact she is suddenly becoming a very different person again, liking the baby and everything."

So at the time of the production of *The Silver Cord* relations between the young couple and Mrs. Howard seem to have stabilized. Yet, of course, *The Silver Cord* represents a lifetime of strong attachment and bitter feeling. While it is not a literal transcription of Sidney's life with his mother and the couple's life with her, it is a metaphor for it. Not accidentally the part of Christina, the wife of the son who escapes the mother, was written for Clare; it is she who in the last act makes a long speech denouncing Mrs. Phelps's kind of mother love, a speech balder in the original manuscript than it was in the theater. For example, the play in print has Christina say, "[D]own, down in the depths of her, grown man that you are, she still wants to suckle you at her breast!" (91). But in the original manuscript Christina says: "[D]own in the depths of her, she wanted to sleep with you herself.... Both medicine and the classics have a name for your trouble, Mrs. Phelps. They call it 'incest'" (III-23). While Clare surely never spoke such words about Sidney and his mother, and had no reason to, yet she surely understood and may well have expressed the Freudian implications of her husband and his mother.

Sidney "would disdain to call" Mrs. Phelps's trouble—or rather her son's—an Oedipus complex (Barrett H. Clark, "Broadway Censorship and a Couple of New Plays," *Drama*, 6, 17). Sidney always insisted that he liked to tell stories of American life, not propound theses or psychological theories. But of course Sidney knew Freud—in 1922 he called *Bewitched* a Freudian fairy tale. But although Sidney's refusal to admit Freud's influence on *The Silver Cord* is altogether too ingenuous, we can understand why he firmly took that stand. For while he may have read Freud, the drama had been worked up from his soul.

Sidney believed that rather than his having sketched his characters from books, good books reflected what he had learned from life. In a letter to John Farrar on August 30th, 1926, he writes that the play is "as you say, appalling, though I did not, in the beginning, intend it to be so. But as it went on and Mrs. Phelps got underway, I began seeing more and more like her and, even, more and more of her in normal mothers." He then goes on to quote from Jung's *Psychology of the Unconscious*, which seems to confirm his observations: "Americans, as a result of the extreme detachment from the father, are characterized by a most enormous mother complex which, again, is associated with the especial social position of women in the United States." Sidney believed then that he did not derive his characters from books but rather that good books like Jung's show his picture to be valid.

At first the play gratified him. On June 17th, 1926, he writes to Roger Burlingame: "I have done with THE SILVER CORD and a nasty little tidbit it is, although mostly funny and very true." On August 3rd in a letter to his mother he seems to think even more highly of the play: "Yesterday Clare read me 'The Silver Cord' and it impressed me considerably as very much the best and deepest thing I have written and as likely to make me no money at all. It will certainly out-do any play of recent years in causing discussion...." But by December 8th, perhaps because of his production troubles with the Theatre Guild, he writes to Arthur Hobson Quinn, "Let me know if you want to see a manuscript of 'THE SILVER CORD'. I am not printing it. [He did.] It is likely to make a good deal of a stir in certain feebly intellectual circles, but it has no real merit." In addition to his having had Theatre Guild problems with the drama, he may have fallen out of love with a play with which he had been passionately in love. Perhaps too he felt as though he had exposed himself in public.

Whatever Sidney's feeling about the play, the critics received it with almost universal praise. They lauded its dramaturgy, its dialogue, its characterization, its wisdom, its wit. Apparently they, like the audience, were stunned by the impact of the play. Burns Mantle, for example, in the *New York Daily News* on December 21st, 1926, wrote:

> Hereafter, I'm thinking, when folks talk of the really fine things the Theatre Guild has done, Sidney Howard's "The Silver Cord" will be one of the first of the plays to be mentioned.

> It ranks with the best of the subsidized productions and with the finest of the dramas the theatre of this town has produced over a stretch of years. It is technically about as finished a job as "Craig's Wife" [by George Kelly, produced in the previous season]; it is even more perfectly acted, and it has a stronger emotional grip.

Joseph Wood Krutch in *The Nation* typically lauds the play while noting its Freudian underpinnings: "In 'The Silver Cord' ... Sidney Howard dramatizes a complex and does it more successfully than anyone else has succeeded in doing since Freud first presented the playwright with a new implement of analysis" (January 5th, 1927, 20–21).

But it is again Stark Young's review that is the most interesting because he takes on full tilt the effect of the comic aspects of the play:

> Miss Laura Hope Crews [who personally and as an actress became a favorite of Sidney] shows sound discernment in giving the note that she does to her portrayal of this mother in Mr. Howard's play. There are those in the audience, no doubt, who think she exaggerates, makes the character much too extreme; and there are those, very likely, who resent the touch of wit or absurdity that she gives to her characterization. But if you have the faculty of hearing the lines in themselves, of making a division between the role and the performance, a distinction between what you see on the stage and the written text of the part, you will appreciate the intelligence and the technical security with which Miss Crews establishes the personage on whom the entire play hangs and the discussion centres.

After giving the plot of the play, Young continues:

> To return, then, to Miss Crews and her interpretation, it is clear that this woman with the extremes that are given her in the lines ... must either be taken as fairly absurd or as a diseased and ominous figure. But for the last to be true and to be taken at the full seriousness of its import, the entire play would have to be deepened and darkened in tone. The dramatic substance would have to be subtly and continuously deeper than it is in The Silver Cord.
>
> But this is not the case in the play; and so it remains to some extent slightly farcical. Its extremes in detail and motivation go quite beyond its substance. No little of its terrific matter and of its powerful motives are used incidentally; tremendous forces out of life are invoked and are managed with great boldness, but both these forces and this boldness remain to a considerable extent incidental.
>
> Miss Crews is right to put that wit into it, to let you know that her character is somewhat absurd and foolish, a woman gifted with words and persuasion, no doubt, but not—in this play at least—to be taken at the full weight of the evil she may work.

When Stark Young talks of the tremendous forces of life that are invoked but used only incidentally, he undoubtedly means that the implications of those invoked forces are not worked through. But the serious implications and the comic are both worked through as we see at the end of the play in Mrs. Phelps's incantatory recitation of its final lines and in her afterthought:

> And you must remember what David in his blindness has forgotten. That mother love suffereth long and is kind; envieth not, is not puffed up, is not easily provoked; beareth all things; believeth all things; hopeth all things; endureth all things.... At least, I think my love does! Robert, "*engulfed for ever*," replies and closes the play with "Yes, Mother."

Clearly, Sidney intended the play to be both comic and serious. He labeled the play a comedy in both the program and in the printed text. He saw the horrific effects of the likes of Mrs. Phelps. But he did not intend the play to be tragic. He did not wish to write a modern *Oedipus*. Nor did he write, as a London critic wished he had, in the modern Strindbergian vein. Sidney, unlike O'Neill, stands very far from Strindberg. Although Sidney admits that his dram is "appalling," it is essentially comic. The movement of the play, as it should, tells us the reason. Escape from the mother is possible. While Robert is indeed swallowed up, David leaps the fence constructed by his mother and runs off with Christina. Thus *The Silver Cord* reflects Sidney's own grittily optimistic temperament and the course of his own life in which he emerged more or less whole. If his mother tried to keep him always as her "boy," his own will and various forces in his environment worked in the opposite direction. If he could manage to break away, many others also can, and the Oedipal mother therefore does not have to appear as fatal. Instead she is the monster who sometimes misses, a comic grotesque.

If *The Silver Cord* is to be likened to the work of any other author, it is to Ibsen, one of Sidney's favorites from the time of his adolescence. A number of reviewers were quick to point out the resemblance, most perspicaciously Joseph Wood Krutch, although he does not actually mention Ibsen in his review. But when he applies the term "transvaluation of values" to *The Silver Cord*, we must immediately think of the importance in Ibsen of reordering principles of behavior. For that is precisely what Sidney calls for in *The Silver Cord*. But there is an important difference between Ibsen and Sidney Howard in *The Silver Cord*. When we are finished with an Ibsen play, much remains ambiguous. Nora in *A Doll's House* may be right when she stresses her infantilism under the rule of her husband, but was she right, for example, to walk out on her children and leave them in the clutches of the very people who kept her a child? Dr. Stockmann in *An Enemy of the People* may be right about the crass, murderous materialism of the town in which he lives, but is his rousing credo at the end of the play, "He is strongest who stands alone," heroic or foolish? And these are the least ambiguous of Ibsen's great dramas. Ibsen may have his final-act rational discussions, but if they settle any of the issues in his dramas, they serve only to open new ones.

Not so with *The Silver Cord*. In the play's final discussion little doubt remains where Sidney stands and how the audience is supposed to feel. First Christina makes charges against Mrs. Phelps:

> Can she deny that her one idea is to keep her sons dependent on her? Can she deny that she opposes any move that either one of you makes toward independence? Can she deny that she is outraged by your natural impulses toward other women?
> You can deny it until you're black in the face: every accusation is true! You belong to a type that's very common in these days, Mrs. Phelps—a type of self-centered, self-pitying, son-devouring tigress.
> Oh, there are normal mothers around: mothers who *want* their children to be men and women and take care of themselves; mothers who are people, too, ... and not be forever holding on to them and pawing them and fussing about their health and singing them lullabies and tucking them up as though they were everlasting babies!
> But you're *not* one of the normal ones, Mrs. Phelps! Look at your sons, if you don't believe me. You've swallowed Robert up until there's nothing left of him but an effete make-believe.... And Dave! ...How he survived it all is beyond me. If you're choking a bit on David now, that's my fault because you'd have swallowed him up, too, if I hadn't come along to save him! Talk about cannibals! You and your kind beat any cannibals I've ever heard of! And what makes you doubly dangerous is that people admire you and your kind. They actually admire you! You professional mothers...! [87–88].

To Mrs. Phelps's accusation that Christina does not know the difference between good and evil, the latter replies: "As a biologist, though, I do know the difference between life and death. And I know sterility when I see it. And sterility, of course is what you offer Dave! Sterility. That's your professional mother's stock-in-trade" (88–89).

Sidney does not leave Mrs. Phelps without an apologia for her life:

> I was twenty, and my husband was fifteen years older than I. Oh, thirty-five isn't old, but he was a widower, too, and an invalid. Everyone told me I'd made a great match. And I thought I had. But before we'd been married a week, I saw my illusions shattered.
> ...I knew at the end of a week how miserable and empty my marriage was....
> [H]e never dreamed of bringing the least atom of happiness into my life. Or of romance.... Only a woman who has lived without romance knows how to value it....
> That isn't true of my life, either. I found it ... and I'm proud to have found it where you say it doesn't belong ... in motherhood.... I found it in doing for them myself all those things which, nowadays, nurses and governesses are hired to do. To spare mothers! I never asked to be spared.

> Think! I was a widow, rich and very pretty, at twenty-five. Think what that means! But I found my duty and I never swerved from it.... I knew that second marriage was not for me. Not when I had my sons. I put them first, always... [89–90].

But Christina, with Clare's "cool and impersonal clarity," utterly rejects Mrs. Phelps's raison d'etre:

> I see! ... [I]t's a very plausible and effective answer. And I'm sure you mean it, and I believe it's sincere. But it is the answer of a woman whose husband let her down pretty hard and who turned for satisfaction to her sons.... I'm almost sorry I can't say more for it, but I can't.... [T]he fact remains, Dave, that she did separate you and me last night and that she separated us because she couldn't bear the thought of our loving one another as we do. And she couldn't bear that because she refuses to believe that you're a grown man with thoughts for another woman. And that's because she still wants to suckle you at her breast! [90–91].

As Krutch suggests, the case rests there, the "whole case of rationality versus feeling, the new morality versus the old." Sidney refused to make his play either tragic or Strindbergian because he saw one side—rationality and the new morality—as definitely right and partially triumphant. For David finally tears himself away from his mother and sticks with Christina. (Did Sidney recognize that David may be escaping the dominance of one mother for that of a wife who will be simply another guide, perhaps a mother replacement?)

If the drama lacks some resonance because it lacks Ibsenlike ambiguity, it is optimistic in the classic tradition of comedy where a member of the older generation is frustrated in her attempt to prevent the union of young people. At the end the union, actually a reunion, takes place, and the festivity at the end of traditional comedy is replaced by the audience's happy knowledge that a child is coming to David and Christina. Mrs. Phelps, like the old men of classic comedy, though truly threatening, turns out to be also foolish and the object of laughter because her attempt to prevent the natural forces of life, and the rules of society which reflect those forces, from working must be and can be at least partially frustrated.

The seeming problem with the play is that Sidney never blinks at the dark side. Instead of farce or constantly bubbling laughter, he gives us, as well as the triumph of the young, such a horror as the nearly successful suicide of Robert's fiancée. And, except for the sliver of laughter caused by Mrs. Phelps's "At least, I think *my* love does!" he ends with the horror of Robert engulfed forever. The resulting serio-comic tone of the entire play, which bothered some critics and seemed to them to make the play less important than it might have been, should make it more accessible to us today. For horror, more often than not in today's art, rarely stands by itself. Rather in both popular and high culture it is often mixed with the comic because we are nervous in the presence of sheer horror and are not altogether convinced of the validity of unrelieved horror. Somehow it can always be alleviated. Only the Holocaust, which occurred hidden from view, seems to stand apart from that generalization.

Yet when we read the play today, it strikes us as somewhat dated. We rarely see the type of Mrs. Phelps today, a woman who does not work and who is absolutely and romantically involved with her sons. But while a Mrs. Phelps may not exist in her extreme form admired by society generally, yet we live in a time when every mother is a mom, and we seem to have forgotten that the term "momism" and its bitter implications ever existed. Where society previously worshipped mothers, it now adores Mom, no matter who she is. Further, in this age of the constant praising of "family values," it is good to be reminded that some women who run their families manage them for their own rather than the families' welfare.

More difficult in the play today is the character of Hester, who seems to be caught between an old-fashioned and new-fashioned girl. On the one hand she says of children: "Have 'em. Love 'em. And then leave 'em be" (13). The remark in the modern fashion seems flippant but unexpectedly valid. To emphasize its validity, the analytical Christina later approvingly quotes it. On the other hand, Hester expects to be totally supported by her husband and expects to do the whole job of bringing up her children without any help from him and even support him if necessary: "You just leave things to me. If we're poor, I'll cook and scrub floors. I'll bring up our children. I'll take care of you whether we live in New York of Kamschatka. The business is up to me, Rob..." (41). Of course in a time of transition a character can be both old fashioned and modern.

Perhaps the real problem is that she wishes to sacrifice herself for Robert. He seems easy to see through. Why would she fall in love with a man who is such a Mama's boy when, according to the drama, she has had so many other men running after her? She remains something of a flaw in the play as do the two boys, especially David, who seems to be passive as the two main women duel. But the women who fight that duel, which is fought in various ways throughout the play, and their meaning, remain exciting and profound.

With the productions of *Ned McCobb's Daughter* and especially of *The Silver Cord* Sidney reached the apex of his theatrical career. He would never write another play which in the popular consciousness reached out to the forefront of the evolving American drama. After *The*

Silver Cord he seemed to be the first of those ranging under Eugene O'Neill. Neither Elmer Rice nor Maxwell Anderson nor John Howard Lawson had attained quite Sidney's eminence. Robert E. Sherwood and Phillip Barry had only begun to write; S. N. Behrman had not yet been produced. Only Eugene O'Neill stood more importantly than he, and yet if Sidney continued in his own individual and courageous way he might yet grow to O'Neill's stature. That is, if he continued working in the theatre.

While Sidney's battles with the Theatre Guild did not prevent the progress of his career, Clare's reputation advanced slowly in this season of growing disillusionment with the guild. Although highly praised for her acting in *Ned McCobb's Daughter*, she did not attract in her other performances the kind of éclat an ambitious leading lady craves.

It is harder to tack down the reasons for Clare's disenchantment with the guild than those for Sidney's. The guild was foolish and shabby in its treatment of him, and its generally grizzly working conditions enhanced his disgust. With Clare we cannot specify any incidents, as we can several with Sidney, that caused her change of attitude, but we do have a story to tell albeit a somewhat mysterious one.

At first Clare seemed to be getting along fine with the guild. "Clare's Guild job is working out admirably," writes Sid to his mother on September 26th, 1926, "—at least, she seems happier now than she has been over her work for a long time." Sid wrote this after his troubles with the guild began; that is, after the guild refused to cast Clare as Christina. But with Clare's happiness at stake and perhaps her good health—she had just recently suffered through a painful afterbirth operation in the depths of the city's heat—we can understand that Sidney would surrender the fight on *The Silver Cord* and even sign the option contract with the guild.

Some time after the opening of *The Brothers Karamazov* on January 3rd, 1927, she writes to Sidney from the dressing room of the theater as she prepares to play for a matinee, "On Wednesday I had a board meeting a most exciting one from 1 to 5:30...." So in January and perhaps a little later she seemed to be happily engrossed in guild affairs. But by February 25 she is ready to leave the guild. "I may add," writes Sid to John Cromwell on that date, "that Clare and Margalo both seem to be leaving the Guild (confidential)." Margalo Gillmore does not leave the guild, but Clare does. However, it takes almost three more weeks before her abandoning the guild was made public.

Her final decision came at the end of a process, part of which, of course, entailed discussions with Sidney. But he did not have the same effect in persuading Clare to remain with the guild as Clare did in convincing Sidney to give up the fight about *The Silver Cord*. An entry in his diary of March 2nd, 1927, reads:

> A day of folly with little sense in it. ...Some time of trying to represent to Clare and for her benefit the possible advantages of continuing as a member of the Guild's permanent company if the Guild directors could be held down somehow by contract terms. I succeeded only in making her unhappiness under them more vivid. I did write out for her a letter embodying my idea of the conditions upon which work for them might be less than a torture, but she is probably right in her determination to escape them at any cost and will hardly present even those conditions.

A March 3rd entry shows Sidney urging a conclusive decision basing it solely on Clare's future pleasure in her work, which can be found only away from the guild: "Clare and [I went] together to lunch at the Plaza where we talked further about the Guild and I kept repeating that her happiness at her work alone matters and that she must quit them if she cannot feel quite happy with them."

On March 15th Sidney writes to his mother: "The papers are agog over Clare's separation from the Guild...," and indeed they were. The *Herald-Tribune* quoted Clare extensively:

> "Perhaps it would be best to say," said Miss Eames, "that I am quitting the Guild because its manner of management does not conform to my idea of the way in which an art theater should be run.
>
> "Artistic freedom, that is what I want. I came to the Guild full of sweetness and light and hoping—but it is too silly to think of the freedom given players by the supposedly commercial minded, sordid managers and producers. I won't mention names, but there are several managers in that class that would give me twice the freedom that I have here.
>
> "I think the Guild has done more for the American Theater in the last few years than any other influence. Let there be no mistake about that. I have the highest admiration for its aims, its literary taste and the selection of its players.
>
> "I may be as crazy as a March hare," she said, "but I know what I want. I want to try my ideas. I can't now. I may make a fool of myself, but I at least shall make the attempt to express my ideas to reach that freedom I want" [March 15th, 1927, 24].

The Times, though its story of Clare's abandoning the guild was briefer than the *Tribune*'s, immediately ran an editorial on the subject:

> Always, just as the world gets beautifully standardized, it shows itself to be more individual than ever. As pessimists reach the peak of their complaints that everybody submits without a murmur to smug convention, and that millions of people are content to do exactly the same things as other millions, the spirit of revolt, of daring originality and of personal independence flame up afresh. A prominent actress announces that she is about to withdraw from the Theatre Guild. The reason is that she finds herself too much cramped by the regulations of the management and the producers. She longs for that perfect artistic freedom which she cannot find within the Theatre Guild. Yet if there was one thing which the Guild set

out to do, it was to encourage spontaneity, to favor the new and the experimental in drama, to be hospitable to bold innovators, and to allow genius of all kinds free scope to run and be glorified. But here it is charged with laying old fogy fetters upon its own actors.

In art this story of endless revolt and perpetual secession is old....

There seems nothing to do but to let a kindly and healing Nature have her way with all these things. She produces the 'sports' and 'freaks' in the artistic world with the same lavish hand that she does in the vegetable world and gives each one a chance to see whether it can demonstrate its right to survive. If it does, the strong probability is that it will swiftly show a tendency to revert to type. The old intense individualist will become a firm defender of group action, and the man who begins as a flaming Radical will finish as the most crusted and complacent of Tories [March 15th, 1927].

The Times's mildly ironic, essentially benign view of the matter gives no idea of Clare's emotional upheaval. And whether Clare would have become an old fogy and a firm defender of group action we do not know, for in a little over three and one-half years she would be dead.

But what new ideas did Clare wish to try? We shall never find out because her brief few years were such that they did not easily admit of experimentation. Perhaps when Clare told the *Tribune* that she wanted to try her own ideas, she had something specific in mind. On March 23rd Sidney writes to his mother, "Clare has been offered a theatre of her [own] to run which I pray God she turns down as it would drive me quite quite mad." But by the following week Sidney seems reconciled to the idea. In an April 2nd letter to John Cromwell he writes: "[A]gain I am flirting with what looks like a real proposition to start a highbrow theatre of which I would be one of the directors and Clare another in a Broadway house backed by a Broadway manager." Whether her quitting the guild came before or after the offer from the Broadway manager we do not know. At any rate, the proposition never materializes, and we shall never know what ideas Clare wished to try.

As to the lack of freedom of which Clare complains, that is almost as mysterious as her new ideas. But we can speculate in terms of what we know. For example, we know that Bobby Jones had only a loose grasp of the technical aspects of directing and that Clare apparently imported him nevertheless for the production of *Candida* that she organized. She seems to have liked having a director who had insightful ideas about a play but who gave her leeway in developing a role. Thus, she obviously went so much her own way in her portrayal of Lady Macbeth that her style clashed with that of the star. Again, *Hedda Gabler* was directed by Dudley Digges, with whom she had lately codirected *The Wild Duck*, implying once more that she had a free hand in developing her role; perhaps she even worked with Digges on the production as a whole. The kind of control she seems to have desired over a production is suggested by Harold Freedman, who thought that the director of *Lucky Sam McCarver* should be someone whom she could prompt. The director turned out to be her husband, who had never previously guided a show and who undoubtedly was grateful for her advice. We also know that Bobby Jones advised him to let Clare fix what he believed to be the abominably lit production.

Clare perhaps had thought that she could work out some similarly loose arrangement with Philip Moeller, who directed most of the plays for the Theatre Guild. Moeller was one of the original founders of the guild, himself a dramatist, and a member of the board. He had successfully shaped the production of *They Knew What They Wanted* and had less happily guided Clare through the double bill of Shaw plays. But despite what should have been a good experience with the director of *They Knew What They Wanted*, Sidney, as we saw, had only contempt for him, raged when he thought that Moeller would direct *The Silver Cord*, and was one of the chief reasons that Sidney wished to quit the guild.

Clare's experience with Moeller at the beginning of the 1926–1927 season did not bode well. She describes in an undated letter to Sidney, who is still at Wiscasset, the rehearsals of Franz Werfel's *Juarez and Maximilian*, the first production of the season:

> My own dear love –
>
> Yesterday we began at 10:30 and by 4:30 when we called it a day there wasn't a living person on the field. Here are some of the questions Phil asked—
>
> 1. What is the difference between confrere and convert?
> 2. What was the Conservative party?
> 3. Was the Archbishop of Mexico a Conservative?
> 4. What is a General of Jesuits?
> 5. What is twenty cavalry?
> 6. What is military police?
>
> etc. etc. etc. ad infinitum et ad nauseum. The company by this time is so utterly dispirited that they have reached the giggling stage. I sit in front with Moeller and Romney (who is the Mexican expert thank God) but really it is disheartening. By noon they are nothing but bolsters thrown on benches. All resemblance to humanity has left them entirely. It is simply so *BORING* that even Alfred [Lunt] has succumbed.

She ends her letter thus:

> I must rush off to rehearsal now my darling. I think and think and think of you all the time—you and my Pearly of Price and I must cheer up or at

any rate not try to bear the whole weight of the world on my little mind for it will crack. For the whole thing is *incredibly* funny.

Love love love
Clare

We can be sure that Clare would have approved of the cast learning thoroughly the Mexican historical and religious background of the play, but apparently it was Moeller's carrying on in his pedantic, dull, and static way that bothered her.

Clare Eames as Carlotta and Alfred Lunt as Maximilian in Franz Werfel's *Juarez and Maximilian*, produced by the Theatre Guild in 1926. Bette Davis played Carlotta and Brian Aherne played Maximilian in a 1939 movie version, called *Juarez*. (Courtesy of the New York Public Library.)

In the seating arrangement here she sits in front with Moeller and the Mexican expert. Is that because she is a kind of codirector or because she is a member of the board? At any rate, there she is a major figure in the company. We can be sure she liked that position, but she knew her place as second to Moeller and could not prevent him from stupefying the company during rehearsals. Perhaps, like Sidney, she found the cast of Moeller's mind intolerable and equally so the thought of having to work with him for the foreseeable future.

Hampering her may also have been the behavior of the guild's board during rehearsals. Jared Brown explains:

> The Theatre Guild had a well-deserved reputation for strained and tense rehearsal periods, largely due to its unique method of collaborative creation. All the members of the Board were welcome to attend rehearsals and to pass along criticism and advice to the actors and the director. This was intended to be constructive, of course, but it frequently resulted in a bewildered group of artists. And there were special runthroughs of each play, the first usually given two weeks before opening night, the second a week later, and often a third at the final dress rehearsal, that were known as "managers" rehearsals. The members of the Board attended these rehearsals equipped with pads and pencils. As the rehearsal progressed, they took copious notes. Afterward they climbed the stairs to the stage and sat around with the play's director. Normally, the actors would be dismissed. In most circumstances the author of the play would be present.... Each Board member spoke frankly—often brutally—about his or her reactions [128].

With such a circus it is a wonder that anyone wished to work for the guild, but more so is it a wonder that Sidney and Clare, both having had experience with the company, wished to sign with them at all, especially on a permanent basis. But perhaps doing three plays in a row in the 1926–1927 season showed Clare the folly of her ways.

The guild had another explanation for Clare's defection. Sidney writes to his mother on May 4th:

> We keep well, though Clare is very tired and more and more distressed by the Guild's bad manners. They have taken to lying about her, now, and to misrepresenting the facts of her resignation. I don't know why people can't say that somebody doesn't like them. I know plenty of people who don't like me and it doesn't make me mad. But they go around saying how much trouble they had with Clare's wanting to play all the leading parts and refusing to work on anything they wanted her to do and how they had to fire her and it is beginning to look as though she will have to threaten them with a lawyer.

In trying to understand the motives of any player we must never discount her being disgruntled with the parts she has been offered, especially if it turns out that she has not been reviewed well in them or that she was reviewed well in a play so poorly received that her acting warranted little discussion.

The guild, having made an exciting production of Franz Werfel's *Goat Song* in the previous season, bought his historical drama about the brief reign, sponsored by Napoleon III, of Maximilian and Carlotta, emperor and consort, in Mexico. Although a few critics in the intellectual journals treated the drama with respect, the ponderous movement of the play killed it for the daily reviewers. Clare, playing still another queen, fared well with the *Times*—"As the Empress, Miss Eames catches the dignity of her part, the intelligence and the high spirit. Indeed, she molds her several appearances into a shapely design in which every detail speaks with eloquence" (October 12th, 1926, 31)—but the other journalists did not single her out one way or another. However, the play was so unsuccessful that it failed to become part of the Theatre Guild repertory program.

But Clare did have one great success that season. It was in Sidney's *Ned McCobb's Daughter*, in which she was again paired with Alfred Lunt. While the drama itself did not fare especially well with critics, Clare (and Lunt, too) received almost uniformly fine reviews. For example, Brooks Atkinson analyzes Clare's acting in the lead role in his Sunday *Times* "think piece":

> Fortunately, the chief roles are played brilliantly by Clare Eames and Alfred Lunt. Miss Eames is usually seen to best advantage in regal parts, like the Carlotta of "Juarez and Maximilian." As Carrie, the dowdy Down Easter, she is queenly only in the dominance of her sharp personality. Miss Eames makes the part glow by sheer intelligence in acting. She has mastered the provincial accent prescribed in the text. In the composition of her role she has discovered the various elements of this gauche personality: the warmth as well as the chill, the high sense of honor, curbed by a respect for the practical; the force, caution and the native shrewdness. All these more or less conflicting qualities she expresses in a many-colored mosaic of acting—no less varied because none of the colors flames. On the surface her Carrie is a drab person, but the human fire does not burn low because it is unseen. Miss Eames manages to convey all these multiplicities faithfully without truckling for the showy applause. Her Carrie is what nowadays we enjoy calling 'vital'. When Miss Eames is suitably cast she is an actress of the first rank, whose mastery of her craft is a talisman for all interpretive actresses [December 5th, 1927, VIII, 1].

Clare had not received such an analytically laudatory review since she had acted Prossie in *Candida*. Atkinson's writing reflects the kind of excitement that makes a legendary reputation for an actress, as does the following review by Stephen Rathbun in *The New York Sun* (November 30th, 1926):

But last night was a Clare Eames evening. Her acting is something to be remembered. The heroic *Carrie* is a stellar part and I can think of no full fledged star who could have played it better, or half as well for that matter. It is a case where a part is greater than the whole, and the rest of the play sinks into insignificance beside it. While "Ned McCobb's Daughter" will not enhance the reputation of the Theatre Guild, it does bring added luster to Miss Eames as an actress.

Clare's third role during her Theatre Guild season was in Jacques Copeau's version of Dostoyevsky's *Brothers Karamazov*. Copeau had directed it in French when the Vieux Colombier played in New York for two seasons at the end of World War I, and he was now to repeat his assignment for the guild's production in English. That Copeau was attempting to lighten the technique of the American company, whose work was sometimes heavy handed, was given a good deal of attention on the theatrical pages (*New York Times*, October 26th, 1926, VII, 4; *New York Times*, November 27th, 1926, VII, 4). But whatever success he had with the actors generally does not seem to have helped Clare much. While *The Times* greeted her performance as one which displayed "dignity, precision and thorough understanding" (January 14th, 1927, 10), other reviewers did not single her out for either good or ill.

Therefore, disappointed with two of her roles, done out of the part written for her in *The Silver Cord*, a success only in *Ned McCobb's Daughter*, Clare had some reason for disgruntlement. Yet all the reasons, the parts she had and the parts she did not get, the chaotic interference of the guild's board during rehearsals, and the possible failure to work well with Philip Moeller still do not quite add up to her cry for freedom, for her vocal desire to try new ideas. The difficulties and irritations she encountered this season are the general conditions of theatrical work, and those specific to the guild she knew in whole or in part before. However, her breaking with the guild might show a general restiveness.

Nevertheless, she does not seem to have lost her faith in acting or in theatrical enterprise. At the same graduation exercise for the American Academy of Dramatic Arts in which Sidney inveighed stirringly against the forces of censorship, Clare also spoke, except that her theme concerned acting:

> Sooner or later you are going to come to the test of the actor, the fine test. You are going to be asked to appear in classics, in which other great actors and actresses have appeared. Those are the property of everyone. Those are the things for which we should work, because those are the things in which we come into comparison with the other great ones. When we make a success in "Turn to the Right," it is very pleasant and charming. If we manage to hold our own against the great actors and actresses of the past, then we can definitely say that we are part of that great tradi-

tion of the theatre. In order to fit yourselves for that final test, you have to do something more than merely escape—merely, I say because it is the most difficult thing to do, to withstand those insidious, cheap, sub-professional shibboleths of the stage—you have to make yourselves into the most sensitive intellectual instruments. Not only do you have to speak and walk,—all those things go without saying, you do that already—but you have to know the literature of your mother tongue, really know it. You have to be sensitive to music. You have to know what the great painters were doing. Yesterday I was reading in one of Shaw's essays where he says the classic drama is the drama from which you feel the great philosophy, the great poetry, and the great statesmanship of an epic emanated, and not its police court trials and its vulgar squabble. In order to be able to give that lofty thing, an actor should be like a hawk who swoops down on his prey, not like a little animal that is reaching up to get it.

Despite her bitter disappointment with the guild, Clare retained her high ideals of theater and acting and the notion that these require the actor to answer the challenge of the great roles in dramatic literature. She continued to believe that a correct preparation for such a career is one that is wider than the theatre itself, that it includes other arts as well. Perhaps, however, most important for our understanding of her emotional tendency at this time is her feeling that an actor must be like a hawk, large and fearless, not like some little scurrying animal. Perhaps it is because she has come to feel like a hawk that she felt caged by the guild and quit.

It is also possible that Clare felt caged by her marriage. While Clare's career moved forward only a little this season, she was generally accepted now as one of the most prominent young actresses of her day, the reference to her "genius" a commonplace. Also her positions in the Theatre Guild Acting Company and on the guild board secured her eminence. Lawrence Langner in his description of Clare as one whose "enthusiasms often carried us along when we began to feel tired and bedraggled" implies both the respect that the guild board felt for her and the confidence by now that she felt in herself.

That very self-confidence may have caused restiveness at home. We know from letters Sidney wrote after this season that he continued to patronize her, believing that she could not manage in a pragmatic, everyday way without his aid. It may be that she, now flying the skies as a hawk, resented Sid's attempting to force her down to earth in her private and professional life. The freedom she professed to lack at the Theatre Guild was also perhaps the freedom she lacked to try her own ideas in both parts of her life.

However, in these two years or so, things on the whole seem to be going exceedingly well for them as a married couple. Sidney enjoys his married life although in Clare's work and induced absence, life seems to lack a special edge, which, of course, shows his great need for her. In the

1926 New Year's Day letter to Jean he writes, "Life is pretty quiet while Clare is at work. I arise at 8:45, play with the baby, eat breakfast, work at the novel [*Jacob Ely*] until one. Eat lunch. Work at other things. Play squash. Dine at six. Work and read in the evenings unless the Sherwoods, who have bought a house around the corner from us, take me to a show. People come here for supper after the theatre which is fun. I go out with the dogs and buy provender at the delicatessen."

Later that year he writes similarly. "Clare being away [in the hospital for the painful post–Jennifer operation] I have been reading." He has gone through *An American Tragedy* ("it misses greatness"), *Microbe Hunters* ("super masculine bed time tales for grown ups"); nevertheless he soon will start dramatizing one chapter of it), Roger Burlingame's *Susan Shane* (he likes it "not alone because it is dedicated to me"), two Jung books ("I've eaten up Jung"), Sandburg's *Lincoln*, and Guedalla's *Fathers of the Revolution*. He then adds: "I had about concluded that one cannot write and read at the same time because I have given over reading almost completely of late years. Now I see that one cannot write, read and talk to Clare at the same time. I think I like talking to Clare best" (letter to Jean, August 16th, 1926).

Clare's letters show similar love and dependency but without the previous self-abnegation. For example, after having arrived from Wiscasset for rehearsals in New York, she writes in an undated letter:

> My darling Sidis—[a favorite loving way of addressing him]
> I got on the train numb with depression and our Pal, the over-acting conductor ... got me a compartment in the Philadelphia car where I sat and thought for two hours and then fell into an unhappy stupor. It was not sleeping really. When we get old, and begin to think that the grass is greener on the other side of the fence and that life is "nothing but" the Old Army Game we must *never never* forget the last six months ... the prismatic glow is the real thing and the dry look of things is the false one. You have made me so happy, my dearest.

There follows the previously quoted paragraph on how boringly Philip Moeller conducts rehearsals. The letter ends with "Philip Leigh [who acted with her in *Lucky Sam*] is playing Bazaine [in *Juarez and Maximilian*]; he ended up playing two other roles] and I think Monty [?] will be in the company [he was not], so that what with Dudley [Digges] and Margalo its [sic] almost the complete C. [E.] Club."

Like any intimate couple exchanging trivial and amusing news she writes:

> So far the bits of gossip are—
> 1. Conway [Tearle?] went home unexpectedly one afternoon and caught Helen in flagrant delit, which accounts for his silence.

2. Louis Calhern is brutalizing Ilka Chase.
3. Lady Lucy [?] is going to have a baby and Basil [undoubtedly Dean, who has been living in the United States) is treating her scandalously.
4. Tallu [the American actress Tallulah Bankhead, who eventually came to be greatly admired as an actress in New York and notorious for her scandalous private life] told Margalo that during rehearsal of *Rain* she had a miscarriage by Basil [undoubtedly Dean again] owing to overindulgence with one of her own sex, and Margalo had hysterics of past horror on the spot.
5. Mary Sherwood has named the dog you gave her Happiness!!!

She concludes the letter with "Fond Fond love ... to Pearlio princess beauty & Rose—" and many crosses indicate kisses.

But we see a faint sign of Sid's irritation with Clare in Sid's letter to Leonard Bacon on December 1st, 1926:

> We have had a hell of a time.... Poor Clare spent last week trying to have pneumonia and, having failed in a really big attempt, compromised on an infected frontal sinus and a temperature of 102.8 when the play [*Ned McCobb*] finally did open, Monday, after a week's postponement. In that condition, which is agony, she gave one of the most memorable performances I have ever seen and scored the hit of her life. Her success brought her temperature down to normal forthwith and she purchased a lot of clothes and hats and now feels much better.

While Sidney's account is on the whole admiring and compassionate, yet his humorous tale of Clare's illness in which she tried to have pneumonia and her immediate recovery after her successful opening-night performance implies perhaps that it would have been equally impressive without the previous hullabaloo of her illness, which scared everyone half to death and delayed the show's opening. Sidney perhaps felt that her illness was a kind of self-indulgence which she did not really require in order to give a first-class performance.

Or perhaps another way of seeing the situation, after the failure of *Juarez and Maximilian,* is that Clare might have been frightened that *Ned McCobb* would be still another failure, that its success and that of the guild's new repertory venture and the well-being of the family's finances depended on her superb performance. The weight of so much on her shoulders might have sent her into a withdrawal through illness, which we have seen before.

But Sid seemed irritated as well as sympathetic to Clare's behavior. Perhaps another sign of Sid's irritation with Clare may be found in the letter to his mother telling of the possibility that Clare might run a repertory company. He asserts that the offer's becoming a reality would drive him mad. The implication is that Clare's various theatrical activities have always driven him at least a little crazy. By the time he writes to Leonard

Bacon about it, he is indeed involved but in a straightforward fashion, as a member of the board, not merely as Clare's unpaid adviser, but he seems to have calmed down about the matter. Finally, however, neither Clare nor Sid became engaged in the enterprise, but what happened at home in the process becomes merely a matter of fruitless though suspicious speculation.

We might not have perceived either in Sidney's letter about the opening of *Ned McCobb* or in the matter of the repertory company any irritation worth noticing, for either or both might be the normal abrasiveness of two married people working together who still love each other, if it were not for two other letters, one a tantalizing missive written on January 21st, 1927, from Leonard Bacon to Clare:

> This is just a line to thank you for your hospitalities and to renew my assurance that the matter of which you spoke to me, while important to you, is nothing to be alarmed about. It has a value which you must find, and which will enrich your life in every way if you can find it. The trouble with things of this sort is that we waste great stores of perfectly good energy upon them without deriving this value which should be the reward of such a struggle. You have, in common with every other person, had a curious psychological adventure, which like every adventure has its painful side. It can do two things to you. It can make you into a neurotic or it can deepen every channel of your existence. You have intelligence more than equal to the occasion. But it may be that something else is needed, which you will have to bring up. As the function which was least differentiated in me was feeling, please do not be angry with me, if I jump to the conclusion that the same was true of you. I may of course be entirely wrong. It might equally well be a want of sensation that is a want of awareness with respect to the actual, existential fact. And like other imaginative people you may have substituted a factitious world in which you live miserably for the real world in which you are so wonderfully equipped to live outrageously happily. If I did not know how bitterly these things can hurt I should have laughed in your face about your difficulties, not from want of sympathy but because it seemed to me the baseless fabric of a vision. It seems to me that our reasoning in such difficulties is often nothing but an elaborate process of scaring ourselves. We say: "How horrible it would be, if such and such a thing were true!" Then part of our nature whispers: "It is true." Whereupon without further consideration we yell, "Oh my god!" and are picked up unconscious by the maid. Most of my horrors were due to the uncritical acceptance of the statement of the whispering voice. The interesting thing here of course is not what the voice accuses you of, but why does it accuse you at all. The answer is that that voice is a part of yourself which has been in some way abused and which is getting even in an easy way. And I think your own intelligence can develop something out of this that may be helpful. What is often called the conscience is very frequently a sharp and dishonest customer who represents not the code of conduct which you believe with your conscious mind, but some set of beliefs which live a wretched existence in a subconscious slum, which your conscious mind has never visited. Some day it might be worth your while

to see how the other half lives, what the stupid, brutal side of Clare Eames really thinks of the Clare Eames that dazzles Leonard Bacon and other intelligent young men. Don't you see, in spite of the queerness of the idea what I am getting at? When you can look at your bad aspect (By the way I've never seen it) without wincing, and accept it, then my dear you will be a very real person, a great deal realer than the author of this letter who nevertheless is really

Affectionately yours
Leonard Bacon.

Patty [Leonard's wife] joins me in love to both of you.

That psychological adventure of which Bacon speaks might be an unwanted arrival from the subconscious. It is tempting to think that it is Clare's jealousy of Sidney, which she has worked up elaborately, coming from the "slum" of her mind, or that it is some horrible fantasy of desire over which her conscience had troubled her. Or perhaps it has nothing to do with Sidney at all. In a 1923 letter from Hollywood Clare wrote of chimeras that frightened her. Perhaps in order to get rid of those Bacon, who was or would soon be analyzed by Jung, recommends that she acquaint herself with the slum of her mind, undoubtedly through psychoanalysis. In any event Clare seems deeply concerned over the psychological adventure she has had, and the experience perhaps implies difficulties in her marriage.

A second letter which perhaps indicates a strain in the union comes from Clare herself. It is dated "Thursday Matinee," and the letter shows that she will play that day in *The Brothers Karamazov*. The debut of that drama having been on January 3rd, 1927, still does not inform us of the exact date of the letter.

> My darling So—[another loving name for Sid]
>
> Since you went away I have been very very lonely for you and I have longed to hear you flouncing up and down stairs singing the litany of the Theatre Guild. I want you back even if you do break tables. And I can't tell you how I look forward to Sunday. I shall arrive at Kingston [Rhode Island; the Bacons now live at Peace Dale, Rhode Island] at 3:30 if that suits you and the dear Bacons.... Everyone seems so boring when you are not here except Jennif. pearl.... Keep on loving me. Don't, don't ever let me think you are fed to the teeth on me, even if you are, my dearest—
>
> Clare

This letter is almost as obscure in its meaning as Leonard Bacon's. We do not know what prompted Clare's remark "Keep on loving me. Don't, don't ever let me think you are fed to the teeth on me, even if you are...." That may be taken as a request or as a warning. Did a violent argument cause him to hurry to the Bacons? Has he gone to stay with the Bacons in anger and disgust at her irrational behavior or because of his chimeras, whatever they were? The matter of his breaking tables is also puzzling. Is that something he did angrily or by some accident, or is it a joke between them? Did she ask him to leave the house? Actually, the letter on the whole seems mild in tone, and so the violent argument that we have speculated that is perhaps its cause did not exist at all.

Sid, accompanied by Leonard, goes to Nassau for a brief vacation in the middle of February. On his return he writes to John Cromwell: "I had a good time in Nassau and feel better for it but something still seems to be wrong with my insides and I'll have to do something more extensive to them. Stop drinking?" (February 25th, 1927). He wrote to Bacon on the same day, thanking him for his company at Nassau: "I have got through no end of creating since yesterday noon and hatched no end of ideas, and it is clear to me that the stimulus lay not in the air of Nassau, which makes not for toiling nor spinning, nor in alcohol, which I have tried before. I should sit down and write me a Baconaid, just a little thing in polyphonic prose. In the meanwhile, bless you for giving me such a good time and bless Patty for letting you go." No mention is made of his painful insides. Perhaps then his sick stomach was not the cause of his vacation. Perhaps his writer's block came from tension at home or with the Theatre Guild, which may also have caused his painful insides.

If Clare and Sidney had not separated later in this year 1927, these letters would not have received quite their puzzled attention. In any case Clare's letter seemingly denotes a problem, surely exacerbated by the difficulties of the couple with the guild. Nevertheless on the surface things went well with them, at least by Sid's light. In a letter to his mother Sid describes the fine and jolly sendoff to Europe after the closing of *Ned McCobb's Daughter* and adds some thoughts about his relationship to Clare:

> On Saturday night, after Ned closed, Lynne and Alfred gave us a party, only eight people and the most perfect Hungarian orchestra I have ever heard. We wandered home a quarter before six. It has been dreary in Wiscasset away from Clare. What an odd thing marriage is! And what a dependent I am, perhaps! My friends amuse me and I love them but if Clare and the baby aren't within whistling distance, I can't enjoy myself. I must be in love or something [June 29th, 1927].

The only one of Clare's letters which we have from the first eight months of 1927 is the one in which she tells him that she wishes him to return even though he breaks tables.

9

Smash!

The always vigorous London theater to which Clare Eames and Sidney Howard brought *The Silver Cord* was not, however, as creatively vital as New York's. The British were bemusedly aware of the difference. A September 1st, 1927, *New York Times* article from London reports:

> AMERICAN PLAYS
> SWAMPING LONDON.
>
> The theatres of London are swamped with American plays in the biggest invasion of foreign plays in the history of English drama. Fifteen plays from the United States and three from France are booked for production during the Fall season at fashionable West End theatres.
> Recording this news somewhat lugubriously, newspapers are asking what is the matter with British dramatists and how is the slump to be explained? One paper asks if English producers are unable to discover merit in the unproduced work of British dramatists, or if they are neglecting promising material?

British producers did not entirely neglect their own. A young Noel Coward had created a *susses de scandale* with *The Vortex* three years earlier, and of the older dramatists, Somerset Maugham and Bernard Shaw were working vigorously, but audiences felt that they had come upon a brave new untried world only with production in the following year of R. C. Sherriff's *Journey's End*.

On the other hand, American plays transported to England are recognizable today, and some have even been revived: *The Butter and Egg Man*, by George S. Kaufman; *Gentlemen Prefer Blondes*, by Anita Loos and John Emerson; *The Second Man*, by S. N. Behrman, and, of course,

The Silver Cord. American musicals to be presented in London that season were by the likes of George and Ira Gershwin and Richard Rodgers and Lorenz Hart. American theatrical creativity ran rich and deep.

The reception of *The Silver Cord* for both Sidney and Clare was all that they could have hoped for. *The Morning Post* wrote, "We were easily and gladly persuaded that, whatever dramatic value we must subsequently award to the play, we were studying a situation contrived by a man of the highest intelligence" (September 14th, 1927). A.E.W. in *The Star* called it a "profoundly interesting play" (September 14th, 1927). Charles Morgan, writing for *The New York Times* from London, compared the play to one by the British dramatist H. M. Harwood that opened the night after Sidney's. "Howard's, though not the great play that it might have been, is an extremely good play, alive, thoughtful and sincere. Harwood's ... is a sad disappointment for his admirers" (October 2nd, 1927, VII, 1). *The Times* of London thought that Sidney did not in his play reach the achievement of Strindberg's *Father* but that he did create an "illusion of truth within the limits of his own scene ... and that, when a subject is as serious and difficult as his, is distinction enough" (September 14th, 1927).

Clare's reviews, if anything, were even more fulfilling. *The Times* of London, catching in Clare exactly the quality which Sidney wished her to exhibit, wrote: "Miss Clare Eames suggests in a firm, clear-cut performance the strength and controlled passion of Christina." *The Star* went further: "In Clare Eames, an American actress, who played the wife with tact and sympathy, we meet an artist of undoubted distinction. Her perfect control and poise, the beauty of her voice and expression are a delight to study." L. E. F. in *The Morning Post* saved his comment on Clare's performance to the end of his review "because it is one such as is rarely seen in this country. Miss Eames is American and the wife of the author, and to me she was utterly satisfying as the calm, collected albeit passionate woman the weight of whose will-power finally triumphs. A most notable piece of restrained, modern acting." The British critics had little difficulty in glimpsing Clare's passion beneath her cool exterior.

As gratifying as their professional lives were, their private lives were quickly breaking into bits. The rapidity with which their permanent separation came at this point indicates that their relationship had been deteriorating for some time, as perhaps Leonard Bacon's and Clare's letter quoted earlier indicate. On June 12th, 1928, Sidney wrote to his mother, "I ... feel more like myself than I have felt in two years." That suggests that the trouble between Sidney and Clare began somewhere in the middle of 1926 and developed during their Theatre Guild season, suggesting again that the restraints she thought imposed on her as part of the

Theatre Guild repertory company and as a member of its board perhaps reflected those she felt at home.

Soon after the opening of *The Silver Cord* in London Sidney left for New York on business, probably to straighten out the dispute between him and the Theatre Guild, which insisted that it had first rights on the production of *Salvation*, the drama Sidney had written with Charles MacArthur. In reading the two surviving letters of that time from Clare to Sidney, we would think that there was nothing wrong between them. They sound like all the loving letters she has written him on previous enforced separations. She misses him wildly, and she chatters on about domestic and professional matters and gossip. The first, undated, reads:

> My Darling Sidney—
>
> I have just got your note from the ship and I can't tell you how deeply I reciprocated everything you felt. Being in London, I have anodyne moments, but at night when I am alone in Montagu Place, I can't bear it. Last night I never slept until six o'clock in the morning, with two doses of allanal. Our business has been very good, and such enthusiasm. When I take my curtain they come down screaming and yelling. To-night Madge Titheradge [an English actress] was out in front with Edgar Park (Who *is* her buddy) and afterward she came to my dressing room and told me that I was one of the great artists of my day. The equal of Velasquez and Shakespeare and oh God. What rot. Aunt E. [Emma Eames] who is in a swell mood came last night and *adored* it. She says it takes her right back to her home life. She adores Lillian [Briathwaite, who acted Mrs. Phelps] and the two boys [Brian Aherne, who played David, and Denys Blakelock, who played Robert] but thinks Miss [Marjorie] Mars [in the part of Hester] is a "Pudding." She told me that I had grown enormously, but that I still brought too furious an intellectual energy to bear on the part and that I was so extraordinarily expressive that I could simply allow things to pass through me (like salts) without making any effort to project them. How right she is. To-night Lillian came back with me and we had a long talk about life and Noel Coward and Hindenburg and kindred subjects and I longed for you she was so amusing and is such a master of narrative. Tomorrow a lot of people are coming for lunch. I dread it in a way but it has to be faced.
>
> All I care about is you and Chrisy-Chro [Jennifer]—who is getting better and better I hope. Darling come back to me soon and love me and talk to me and spoil me. And tell me I'm the only one who could ever matter to you. I love you darling.
>
> Your
Clare

The second letter is similar in mood with her stream-of-consciousness chatter and sprightly asides of her own activities.

My own darling Sidis—

I can't tell you how I feel without you. Here it is ten o'clock and Aunt Emma has just left and I never went to sleep until five o'clock in the morning [when I finally took allanal] because I was thinking of your empty bed and trying to say—Sid

What?

Snoring on and then some crack that would keep me going for weeks. I was so sleepy when you left that all I felt was an awful oppression, like the feeling when you come out of an anesthetic. Is that a lump in my body or a pain? You think. But when I woke up, about twelve, it really came over me, and I felt awful. Brian (kind thing) took me to lunch and Pavlova afterward and she was very silly, except in The Swan where she was so piercingly augustly beautiful that she made me burst into floods of tears thereby disgracing the good David who pretended not to notice. (Very different from my So.) I had a quiet dinner with May [Whitty, famous British actress and Margaret Webster's mother] who was eloquent on the housing situation and went to the theatre where I didn't play very well to a *packed* house, but when we took our calls through the tabs after the second act the house cheered and cheered me. To-day, as I didn't sleep, and woke at noon to a hurried cup of coffee and then to see Aunt E. who is *adorable* and very well. We lunched together and Jennif Pearl came to call afterwards and loved our E. who let her wear her pearls and Jennif kissed her and when we got home wanted to know when "Booful Aunt Emma coming back." Then I had tea with May and Ben [Webster, May's husband, also a well-known actor] and then E. dined here and she has just gone home. I love seeing her and she is in her most adorable darling human mood. But *oh* how I miss you. You can't know how *knitted* I feel to you. If you have a pain I feel it. Darling darling. Come back soon and confound the Theatre Guild....

Goodnight my own dear husband. I shall write very soon again. I send you the best love I have.

Your
Clare

As loving as these letters are, the telegrams that she sent Sidney to New York indicate a quite different story. The first, received in New York on October 5th, 1927, reads:

> DEEPLY MOVED [letters] JUST RECEIVED NO WIRELESS RECEIVED SHIP DO NOT DESPAIR BUT AGREE JUNG ESSENTIAL BELIEVE [always] I AM HERE TO HELP YOU LOVE PLAY SALVATION WILL SEE ALEC [Woolcott] BEATRICE [Kaufman, George's wife] SO DIFFICULT TO EXPRESS DEPTH LOVE SYMPATHY ALSO RELIEF YOU HAVE PERCEIVED NECESSITY DO CONSULT BOBBY MY DEAR

The telegram is partially mysterious, but we can discern some things. Sidney intended to consult with one of the great founders of psychoanalysis, Carl Jung, whom he greatly admired. When Sidney went to Nassau earlier in the year, he had mean insides and writer's block. The writer's block, certainly, and his mean insides, probably, were signs of important psychological difficulties that undoubtedly worsened with time. They may have been caused by his deteriorating relationship with Clare, or they may have helped cause the increased tension between them, or both. Whatever the reason, his psychological state now reached a point where he felt it necessary to consult Jung. When Clare expresses relief that Sidney perceived the necessity for seeing Jung, it seems apparent that she had been urging him to do so, probably to save their marriage, perhaps simply to save himself.

Becoming a patient of Jung seems to have been almost a fashion among Sidney's friends. Leonard Bacon had felt the beneficial effects of Jung's treatment a couple of years earlier, and in the previous year Robert Edmond Jones (Bobby of Clare's telegram) had been an enthusiastic patient.

Clare's telegram does not necessarily show that things had gone wrong between her and Sidney although we might suspect that they had. Her next telegram, however, seems altogether innocuous, but Sid's reply tells us something very different. Clare's telegram was received in New York on October 10th:

> DARLING LETTERS RECEIVED REJOICE HOPKINS LONGING TO SEE YOU FOR LONG-LOVING TALK DON'T LET THEM DOUBLECROSS YOU AGAIN EVERYTHING HUNKY DOREY HERE LOVE
>
> CLARE

Written on the back of the telegram is Sidney's reply:

> Who is going to take care of you
> I can make out
> I couldn't move last week,
> But I can now

Given our knowledge that a rupture in the marriage was in progress, the first line surely indicates that there had been a discussion of separation or divorce and probably implies that Sidney did not believe that Clare could get along without him. She, on her part, may have thought that he could not get along without her and his consequent reply "I can make out." While she may have relied on Sidney, as he believed, for practical matters, he seemed entirely dependent upon her psychologically, emotionally, and artistically. But, he seems to assure her (and surely taking his courage in both hands) he can and will manage.

Then Sidney refers to an illness he suffered while in New York. It is, of course, possible that the second line of Sidney's reply refers to his illness, meaning that he can manage now, the third line indicating that he could not manage in the previous week.

Sidney spent some of the time in the United States recovering from his illness with the Bacons at Peacedale, Rhode Island:

> My dear Leonard—
>
> I never apologized to Patty and you for making a bore of myself what with pajamas, pills and all. I never wrote you a bread and butter letter. Now that I am far at sea, all these things come over me in great waves.
>
> I have been bored stiff on this ship and found no amusement but that of giving up alcohol which, odd though it may sound, seems to have done me no end of good and I may even keep it up for a spell, at least until I have got round to sleeping properly again [October 30th, 1927].

Later in the letter he requests Bacon to "send me a word to Jung...."

On October 31st, the next day, he writes his mother, "We dock tomorrow. I shall hope to see Clare at Southampton. Wireless messages of welcome are already arriving from my actors and managers."

Clare, however, apparently did not meet him at the dock: "I found Clare recovering from a badly sprained ankle," he writes his mother on November 14th, "and Jennifer, who met me at Southampton [presumably sent in Clare's place], a fluent conversationalist." The reason that apparently Clare failed to meet Sidney at the dock, we learn from Brian Aherne's autobiography, may have been related only partially to her having a sprained ankle.

According to Aherne, who played David in *The Silver Cord*, writing some forty years later in *A Proper Job*, Sidney returned to the United States some two weeks after the opening as the play began a substantial run. Aherne writes:

> It wasn't long, perhaps a few weeks, to the evening when she looked at me and said unsteadily, as if she feared the answer, "Brian, you do love me, don't you?"
>
> I fell on my knees beside her. "Oh Clare," I said, "I adore you!" [Aherne, 140].

Aherne, a young actor brought up in a middle-class family in northern England, had recently returned from a successful Australian tour during which he had played leading roles in a repertory of James Barrie plays. After some difficulty in finding a part in England, he applied for David in Sidney's play. At the interview he "saw Queen Elizabeth in a red coat, sitting on a chair with a cigarette in her hand.... There was no doubt about it, for I was very familiar with the portrait of the young Queen Elizabeth in the National Gallery, the lean proud face, the high forehead, the enigmatic steady eyes, the aquiline nose just slightly off

Brian Aherne, in a promo shot taken in his Hollywood days, around 1940. (Courtesy of the New York Public Library.)

center, and the air of high breeding, intelligence, and wit. I sat down and stared at her. Surprisingly, her hair was brown, instead of red. One of the men spoke to me, and I stammered some reply." After some discussion of Aherne's experience, Sidney asked Clare what she thought of working with him. "She regarded me steadily for a moment ... 'I don't think ... that I could object to acting with the Hermes of Praxiteles'" (Aherne, 138).

Clare's affair then with the Hermes of Praxiteles began shortly after Sidney left for the United States, for, as we shall see, Aherne's timetable is correct. Sidney went to the Continent soon after his return to England probably at Clare's request or because of difficulties between them, undoubtedly exacerbated by her affair with Aherne (of which, of course, Sidney knew nothing).

On November 14th Sidney writes to his mother from Italy, where he has been staying with his friend, the novelist Roger Burlingame:

> This is a surprising address. A cold one, too, but pleasant and restful. I go from here to Zurich where I shall met Jung and discuss with him the possibility of studying some psychology under him in his university seminars this winter. I don't know that it will come to anything, but he has asked me to come see him, being interested in my play.... The [Richard] Myers family was sweet in Paris. I stayed with Aunt Emma. I shall be back in London for Thanksgiving with the family. I leave Burlingame here to spend his winter....

Clearly he has been on the continent for some time, long enough to have stayed with Emma Eames and seen Dick Myers and his family and, as we shall see, to buy clothes for Clare in Paris, and to stay in Italy with Roger Burlingame. Obvious also is that when in New York he never mentioned to his mother anything about his marital or psychological difficulties or that he was going to Jung as a patient. With the prospect of remaining at Zurich for quite some time, he lies to her about his reason for going there. But the Bacons, we shall soon observe, undoubtedly knew about his marital troubles and why he wished to see Jung. Interestingly, in Bacon's letter to Clare in early 1927, we inferred that Bacon thought she ought to see a psychiatrist, but it is Sidney, and Clare as well, who now believe he ought to see one, and probably both believed that his psychological difficulties were the source of his marital discord.

Clare continued to correspond with Sidney; there is an undated letter to him probably at Zurich:

> Sidney dear—
>
> Thank you for taking all that trouble about the clothes. I am sure they are lovely and it made me so happy to hear that you had a good time with that angel Aunt Emma. My own doings have been nothing, except that I am trying to keep my performance up to scratch. It seems all right. I shall be so glad to see the dear Myerses—on Wednesday I went to lunch at Lady Seaforth's who is supposed to be the ugliest woman in the world. To-day Jimmy [?] gave a tea for me at May's which was nice but tiring. Jennif is well and talks of her Fallo.
>
> There is so much for me to say to you that I can't say in a letter. But I too have known some *very* bad moments in the last fortnight—Don't be upset but I always turn to you when I am a little down in the mouth. This evening I am quite gay however and so so glad that you are seeing our friend and so anxious to hear the out come.
>
> Always your loving wife.
> *Clare*

"Our friend" undoubtedly is Jung. Despite Clare's eagerness to know the result of Sidney's interview with Jung, her mild tone in this letter presents a sharp contrast to the emotionality in her letters to New York, the alteration unquestionably the consequence of the progression of her affair with Aherne.

To Leonard Bacon Sidney writes enthusiastically of Jung, who, however, refuses to take him on as a patient. Bacon seems to know that among Sidney's motives for seeing Jung are his marital difficulties:

> Dear Leonard:—
>
> Jung was great. I talked to him for two hours or something yesterday.... I wasn't prepared for him to laugh so much. He seemed to me, besides, an enormous thinker far more interested in thinking about people than in doing anything much about them, tremendously interested in his vivid description of his work, in stating in powerful metaphor. I'm sorry there's no opening for me here at present. It's exciting, plunging and throwing one's dirt about oneself on the table like poker hands in a heap. And about one's relations, too. It brings the cad out in one. That's always fun. To have the cad brought out, I mean.

I'm off for London now. When I got there [on his return from the United States] I found the performance very bad indeed and Clare concentrated on being very sweet on Osbert [Sitwell].... Osbert has too much humor to be a joke but not quite enough vigor not to remain a patrician amateur. I think that's just and not prompted by jealousy repressed for appearance's sake. I don't know what happens to me at this point. I expect I stay in London, guard my hearth and home and write for a living... [November 20th, 1927].

That Leonard Bacon knows about the difficulties between Clare and Sidney seems clear by the casual way in which he mentions Clare's being sweet on Osbert Sitwell and by Sidney's use of the traditional phrase "guard my house and home" for a husband's defending his domicile from intruders ready to steal away his wife. But it seems obvious that Clare's attention to Sitwell is merely a way of misleading Sidney about the real object of her affection. It would almost certainly mean the end of Aherne's job in *The Silver Cord* and an open break in the marriage if Clare revealed the truth.

The open break was to come, however, soon after his return to London. On Thanksgiving day Sidney writes to his mother that "Clare is not at all well, alas," and on December 5th, again to his mother, he writes, "Clare is having her annual breakdown rather early this year. I am shipping her off to a hotel tonight to sleep away from the healthy but riotous Jennifer."

Sidney's term "her annual breakdown" indicates his exasperation with her, implying that the breakdown is willful or at least unnecessary. Clare's stress now seems more psychological than physical; but we noticed earlier, when Clare's physical illness delayed the opening of *Ned McCobb's Daughter*, that Sidney's tone about it has a sharp edge as though then, too, the illness was unnecessary and therefore psychogenic. But by that time the tensions in their marriage were already building and seem to have contributed to Sidney's physical difficulties, as well as to Clare's, causing his trip to Nassau. But Sidney counters illness. Clare relies on it not only in developing her roles but to serve her other psychological needs.

Clearly the last two or three years have been nervewracking in her personal life and in her career. There were the difficulties of conceiving and giving birth to the child, followed in the summer of 1926 by the painful operation that resulted from childbirth. Between the two hospital stays came the failures of *Lucky Sam McCarver* and *Little Eyolf* as well as the mediocre reviews of the Shaw double bill. These brought on a physical "breakdown" in early 1926 which initiated their seemingly happy European cruise. In the fall, rehearsals of *Ned McCobb's Daughter* resulted in the illness of which Sidney was suspicious and which delayed the opening of the play that year. Outside of her first-class reviews for *Ned McCobb*, her season with the guild proved disappointing as was her tenure on its board. Her quitting the guild became a matter of public controversy. So when she arrived in London Clare was understandably on edge. But her reviews for playing Christina were wonderful, and that should have soothed her if she wished to be soothed.

To his mother Sidney disguises the seriousness of Clare's behavior by referring to Jennifer's noisiness as harmful to Clare's well-being. But their marriage had reached its wreckage; it had hit the rock against which Clare had warned four years earlier. But the cause did not lie in Sidney's philandering, as Clare had feared. The reasons were mainly subterranean.

Certainly the alluring Brian Aherne contributed the immediate cause of her leaving Sidney now. But not only did the unusual charms of Aherne attract her, but her life with Sidney pushed her away. No matter how much Sidney succumbed to her variegated wishes, precisely because she had such a whirl of desires, Sidney insisted on the controlling hand. "Who will take care of you?" he had telegraphed her, and he now writes to his mother, "I am shipping her off to a hotel." Both occasions see him in his apparently customary role of the traditional husband who must watch over his wife. Early in their marriage Sidney evidenced a certain overbearing quality in his attitude toward Clare, an insistence that she live up to what he thought right. With time, there was a good deal of equalizing. Still, for him the notion that Sidney must take care of Clare remained, a habit of mind to which she could no longer consent.

Hal Rhodes, writing to Sidney on May 21st, 1928, recognized that there had been a strain in their marriage. He states the cause in too simple a fashion, and yet his observation possesses an essential truth:

> My dear Sidney:
>
> I was always afraid that your marriage was too good to be true. I am of course very sorry at what has happened, but I am not surprised. I am fond of Clare and I don't blame her especially. It is merely that she is not domestic and it has turned out that you are....

Both Clare and Sidney had compromised and sacrificed as others do in the course of a marriage, some couples thus ending in happy unions, others in misery. For Sidney the compromises and sacrifices were worth it; Clare was in many ways his partner and the staff of his life. For Clare they were not worth it, even with the child, for finally the interchange of dependencies (as well as the sharing of pleasure), the very heart of the domestic scene, interested her not at all. She was a hawk.

This required that she divest herself of her responsibility for Sidney. He heavily relied on her for professional aid, which she apparently provided with pleasure. But beyond that Sidney, a sensitive instrument himself, a major rising dramatist whose family depended on his large income, needed peace and quiet for effective work and a generally nurturing environment, for which Clare as his wife felt responsible. She had mentioned such a responsibility in a letter to him from Cleveland before her marriage. Separated from Sidney, the hawk need no longer be bothered by this burden.

How much of an unsatisfactory sexual relationship contributed to the break is, of course, uncertain. Their early sexual difficulties, if any, were resolved during their 1923 summer sojourn in Europe. Now, if sex, for emotional reasons, once more became unsatisfactory, and Sidney's later letter indicates that there were sexual problems, Clare turned to the extraordinarily handsome Aherne for both sexual and emotional comfort.

Further, Clare, six years Aherne's senior, became in fact Aherne's teacher. By his own testimony, he was a callow young man who knew little of the great cultural traditions of Europe, and Clare taught him about literature, history, and art. His family and friends, he wrote, neither read nor discussed poetry, and he therefore thought his interest in it foolish, but Clare on the contrary encouraged it. The great poets—Keats, Shelley, Wordsworth, Browning—were woven into the very fabric of her life. She gave him books, the first being *Anna Karenina*, "which made a deep impression on me because I seemed to see a parallel between her story and that of the tragic, romantic Anna, and I feared that I might become her Vronsky." She continued to supply him with novels such as *War and Peace, Sons and Lovers,* and *Of Human Bondage,* and the work of biographers such as Lytton Strachey, Lion Feuchtwanger, and Stefan Zweig. She plied him as well with philosophers. One would think that he would have developed a case of indigestion. Instead, he asserts, "All this was heady wine for me" (Aherne, 141–42).

Seemingly, not only did Clare wish to break out of the restraints imposed on her by Sidney but she now wished to take Sidney's role. She wanted the controlling hand. With Aherne, rather than through her seniority in age, this came through her cultural superiority, undoubtedly augmented by her greater experience in the theater as actress and director.

Having moved in her marriage and in her career to positions of independence and strength, although she had yet completed neither of these moves, she now in her new personal relationship with Aherne, assumed the role of "cher maitre," which seemed desirable and right as she sought the goal of "freedom."

Sidney and Clare never again lived together (they were briefly under the same roof in their house in Manhattan in the fall in 1928). Supposedly to help them resuscitate their marriage, they went separately to the same psychotherapist, a Dr. Baynes. Clare continued staying at the hotel to which Sidney had "shipped" her, a procedure which may actually have been the result of her manipulation. From her hotel in Piccadilly, she writes in an undated letter to Sidney at Montagu Place, where he was still living with Jennifer:

> Sidney dear—
>
> I am ever so much better, sleeping and eating better and generally trying to relax into a good mind. A dreadful fiend from hell in the shape of a puppy, who whatever its sex, was a BITCH, the Mabel Terry Lewis [a well-known English actress] of dogs, yapped from 11:30 until 4:00 on Thursday night, only snatching a few moments measly rest from time to time. Just long enough for me to imagine that its screaming had stopped. I beseeched the hall porter to go out and shoot its owners, but he couldn't find them. Last night I had a great success at the theatre, probably undeserved. But it was great fun to see that kind of leaping welcome from the audience when I took my calls. Lillian [Braithwaite] coughs like a seal and is, I believe, entirely booked all day with Debrett and Burke [the authors of books of who's who in the British peerage], so that naturally, not being able to cough with her toney friends, she vents her mucous membranes on the public. I saw Baynes yesterday. He is really a most soothing and heartening person. He says that this establishment of a distance is frightfully important now for both of us. He asked me to dream for him, but try as I might, last night, not the vestige of a dream could I remember even on the instant of waking. They will come, I suppose. You and I have swapped appointments on Monday because 5:20 (the only vacancy) did not give him enough time. (He says I am all messed up at the back of something.) Well God knows I have led a discreditable life and I shouldn't mind having to admit it to someone who can help us both.
>
> When I am with you I am very fond of you and mostly unhappy. Here, I have been more peaceful and still very fond of you. We mustn't lose heart my dear. I no longer regret my Gregers Werleism because it may be the beginning of something resembling a real union please God.
>
> I shall see you on Monday at Hugh's [probably Walpole], at 1:15. Have a good time on Sunday, and remember that the good Dr. Pangloss may sometimes have been right when he said all's for the best etc.
>
> Love
> *"Clare"*

Gregers Werle is a character in Ibsen's *Wild Duck*, the play that Clare had codirected for the Actors' Theatre. Werle, one of the drama's chief characters, blindly insists that the absolute truth be told to the destruction of the very people he is trying to aid by truth telling. If it is that aspect of Gregers's character to which Clare refers, we may guess that the truth she told, which smashed her marriage to Sidney, is that she wishes to escape the now miserable bonds of marriage with him, at least temporarily, until the restraints no longer seem to cut. She may well have told him that she has ceased to love him, for while she says that she is very, very fond of him—she says it twice—neither time does she say she loves him.

But if Clare permitted her Gregers Werle truth telling to break up her marriage, it did not go so far as to include the revelation of her affair with Aherne. She energetically covers her tracks when Sidney guesses that she is conducting an affair, although he does not light on the correct person, in a letter she leaves for Sidney at Montagu Place, where Sidney and Jennifer still resided:

> Sidney Darling—
>
> I came over here post-haste from Dr. Baynes to see you. He told me you are terribly upset because you thought I had a *lover*. My dear dear Sidney. What can I do or say that can disabuse you of such an idea. Last night I was getting undressed when Reggie [Reixach, a rich, sexually neuter friend of Clare and Aherne; in Richmond Reggie owned Trumpeter's House, built by Christopher Wren], Prince George Charebar [?] and Adze [?] and a girl called Millen stopped to see if I were in and ask me to go to Trumpeters which I did, not leaving a message which I should have done. I give you my word that if I had a lover or wanted one even, I should say so. I am *not at all nice*, but there are some kinds of duplicity of which I am not capable, disorderly and careless and cruel as I am, and one of them is to tell my husband that he is the only man who matters to me and then fly high with someone else. Baynes says its [sic] a good thing you had this doubt but I can't bear the thought of your suffering for nothing, when I have made you suffer for so much that is real. Please please dear come to Lady Colfax's or to the Theatre. I did so much want to say this to you face to face—the reason I didn't say anything when we were walking up the street was because I thought that was what you were thinking and I was sore. I told Baynes this and he told me to tell you.
> How could I do such a thing.
> Dear dear Sidney who I am trying to find my way back to please forgive me.
>
> Your loving
Clare

Relying on her reputation as a straight shooter, Clare hopes to get away with her downright lies. Brian Aherne's autobiography, written forty years after the event, was not wrong about when the affair began, for Sidney, in a letter to his mother on June 29th, 1928, when he finally found out about the relationship, confirms Aherne's date: "The affair would appear to have started almost immediately after the play opened and to have been pretty public property in the company and in our house." There is no doubt that Clare, for all her Gregers Werleism, not only withheld information but told lies made more outrageous by her reputation as a truth teller. This is no longer the Clare, guiltless and carefree, who aims for the truth at any cost. She is now like anyone else in the midst of a separation and possible divorce, wishing to look as good as she can should she decide on a reconciliation, and wishing as well to save the face of her lover. She says that she is the same old square shooter Clare, but she now, understandably, says anything to prevent herself from being caught, the typical liar in an adulterous affair.

With all his personal troubles, Sidney still has a play, *Salvation*, to put on in New York. Written in collaboration with Charles MacArthur (who in the previous year had, with Edward Sheldon, been the author of the scandalous and successful *Lulu Belle*), *Salvation* was to be produced by Arthur Hopkins. Sidney awaits word as to when rehearsals will begin. Finally he telegraphs his mother on December 20th: "SAILING MAURETANIA TOMORROW CHRISTMAS LOVE ALL." "All" includes Jean and Duncan, who are celebrating Christmas in New York with Helen Howard. But Sidney cannot stay for Christmas with his wife and daughter. Clare writes him from the theater on Boxing Day, December 26th, 1927, a day for storing Christmas presents in boxes, a holiday in England. She tries to lend him Christmas cheer by describing Jennifer's Christmas but also attempts to soothe his feelings about their marriage:

> Darling Sidney –
>
> When I kissed you goodbye in that soulless lobby, I thought my heart would break. You looked so *forsaken*. You mustn't believe that you are, dear. Really. And in your heart I am sure you don't. As to my being in bed with Ivor [Novello, a handsome and popular English actor]. Oh what a treat. If you really give me permission to lie by the side of the lissome body I might take advantage of it, although Eddie [?] would probably be there first. Walter Creighton [?] turned up last week. I was so glad to see him, as funny and good and wild as ever.

After giving Sidney some information he desired about a religious matter, she continues:

> Miss Jones [Jennifer's governess] and I filled the Pills [Jennifer's] stockings on Xmas eve with your policeman, the pocket lamp, a tangerine, a fascisto soldier (from R.B. [?]), a bottle of barley sugar fish, and a soap bubble set. Her little woolen stocking, if you please. She kept talking in her sleep. In the morning, she woke up and said "baby two more days and Santa will be here." When Miss J. told her he had come she wasn't much impressed, nor did she thrill over the contents of her stocking. But when she saw the Tree and the Dollhouse and the little stable with 4 horses (2 saddle[s] and two carriage[s]) and a coachman, that I had got her, and she was lifted to the 4th dimension of excitement. She became quite still and demolished the arrangement of the dollhouse (so carefully ordered by us

9. Smash!

the day before) in about a minute. She put the cook to sleep in the master bedroom—and the litta lavatory in the dining room. The tree was magnificent with light, and the usual red balls and things. Plenty of tinsel. When she finally [went] to bed, with her darling little face literally drawn with [?] and a surfeit of happiness, she wanted to know if Santa would come again to-morrow. Your beautiful cyclamen was a great comfort, darling, because I missed you so terribly. My Xmas wasn't bad, but it was Hamlet without the Prince. Darling Jennif was the point—the play—but the leading part wasn't on the Atlantic. In the evening Miss Jones and I went out to Trumpeters to help entertain the twenty worst cases of permanently disabled veterans from the Star and Garter Hospital. It was a most touching and terrible sight, but at least it gave me the sense that I was giving someone pleasure, as I plyed them with beer and cigarettes. How sweet and how easy to talk to! Just like Tolstoi's soldiers. I have lived in the theatre since Matinee yesterday and to-day (I am finishing this letter Tuesday) and a dreadful blizzard and no taxis! Really it is awful. Last night one couldn't even get on the buses. I finally found a taxi in Shaftesbury Ave. with his flag down and I can tell you he held me up in fine style.

I have read *K.M.*[Katherine Mansfield]*'s Journal.* Wonderful....

...Well dear Freind [*sic*], I must now draw to a close as I want to catch the Acquitania.

Love me, darling Sidney, and try to be patient with me. I love you, more deeply than you know.

Yr
Clare

Despite Clare's plea for patience, Sidney could no longer tolerate dangling while Clare made up her mind. Being suspended in air prevented him from working. Furthermore, he could not abide ambiguity in feeling among people: "I dislike being baffled by relationships," he had written Jean back in 1921. Having been baffled long enough, three months at the very least—actually, he was to write his mother that he had been unhappy since the fall of 1926—by January 21st, 1928, he informs his producer in England that he does not plan to return there "for a considerable time." On January 29th, he explains his state of mind to Roger Burlingame, who had invited him for a visit to Italy:

... I wish th[a]t my plans fitted into yours and that they led me toward Portofino. Alas, they keep me indefinitely in New York.

I have decided against returning to England and returning to Europe, not to England, savors of driving my point home a little melodramatically. My decision arises from the tone of Clare's letters which certainly shows no improvement in the warmth of her attitude toward resumed relations and seems to indicate an all but inevitable parting of the ways. I don't want to go through any more of the recent agony or to go back from the little distance I have progressed along my own road alone. I have a lot I want to write about. I shall send for Jennifer as soon as those damned Knoblocks [Edward Knoblock, the writer, who rented his East 82nd Street house and whose house the Howards in return have rented in London] get out of my house and go back to their own in London and sit here and work until it is time to move north to Wiscasset. I may even abandon Wiscasset as a haunted house and go to my sister in California for the summer. You see, Italy, spring there, peace there, your society there—the which I miss like sin and fury here—are all cut off by a very sound reluctance to make a gesture which, however honest, would look defiant and who cares.

Clearly, Sidney has made up his mind that the separation is virtually certain, and with his typically pragmatic grit he has decided that he must go his own way. But by refusing to return either to London or to the Continent, by refusing to appear flippantly defiant, he shows the deliberateness with which he was proceeding in the now tricky relationship. He does not wish to jeopardize the possibility of a reconciliation, but he wishes to show Clare that he has done all he can toward a reunion and that it is now up to her either to return or to cut and run.

While his personal life has been shattered, Sidney has been working hard in the weeks since he has been home attending the rehearsals of *Salvation* and its out-of-town tryouts. Of this he writes to Burlingame:

How good [Osgood] Perkins is in "SALVATION!" He is giving the performance of his life and will come off with flying colors when the play opens at the Empire next Tuesday night. They will all come off with flying colors, I believe, for I have not often seen any play so well acted throughout. As to our [the authors'], part I am considerably less happy about that. I have a feeling that the theme is too big for our treatment and an added feeling that a simple story about a nice girl who happens to become an evangelist will strike milk and waterishly upon minds convinced that the clergy spells villainy and hypocrisy which is the clerical fashion these days in works of fiction [January 29th, 1928].

Sidney was correct about his expected failure of *Salvation*. It lasted about a month. But he was wrong in saying that one reason for its failure would be the writers' excessive kindness to the clergy. On the contrary, critics complained that Howard and MacArthur were altogether too cynical.

Despite his sense of impending failure, Sidney enjoyed MacArthur's antic disposition. In the same letter to Burlingame quoted above, Sidney writes:

Charlie goes on being delightful. A reporter asked him why we were collaborates. "Because I'm a fairy," he said, "and my collaborators are so good-looking." His engagement is again broken off and this time, when Helen [Hayes] came back to him to resume, she found that he had hocked the ring for five hundred berries. He told her that she could have it back if she wanted to redeem it....

But Sidney in the letter to Burlingame keeps returning to his state of mind and to Clare and to his frenetic activities resulting therefrom:

> I have been gadding, drinking a great deal, remembering your remarks on the subject of not-working as a positive activity. I have been gay, god damn it, I *have* been gay! I am said to be rejuvenated. They tell me I have not been as I am now since before my marriage. Everyone who sees me tells me so. I have enjoyed myself to beat the band, too. I have danced and sat in drinking emporiums and entertained folks and refused to give a whoop about the play or anything. I have associated largely with wastrels. They are good for one. I leave things matrimonial to decide themselves. I shall not have any decision to make. There is strength in non-resistance. Also, in being completely prepared for the worst.

While Sidney sat tight and tried desperately to have a good time in the midst of his misery, Clare was also suffering. But we must remember that genuine though her suffering, she was carrying out her desires.

We have two letters and four cables from Clare to Sidney in this period. Of the cables, one says that she can't understand why her mail has not reached him (November 18th, 1928), two wish him good luck with the production of *Salvation* (January 24th, 1928; February 13th, 1928). The final cable expresses a "KEEN WISH I COULD SEE YOU," to which Sidney, determined to remain in New York, replied: "Want desperately to see you but don't you think best continue present status until you feel certain enough to return. Stop Hard for me to maintain two households." This last refers to his request that she send him Jennifer.

Although the tones of the two following letters are very different from each other, they seem more accurately than the cables to reflect Clare's conflicting emotions.

The first, by its reference to Christmas having been "last week," indicates that it was written in the first week of January 1928. The letter is full of pleasant gossip about a party for Jennifer, theater news, and other such matters:

> My Darling Sidney—
>
> Last week was indeed a whirl. First Xmas and then 4 performances in succession and then, on Thursday, Miss Howard gave a Rout. She wore her pink velvet... We pinned the tail on the donkey, and had a peanut lunch, (all the peanuts were conspicuously hidden and then Jennif couldn't find any so I had to giver her some) and a high tea with crackers.... Last year, if you remember, the children never spoke. There was not a sound except Blaine Damrosch's crying. This year, they didn't talk to each other either; they simply opened their jaws and screamed a gorge deployee from 3:30 until 6:45. Jennifer ignored her guests for the most part, but she had a lovely time.... Jennif & I went to feed the swans and ducks in Regents Park on the coldest day in the world, but oh so beautiful, all blue and gunmetal and shivery, and Jennif with a pink face and white fur coat and hat, and white leggings throwing bread to the greedy birds. Last week our business was pretty bad but this week it has picked up and the houses are most enthusiastic. On Saturday night we had quite an excitement. Marjorie

[Mars's] nose began to bleed terribly in the hysterical scene ... we had to bring the curtain down....

She continues in this breezy way until the meaningful paragraph:

> All my thoughts are gradually straightening I think. Of course Baynes is away, and I don't know whether I understand him anyway, but at any rate, I feel as if I were *resting* for the first time in, literally, years. Not sluggishly lying in bed and trying to get enough strength to meet the simplest demands on me, but resting fruitfully.

Clare indicates her relief that she is without Sidney, presumably without Sidney watching her, whether it be the loving, the tender, the irritated, or angry Sidney. Without him she sleeps more deeply and breathes more easily.

The other letter of this period, highly emotional, written on February 14th, 1928, does much to explain the crucial paragraph of the letter just quoted:

> Darling Sidney—
>
> It is a most unhappy woman who writes to you. I think that to-night I have just touched the Nadir of all I could ever feel of pure sorrow. Baynes told me to write and tell you exactly how I feel—but how can I? In the first place, I don't write well enough and in the second I chop and change so. I am bound to you in every conceivable tie, including a beloved baby; and I am often overtaken by the most penitent rushes of tender feelings toward you, when I long to call you my So and remember with you all the happy times we have had to-gether. And yet, in a queer way I can't explain or ever describe, I am afraid of you. I didn't tell you about my Sunday night show because I was afraid to. Why? Am I afraid of being hurt? Or am I just constitutionally a coward? Or is there something inside me that I am trying to protect? And then side by side, I have unreasoning reluctance and fear, and the most devoted gratitude, respect and love. I can't make out whether you want me still or not. I look so awful I can't imagine anyone's wanting me now—I really look ill. Self contempt and regret and longing and loneliness and fear of the past the present and the future are not salutary companions. I told McLeod [one of the producers of *The Silver Cord*] I would produce [direct] *The Silver Cord* [for touring] because if you are to get anything out of it, I couldn't leave [it] to be bungled. Your refusal to put on Ned McCobb has cancelled that. So what is it really that you want me to do—try to earn a little more money over here and then come back or what? My horrible inhibition about writing held me for weeks. I was so stiff with unhappiness that the thought of saying anything but woe! woe! was simply impossible to me. The news about *Salvation* is heartbreaking. Darling Sid. Such a beautiful play out of its time and place. What you say about the English stage may be very true. I have other ideas about it (not denying yours) but too long and involved to write out. Will all this about my feelings simply seem a perverse medley to you? & will you real-

ize that from the bottom of my heart as I am a woman and a human being, *I want to do the right* thing? Please please try to believe, darling Sid, that my impulses toward you are so strong sometimes that I weep for my Sidis and then this fatal other thing comes to kill it all. Everything is so intangible and yet so terribly terribly real. If it hadn't been for Baynes I believe I should have gone mad. I am sending you my—our Pearlio, the darling of my life, whom you think I don't love, oh god. You see in all this I am so completely at your mercy. Not that I don't see that you should have her now—after all your suffering is probably much more than mine—but I mean in other ways. Well whether I am at your mercy or not, you are my husband and I am glad you liked me, although such has not always been my impression. But I know you do dear Sid. Will you cable me on receipt of this letter—"do not think you are a God damned fool of a bitch" or words to that effect.

> I send my love, dear.
> Clare

The central reason for their separation now seems clear: She was afraid of him. "Or," she adds, "is there something in me that I am trying to protect?" Perhaps her fear and her self-protection are not alternatives but two sides of the same coin: She fears that he will crush her very essence.

In a sense Clare wanted no inhibitions, no fence around her essential self. Guthrie McClintic, the director, Katharine Cornell's husband, wrote that Clare was "dynamic, without fear of any kind. She heard 'wild harps' playing and that was what she was gunning for..." (McClintic, 184). Even though McClintic badly mixes metaphors, he seems to understand something about Clare, who, despite the emotional whirl in which she finds herself, will brook no interference, from Sidney or anyone else, in her attempt to evoke in her work and life the wild harps playing in her soul.

In this same letter quoted above she writes, "You see in all this I am so completely at your mercy." She refers here in part to sending Jennifer to him. We suppose that she must send the child because he holds the purse strings. If he says that he cannot maintain two households, she must for that reason abide by the decision, her income as an actress, although good, being only a fraction of his.

But she insists that it is not only in the matter of the child that she is at his mercy. One consideration seems preeminently to fit her meaning. She appears to desire his approval for the course of action she has adopted: "... [W]ill you realize that from the bottom of my heart ... *I want to do the right* thing?" Sidney's strong moral stance hovers over her, reinforcing similar moral feelings she has brought from her own family life.

Clare's ambivalence toward the marriage and toward Sidney appears genuine. However, she self-protectingly omitted her affair with Brian Aherne. Exactly what the Aherne factor was in her feelings is difficult to gauge. For the most part Aherne pictures their relationship as idyllic, but it could hardly have been so for Clare. Surely her relationship with Aherne and its secrecy increased the agony and prevented clarity in making her decisions about Sidney and her marriage. But she continues the affair and continues to hide it.

Toward the close of her letter Clare asks Sidney to cable a response upon its receipt. At the end of Clare's letter he writes what will be his telegraphic answer: "Darling your letter gives Jennifer and me new hope you will find your way back to us Love." This is a surprising response, for it seems to an objective reader of her letter that there is less than an even chance that she will return to the marriage. We must conclude that Clare's letter, as uncertain as it is, had to be more encouraging to Sidney than her previous ones, showing that his outlook for a reconciliation had been bleak indeed.

On March 15th, five days after the closing of *The Silver Cord* in London, Sidney wrote Clare a letter at times angry, at times distressful, even seemingly patient, and finally poignant, outlining his tenuous position:

> I ... asked you when you are sailing. I don't mean to keep after you. It is hard as the devil not to have at least some idea, that's all. You must realize that. You told Miss Jones that my letters have always scolded you. Now, I ask you! Have I scolded except about writing? And can't you realize how damnably hard it has been on me to keep my head above water without so much as a straw to cling to? You, who told both Miss Jones and Baynes that you were writing constantly because you knew damned well that you weren't doing the right thing by me. Shame on You!
>
> I saw Baynes [who was visiting the United States] this morning, the same heavy going, well meaning blunderbuss I saw in London, always leaving what he has to say in high cloudy psychoanalytic phraseology and leaving me as much confused as when I came with another appointment for more confusion on another day.... It's all beyond me. In all honesty, my darling, I don't know how much longer I shall be able to stick this walking in darkness in your regard nor do I know how much damage to our marriage may already have been done by same. The way I look at things, you know where I am, what I have been doing, where you stand with me. I have no such security toward you. If you come back you will be able to put your finger on me. What shall I have to put my finger on? I don't know that. Baynes says it's an incomprehensible business. So it is.... If sex has got pushed aside sometimes, if each one of us has felt that the other held something back, each one of us only had to say so. I said so some, not enough. I think that I was too deeply flattered by your telling me that I had sexual tact. I know, and this will shock you, that I should, and could, not have given you or expected of you the sexual brutality that I have known in long past relations with other women. I may add that what you gave me, though too reticent, brought me more happiness tha[n] that. No, darling,

I am no Earle Larrimore [a member of the Theatre Guild acting company who was a homosexual]. And to conclude sexually, I know that we have both worked too hard on too little comfort and too much worry to have preserved the vitality required for perfectly expressed and generous love. But there you are and it remains a queer mess. Only I must hear from you, darling, I must, I must, if our lives are not to become hopelessly estranged. Suppose you conclude, presently, that life with me may not be as bad as it has seemed and come back and find that I am no longer, through no fault of my own, at your disposal, that my life has got its own impetus and no longer needs you in it. Would you not, then, blame yourself for not making that little effort of giving me some contact with you? Aren't you playing your separation cards before you are entirely sure that separation is what you want? I have wondered if you wanted, and were trying to force me to ask for, separation. Permanent separation, I mean. I have been so baffled and so distressed. And yet I have managed so far to keep anger out of my feelings. Only don't ask the impossible. Even if we do split, why should we stain a one time happiness with anger. Anger will make us do things to each other and say things about each other. We have so little to do that is not good, you and I, and what, after all, have we to say against each other? And anger will come, my dear, and poison us if you are not very careful. Think, I beg you, before you invite its coming. I have done something which I venture to call heroic—at least in the effort it has cost me—in keeping it down so far in the face of the fact that I knew that the worst of my distress (not hearing from you) was wholly needless all of the time.

The next paragraph is half taken up with gossip and activities: the "gravely ill" Robert Sherwood's "eighth week of illness" which has brought out the "niceness" in his wife, who has "behaved like ... a thoroughly competent little angel"; Walter Gieseking, the "greatest pianist I have ever heard at Bach and Debussy and one of the greatest artists I have ever seen at anything"; Zoë Atkins, whose "buddy" he has become "for writing such a marvelous play as 'The Furies' in which Laurette [Taylor] does acting such as I have never seen any actress do."

But eventually the chitchat leads him back to their situation.

I am trying to find out what the [John] Marquand plans are for Wiscasset. If they are not going there, I may go to California. Unless you come home, that is. It is hard for so many reasons not to know where you are and what you plan to do. I am really at the point of asking you to decide one way or the other. Say one of three things. Say that you are not coming back and want a divorce. Say that you are coming back later and about when so that I may live at peace at least until the date you name. Or come back. One of the three and, for God's sake, say it soon. Make up your mind. Imagine what this uncertainty would do to your work if I were practicing it on you and make up your mind and tell me. If you do not want to hold me, set me free. I fully appreciate what your own uncertainty must have caused you to suffer. But try to see my side as well as yours and try to realize that such a trial cannot but come harder on creative than on interpretive work. In the very nature of things that must be so. You have outer forces to make you do your work. I have nothing to stand between me and harassing thoughts except my own will to work and that, my dear, is almost in abeyance under this strain. Now don't say or think that I am scolding. I am only pleading for mercy from the woman I love. And I make no claim on her which she is not ready to welcome. What I say is, if marriage between us can not happily become a communion (paraphrased if not quoted) let us have done with marriage; one or the other before we both go broke and mad together.

So much for gloom. Jennifer has just come in from shopping for shoes in Mother's car. When Leonard [Bacon] was here, the other day, she came in to tea for a cookie. When she saw Leonard she returned abruptly through my study. Leonard asked her why she didn't stay longer and, as an exit line she said: Well, you know, I'm rather shy. She refuses now to call me Fahlo any more. Father, she says, I love that name. She talks about you all the time and makes up stories of what she does with you. She said she went to the Zoo and saw a Giraffe and Munna and Munna was feeding it cereal with a spoon.... Miss Jones tells me that you told her you were disappointed that I had not come over to take the family to Switzerland. If you had told me that we should have gone. Don't keep me in the dark any longer, please, my dear. Don't.

After his signature Sidney adds in his handwriting: "Three weeks ago I signed two letters by your old name for me ["Sidis" or "So"]. I've lost my nerve again now."

On top of the first page he adds, again in his handwriting, "P.S. if you are staying on for 'The Silver Cord' road tour, for God's sake forget about it. I don't care whether its [sic] good or not or whether it comes off or not. What happens to my plays in England interests me about as much as what happens to them in Boston."

Sidney begins the letter by stating that he is not trying to hurry Clare and ends by urging her to decide soon. Uncomfortable in any state of suspension, Sidney suffers even more deeply in this situation because he is clearly still in love with his wife and does not want to prevent the possibility of her returning to him. Yet, his gritty self says that if she is not, he will get on with his life.

Sidney, who has always prided himself on his right-minded ethics, or at least has criticized others for failing to be ethical, is trying to behave according to high standards in this crucial test. His refusal to shut the door to reconciliation implies forgiveness for whatever Clare has done, and he regards her refusal to stay in touch with him as her worst fault. He wishes to act as Tony toward the wandering Amy in *They Knew What They Wanted*.

He has tried to repress his anger, perhaps not as successfully as he claims he has, for he knows how damaging that emotion can be psychologically and spiritually, damaging the possibility of future intimacy or embittering the possible divorce proceedings. His expression of "heroic" efforts to repress it smacks of self-pity, yet in battling anger at obviously great cost to himself, he shows patience, courage, and fortitude.

Sidney remarks that the pressures of their work prevented them from "perfectly expressed and generous love." That is, the heavy demands of their careers caused sexual as well as emotional problems. Both were at fault for withholding satisfying sexual pleasure to the other. Yet on the whole, he says, he gained more satisfaction from her "too reticent" lovemaking, presumably because it was deeply loving, than in the brutal, undoubtedly exciting, liaisons he had had before he married. But the sexual difficulties, for a long time unexpressed, helped bring about Clare's decision to engage in her affair with Brian Aherne, whom she was now reluctant to leave.

Clare's response to Sidney's urgent letter was to sail back to the United States toward the end of March. "She felt she owed it to her baby, to her family, and to her marriage vows to make one more effort to reconstruct her life there," writes Brian Aherne, "but," he adds, "I think we both knew she would come back; and so she did, in three months..." (144). It was not even three months, for on April 30th, Sidney writes to Leonard Bacon that "she came back to this country last month" and is "returning to England this coming Friday." Her decision to try for a reconciliation, as Aherne indicated, seems to have been half-hearted. In the letter to Bacon Sidney reports: "Clare has decided on a permanent separation.... She has been almost all the time with her people in Cleveland."

Clare's speedy flight to Cleveland may have been hastened by this unlikely story that appeared in a newspaper report at the time divorce proceedings were filed in 1930. Friends, the story says, attempted to bring about a reconciliation:

> On one occasion in New York [and this visit early in 1928 could have been the only such occasion], Miss Eames was escorted to Howard's home without being told where she was going. Mutual forgiveness was expected as a result of the pathetic scene when Miss Eames walked into the strange drawing room and found Howard sitting at the Fire with little Clare on his knees. However, the friendly scheme did not work... [undated in clip file].

It is unimaginable that the straightforward Sidney would have participated in such a sentimental plan of entrapment. The story is further suspect because the drawing room, since it could only have been at East 82nd Street, would not have been strange to Clare. The kernel of truth in the account lies in its sense that Sidney was ready for a reconciliation with mutual forgiveness while Clare was not. The facts might be wrong, but the public perception of the situation was not. Such stories, however, published and unpublished, making the rounds, must surely have sent Clare running from New York.

Writing Sidney from Cleveland on April 24th, Clare confirms the newspaper insight and appears to possess more assurance than she has shown thus far:

> Sidney dear—I was a very unhappy woman the night I went off from you; and I still am, although less so—because somewhere, like the vague apprehension of a discovery, I am beginning to feel a way out, as if I had antennae. What that way is, and how it will be trodden is a mystery, but I know that if I wait very quietly I shall know. And it will depend on me. You will of course play your part; but when it is opened to me I shall be the responsible one. You tell me I live in the Empyrean and all this, after all, may be an unpragmatical dream: I believe it, anyway.... How is my Price [Jennifer]? And you?

After her signature she adds:

> I am going to send this letter anyway although I am afraid it will irritate you.
>
> Love
Clare

Although her behavior with Brian Aherne has hardly been puritanical, yet her waiting upon an inner light to shine her way to the right path is in Clare's case consonant with the puritanism she was taught as a youngster. We are reminded of her writing to Sidney that their material success was a sign of their inner grace. At one point she tells Aherne, "Be true to the God within you.... Listen to your own secret heart, and you can do no wrong" (144).

The paradox of Clare's position here can be understood by a brief reference to *Pilgrim's Progress*, the great puritan allegory. Early in the book Christian, after begging his wife and children to accompany him on the road to Heavenly City, runs off without them when they refuse. As they cry for him to return, he puts his fingers in his ears shouting, "Life! Life! Eternal life" and continues running.

The problem with a person seeking God's light is that he will do anything to find it even at the expense of others. We may well sympathize with someone seeking redemption; we may well admire the devotion, tenacity, and the depth of his interior life. But these sometimes, perhaps often, come at a cost to those who love him and whom he presumably loves. The spiritual self is a hard taskmaster and brooks no other, sometimes to the point of utter indifference to the fate of loved ones.

Thus when Clare writes in this letter that she will wait "very quietly" until the way is opened to her and intersperses her remarks with "You will of course play your part; but ... I shall be the responsible one," we have the sense that she seeks only her own salvation and that the outcome for others once her decision is reached matters little. Guthrie McClintic wrote of Clare that she heard "wild harps playing." But listening for them hardly helps her to hear the groans of pain from those who love her as she waits.

In addition to pain, Sidney must also have felt an ironic amusement in Clare's postscript—mischievous or not?—"I am going to send this letter anyway although I am afraid it will irritate you. Love Clare." Perhaps her closing line before her first signature was even more bitter for Sidney, "My dear Sidney, who means an awful lot to me." Certainly both endings of the letter show her deep ambivalence toward Sidney and her marriage.

Sidney believed that Clare made her decision for a permanent separation "seriously and coolly" and that they were now faced with "looking for some less than utterly foul way to get divorced" (letter to Roger Burlingame, May 7th, 1928).

With all this, the professional lives of both proceeded. Before Clare returned to England, she signed a contract for a film, *The Three Passions*, to be directed by Rex Ingram in Nice (Aherne, 144). Sidney meanwhile intended to return to serious playwriting, mainly an adaptation of *Camille* for Ina Claire to be produced by Jed Harris. This would really be a new play based on the autobiographical affair of Dumas fils and Marie Duplessis (Letter to HH, May 4th, 1928).

The better to ready himself for a writing stint after his psychological trauma, Sidney goes on a western vacation in New Mexico with Jean and her husband, Duncan (letter to HH, May 4th, 1928). He had wanted to take along Jennifer, whom he now leaves with Miss Jones, but he could not afford it. "It's the first thing I've wanted to do for two years and I've spent so much money doing things I didn't want her [Clare] to do, that I couldn't afford it. Self-indulgence" (letter to HH, May 8th, 1928). On his way west he is haunted by the "possibility of Clare's return before I have had enough hard earned peace to get some work done in. How terrible not to want to see the person one loves best! Or to be afraid to see her!" The vacation will consist of "cliff dwellings and the aboriginal past. Then a few, very few, days of Berkeley. Then Maine and work, work, work, in which is salvation to me" (letter to HH, May 15th, 1928).

Sidney then tells us something that causes the greatest puzzlement for us in attempting to understand Clare's behavior in this whole divorce proceeding. From his trip, Sidney says, he will send Jennifer "post cards which she loves. If only Clare might feel some impulse to do such and keep her memory green. Jennifer misses her but not at all in the right way. Not happily, but wonderingly. Not with any picture of where she is and what she is doing, but only with a sense—an aching sense, I'm sure—of lack, of an essential omitted. Which, of course, is actual...."

After Clare's spring visit to the United States, she lived with Jennifer for a brief period when she returned to New York to do a play in the fall of 1928. At Christmas of the same year she sent Jennifer to Sidney in Berkeley for the holidays, and the child remained with Sidney for the rest of his life, never again to see her mother. Clare wrote her a Christmas letter in 1928, but for the less than two years left to her, Clare failed to write anything more to Jennifer. During the two separations of 1927 she also never wrote to her daughter.

We can more or less understand why Clare left Sidney and the way in which she left him. But her treatment of the child defies the comprehension of anyone who has come to think of Clare as humane. Why in almost two years of her remaining life did she not keep in touch with her child? Granted that she was not domestic, that perhaps she felt, in the vulgar language of newspapers, that a "child cramped her art," that in the harsh theatrical world she now had to navigate alone a child would be a hindrance. Yet it would hardly take much effort to maintain a correspondence. Even if she found it wrenching to write to a daughter whom, in her circumstances, she could not see, yet she surely must have understood how painful it was for the child to hear nothing from her mother. Surely, she loved the child. Any resentment Clare might have felt for the physical and psychological pain she withstood in trying to conceive and in bearing her must surely be gone in the wonderful reality of the child. We can only draw a blank in attempting to explain Clare's behavior in this regard.

Yet Sidney, writing to Richard Myers on June 12th from Maine after his healing vacation in the West, says that Jennifer "promises to be one of those bones of contention and Gawd knows what will happen or how much I shall be able to retain of her. For the moment I am doing what I can to give her a peaceful and healthy summer and I intend to do what I can, quite ruthlessly, to continue giving her a peaceful and healthy life ... mother or no mother." In a letter to Helen Howard on the same day he repeats his "ruthless" determination to give Jennifer a peaceful life. He then adds, "I am still very deeply in love with the lady and lonely as a lost soul without her. But I am on my own feet again and I know that I have a man's sized job in Jennifer." Later in the letter he says that Clare "will not have the sense to sit tight and keep quiet as I am doing. Or the taste. She will talk to cover her desertion of Jennifer because the old-fashioned virtues still have enough life in them to condemn any woman who deserts her child.... Clare will have a hard time to prove anything against me while, with my private record as a husband and father likewise, I am still supporting her even after her desertion...."

Brian Aherne in his autobiography talks of Clare's lack of money at this time in her life (142–43). We do not know how much money Sidney was sending Clare, but apparently it was enough for what he considered adequate support, and from the generosity we have seen in his life, that would hardly seem to be a small sum.

In a later paragraph of the June 12th letter to his mother Sidney writes again: "I am as much as ever in love with Clare and as unlikely as ever to get over being in love with her, admiring her, missing her, wanting her to come back. But I have seen that there is no hope of getting her back on any tolerable basis...." He continues: "I mean to make Clare ask me for a divorce. Then I shall give her one. I have no intention of separating mother and daughter. But I mean to establish and maintain security for Jennifer's childhood under her own roof here [in Maine] and in New York...."

For Clare, now that she had made her decision for a permanent separation from Sidney, there was no hiding her relationship with Brian Aherne. He met her in Nice, where she was filming *The Three Passions*, and they drove north through Italy and Germany. However, when they reached London, they did not live together. "I suppose," asserts Aherne, "we were too proud, we had too much respect for our families, and above all for Clare's child to do other wise. We were not light or irresponsible people, and the great emotion which overpowered and possessed us both was not without an element of sadness" (159–60).

Word filtered back to Sidney about Clare's affair, but the talk did not immediately identify her lover as Aherne: "I have heard much gossip of a boy friend and other things less agreeable [whatever the latter means]. I should like to believe in the boy friend, that he is worthy of her, will make her happy and a duchess, if possible" (letter to Richard Myers, June 12th, 1928). But by June 26th we see in a letter to his mother from Wiscasset that it was all out:

> Letters last week upset me somewhat again, for everyone in London rushed, ostensibly to sympathize for the way Clare is acting and, actually, to tell me, by every form of stinking British innuendo, the name of my successor. Which same distressed me for Clare as much as it grieved me for myself because, if he is actual, he is a bad choice, being a bounder and some seven or eight years her junior. I am further distressed by the inevitable indignity of my position, if he is actual. I know that I have no reason not to believe in him and I know that I have even less reason to expect anything like candor from Clare.

It is clear now that in making no attempt to hide her relationship with Aherne, Clare had definitely determined upon a divorce. However, whatever discretion she previously used seems to have been reserved for the general theatrical community and to the public, for in a later letter to his mother Sidney writes, "The affair would appear to have started almost immediately after the play opened [Sidney here confirms Aherne's account] and to have become pretty public property in the company and in our house." Apparently, as long as Clare wished to keep her relationship with Aherne quiet outside the cast of *The Silver Cord*, the company accorded with her wishes and never wrote Sidney. Of course, if members of the cast knew, many others knew as well, but the British sense of individual privacy seems to have prevailed. However, once Clare was open about the matter, no one lost any time in writing Sidney "by every form of stinking innuendo" of Clare's affair.

But now there were further problems. The first had to do with the form of the divorce. At the time, and for a long time afterward, the only ground for divorce in New York state was adultery, which could be proven only if one of the parties was caught in bed with another person. Commonly, the husband consented to be found in bed with a woman he did not know, have his picture taken, which was then presented in court, and in the course of time the divorce was granted. Since in Sidney's case Clare was the person who had committed adultery, one possibility was that he seek the divorce on that ground. But that entailed certain disagreeable procedures: "I detest the idea of divorcing my wife. I detest everything that employs detectives and furnishes the papers with such copy. There is nothing for me to do but sit tight and grit my teeth and write like a demon and, in time, something will come to me as a course of action" (letter to HH, June 26th, 1928).

But that, he contends, requires Clare's cooperation. The present uncertainty will surely "bring injuredness and enmity with it and I should so have liked things to have ended without either of those. Uncertainty is a cruel business and Clare has hit on a most skillful method for torturing me." As we saw, uncertainty is one of life's characteristics that Sidney hated more than did most people.

Nevertheless he still refuses to take the seemingly easiest path, that of proving adultery on Clare. One reason derives from a sense of responsibility for Clare's behavior. "I cannot bring myself to putting detectives on Clare and securing a divorce for infidelity. Infidelity on the part of either a wife or husband is always, I believe, partly the injured party's fault. I mean that Clare, with her fineness and moral fastidiousness would never in the world have fallen in love with Aherne had I made her happy." He hastens to add, "I don't to be sure, know what it was that I did or left undone, but something must have been lacking from her point of view" (letter to HH, June 29th, 1928).

There was still another problem: "I shall do my utmost," Sidney continues, "to have her persuaded to divorce me and to resign custody of Jennifer at the same time. Failing that, I shall do my utmost to divorce her and retain custody of Jennifer." That is, he was determined to keep Jennifer if he possibly could, and he thought that he had a pretty good case. He writes to his mother in Europe on July 5th:

> Jennifer and I are getting on well enough however much we may miss my darling Clare.... The works are pretty public property, now, thanks to Clare's unbridled tongue and she will almost have to do something about it. The longer she postpones moving, the stronger my court hold is on Jennifer. It's two months now that no word has come from her during which Jennifer has had two illnesses of which she could not, for want of an address, be notified. I think that I am safe. So let's not worry. Clare has her case and her right to her own idea of happiness. Jennifer has her case and her right to a quiet childhood. She's getting one at present. I hope that Clare is getting what she's after.... And once more don't be alarmed at libelous statements made about me if you hear them They cannot hurt me in the long run. Unproven libel boomerangs the libellor [sic]. I am playing a waiting, cautious game to protect Jennifer and that is the ball on which we must keep our eyes letting the horseflies buzz and bite as much as they like....

Sidney's intention of protecting Jennifer showed good instincts in this situation. Nowadays, when divorce is commonplace and much research has been done on the effect on children of divorce, we know that the more the children are shielded from the conflicts involving their parents in the course of the proceedings, the better off they are. Clare, of course, may have had the same feeling as Sidney, and that may be the reason that Jennifer did not hear from her. Clare may have mistakenly thought that even a letter from her would be disturbing, especially if, uncertain of her future, she was unclear as to what to write in it.

Clare finally decided to move: On July 9th, Sidney writes to his mother: "I have just been talking to Haydie [Clare's sister] over the long distance and she tells me that Clare has written her lawyer to get in touch with me. When he does I shall refer him to Hess and Angell [his lawyers] and keep myself as much as possible out of what has turned my personal tragedy into a sordid and sexy mess."

Clare's action prompts Sidney to write a careful letter to Clare on July 17th:

> Dearest Clare:—
>
> Haydie tells me that you are writing to lawyers in Cleveland. I urged her to do nothing which might hurry you in any direction which you do not see quite clearly. I realize, however, that three months have passed since we parted in New York last April and nearly a year since our separation began. You may, therfor [sic] have come to some conclusion.
>
> What the conclusion is I shall, I suppose, learn from your lawyers. What your wishes concerning it are I cannot expect to learn from them.

You must realize that anything that is done must either be done by me or with my cooperation. I urge you to write me telling me explicitly and candidly just what you want to do or have done about this marriage of ours and why. Lawyers will look for me to act in my own interests exclusively and leave me no course bu[t] to do so. I hope that you believe that I am ready and eager to consider your wishes.

But I don't mean to press you toward divorce or to object to an indefinite continuation of the present situation. I am afraid, however, that things left to drift, may come to a head at some time most inconvenient to either you or me and that some situation may arise in connection with either Jennifer or my work that would oblige me to act on my own account. Unless, that is, you and I come to a complete understanding. There is, after all, no reason for anything but the most complete candour on your part. Haydie only confirmed what I already knew [clearly, he refers to her affair with Brian Aherne].

So please write to me. My usual rehearsal troubles begin this year toward the end of August and I want very much to enter them knowing that nothing is going to surprise me before they are over. Suppose I say that I shall look for a letter from you by the 15th of August and put this matter out of my mind until then and that, unless you write or cable to the contrary before then, I shall feel at liberty to use my own judgment after that date.

Jennifer is top notch, loves life in Maine and will welcome you so happily when you again feel like seeing her. I have moved the best of my National Portrait Gallery [the pictures of Clare in her various roles in the Wiscasset house] into her nursery to keep your memory not only green but blossoming. All good things to you, always, my very, very, dear.

Not only does Sidney desire no surprises while he is preparing his new plays for presentation, but he is obviously trying to avoid legal conflicts that will embitter their relationship, one that must continue after their divorce since they share a child. There are extant, so far as we know, a few letters from Sidney to Clare. The tone of the greater part of this letter, that of a patient father to a recalcitrant child, while it may show that he still loves her, perhaps even still has hope of a reconciliation, confirms the notion as to an important reason why Clare left Sidney.

But before Clare could reply, Sidney hears from her lawyers. Sidney writes to his mother on July 19th, 1928:

> This is just to tell you that Clare's lawyers have started.... Our story is that Clare can have her divorce if she will surrender any claim to Jennifer.... Clare is coming back to fight at once. I shall pray that I don't have to see her and Hess and I will try to dope out something legal which will prevent her snatching Jennifer on her return.... To have meant well and done almost as well as one meant and to have, as they say, nothing to reproach oneself with cuts little ice in this world these days. However, Clare has the divine spark and I'm a plodder and it's the business of plodders to keep the divine sparkers going and that's what I've been doing all this while

since I married Clare and here's one more effort I've got to make before I'm through, let her walk over my work and fight like hell against any abuse whatsoever and however public for that little party who is now passing the window in a red bathing suit on her way to the daily swim.

Understandably, Sidney feels sorry for himself. More interesting is Sidney's observation, in words other than we previously noted, that Clare lives in the Empyrean while he is earthbound. Although Sidney stops his self-pity, he never loses his sense of the difference between their natures, the nature of their creative efforts, or the painful necessity of his having had to sacrifice his work for hers.

On July 23rd, he writes to his mother that his previous letter, the one just quoted, was written "in pretty low spirits," but he now wishes to "correct some of the impression." His lawyers

> absolutely refuse to tolerate the idea suggested by the Eames family of a collusive divorce [one in which he would be photographed with a woman he did not know and thus take the responsibility of the divorce upon himself]. They further assure me that, as long as I continue to provide a home for Clare and the baby and do not exclude Clare from the home, she has absolutely no legal right to take the baby out of it…. I sit tight, refusing to consider anything except custody of Jennifer. There are three possible outcomes or courses in view. 1. Clare allows me to divorce her under the laws of New York State, i.e., for infidelity, I retaining custody. 2. I go to Reno and divorce Clare for incompatibility, Clare resigning custody. 3. I do nothing, cease to support, but continue to provide and extend hospitality which she will never in God's world accept and which leaves Jennifer entirely at my disposal.

Later in the letter Sidney writes:

> I am in love with her and I shall continue to leave all doors open with all sincerity. I don't believe that there is any possible basis for a reconciliation, but one never knows what miracles may not happen and I am not, in later and in even lonelier days, going to reproach myself with having acted in pride. Clare is closing doors herself, with all suitable rapidity. Let her finish the job herself. Then I shall not have to tell myself that I did any of it. I know I'm right to watch and wait.

After this flurry of activity, Clare is once more incommunicado. On August 24th, Sidney writes to Roger Burlingame:

> About July 15th last, her lawyers wrote me at her behest to ascertain on what terms I would give her a divorce. I was then informed that she has generally announced her intention of divorcing me to marry Brian Aherne who played David in London. Since the middle of July, however, as I have ascertained, neither her family nor her lawyers have been able to get into communication with her and I have even heard indirectly from her lawyers

asking me to give out where she is to be found, which I know but I'm damned if I'll tell. For a while all of this about threw me.

Clare's exasperating behavior leads him to make two proposals collateral to the divorce. On the same day that he writes to Roger Burlingame, he also writes to his lawyer Ernest Angell:

> I am wondering if I had not better make another will leaving all my property to Jennifer. I know that, under the present one, Clare cannot touch capital. But I have to face the fact that she seems to have come pretty much completely under the domination of Aherne, who is, at best, only a Cockney actor and who, according to rumor, at least, is now getting from her every cent that she has. This influence does not seem to be quite ideal for Jennifer's up-bringing. I am further wondering if a new will can go so far as to name my sister exclusive guardian. I know that such a nomination is not binding in any court but I should hope that it might, in addition to the contrast of Jean's notable responsibility, of Clare's evident lack of same, have some weight in protecting Jennifer from future bad influences and neglect.

In a later paragraph he writes: "I shall, on your advice, continue to deposit monthly cheques to her account."

On the next day he writes to Jean summarizing the reasons for his wishing to name her Jennifer's sole guardian should he die:

> When [Clare] left New York on the 20th of April last, she left no address through which any news of her child could be transmitted to her. She has never, since that date, either directly or indirectly, made any enquiry concerning the child's well being or given the least sign of interest in the child's existence. This cannot but impress you as it has impressed me as evidence of more than ordinary irresponsibility. Reluctantly I have come to recognize it as indifference to the child on the part of the mother.
> My assumption is confirmed in a letter written to me by Mr. Richard Myers... reporting a conversation between himself, his wife and Clare held in their apartment about the middle of last month. This letter reads, in part, as follows:
>> "But hang on to Jennifer. Aunt E. (Emma Eames) and all of us agree that she should be in your care and A.L. (Mrs. Myers) told this to Clare who agreed quite glibly that J. should be with you."
>
> Of this letter I must say that both Mr. and Mrs. Myers are proven loyal and disinterested friends of both Clare and myself.
> I submit further reason. Clare's guardianship of Jennifer will, in my opinion, throw the child upon the hands of its grandparents. I most strenuously disapprove of the kind of upbringing she would receive at their hands.... On the other hand, if Clare retains Jennifer and keeps her with herself, the child will be exposed to the influences of the life with which Clare has involuntarily associated herself, influences which viewed in the most charitable light, bode ill for the development of both mind and character.

Sidney's last remark about Clare's influences which would be harmful to Jennifer if the child were left to her refers not only to the (according to Sidney) baleful Aherne. Writing to Roger Burlingame, he says that Clare has returned to "her world of fairies and lesbians and yes-guys after her brief sejour in the respectable intellectual middle classes of Yorkville" (the location of their East 82nd street house). He here contrasts his way of life and that of his friends with a world of volatile relationships, unstable homes, shallow minds, and men and women of untrustworthy character that he believed Clare now frequented.

On the one hand it is easy to know why Sidney makes the sharp difference between his life and the one he supposes Clare now lives. He was homophobic (although tolerantly so), hardworking, stable, monogamous, extremely intelligent, and highly respectful of people who know the "right" thing to do. Abstractly he had great admiration for those of the "good" middle class. On the other hand, Sidney actually lived very little among the middle class. With all his complaints about the theater, with all his determination at various times to give it up, he never did, for its excitement and creativity were alluring. His friends were the creators of art, drama, and literature, such people as Katharine Cornell, Alfred Lunt and Lynn Fontanne, Charles MacArthur, Roger Burlingame, none of them leading ordinary middle-class lives or possessing the merely middle-class virtues if they possessed them at all. Although he himself lived a life that somewhat resembled that of the middle class, for the most part his friends were the loose-living creators of art. Between them and Clare's friends before and after Sidney there really was a matter of a degree of difference. Nevertheless, he continued to use Clare's environment as one of the counts against her.

On September 24th, he receives word from Margalo Gillmore, "who keeps in touch," that Clare will sail on the *Mauretania* in two weeks. (Whether Margalo Gillmore keeps in touch with him, Clare, or both he fails to say.)

To learn of Clare's state at this point we must turn mainly to *A Proper Job*, Brian Aherne's autobiography. Of his relationship with Clare he, of course, gives a quite different view from Sidney's. But he is not altogether accurate in his account of Sidney's relationship with Clare.

Of his relationship with Clare Aherne wrote that she "flooded" his heart "with comfort and happiness." He would ask her "how it was possible that she should love me. Shaking her head just a little and smiling tenderly, she would reply…: 'You're just my idea'" (a fascinating remark suggesting that the Brian Aherne with whom she was in love was someone of her own devising, but that is perhaps true of anyone who is in love) (140).

Just as Sidney presents a cynical view of Aherne's emotions, so Aherne interprets Sidney's feelings coldly: "He [Sidney] did not care for Clare, but he cared deeply about what people said, and he felt he was placed in a humiliating position. He cut off financial support, refused a divorce, and insisted upon the return of the baby and the nurse" (142–43). While the last two items were true, and Sidney did feel himself to be in a humiliating position, he clearly continued to love Clare, and he did not cut off financial support, and he did not refuse a divorce. But after forty years, when Aherne wrote the book, if he forgot exactly what happened, he may be pardoned. Of course, he may always have believed his assertations to be true.

But Clare had problems other than those of the heart. Aherne tells us that despite her great success in *The Silver Cord*, she could not find work. She did act in a Sunday night Stage Society performance of Jean Jacques Bernard's *L'Ame en Peine*, which James Agate was to remember: "The late Clare Eames, in her beautiful and memorable performance for the Stage Society three years ago, was largely helped by a personality which suggested the unrest occasioned by a soul too eager for the body" (Agate, 63). We cannot help but think of Sidney's remark that Clare had the divine spark or again of Guthrie McClitick's observation: "She heard 'wild harps' playing and that was what she was gunning for...."

Nevertheless, despite that apparently magical performance, she did not immediately get another role in England. However, Gilbert Miller offered her a part in the New York production of Maugham's play *Sacred Flame* in New York, which she accepted because of "her financial straits, her longing to see her child, and her hopes of one more appeal to her husband..." (Aherne, 150). Since we do not have any of Clare's letters to Sidney for this time, we cannot know of any appeal she previously had made or what appeal she now intended to make. According to Sidney, she had all this time been frustratingly silent.

The New York critics hated the Maugham play, very different from his usual comic mode, in which Clare returned to her native stage. But they generally greeted Clare with admiring reviews. The often-skeptical Brooks Atkinson of *The New York Times* remained skeptical: "As the nurse, professionally accoutered, Clare Eames seems to overreact to the heroics and to endow melodrama with the splendid coloring of Greek tragedy. It is perilous in the acting, to adorn dramatic trifles with tragic substance; it gives the secret away" (November 20th, 1928). But other critics were more sympathetic. For example, St. John Ervine in *The World* said, "Miss Clare Eames magnificently portrays the taut devotion of Nurse Wayland" (November 21st, 1928), and Richard Lockridge wrote that "Miss Eames ... makes Nurse Wayland an unforgettable portrait of

9. Smash!

a twisted, desperate woman—pitiable and agonizing..." (November 28th, 1928).

In her private life Clare seemed at first to be straightening things out with Sidney:

> Clare got her lawyers on my head and we fought alimony and custody and I sat tight but that was bad and then, everything being arranged for Clare to get her freedom under the law of Ohio for cruelty and gross neglect of duty, the tabloids waited upon her to ask if she had anything to add to the truth about the divorce and thus informed her that her London romance is all but public property and she will become same the moment she gives the press a divorce to hang it on and she dropped everything and headed for 157 [their home on East 82nd Street, presumably to show that she and Sidney were still together] in blank terror that she may have to pay for her behavior in the form of a somewhat dented reputation [letter to Leonard Bacon, November 9th, 1928].

Clare's "scuttling" into 157 made Sidney scuttle right out, leaving Jennifer with her mother. He had been offered contracts in Hollywood before, and now he accepted one from Samuel Goldwyn for a short stint there, expecting to return to New York in December. His New York season was now spoiled. Of the three plays he had planned for it, only *Olympia*, a translation from Ferenc Molnar, was produced, and it ran a mere 39 performances. *Fête Gallante*, the play about Marie Duplessis and Dumas fils, was never produced. "I shall probably never show that to anyone," Sidney wrote in the following year to Arthur Hobson Quinn (October 15th, 1929). *Yellow Jack*, the play taken from *Microbe Hunters*, he could not finish and in fact did not feel it ready for the stage until the mid-thirties.

Sidney did not return from Hollywood in December. He became an extremely successful film writer much in demand now that the talkies were here. He always came back to the stage, however, regarding it as his major artistic enterprise, but never, for the rest of his life, did he give up the very large income that he commanded in Hollywood.

Although Clare's play was a failure, she remained in New York for unfortunate reasons. Sidney writes his mother on November 13th, 1928, "her doctors think she has something the matter with her for which they are making x-rays." For this "something the matter with her" she needed yet another operation.

10

Divorce and Death

Clare and Sidney paid a terrible toll for the emotional turmoil in the years immediately preceding their separation and those of the divorce negotiations.

In 1920 Sidney wrote: "The world was not made to be reformed. It was made for men to struggle against despair and hope together." In this difficult time of his life he lived up to, as he always tried to do, his cross-grained credo. Clare forced the separation and the divorce on him, and he accepted them with painful stoicism but with the underlying expectation that his life would eventually recover, that he would one day resume an emotionally nourishing relationship. But repressing his anger, especially in the face of Clare's silences, and his usually successful refusal to indulge in self-pity came at great cost, often depression and the inability to work on his plays. In 1930, when he looked back over the four years since the production of *The Silver Cord*, he found that he had wasted four of his most productive years.

Fortunately, in this period he was able to start a highly successful new career, screenwriting, which proved wonderfully lucrative. Not only was it able to divert him from worrying excessively about his failure to work on his dramas but it allowed him to pay for his high divorce expenses. Indeed, the remuneration from this new career was so great that he was never able to give it up altogether. Still, he found it artistically unsatisfying and in the deepest part of him felt it to be a barren use of his time.

Clare desired the separation seemingly to fulfill herself without Sidney's hovering presence and without the necessity for providing the requirements of his work. The love to which she then turned, according to Brian Aherne, gave joy to them both. In the theater she achieved a few successes and thus maintained her status as a major actress. But when we consider that when she came to England she left a leading role in the most important repertory company in the United States, membership on its Board, marriage to its "American" dramatist, the general acceptance of her work as an actress of "genius," and a growing reputation as a fledgling director, we realize that she had indeed been a major force in the theatre. In the last years of her life she never recovered that power. Among the major obstacles preventing her from developing a career in England was the Aliens' Restriction Act of 1921, a law never intended to be applied to the theater, but then it was so applied that both Clare's career and finances were limited (Aherne, 163–65). Her bad health also prevented the growth of her work, and then it killed her.

For Clare, the divorce negotiations resulted in twisted feelings, often in emotional paralysis, apparently preventing her from even writing to her daughter. This surely struck deep into her soul. Life, that is, behaved in its usual unpredictably baleful ways. Like Sidney, Clare apparently faced her problems with courage. Had she lived, her career might have returned to its full effectiveness. But in her last years, though Clare may never have regretted leaving Sidney, she never fulfilled the hopes for which she left him.

Probably early in January 1929 Ernest Angell, Sidney's friend and lawyer in the divorce proceedings, asked Sidney for a copy of a letter Clare had sent him on November 28th, 1928. He replied to Angell: "I have spoiled a genial Sunday morning reading Clare's letter of November 28th of which you have asked me to send you a copy. I shall not send you a copy of all of it. I transcribe herewith such passages as can have any bearing on matters."

Sidney had written Jean on January 7th that the letter "seems confidential even for a lawyer's eyes." He himself will decide whether Angell "really needs it, and if he does, copy it myself and keep the original in the Bank of Italy here." We do not possess any part of the original letter. The section of it that Sidney sent Angell follows:

> Sid dear, I beg you to postpone your return from California as long as possible. I don't want to keep you out of your house, but I am sure that, for Jennifer's sake, you don't want to have her mother placarded in the tabloids. I realize I am asking a great deal and, if you want me to, I am willing to send her out to California for Christmas. On the other hand, if you really want to come home, we might be able to pull it off pleasantly enough living in the same house for a few weeks. I don't see why not, if the situation is *net*. But that all depends on your feeling. I don't want to cause you any more pain than I can help. And I have suffered, too, dear Sidney, as much as you, but in a different way; compunction and regret ands self-contempt are very real torments. And I shall continue to pay for this. I know. We cannot inflict suffering on any one, even involuntarily, and

hope to get off Scot free. The only thing I implore you to help me to avoid is a ghastly scandal. For Jennifer's sake, if not mine, I simply *cannot bear it*. The thought that she should be looked upon as a Poor Little Thing. Let us, oh, let us be brave and splendid and self-respectfully [sic]. I am willing to bind myself to anything. (I am so afraid you won't believe me.) If we are divorced and the court awards you the custody of the child (now be patient this is not a hidden attempt to get her) there is no hope that a terrible scandal won't break. But, if you allow the Court to award me the custody, I promise to bind myself to any kind of legal instrument you and Angell see fit, to make no attempt to take her away from you and to trust to your good will to let me see her. This would put me in your power absolutely and, if I did break my word (which I solemnly swear I won't) you could always raise a most awful stink by disclosing the nature of the document to the court. I have spoken to Ernest about this and he seems to think it not impractical. Dear Sid, I beg you to believe that I am writing with my heart's blood. I stand to lose everything. You and my darling Pearlio and Brian. For as to him, I am not decided. But I can't look to the future any more. If I find myself quite alone, I have to put up with it and take my medicine. I can not hope to postpone punishment and my own private castigation that the Lord will certainly see fit to inflict on me will be, and is, bad enough. I still want to save the remnants of dignity for you and Pearlio and, to a lesser degree, myself, to build what we can on. And no child can be a fine spirit if she is taught that her mother is a disgrace. I don't mean by you, dear, but by the very air she breathes. We *must* enter on a conspiracy of silence as far as she is concerned.

Sidney ends his letter to Angell with the following: "You can see from that much how tragic a cry of fear the letter is. The balance is intensely personal and of no interest. I should not want any eyes but yours to see even what I have copied herewith nor could I allow any of it to be used against Clare. Whatever else her feeling toward me may be, she trusts me completely. What a contradiction the poor girl is, what a mixture of modern freedom and ancient fears!"

When Sidney characterizes the letter as a "tragic cry of fear," he sees it only as self-protective. Clare, we know from one of Sidney's earlier letters, had fled to their house to avoid scandal. Once divorce was definitely in the offing, she feared that there would be then a hunt for a reason, which would be easy enough to find, for rumors were everywhere. Further, she believed, if Sidney sued for divorce with desertion as the reason and the custody of Jennifer awarded to Sidney, she would be seen as a "disgrace." Almost never at that time was the husband given custody of the child. The woman would have to have committed acts of moral turpitude, and adultery was so understood. If the man committed adultery, most people thought of it as a minor blemish. But in considerations of awarding custody, a man's adultery normally would not be taken into account, for the woman in most cases was regularly given custody. But if she were not, everyone thought of her as adulterous or worse.

In this situation, even though Sidney did not intend to charge Clare with adultery, the newspapers would attribute such behavior as the court's reason for giving custody to Sidney.

Whether or not the scandal at the end of the twenties would have been as terrific as Clare feared it would is a question. Whether or not it would have hurt Jennifer more than Clare's failure to write her daughter is also a question. We have to realize that after no contact with Jennifer for about six months, she is, as she writes this letter, living with her daughter at 157 East 82nd Street. Previous to her briefly seeing her earlier in the year when she had returned to the United States, supposedly to try for a reconciliation, she had not been in touch with Jennifer at all for about six weeks. After she sends Jennifer to Sidney at Christmastime of 1928, she will write one letter to her daughter, who will then neither hear from nor see her mother for the rest of Clare's life. Clare's concern for Jennifer, then, expressed in the letter, we may agree with Sidney, is in large part self-protective. But we may also assert that consciously Clare genuinely believed that she was looking out for Jennifer's best interest. For the Victorian era still hovered darkly above the early twentieth century; the possibility of scandal seemed real, and the modern addition of the tabloids to cry out unseemly tales would make it all the worse. As things worked out, however, the divorce did go the way Clare feared, but neither Clare's career nor her public character seemed to suffer by it; nor was Jennifer's life made worse by that aspect of the divorce.

When Clare implies that the suffering she has inflicted on Sidney was involuntary, she insists that her leaving him was neither willful nor the outcome of lust for Aherne but a need that came from her very being, the puritan call of her inner self. Sidney denigrates her inability to control such behavior, labeling it "modern freedom." In the sense that she left him not because he committed adultery but because she simply could no longer live with him, she is indeed acting in accordance with the dictates of "modern freedom." The distinction between Clare's professed motivation and that of the contemporary woman who divorces her husband because she desires the freedom to develop her work and her career may seem trivial. But to Brian Aherne she had said, "Be true to the God within you." She felt she could act only after compliance with the word of the God within. However, even though Clare spoke the language of puritanism rather than that of the liberated "new" woman, her action may also be seen as compatible with the new woman's seeking self-realization. While Clare never speaks of herself as a new woman, she had to be influenced as well by that prevalent phenomenon.

Whether she be puritan or new woman, there can be little doubt of the pain she felt for the pain she caused. The same puritan self that gave her assurance for divorcing Sidney also gave her guilt for the hurt she inflicted; she held herself in contempt; she castigated herself. Being a new woman in no way relieved her of her self-punishment; in fact, it only added to it. Clare would never wish to return to Sidney; she felt herself entirely justified in leaving him, and yet we can entirely believe in the pain that came from it.

Clare's relationship with Jennifer brings up other questions. Her offer to send the child to the West Coast for Christmas is surely related to Clare's forthcoming operation and her subsequent period of recuperation. Certainly, she felt, Sidney could provide Jennifer with a happier Christmas in Berkeley than she, a convalescent mother, could give the child in New York.

We can offer some logical explanation for Clare's apparently easy willingness to give up the child altogether. On the one hand, with jobs coming uncertainly, despite her high professional reputation, Clare would be earning much less than Sidney. Even with substantial alimony and child support which the court would award her, she could not offer Jennifer the ease of life Sidney could with his large income, very large now that he was earning a Hollywood salary. Perhaps more important was her correct understanding of which she wrote to Sidney: "I can't look to the future any more." She left Sidney for her unhedged future, but how she would develop her career seemed clouded. However, as we shall see, she wished to do so beyond stumbling from part to part. But in that effort Jennifer would be a burden, robbing her of the long hours necessary to developing a theater, or to traveling with a company. Sidney, on the other hand, with a career as a writer already established enabling him to have secure and definite places to live, having also an extended family (Clare would lack one in England) could offer Jennifer, in addition to ease of life, a stable landscape in which to grow.

Many can understand Clare's position in this matter, but few would understand her failure to see or write to her child for the six months before she returned to the United States to play in *The Sacred Flame* or her failure to write more than one letter to her daughter from the time she left the United States in late 1928 until her death in November 1930. We must register the shock of Dick Myers, who seemed to like Clare, saw her in London when he visited that city and invited her to his house for dinner when she twice visited Paris. Myers wrote to Sidney on July 4th, 1929, after a conversation with Clare: "The thing that astonished me is that she can go on ad libitum without seeing or hearing from her child."

Meanwhile in late 1928 Clare had to worry about her operation. She had originally retreated to the house on East 82nd Street owned by her and Sidney in order to escape scandal. She wished to continue in it not only for appearances but because of the recovery period following the operation. This becomes clear in a telegram Ernest Angell sent Sidney on December 14th, 1928: "Clare desired return to house for few days before going Cleveland stop Believe this is solely for recuperation and have told her to do this stop On leaving she desires take flat silver coffee service and two gold trays wire confirmation my understanding that these are hers stop See to it personally that her temporary stay at house does not interfere with closing plans" (The closing concerns not only the sale of the house but its shuttering because the owners, Sidney and Clare, are absent.)

In a letter to Jean on December 15th, Sidney shows both anger and cynicism at Clare's desire for the flatware and trays:

> I wired Angell to tell Clare to gut the house if she likes but to clear out completely. My goat was got finally and forever by her selecting, to take away with her, the only objects of really monetary value which I have ever possessed. I thought that was just the least bit shrewd of one who lives, by her own admission, wholly in the Empyrean. I suppose that real breeding is the same in the Empyrean as here below. I shall have difficulty with Mother because about half the flat silver now being removed belongs to her. I am keeping my eye on Jennifer and the more Clare's wanders to gold trays and mother's silver, the better for me.... Take the baby but give me the gold trays!

A few days earlier, speaking, we presume, of those same trays, Sidney had written to Jean, "My heart will always bleed for those Henning trays, though. I worked so damned hard to pay for them" (December 12th, 1928).

Of course, by current standards, Clare had as much right as Sidney to those things, even his mother's flatware given, after all, to both of them. Not only that, but Clare, Angell's telegram implied, asked for Sidney's consent to take the stuff. Actually, Sidney's objection seems less to Clare's taking these items than to there being no previous discussion between them of the division of the property.

On his part Sidney was engaged in somewhat secret maneuvers. On December 12th, 1928, he telegraphs his mother, "Best not divulge this plan to Clare and [her] mother as unwise they know how long I intend keeping Jennifer west." The plan was to keep Jennifer out west for the winter. Now that he knew she was coming, he intended to take her to Hollywood after the Christmas spent at Jean's. Christmas included also Sidney's mother, who, according to form, refused Sidney's several invitations to Jean's, only to change her mind at the last minute when she accompanied Jennifer and Miss Jones out west.

Back in Hollywood the day after Christmas, with Jennifer still at Jean's, Sidney wrote his sister:

Dear Jean:—

Use your own judgment about the following. I should be glad if you would talk with Miss Jones somewhat as you did with me yesterday morning, expressing yourself about the disturbing influence of Clare's sporadic relationship with Jennifer and about Jennifer's need for an anchorage. I have no doubt of Clare's love for the child, but I see it as disturbing and not beneficial because it is wholly emotional and selfish, not maternal or considerate. It always seems to me desirable that Miss Jones, who is so much a part of my solution to Jennifer's problem, should understand the problem itself and yet it is nearly impossible for me to explain my position for fear of involving her and of presenting myself in a vindictive light. There is, for example, the immediate question of whether or not to answer those telegrams with some description of Jennifer's Christmas. I shall do nothing about them. I had rather that nothing were done. But I don't know how to tell Miss Jones to do nothing. My reason for doing nothing is that I prefer that to continuing to cooperate in Clare's performance regarding Jennifer and that is not at all, as I need hardly say, vindictive. However, Miss Jones ought to realize that. And you, being detached, can explain it better and far more convincingly than I.

It is difficult altogether to understand Sidney's attitude. In the first place we do not know to whom Clare addressed the telegrams. If she addressed them to Sidney and to Jean, we can easily comprehend why he did not respond to them and why he did not wish Jean to respond, either. Clare came and went as she pleased in Jennifer's life, and certainly, as Sidney pointed out, Clare did not supply Jennifer with the kind of parental stability children require. He believed he had a right to exclude Clare to reduce the confusion and strain upon the child. On the other hand, one of the telegrams might have been addressed to Jennifer. Clare might thus be making direct contact with her child, rightly expecting Miss Jones to act as the medium through which the child responded to her mother. Sidney then had no right to come between a child and her parent. Simply the knowledge that the parent is there, even if she arbitrarily comes and goes, is better than absolute absence. Sidney disclaims vindictiveness, and Jean's apparently having originated the idea in the first place implies that it did not begin with him and therefore was not energized by anger. Yet he latched onto it strongly, and we can only wonder how much the Henning trays and the flatware entered into his decision—besides his anger at her leaving him. He had recently said of Clare's behavior in taking them: "My goat was got finally and forever." At any rate his refusal to answer her telegrams may have encouraged Clare to reassume her silence if she needed such encouragement at all.

In Hollywood Sidney signed a lease for a small house where he, Jennifer and Miss Jones would live while Sidney wrote for the movies, and he found a playschool for Jennifer (letter to Jean, November 31st, 1928).

His movie contract was with Samuel Goldwyn, the legendary film maker who settled early in Hollywood. Although as rude in manner as the other Hollywood pioneer producers, Goldwyn in his series of independent companies managed to make a number of films that were both popular and critically respected, and some stand up to this day. He had the good sense to hire such distinguished writers as Sidney Howard, Lillian Hellman, and Robert E. Sherwood, and such an insightful director as William Wyler, such an inventive photographer as Gregg Toland. These artists, irregularly working together, created over the years such fine films as *Dodsworth, Dead End, The Little Foxes,* and *The Best Years of Our Lives.*

Sidney originally went to Hollywood to escape Clare, to work as a writer when he could not, in the turmoil of separating from Clare, function as a dramatist, and to make good money. He meant to stay a month, but first with Clare continuing on in New York, then with divorce proceedings developing into a monster feeding on money, he signed a series of contracts that kept him in Hollywood for two years, except for a few months to write a play and see it onto the boards.

At first he found the work "fascinatingly interesting and difficult without being at all too hard. I mean, the difficulty has been, not driving work, but [that] the adjustment to an entirely new medium and my round about way of telling stories through detailed characterization needs much adjustment to photography" (letter to HH, November 22nd, 1928). But he soon found the group work, the comparatively small power of the writer, and the shoddy standards so agonizing that he longed to return to playwriting. Also, even though he seemed to be welcomed by the "good and great of the picture industry," he was "lonely away from my friends. That has cured me of any idea I once had of living out of New York" (letter to HH, November 28th, 1929). That loneliness, he writes to his mother, was apparently ameliorated by "some thoroughly pleasant things ... happening lately including the descent of Clare Kummer [a popular New York dramatist] and Roland Young and his wife at the Beverly Hills Hotel up the street. And of Lawrence Stallings. And of George Abbott. All of New York seems to be coming here." Sidney adds prophetically, "I doubt if much of it will ever come back." Also arriving soon is a person who must have been a sharp reminder of Clare: "Dudley Digges is coming, too, to act in two of my pictures." But despite the arrival of those personalities and perhaps because of the stab that might have come with Dudley Digges's name, he ends this part of the letter with "I am sick of sunshine" (March 2nd, 1929).

Nevertheless the money held him fast in Hollywood. In the midst of his depression he seemed in a backhand, almost shamefaced, way to enjoy his success. In a letter of December 10th, 1928, to Jean he apologizes for deserting art to sign a second contract: "Before you stamp your foot and cry 'Perfide!' ask Duncan if he can't remember the day when he took quite a bit of trouble to earn a thousand berries a week and pick up more than that in experience." On December 28th, 1928, he writes to Leonard Bacon, giving his desperate travails an amusing twist:

> This Hollywood is funny a good deal of the time, tiring some of it but never real enough to take anything out of one and it pays extraordinarily well. They give me thirteen hundred per week to be kicked around and, at that figure away from New York, I don't at all mind being kicked. I write talking sequences as they are called for the most God awful pictures and when I am really up against it for something to give my characters to say, I remember an old joke or two that I once read in Judge and thus get a reputation for being a wit. They brought me in a Conrad story the other day with orders to "pash this up a bit." Did I not pash! That story is now only one long orgasm and it is produced as "from the magic pen of Joseph Conrad." All this must shock you terribly. Never mind. I'm no longer worrying about my own troubles and I should worry about Joseph's.

Then again to Jean, this time on January 15th, 1929, he writes:

> I see plainly that I shall very soon stand in need of moral support again. These people like what I've done on [Bulldog] Drummond so much that I am now getting propositions which will, literally, make a millionaire of me if I haven't the courage to refuse them. Goldwyn will actually give me a long contract on a sliding scale beginning at $75,000 a year with, thrown in, royalties on any original pictures I write. Sister, dear sister, I don't need that much cash, do I? And I do need to write plays and a novel or so before I'm finished.... Famous Players is just girding its loins to make what they call a REAL proposition and I'm afraid to go to the telephone on account of weak character.

With all his complaints three films from this period went out under Sidney's name: *Bulldog Drummond*, *Raffles*, and *Condemned*. All of them received critical approval, made money at the box office, and the first two at least remain interesting today.

But Sidney's personal problems continued. In the January 15th letter to Jean just quoted Sidney writes: "A night letter from Mother informs me that Clare sailed for England on January 5th. I had not heard of that before. It will mean, probably, that she has abandoned her divorce plans because she can't very well work a Cleveland residence in London. Well, a letter from Ernest is on its way, and according to Mother, he now says that I must do things myself."

Clare's return to England was undoubtedly the result of a conscious choice between divorce proceedings and her career. The popular actress-manager Gladys Cooper decided to produce *The Sacred Flame* in London despite its New York failure. She offered Clare her New York role of Nurse Wayland, and Clare clearly saw it as an opportunity to resume her lapsed career in England. As far as her profession was concerned, she chose correctly. In fact both the play and she fared much better in London than in New York. The London *Times* concludes its review:

> But the evening's honours are shared by Mr. Maugham with Miss Clare Eames. Her study of the nurse is an exquisite piece of delicacy and judgment. How steady is her reserve, how unmistakable are the gleams of passion beneath her coldness, how overwhelming in consequence is that passion when it breaks into flame! Hers is a lovely performance, charged with wisdom lighted by its restraints, enriched continually by perceptions not of the mind but of the spirit [February 9th, 1929].

Charles Morgan, writing in *The New York Times* under the heading. "LONDON ONCE MORE REVERSES A NEW YORK VERDICT," praises Mr. Maugham: "[H]e seems to have been brilliantly successful in making the motives and inclinations of his creatures neatly interlock." Comparing *The Sacred Flame* to Maugham's immediately preceding play, *The Letter*, he says that the former "has a dignity and a freedom from sensationalism which the earlier piece conspicuously lacked." But again the climactic final paragraph is reserved for Clare:

> But Clare Eames is an artist. You know her merits too well for it to be necessary to analyze them here. It is true that she has the best part in the play. Mr. Maugham's study of Nurse Wayland is flawless.... He has given the actress every opportunity. But Miss Eames brings to the part something that no other actress except Dorothy Green [a highly admired British player] could bring to it—a magnificent steadiness, an extraordinary reserve of tragic power, a perpetual suggestion of nature fighting against an imposed control. She gives to the play that touch of beauty it lacks elsewhere [March 3rd, 1929, VII, 2].

But illness again intervened to prevent Clare from completely enjoying her triumph. Sebastian Shaw, who was in the cast with Clare, remembered several decades later, "One night in the wings Clare Eames told me she was soon going to die, and she used to faint on the stage occasionally because she was already very ill" (Morley, 128).

Despite her premonition and her occasional fainting. Clare apparently failed to see a doctor, for Brian Aherne seems surprised when he went to pick her up at the stage door one night that she had been replaced by her understudy. Finding Clare in her apartment with "severe abdominal pain," he telephoned their friend Reggie Reixach, who sent his doctor from Richmond. The physician placed her in his "'nursing home.'" Major surgery followed to be succeeded by a six-month recovery period (Aherne, 160).

We suppose that Aherne called Reggie Reixach because the latter was a good friend to both Clare and him and rich enough to take care of any expenses that might arise from an illness. But why did Reggie's doctor take her to his "nursing home" rather than to a standard hospital? Why is *nursing home* in quotation marks? What was the exact nature of these abdominal problems? Brian Aherne is silent on all these questions.

Sidney hears about Clare's illness almost three months after its onset when he is back in New York to mount a play. Margalo Gillmore, who had a success that season in *Berkeley Square*, informed Sidney of "how seriously ill Clare has been." He telephones Mrs. Eames, who

> told me that she does not know Clare's address, that she has not heard from Clare since June and that Clare was operated on for something mysterious early in August (the 9th) and was then (at the end of October) just able to walk a little. She had the news from Clare's brother [Bud] who lives in Cambridge, England. Clare had nearly died when they took her out to some sort of resort in Cornwall. I managed to get a thousand dollars to her through her lawyer and Angell who understood it to be a gift without any implications on my part and she is now said to be in Italy with a nurse. One aspect of this that shocks me just a little is that none of it seems to touch me at all personally. It seems to be something which has happened to a friend with whom I have got quite out of touch [letter to Jean, November 23rd, 1929].

Sidney had paid for Clare's operation in the United States in the previous December and, despite his apparently diminished feelings for Clare, he paid at least in part for this one. Further, when Mrs. Eames asks him to find "some desert resort where she could get back on her feet again as soon as she is well enough to be brought back to this country," he almost immediately writes to a friend to find one.

But Clare did not return to the United States to recover, nor, so far as we can tell from Brian Aherne's memoir, did she go to Italy with a nurse. "I was used to being short of money," writes Aherne, "and my wants were small, but Clare's situation was now grave indeed, and had it not been for Reggie's kindness and hospitality I don't know what she would have done. Sitting on the terrace of his lovely garden that bordered the Thames, she slowly regained her health" (163). Aherne makes no mention of the thousand dollars that Sidney sent Clare.

When Clare recovered, she accepted an offer to appear in an all-star revival of *Milestones*, a multigenerational play by Edward Knoblock and Arnold Bennett first performed in 1912. Clare's character was central to the drama, that of a young woman who breaks her engagement and regrets it later as an old maid. Brian Aherne writes enthusiastically that

Clare Eames in romantic youth and disappointed old age in *Milestones*, her last production. (Courtesy of the New York Public Library.)

in this role Clare "slowly aged from a young, vibrant, romantic girl to a tired old woman.... [I]t gave her the chance to give what was possibly her greatest performance" (163).

Soon after the limited run of *Milestones*, Clare was offered the part of Beatrice opposite Baliol Holloway as Bendick in *Much Ado about Nothing*. Holloway, who had played on both sides of the Atlantic and had worked with many of the same actors as Clare, perhaps knew of her intention of a few years earlier to play Beatrice. But again her desire to act the part was frustrated.

The British Aliens' Restriction Act of 1921, meant to prevent large-scale cheap labor from entering Britain after World War I, had an unexpected effect on the theater. For the government insisted that the law applied to the theater as well as to any other field. Only exceptional talent would be granted permission to play, and the arbiter of that talent was the minister of labor. He refused Clare permission to play in *Much Ado* (Aherne, 165–67).

Aherne received Hollywood movie offers, and Clare might have continued her career in films, but both tended to look down on films as a career. Further, according to Aherne, Clare was very reluctant to meet Sidney again, who, as we know was successfully ensconced in Hollywood. Instead of pursuing their careers in the movies, they pooled their resources for a presentation of *S.S. Tenacity,* to be translated and directed by Clare with Aherne in the cast.

The production of *Tenacity* may have been the first in a program of Clare's future plans. On November 30th, 1929, Dick Myers wrote to Sidney:

> Clare arrived in Paris last night and promptly telephoned us. She came for dinner—and really looked better than I have seen her look for a long while. She was all afire with a new idea for presenting the works of the newer French playwrights in London—translated, of course,—and with herself to direct, and occasionally play. She wanted some letters of introduction, which I gave her. Her recent operation seems to have helped her physically—but I still think she has a wild look in her eye and even last night she got more and more excited until she was in a state bordering on hysteria.

There is now surprising news of Clare's new religious ideas:

> Incidentally she says she is thinking of becoming a Catholic—(Alice Lee is sure that she has already become one; she raved about Rome, St. Peter's, the Church, and was going to mass at Notre Dame early Sunday morning.) She didn't mention you—and I'm glad she did'nt [*sic*], but she said she was trying to earn enough money so she could prove she could support Jennifer.... [S]he seems perfectly contented with her English life, and evidently plans to stay there.

On December 31st, 1929, Myers again writes Sidney:

> Now about Clare—she is far from being at death's door. It is true that she was ill last summer, but that is all over. At present she is preparing to act in a series of French plays in London (translations of course) & she dashed right over to Paris two weeks ago to get the rights for one—accom-

panied by Mr. Brian Aherne. I don't suppose it is any news to you that her affair with Aherne is "common talk" in London & yet Clare acts so innocently when she talks to us, that it is almost insulting to our intelligence. She even had him call for her at Poirets [apparently her poverty, after all, did not force her to give up purchases at that establishment] where she was getting some clothes—& of course, the quick intuition of Mme. Helene saw the situation at once. Both Alice Lee and I think that Clare is in a strange state of nervous tension—she is truly an exaltee....

I believe Clare plans to marry Aherne—& become a Catholic! So London friends say—& she herself told us she was thinking of becoming a Catholic; & she wouldn't do this, if it were not for Aherne.

There is no evidence that Clare became Catholic. (The Episcopal service was recited at her funeral.) But if she had, it would not have been because of Aherne, whom Myers probably thought to be Catholic because of his Irish descent; but neither his Irish nor his English forebears were Catholic (Aherne, 8). It is unlikely that the iconoclastic Clare was serious about converting to Catholicism. Perhaps she was trying on for size an idea that for the moment, because of her current emotional difficulties, appealed to her.

However, these difficulties were certainly the cause of her "strange state of nervous tension." Her situation was now worse than it was when she first separated from Sidney. Since the previous February he, on Angell's advice, had cut off her allowance with the hope that she would do something about the divorce. Her remark that she was trying to earn enough money to prove that she could support Jennifer shows a sense of guilt about her strange behavior toward her child. Although she and Aherne were not living together, they were openly engaged in their affair, at least in London (her foolish attempt to hide it from the Myerses undoubtedly added to her tension that evening). It may have been brave of Clare to acknowledge her relationship in London, but it was undoubtedly a trial for a woman who had come from her conventional background. The illness that brought her to death's door and her long and difficult recovery that, according to Aherne, had not yet ended, surely aggravated her nervous condition and intensified her premonition, remembered by Sebastian Shaw, that she was going to die. Now in addition to her other pressures, she was evolving a program that would test whether or not the lonely creative road she had chosen was worth what she had given up.

When in July 1930 her program began to materialize in the production of *S.S. Tenacity*, presumably the first in a series, her tension must have reached a very high pitch. For by then she had discovered that the ministry of labor would prevent her taking any job a producer wished to offer her. Nevertheless, she courageously went about her creative tasks and directed the play.

Clare gave a small role in *S.S. Tenacity* to Margaret Webster, who in the 1930s and 1940s was to become the premier director of Shakespeare in the United States. Webster, the daughter of the popular and influential May Whitty and Ben Webster, had met Clare and Sidney at Hal Rhodes's in Venice in 1923 and had been impressed by their "life enhancing" force. In the late 1920s she seemed to be rudderless, and she credits Clare, while acting in *The Sacred Flame*, with bringing her out of her funk. "Clare Eames ... turned my eyes outward. I stopped being what Shaw calls 'a selfish little clod of ailments and grievances.' She encouraged me to hope that I had something to give and not just something to get. A little Life Force flowed back into me" (Webster, *The Same Only Different*, 345). The words Clare used, as recounted by Webster, were trite, might have been and probably were spoken to the aspiring actress by others. But certainly it was Clare's "life enhancing" force, her sense of high calling, her accomplishments as an actress that inspired Webster and caused her to remember Clare's effect on her four decades later.

But the aid that Clare gave her did not prevent her from evaluating objectively Clare's directorial abilities at this time: "She had not yet fully mastered the art of imparting to others what she could do herself; but she was enormously stimulating and brimming over with plans for the future."

The London *Times* review of the production makes no mention of the direction but finds that the play has the "veracity, though neither the brutality nor the vigour of a Maupassant story, especially as it is no less delightfully acted now than by the Stage Society [ten years previous]" (July 30th, 1930, 12). Clare and Aherne lost forty pounds on the production, but it was a modest and promising beginning for Clare's plans.

Clare's choice of *S.S. Tenacity* in her series of French plays may have been accidental. Perhaps she was able to acquire the rights easily; perhaps she felt that it would be easy to begin with a play she knew. Yet there seems to be a certain oddity about her choice. *Tenacity* in a sense began Sidney's career, for while translating it, he found a way to his original compositions. Although Clare was the creator of the current London project and the producer and director of its initial play, she may have felt that she was not the true source of its power unless she was also somehow the dramatist, that is, the translator. She wished to become *chère maitresse*. It is as though in seeking her own maturity, she was imitating Sidney when he found his.

Meanwhile Sidney had been growing increasingly disillusioned with his Hollywood enterprise though it paid him extremely well. His return to New York to see his play on stage only made greater his desire to escape his golden shackles. In a November 23rd, 1929, letter from New York to Jean he writes, "My one idea is to break with the pictures. If I can, oh, if I can. I came back here and, to my surprise, found myself completely myself once more and rarin' to go and write no end of things and I says to myself, says I, what in hell are you doing in that stinking, false world of Hollywood where machines and money displace life and art."

There were reasons other than the desire to escape the expressionless, greedy world of Hollywood for him to return to the theater. On April 6th, 1929, he wrote to Jean of his desire to "regain my position in the theatre." On July 12th of the same year he wrote to Ernest Angell: "[G]etting a play on has become a mania with me. It's very important to me and my future."

We can easily understand Sidney's anxiety. He had not written anything original for the stage for more than a year, and that was the unsuccessful *Salvation*, the collaboration with Charles MacArthur. He had produced no solo work since *The Silver Cord* in late 1926. When he left New York for England in 1927, he was the esteemed author of two recently successful and respected plays, one coming hard upon the other, produced by the major art theater in the United States. At that time great things were expected of him. On May 6th, 1930, he wrote, "Its [*sic*] awful to have started out with the promise I gave and fall as far as I've fallen in these last four years since I finished 'The Silver Cord'" (letter to Polly).

Sidney is correct about his lost position only in the sense that since late 1926 to the point in the fall of 1929 when he returned to Broadway with a play written alone, Broadway has blossomed with serious drama, not necessarily drama that is tragic or filled with pathos, but drama with serious intent though it may be comic. New playwrights appeared, and even when they seemed merely to entertain, their work had an expansiveness and sheen previously absent. Older dramatists also extended their range. Eugene O'Neill, for example, now taking Sidney's place as the Theatre Guild's "American" playwright, produced the nine-act, five-hour *Strange Interlude*, a Freudian drama bringing a sort of Joycean stream-of-consciousness technique to the stage. To everyone's surprise this daring adventure proved to be an immense success both on Broadway and on tour. Elmer Rice, who, though one year younger than Sidney, began his career as long ago as 1914, produced in his 1929 drama, *Street Scene*, another of his periodically successful experiments in theatrical technique.

Further, Sidney's friends were advancing their cause on Broadway. Robert E. Sherwood, who had been the movie critic on the old *Life* magazine, wrote a successful comedy in *The Road to Rome*, and he continued working. Charles MacArthur, after his failed collaboration with Sidney on *Salvation*, joined with Ben Hecht to produce in 1928 that roaring, now classic, newspaper comedy *The Front Page*. In the previous year George S. Kaufman, joining with Edna Ferber, wrote the successful satire on the Barrymores in *The Royal Family*. Philip Barry, whose comedies Sidney admired, produced in 1928 the play *Holiday*, which Sidney enjoyed and respected. S. N. Behrman, who had attended Baker's class at Harvard with Sidney and whose comedy Sidney felt during his Theatre Guild season that the producers were favoring over his, saw the critics treat that play, *The Second Man*, estimably.

Sidney, slogging away in Hollywood, worked hard to make money but simultaneously to clear some continuous time in which he could write a play that would enable him to reenter the Broadway scene with a flourish. He was able to arrange things so that he could be away from films from May through the fall to work on things theatrical, expecting occasionally to be recalled to Hollywood. When the lease on his house in Hollywood ended in April, he sent Jennifer to live with Jean at Berkeley, which he made his headquarters for playwriting. When ready for production he expected to go to New York, return to Berkeley for Christmas, then return once more to Hollywood for a stay after Christmas, visiting Jennifer weekends.

He had several plays in his mind. There was the revision of *Fête Galante*, in which he had already lost interest, the completion of *Yellow Jack*, the drama taken from a chapter in Paul De Kruif's *Microbe Hunters*, and a play originally for Clare and which finally became *Alien Corn*, to be produced by Katharine Cornell, who also played the leading role (letters to Harold Freedman, January 7th, 1929; August 3rd, 1929). But all these were pushed aside for the comedy he informally called his marriage play. It was at time variously titled "A Man Taken in Matrimony," "A Play for Married People," but finally produced by Arthur Hopkins in December 1929 as *Half Gods*.

Sidney insisted that the play was "completely impersonal. No one who has read it sees any trace of autobiography in it. It was planned before divorce crossed my path and discussed with Clare" (letter to Ernest Angell, August 27th, 1929). Of course, while the plot may not resemble the story of Sidney's recent life, surely its spirit derived from his personal experience. Further, pieces of the dialogue and some situations reflect Sidney's relationship with Clare. He had written to Barrett Clark on June 26th, 1929: "I have spent a blissful month on a play called 'HALF GODS' in which I am trying to get down some of American womanhood's revolt against marriage, kidded, of course, but still pretty much as I see it and have myself experienced a phase of it." So, while Sidney tried to generalize, the ideas come from the core of his being.

When *Half Gods* entered the Broadway competition, characters in dramas about the relations of men and women, marriage, and divorce had been tread the boards for about thirty years; throughout the twenties, writes Brenda Murphy, "the major topics for discussion plays continued to be marriage, women's equality, and divorce, with the last two closely linked" (Murphy, 165). Sidney's contribution to the subject asserts that marriage between two people who love each other, even if it is not a bed of roses, is good. Modern notions that women's self-realization is important point women in the wrong direction. Even being good at their jobs doesn't matter because those jobs can always be filled by someone else. There is nothing wrong with women taking jobs as long as they know that their first obligation is to their families. Men, in his view, ought to remain the major breadwinners. Marriage may be full of disagreements and fights, but for two people who love each other, it is a kind of splendid agony.

The play involves a successful young lawyer who complains of his wife's demand that they go out every night and of her incompetence at running their home. He cannot obtain the eight hours of sleep he needs each night to conduct his business the next day. For her part she sees his insistence that she can be nothing but wife and mother as limiting her options. Marriage, she believes, prevents her from the free personal and business choices that would allow her full development. The wife, Hope, becomes so unhappy that she leaves her husband, Stephen. Despite the efforts of both a friend and a relative, they fail to reconcile until she is about to leave for Reno, when she slaps Stephen, who knocks her out with a return punch. In the next scene Hope asks Stephen to return not because he punched her but because she realized the foolishness of their seeking a divorce. What matters is that they love each other and that marriage isn't meant to be happy at all! It's meant to be one long knockdown and drag out battle royal between two people who can't live without each other (*Half Gods*, 197). Despite Stephen's skepticism that the marriage will work and his knowledge that the peace for which he has been yearning since the play's first scene will always elude him, the couple seems to have gained the knowledge from the Emerson poem "All to Love," from which the play's title derives: "Heartily know, when halfgods go, the gods arrive." That is, the romantic conception they had of each other made them only half-gods. The ability to cope with the strange and familiar turns of the other's personalities makes them gods.

If Sidney wished to write a play which generalized about the relation of men, women, marriage, and divorce in modern times, he however took material "as I ... myself experienced a phase of it." There are pieces of dialogue and situations that are reminiscent of Sidney's life with Clare. For example, when Hope tries to make Stephen understand why she must leave, she explains: "Steve is a great man! ... I'm not kidding you! You're the greatest man I've known.... Just the same I've been so horribly unhappy with you that I couldn't, I simply couldn't endure things any longer..." (45–46). That sounds just like Clare, who continued to admire Sidney as a person and a dramatist but found living with him impossible. What emphasizes the parallel is that Hope's sentiments fit Sidney, at least according to Clare, but not Stephen, a successful lawyer in a prestigious law firm, but nothing about him indicates greatness.

Similarly, the Hope who exclaims to Stephen that she is "so much finer than you are! So much more sensitive!" (72) recalls the Clare who, according to Sidney, thought of herself as living in the Empyrean while Sidney's two feet stuck him on earth. We are reminded again of Clare when Hope asserts: "A time comes when a woman simply has to think of herself. I've got to get my place before it's too late" (50). Again like Clare, Hope easily surrenders her children to her husband in the course of the divorce settlement.

And Steve reflects Sidney. When Steve insists, "Well, I refuse to take a tart to a hotel, hire detectives to catch me in bed with her and let the papers make a mess of my good name" (122), he echoes Sidney's similar refusal. In Stephen's continual cry for peace for the sake of work we hear Sidney's cry as well.

But when we approach the comedy biographically, Sidney seems to have cheated. For, while Hope desires a position in the marketplace that could well do without her, Clare did not simply out of the blue sky decide that she wished to realize herself. She had always been an artist successfully bent on developing herself. In Sidney and Clare's home there was a more difficult situation of two highly sensitive, successful, complex individuals who could not altogether satisfy each other's array of needs. In *Half Gods* Sidney reduced this complexity to the situation of a successful husband and a foolish wife.

That is not to say that the play fails to show the workmanship of a first-class comic dramatist. Sidney gave up the structure of the well-made play that functioned smoothly in *The Silver Cord* for a fluid drama in several scenes, preferably without an intermission. The play seems to grow organically from the opening argument of Hope and Steve and branches out to the various scenes which derive from that argument. The characters are carefully shaped, the scenes are firmly built, the dialogue has life, and a farcical scene toward the end could probably be played uproariously. Yet a central failing persists, that the two chief figures seem to be very foolish and somewhat lacking in intelligence.

Of the contemporary reviewers, only Richard Lockridge enjoyed the play:

> Here and there along Broadway are plays more dramatically compelling tha[n] is "Half Gods"; there are a few, a very few, which are funnier than is Mr. Howard's play in those many moments when he let himself go into satire or travesty or simple intellectual spoofing. But it is hard to think of any in which the quality of clear, free intelligence is more mani-

10. Divorce and Death

fest; any which says keener things more gracefully; any which maintains a saner balance on the delicate tightrope of objective observation [*The Sun*, December 23rd, 1929].

If only the other daily reviewers thought as did Mr. Lockridge, Sidney would have been joyful indeed. But to a man they lambasted the drama, partly because their expectations of a Howard play were frustrated. John Mason Brown speaks for them all:

> Though the present season has excelled in its disappointments, even the keenest of them has not been more bitter than was the floundering tract on marriage which arrived at the Plymouth on Saturday night under the name of "Half Gods."
> If "Half Gods" was particularly disappointing it was because there were at least two persuasive reasons for assuming in advance that much might be expected of it. For after all, it came not only as an Arthur Hopkins production but also as the first play to reach Broadway in almost two years from the pen of the same Sidney Howard who—before he journeyed to Hollywood—had established himself as one of our leading dramatists by writing such vigorous and expert plays as "They Knew What They Wanted," "Lucky Sam McCarver," "The Silver Cord" and "Ned McCobb's Daughter."
> In "Half Gods," however, there are—with the exception of the first scene—scarcely any traces of the skill or the sophistication which are rightfully associated with the work of both Mr. Hopkins and Mr. Howard.

Brown later adds: "Indeed, if the sad truth must be known, 'Half Gods' is a muddled and ingenuous mixture of sugary sermonizing and sophomoric farce that is blessed with few virtues at all."

If Brown seemed to confirm Sidney's nightmare that he was no longer up there with the best of his contemporaries, Joseph Wood Krutch's review in *The Nation*, pointing to Sidney's personal life as the origin of the play, was perhaps even more painful:

> It is, I take it, no part of a dramatic critic's business to inquire too closely into whatever private reason a playwright may have for changing his opinions. If, for example, Mr. Sydney [sic] Howard once thought very well of both women and Freud, he has a perfect right now to denounce the two of them in good round terms without thereby giving me any license to speculate publicly upon the causes of the change. But the artist should earn his immunity by assuming a reciprocal obligation. It is his business to cover up with the impersonality of art the private feelings which inspire him, and accordingly when Mr. Howard, excellent playwright that he is, exhibits before the world a drama like "Half Gods" ... it becomes my duty to say that the play give every indication of having been written in some kind of a private pet; ... Passion is the *sine qua non* of drama and even anger may occasionally serve the playwright very well, but a masterpiece cannot be founded on mere irritation even though, as seems here to be the

case, that irritation nourishes a delusion of grandeur and believes itself to be moral indignation [January 1930, 52].

But that fall in New York brought some compensation for his professional failure. On November 23rd, 1929, Sidney writes to his sister, "I'm afraid, dear sister, that I've fallen in love. And that doesn't help matters when a divorce is still a year and four months away from me.... How can you say: please marry me a year and four months from now? Certainly you can't say it to anyone with Polly Damrosch's sense of humor."

Polly's full given name was Leopoldine, the third of the four daughters of Walter and Margaret Blaine Damrosch.

Walter Damrosch, one of the most eminent figures on the New York musical scene, had conducted the New York symphony for over two decades, was central to the founding of the New York Philharmonic Symphony, was one of its first guest conductors, and he was a radio personality as well. But not only Walter figured prominently in New York musical circles; the Damrosch family spread its influence wide and deep. Walter's brother Frank was central to the founding of the Juilliard School of Music and his sister Clara to the Mannes School of Music. With other organizations with which members of the family were associated, Damrosches permeated New York musical performances and educational life.

Politics also played a part in Polly's background. Her mother was a daughter of James G. Blaine, the Republican presidential candidate in 1884 and twice secretary of state. Polly was thus from distinguished families on both her mother's and father's sides.

"Polly was the most musical of the four Damrosch sisters and by universal report the prettiest and the sweetest." As the most musical of her siblings, she was "perhaps closer to her father than the others." According to Sidney she possessed a sense of humor, but "her friends felt in her at times an intensity which suggested to them that she would fall in love only once and then forever..." (Martin, 325). It was this attractive, humorous, obviously intelligent, musical, intense woman of thirty with whom Sidney fell in love. An observer might describe Clare in the same way except that Polly lacked professional ambition and therefore lacked Clare's threatening power.

Sidney and Clare had known the Damrosches for years. When Sidney came to New York to mount *Half Gods*, it was natural for him to look them up. The renewed acquaintanceship with Polly apparently quickly turned to love. By December 16th, when he is on the pre–Broadway tryout for *Half Gods*, Sidney is writing love letters to Polly. In the next year from Hollywood the vast majority of his frequent letters and telegrams go to her.

In one, written on December 29th, he describes his hare-brained and

10. Divorce and Death 263

hair-raising trip from New York to Berkeley, determined to share Christmas with Jennifer.

> Polly dear:—
>
> I had such a hell of a time beginning practically the moment you left me at the station. I woke up with a cold that would have done Donn Cook [the actor who played Stephen in *Half Gods*] proud in the scene nobody knows in the play nobody will ever go to see. And we missed my train in Chicago for no reason at all. And we missed the Western Air Express in Kansas City. And when I found that it was gone, I kicked my porter back down the depot stairs to the train I had just left and just managed to catch it again, thrusting bills and telegrams on people and did manage to catch the T.A.T. plane at Clovis, New Mexico ... it all but drove me mad when we got to Albuquerque and the central motor wouldn't start and we had to wait an hour and a half. I sent wild telegrams of a very melodramatic life and death character to Los Angeles to have the San Francisco plane held. I put on such scenes for the benefit of the pilot of the transcontinental plane. He left out two stations in my behalf—just skipped 'em—and the plane was held and I did get to Berkeley on Christmas Eve, a good deal more dead than alive, but I did get there.

The problem of Sid's divorce, still unsettled at the time of this letter, hung over his relationship with Polly. But there was another, perhaps more important, problem pressing Sidney. He indicates it when he writes on October 10th, 1929, to Leonard Bacon about *Half Gods*, on which at this point he is still working. "My play is fine at both ends but not so good in the middle and has to be developed thereabout. Like its little master in that. No, I won't make dirty jokes." We could easily pass it over as a quick shot at a joke but that he repeats it several times in subsequent letters to various people. Even then we could regard it simply as a joke he enjoyed repeating. But a letter to Polly implies that these jokes were a Freudian way of his relieving his mind of a problem that bothered him.

Replying to one of Polly's letters, he writes on February 19th, 1930:

> I *am* afraid of making you unhappy, or, rather, of not making you happy, but my doubts, believe me, darling Polly, are neither of my love for you nor of my happiness with you.... But my self confidence has been badly jolted by the beating I just took on Broadway and I Can't [*sic*] get over the has been feeling about my talent. More than that, though, I've got what might easily be called an inferiority complex out of the failure of my first marriage and this is going to be hard as hell to say but it has got to be said and you'll just have to be an angel and a bit more and realize how hard it would be for any man to say. This is it. Though I shall never understand or excuse Clare's behavior about this divorce and particularly her indifference to Jennifer, I could not divorce her in New York because I could not honestly or fairly blame her for laying herself open along those lines. And the reason why I could not blame her is—damn it this is hard to say— that I have come to realize that a tubercular boyhood, malaria [contracted

while he was in Albania on the ambulance corps], a semi-broken back in the war and other minor mishaps of thirty-eight rather over-strenuous years have left me something short of a woman's ideal of what a shiek [*sic*] should be. I don't mean anything terribly dire by this. Jennifer is patently my child. None the less I am painfully conscious that there are a good many Gungha Dins around me. In the romantic sense better than I. I know, so clearly, that this is the secret of my fear regarding you because I am not unmindful of the deep importance of perfect romantic happiness. To you. To what the Irish would call the glory of you. I know that I should be perfectly happy with you. I can't help being afraid that I might fail you romantically, fall short of what you expect of a lover and a husband. I can't fairly deny the possibility that I may well have fallen short of what Clare expected.

The New York divorce to which Sidney refers is not one in which he would be found in a room with a woman unknown to him. At one point he "got desperate in New York" about the divorce and decided that he would set detectives on Clare, find her *in flagrante delicto* and sue her for adultery, then the only grounds for divorce in New York State. However, under Polly's persuasion and Jean's he decided against it because "Jennifer can't have a stink behind her" (letter to Polly, December 28th, 1929).

Sidney's feeling of sexual inadequacy came up at the beginning and at the end of his marriage. For the difficulties at the later time and perhaps for those at occasional times throughout his marriage, Sidney blamed the couple's stressful and time-consuming work schedules. But now in 1930, with his background of sexual uncertainty, he sees himself as the main source of the problems, especially as Clare immediately went to another, very attractive and apparently sexually assured man for comfort.

Yet he says that he does not mean "anything terribly dire by this." Sidney had had a sex life before he married Clare, and he apparently had one in Hollywood before he met Polly. He wrote to Jean from New York that he had so much work to do that he is "taking the veil and going on the wagon" (November 23rd, 1929). And there are other such hints in various letters of the time. So Sidney's sexual difficulties, nothing "dire," were lapses of one kind or another and important only insofar as the women he was with regarded them as important.

So far as we can tell, Clare did not usually so regard them. Nevertheless, the emotional beating that she inflicted, given Sidney's probable residual sense of sexual inferiority, seems to have had a sexual impact. Sidney, in a letter of December 28th, 1929, writes to Polly:

> I had a long talk with my sister who is very wise. Troubles like mine are emotional infections. They have to work out. A man who [is] emo-

tionally infected isn't of any use to any woman. It isn't what you call Clare-minded. It isn't really. It's just a kind of poison mixed with inferiority complex and having been so mad for so long. Polly darling, you've got to believe it's coming straight. You've made life worth living again for me. That's deja quite a bit. I think of you all the time from getting up in the morning to going to bed at night. Particularly then.

Sidney, badly hurt by the breakup of his marriage, shows his determination to survive by falling in love with a Polly who, he perhaps knew, would soothe his wounds. And she seems to have done so, for Polly and he apparently had a joyful and flourishing union.

But most of Sidney's letters from Hollywood concerned his attempt to escape his Goldwyn contract so that he could write plays again. But then there was the divorce process. The last contract Sidney signed with Goldwyn in this period paid him $1500 a week for thirty weeks. When Sidney asked Goldwyn to release him from the contract, the producer refused, but Sidney took the denial with some equanimity because the divorce he finally chose would be costly.

When Clare first returned to England to do *The Sacred Flame* in early 1930, she apparently kept in touch with her lawyers and tried to work out some agreement with Sidney, but things did not go well. "Jennifer remains the sticking point." Clare earlier seemed to be easily surrendering Jennifer but apparently changed her mind. Sidney believed that "Clare is not strongly held to her, but not unnaturally, she flinches from giving her up." Dick Myers's letter of November 1929 implies that getting custody of Jennifer still seemed important to Clare. Yet in the whole period from Christmastime 1928 to her death, she wrote only one letter to Jennifer. The letter, which was obviously written a little after her return to England in 1929, follows:

54 Fulham Road
S.W.1

My own darling Jennif –

I want you to tell Miss Jones all your news, my precious and send me a message that I can carry around with me here in London. You are in such a lovely sunshiny place while Mamma is in such a cold one. Do you remember last winter? It is even colder now. I go into the Park quite often to see the ducks and think of my Pearlio-Price. They are lovely now. There are pelicans who can swallow Dozens of Fish Whole—and herons who stand so still they look like statues and storks (only the storks haven't got any babies in their mouths) and geese and gulls and beautiful stately swans. When people throw bread to them they all scream and flutter on the water and dive to the bottom for crumbs.

I am so glad you like the pink Beauty that Santa brought you, and the pretty blue one too. My darling child, all my love and thoughts and wishes go with this to you, little chunk.

My darling.
Mama

In this tender letter we hear Clare's direct voice for the last time. The letter shows her ability to enjoy herself with Jennifer, to know the kinds of things that give the child pleasure, how to describe them for her in vivid word pictures. In short, it shows Clare's empathy and love for her child. Yet she would eventually give up her daughter to the sole custody of Sidney.

Until then there was much to be got through. The Eames family's participation in the divorce process exasperated Sidney, a good deal of the usual divorce turbulence erupted, and Clare is silent again. Sidney wrote to Angell on May 30th, 1929:

> Clare and I have not corresponded. I have, on three occasions since she returned to London [in early 1929], written to her. Once to send her some photographs of Jennifer taken on the child's fourth birthday, once to report on Jennifer's change of address and once to ask for her surgeon's bill for her operation last December [1928 in New York]. Each letter has been perfectly friendly and has contained a certain amount of detail regarding Jennifer and regarding my own plans. None of the three has been answered and I did not expect or want any answer.... My chief regret in this business is that Clare's persistence in a truculent attitude towards me is going to make future relations regarding Jennifer just that much more difficult. I don't anticipate writing to her again before Jennifer again changes her address. I believe that Miss Jones has written to her once in a reply to her single communication with Jennifer, a note which arrived in Beverly Hills late, I think, in January. I should like to have that surgeon's bill, by the way. Clare is simply tossing it aside and the poor devil is whistling for his money. As I think I told you, she did not use the money Shurmann demanded for the purpose intended. I got a bleeting letter from him last month.

Although relations between Sidney and Clare are now strained, he did not carry out the intention to cut communication with her, nor did he prevent Miss Jones from answering Clare's letter to Jennifer. In fact he is very angry that Clare has written only once. It is one reason that he wrote to Angell on April 26th, 1929, that he is ready to *sic* detectives on Clare in London if she will not divorce him in Cleveland and grant him custody of Jennifer: "...[I]f she won't, Ernest, I don't see any way out of detectives. I really don't. Jennifer's getting the break of a lifetime under my sister and I'm not going to wreck it to save the looks of things for a lady who let five months go by last summer without a single enquiry and who has thought one note sufficient attention for the past four months. Jennifer deserves better of her mother than that and she's getting more from Jean in a few months than Clare would give her in years."

Sidney eventually decided against the New York route, which would involve detectives, and against Reno because of the "filthy crowd there." After he realizes that he cannot "count at all on the ... likelihood of Clare's taking any trouble about this business," he opts for a California divorce. "Desertion in California is simple and inconspicuous and has the dignity of being what really happened" (letter to Haydie Eames, January 20th, 1929).

There were some problems, however, about the California divorce. One was the matter of money. The law for divorce in California was for a community property settlement; that is, any money earned in the course of the marriage was to be divided equally between the husband and the wife. That presented a number of problems such as whether or not to divide equally between Clare and Sidney the money that he had earned since he was working in California. "Sam Goldwyn says: 'get yourself a Jewish lawyer, these Christian lawyers are a menace.'" But Sidney continued to keep his eye on Jennifer, and the terms he intended to exact he grimly stated to Haydie, Clare's sister (December 20th, 1929):

> About Jennifer. This is the disagreeable part. I have no desire to keep the child and her mother permanently apart but I shall oppose any arrangement which does not award me full custody. I believe that children are more important than their parents. I do not believe that either Clare or I have any rights over Jennifer which are comparable to Jennifer's right over us. In demanding custody I am considering Jennifer, not myself. Clare has never shown herself disposed to take any trouble on the child's account. During the last two years when she has ignored the child's existence I have been able to keep her in a life and atmosphere which could not be well improved upon for the development [of] her life and character. She is an exceptionally impressionable child and I am determined to protect her from the neurotics of the life Clare is leading. I shall always be willing to arrange and underwrite any visit Clare cares to pay the child and when Clare can convince me that she can have the child with her for visits without any detrimental effects I shall be happy to be convinced. For the present Jennifer has coming to her more consideration and better chances than Clare has ever shown any sign of offering her. Egomania like Clare's is not of much value to a child.

By today's standards Sidney's assertion of the child's rights over the parents is enlightened. In most divorces the child is the only real victim, and its interests should be the main consideration. But Sidney's attitude beyond this is high handed. He not only wishes to receive full custody, but he will decide on all and any kind of visitation rights with Clare counting on his good intentions for not keeping mother and child "permanently apart." Sidney's attitude is understandable, for Clare had been neglectful, but it is also an extreme version of an outlook that contributed to Clare's decision to seek a divorce.

His absolute stand was urged on him by Jean in letter after letter. At the time of these remarks to Haydie, December 1929, Jean had been caring for Jennifer since April, and he believed, as did Jean, that Jennifer had been flourishing there. Jean was as determined as she could be in the circumstances to keep Jennifer out of Clare's hands, to keep Sidney's influence, with hers reinforcing it, the single important influence in Jennifer's life. Sidney had such faith in Jean that whatever weakening he may have felt in resisting Clare's desire for custody was strengthened by Jean's urging. This fragment of a letter from Jean demonstrates her attitude:

> I know I dont [sic] need to say this, but cant [sic] help repeating my *prayer* that you will not compromise on your complete custody. No sharing, no months in one place & in another, even though you may want to please Clare, or may think it cruel to her to deprive her completely of Jennifer during her growing up. The point really is Sidney that she *does not care*—and that is the important thing—you would subject the child to divided and bewildered loyalties, & she would have the right to ask you later "If you knew it were better for me to have a single peaceful childhood—why did you subject me to this confusion?" She is so young that there will be no pain for her—no missing—no loss that you cannot, since you must, make up to her. Better far for her mother to completely disappear from her consciousness than to have the pitiful bewilderment, and the secret questionings—and the evasive un-convincing answers that must be given. When she is older she will have at least understanding—I think the very saddest aspects of these arrangements is the division of the child. It is the veritable cutting in half of the Soloman [sic]—and you can & will give her everything that you believe and *know* to be a good equipment for having work & fun out of life and taking it galantly [sic] & as with wings— but nothing that can be helped by her throwing her periodically into that very alien group....

Jean's view is one that arouses a controversy that goes on to this day, the other side being that a child needs both his parents unless one of them is egregiously cruel or immoral, that judgment being made by the court rather than by one of the parents. But it is important here, however, to know that Sidney's attitude was reinforced so that it gave vivid life to the notion that Clare was indifferent to her child's welfare, that her environment was careless and perverted and her future uncertain. It is this notion, constantly shored up by Jean, in whose wisdom he had great faith, that locked in Sidney's grim determination to take his stand.

Suddenly the deadlock over the matter of custody was broken. "Whoever had the idea," wrote Sidney to Haydie on January 8th, 1930, "of my sister's rather dominating the Jennifer question is a bit of a genius because there you have a point of view which is concerned only for the child's good." That is, it would be Jean who would make any disputed decision as to visitation rights. Ironically, it was undoubtedly Clare who had the "genius" of allowing Jean to dominate the Jennifer question because Clare, like Sidney, had faith in her wisdom. At any rate, if Clare didn't first think up the idea, she certainly had to agree to the provision. Whether Jean would have decided the various disputes to Clare's satisfaction remains a question. But Sidney was joyous because the solution not only suited him but broke the logjam into which his life had recently been set. "I felt, when I had Ernest's telegram about it, that I had come into several million dollars" (letter to Polly, January 14th, 1930).

The matter was not yet over, actually, because there still had to be agreement over the property settlement, not an easy job. Sidney tried to escape the exact terms of the community property settlement because he thought that such an arrangement would leave him with too little money for all the slogging work he had done. Clare caused problems by withholding from her lawyer, as she had some two years earlier from her psychoanalyst, that she was having an affair with Brian Aherne because she did not wish her father to know of it (letter to Haydie Eames, January 29th, 1930). However, those obstructions were also broken with Clare receiving a cash settlement instead of alimony, and by March 1st, 1930, Sidney had an interlocutory decree, which would be made final one year from that date and allow him to marry.

Despite his anger at Clare and contempt for her way of life, he still believed that his work in the theater would suffer without her aid. In a letter to Barrett Clark he says: "If I can still write for the theatre without Clare's invaluable advice and guidance, I shall certainly go on writing for the theatre" (June 26th, 1929). We also see that for all his previous railing against the theater that he now has no intention of giving it up. He also writes to Clark: "I think I am interested, now, in trying to dramatize what these people of ours are thinking about, not in a critical sense, but as it is heightened by some kind of intensification that comes automatically with dramatic condensing." The program does not sound very different from the one he announced to his mother when he was a young man. Not surprisingly, just as Polly seemed to be Clare without the threat, so in terms of his work he also desired Polly's help without her turning into the full-fledged professional that was Clare. He tells her in a letter of January 3rd: "What my plays need is you to say: 'Sidney, I don't believe that place.' Because I feel so well when I'm writing that I believe damn near anything. Only you won't make me have good taste, will you? Promise me that. I hate good taste in artists as I hate the very devil. I hate good judgment, too." Perhaps the Damrosches with their high-and-mighty background specialized in good taste. That was a quality, at least in terms of artistry, that he did not have to fear in fearless Clare.

But it was not only in his work that he missed Clare. At the end of a letter, his last to Clare, on May 6th, 1930, in which he discusses mostly business matters, he writes: "I miss you somewhat less—not much, but somewhat...." On the same day he writes to "Polly Dearest: Do you miss me anything like as much as I miss you? Everything you say or do is so damned fascinating and important to me."

The divorce now being achieved, Sidney's next step was to finish with the studio. "Goldwyn called me into his office on Friday," he writes to Polly on July 13th 1930, "and presented me with a cheque for five thousand, saying: 'Have your holiday on me.' Laugh that off."

Again, to Polly, on July 19th, 1930:

> Sam called me in. Offered to tear up my contract and write me a new one for two years exclusive service with my residence out here to make me independent. Independent. [Arthur] Hornblow [Jr.] says it means three thousand a week or a percentage of profits. That's independent all right. But not independence of Sam. Sam talked lugubriously of future responsibilities, he, too having heard rumors. And charmingly added that if the lady is the one he thinks and she is agreeable, he would be charmed to give her a job too, so that she wouldn't be bored!!! ... I turned the proposition aside rather than down. I said, admitting and denying nothing about you and me, that if there were any truth in such rumors, I couldn't consider any job which involved living away from New York without consulting you.... Three thousand a week less twenty-five thousand a year for living, is a quarter of a million put aside in ten years. Not a fortune, but a good ten thousand a year more of secure income which is a bit more than I have as it is. One may turn away from but not laugh off such an offer.

Finally, he gets away, says his good-byes in Berkeley to Jennifer, Jean, and Duncan, and sails to Europe on August 1st, where Polly and her family have already gone. While in Paris he consults with Marcel Pagnol about a translation of *Marius* on which he had been working. Joining the Damrosches, he goes off on day trips with Polly, "heavily chaperoned" (letter to HH, August 31st, 1930). He had asked Polly to live with him until they could marry, but she refused (August 15th, 1930). Finally, the Damrosches return to America, and Sidney settles down in Portofino in October with Roger Burlingame, determined to finish at last the first draft of a play before returning home (letter to Polly, October 12th, 1930).

He was now in the midst of a plagiarism suit on *The Silver Cord*. For this he needed Clare's help, for she had first told him the story on which the drama was based. He thought that there might be some difficulty about obtaining Clare's deposition in his favor, but on November 8th he writes to Polly: "A worry is lifted from the chest, however, by [a letter] from Bud Eames saying that Clare's Silver Cord affidavit is now in the mail en route."

Later the same day he sends the following telegram, apparently to his mother: "Received word this afternoon Clare died this morning following another operation."

Still later the same day he writes:

> Genoa
> Nov. 8th

Polly my darling :—

I'm writing this from a boat in Genoa. I'm here on the chance of chartering a plane to Paris tomorrow morning. Bud having asked me to come to London. This is an inconceivable and shocking tragedy and it came in a telegram from Bud—he is Clare's brother—with no warning, no presentiment, even, that she was even severely ill. What wouldn't I have given for a word from you today. Lacking one from you I can't turn in until I've sent one to you. There's no grief in this for me because there isn't any grief in life without personal loss. But there's shock and horror and rage at the extinction of that unnegotiable but so vibrant life. It's two years ago today that she and I parted and I went to Hollywood to get well. I'm even a little horrified at how well I've got. Today has been an acid test of it. Mixed up with a thousand pangs of wishing harsh thoughts unthought and harsh words unspoken. I don't know what I'm writing, darling, only that I'm writing to you. This tragedy of hers has been so tragically complete and completed. Life hasn't any right to be so definitely and brutally punitive of what, at the worst, was no more than a piece of willful folly. Career gone, health gone and, now life, too. And I've got everything and you, to boot. I'm shocked at this whole business. Even at Jennifer in California. Do you know what I mean? There *is* Jennifer and Clare is dead. My Gawd how I wish that I had you where I could get at you. It's *frightening*, that's what it is. I told her once, in a figurative sense, that she couldn't make life work for her. And I was right. She's done everything but live. I've thought of you so much today. Rog has been a saint and talked about you. You can't mind my raving this way. You can't blame me. I *have* needed you today. That look you have from Vienna. I see why you went [back to the United States rather than stayed in Europe with him] so much more clearly than ever. Clare wasn't true to herself. She threw herself away. Now she's dead. But that's too much. One ought to have a chance to come back. I nearly cabled you to ask you to destroy my last letter unread because, for want of anything better to say, I was flippant about a dream about bad news. Oh, my darling, I've made a god of life—as—life and worshipped so long and so hard now that I'm looking it in its Moloch joints. I feel like a very small boat in a very large ocean in a very high wind and I want to throw an anchor around your neck. Jennifer's left. Jennifer. Why should she be shocking? She isn't really, of course. But there was Clare with so much to give the world. So much more than I ever had. What is this life business we're all in for? I'm terrified of it, that's what I am. I tried to think of something to cable you but the evening papers must already have come out with the news by the time I heard it. I hope there isn't a plane to London tomorrow. If there isn't I can't get there until Monday night and Bud may wire me not to come. I dread going as I've never dreaded anything on earth.

> Seeing those people she gave her life to after she went out of mine. Am I going to mail this? I've never loved you so much as tonight and if I'm afraid to go down on my knees and cry out my fears and doubts and bewilderment to you, where are you and I at? Polly, it's too like Anna Karenina to be true. Oh, my darling, my darling, it's a very shaky fiancé you have tonight. Ought I to have cabled? I couldn't think of what to say. I couldn't think, only be horrified. I love you. I hope to Gawd you're loving me tonight.
>
> Sidney.

On November 10th he cables his mother: "VERY GLAD I CAME SERVICE TOMORROW...."

Again to his mother he cables: "CLARE BURIED RICHMOND YESTERDAY AFTERNOON NO TIME LETTERS WILL TELL YOU PARTICULARS WHEN I SEE YOU...."

On November 13th, Sidney writes Polly from Paris:

> When I wrote you I was in Genoa trying to get to London and pretty groggy from the shock of Clare's death. I did get there, not all the way by plane, because that proved to be both insolubly complicated and impractically costly.... I'm glad I took the train. I got it at Turin. There was my mother on the platform of the Gare de Lyons at six A.M. Monday morning with English money to get me across. I had lunch with Bud Eames. I'm terribly glad that I went apart from the quite ordinary gesture of being at the funeral. Bud is a frail reed but a good fellow and normal and he was having a hell of a time with the cheap histrionics of that second rate gang with whom Clare had allied herself. It was a painful two days. Not in anything that happened but in the dreariness of the picture it gave me of these last three years of which I had heard such fragmentary and vague reports.
>
> I was distressed immeasurably by that and there was murder in my heart as the conviction grew clearer and clearer that she had been killed by London surgery of a very inferior quality.... I spent ten minutes in a cemetery chapel, paid some bills and blew over here to spend last night and see Aunt Emma, whom I found very poised and lovely.... I lunch with her today and go back this afternoon to Italy.... I want to get back to you so desperately, my darling. We can be married now whenever we like, a decent interval, I suppose.... Aunt Emma has heard all about us and sends you her love.... I'll always see [my mother] standing in the Gare de Lyons in that cold grey dawn last Monday morning.

Sidney finally returns to Polly in New York and then goes out to Berkeley for Christmas with Jennifer. On December 25th he writes to Polly: "Damn it, why didn't you marry me and come along? On the other hand, I must admit, it would have presented its seamy side because Jean, thinking of Jennifer's welfare, had left telling her about her mother's death until Christmas Eve, figuring that the child could find out by going to church and lighting a candle to her mother and having me on hand to stave off some of the forlorn feeling. And that in itself would have made things a bit difficult for you...."

On the next day he writes Polly again: "I thought, while I was talking this morning to Jean, that it's the first time in years that I've talked to her about anything but my own troubles. I haven't any more troubles."

Epilogue

Brian Aherne recalls in his memoirs that one evening as he was working late at a film studio, he received a call from Margalo Gillmore, who had been dining with Clare at the Robert Sherwoods', that Clare had suddenly fallen ill; a doctor had been called and announced that Clare had "eaten something that had poisoned her." He gave her a sedative and put her to bed. Although Aherne, because of Clare's medical history, was uncomfortable with the doctor's diagnosis, he accepted it because Clare seemed better the next day.

"Suddenly Clare was ill again, with severe abdominal pains, and once more back in the old nursing home in Richmond." She endured another operation for an "intestinal stoppage." That was on a Monday. Overnight Thursday into Friday surgeons operated once more. On the Friday night after his theater performance a car waited for Aherne at the stage door. When he arrived at Richmond, Clare's "eyes, wide and terrified, were fixed on me as she fought for breath...."

> The doctor said that she might survive if she could sleep, but as a storm raged outside, Clare died.
> Four days later I stood before an open grave in Richmond Cemetery. Reggie was beside me.... Kate North pressed a bunch of violets in my hand. It was dark, damp and cold, and I shivered as I watched the wooden box being lowered into an oblong hole newly dug in the wet earth. As it came to rest, there was a pause. I stepped forward and threw in the violets, then I turned and stumbled down the path. I ... began running, desperately, blindly seeking a way out of that terrible place [168–71].

According to Aherne he continued running blindly for the next twenty years.

On November 9th, 1930, *The New York Times* headed its story on Clare Eames's death,

CLARE EAMES DEAD;
BRILLIANT ACTRESS

A subhead reads: "Enthusiastically received by Critics/and Public—Had Made Reputation Before Going Abroad" [31].

Under the heading of "CLARE EAMES BURIED" a story of November 12th said:

> Simple but impressive funeral services for Clare Eames, American actress, who died at Richmond on Saturday, were held this afternoon in the chapel of Richmond Cemetery, where burial later took place. Her brother, Hamilton Eames, was present, was well as many American and English friends, including those with whom she had been associated in the theatre.
> The Episcopal service was read. There was no music. The little chapel was filled with flowers.

On November 15th *The New York Times* printed on its editorial page "A Tribute to Clare Eames":

> In her short life Clare Eames made a profound impression on many of the players with whom she came in contact. She was an aristocrat of the theatre, and to audiences as well as to her friends her rare poise and dignity were a welcome influence where so much is pose and tinsel.
> Katharine Cornell, who knew her for many years, was playing in Cleveland when news of her death came. She did not speak of her personal grief ... but only of how our theatre would miss her.
> "Her artistic integrity was absolutely complete. She would have nothing to do with anything she could not believe intensely as an artist. She believed with all her soul in the fullest freedom for the artist, and she was an inspiration to less dynamic folk. Her intelligence, her force, her courage, her taste were constantly making themselves felt on all with whom she came in contact. There was something Elizabethan about her."
> That is not all MISS CORNELL said, but it expresses part of what those who knew CLARE EAMES only through her acting must feel. The authority and solidity of her work made her a figure of distinction on our stage and justified the influence on others which thirty-four years would not warrant in a personality less regal.

On November 23rd theater people sponsored a memorial service for Clare at the Little Church around the Corner in New York, which they regarded as "their" church. Among relatives attending the service were Clare's mother and Emilio de Gorgoza, "noted baritone, whose wife, Mme. Emma Eames, is now living in retirement in Paris." Among theater people who attended were Katharine Cornell, Brock Pemberton (the producer of *Swords*), Margalo Gillmore, and Robert Edmond Jones. The church was filled to capacity.

Speaking were Frank Gillmore, Dudley Digges, and Robert E. Sherwood. Gillmore spoke in his office as president of the Actors' Equity Association and certainly as her friend: "She possessed the spirituality of the artist and compelled attention like a torch. Sometimes, like the flight of an eagle, she would rise to unusual heights in her acting." In addition to thinking of her as comparable to an eagle, perhaps to himself he remembered her gaiety and high spirits, her kookiness when Margalo first brought her to his house for dinner.

Digges, who codirected *The Wild Duck* with Clare, "characterized her as 'an inspiring spirit, a direct and fearless woman.... [H]ers were the qualities martyrs were made of.'"

Sherwood said that he had taken his first play to Clare "to receive the advantage of her extraordinary judgment and intelligence." She praised it highly, he said, "not because it was good, but because she was a very great friend." Miss Eames, he declared, "was a great artist, but the greatest evidence of her artistry was in her own life." Sidney would not have agreed with this last appraisal by his very good friend and best man at his wedding to Clare.

Despite his saying so, Sidney Howard's troubles were not at all over with the death of Clare, nor would he have said so if he were speaking in all seriousness. Nevertheless, with Clare gone, he had a new and apparently brighter life to face. And it seemed to work out that way, for Polly and he were a happy flourishing couple. In the course of time came three children, Jennifer found a mother, and eventually Sidney bought a farm in Tyringham, Massachusetts, in the Berkshires, for the country place he always desired. In New York City the family continued to live in the East 82nd Street house that Sidney and Clare had bought, but it was renovated for Polly's benefit.

All seemed to be complete. But Sidney was dissatisfied with his professional life. He continued his financially remunerative work for films, but after the failure of *Half Gods*, he began to feel as though his talent for the theater was diminishing. On June 9th, 1931, about five months after his marriage to Polly on January 10th, he resumes his diary:

> I began this diary as a record of my forties upon which I enter, now in a few days. I leave the thirties without much regret. They began well, went very sour indeed and ended ... with my career in some darkness still and likely to be on a permanent wane: let us hope not too swift a wane.

He goes on to discuss his responsibilities and financial problems, then continues:

> I am responsible for four contracts, the pictures of "Arrowsmith" [from the Sinclair Lewis novel] and "The Greeks had [sic] a Word for It" [the 1930 Broadway hit comedy by Zoë Atkins] and the play scripts of 'Yellow Jack' and 'Alien Corn.' At the present moment "The Greeks" has been submitted in first draught and the first draught of "Arrowsmith" is in work. "Yellow Jack" has lain partially completed for three years and "Alien Corn" is within a few weeks of completion....
>
> My powers are slowing down. I tire more easily and write less easily and my reputation, which formerly stood me in good stead, has practically ceased to exist through my long connection with motion pictures. I mean, if possible and at whatever effort to reestablish that factor in my life through these two plays plus one on the Versailles Conference and another, probably about Southwestern archeology and in addition to that to publish, within the next eighteen months a novel and another volume of short stories some of which are already written, others of which I have in my mind. The novel will be 'Jacob Ely' which has been under weigh [sic] since the month of January 1925 and on which I did my last work in the spring of 1928. In other words, I am recommencing things just fifteen days before my fortieth birthday at a time in my life when, by the standards of all but the greatest writers, I have very little chance of getting anywhere. Creative talent survives forty only in the greatest minds and I have no illusions about belonging to that company.

On June 11th he writes in the diary of *Alien Corn* and *Yellow Jack*, both of which were conceived in the twenties while he was still married to Clare: "If either goes then I have layed [sic] to rest the ghost of Clare's inspiration without laying which I can never be a free writer...."

By saying that he wished to lay the ghost of Clare's inspiration (the Freudian implications of those remarks may go unpursued), Sidney apparently means that even though the dramas were conceived with Clare's inspiration, they had now so far developed beyond her that their success was independent of her.

About six years later, on November 25th, 1937, Thanksgiving day, he writes in his diary:

> I have just found and read through a page of a diary which I began six years and some months ago in a state of depression at the prospect of entering my forties. I was then enceinte, so to speak, with "Alien Corn" and "Yellow Jack" and at work on the picture scripts of "Arrowsmith" and "The Greeks Had a Word for It." I was filled with gloom at the increasing sense either of my failing powers or the expose [sic] of my talent for writing as the flimsy thing that it might turn out to be.
>
> I suppose that I am now at even a lower ebb of depression. Diaries are as good a way as any to work the self-pity out of one's system. At this present moment I am strapped and have just produced the play "The Ghost of Yankee Doodle" and taken the critical beating of my life for it. I have in prospect only the job of writing the definitive saga of Pan-American Airways for Goldwyn and little or no genuine impulse to do anything about it....

> If I count my blessings of the past six years they add up to an impressive total. Though the falling powers as a writer have continued to be more and more manifest, I am married to the most perfect of wives and have two more completely lovable and fascinating children. I have an enchanting house to live in here in the city and a more than enchanting farm in the Berkshires. Apart from my work and my financial difficulties I am a man to be envied by any onlooker.

He goes on to discuss how he might manage his "financial difficulties" and then continues:

> I am planning to spend next winter in Tyringham on this same novel which has been so long projected and so often postponed. I am in doubt about writing any further plays. My gift for the theatre, such as it was, seems to have failed me. If I try another I have three ideas all of them partially worked out.... In two hours I shall be, with all my family, at the Damrosches for Thanksgiving lunch and that will be warm and fun as everything in that house is. I look forward to that. Tonight we dine with my mother and take her to see a play. I shall look in on my own matinee this afternoon.

He discusses then the faults of *The Ghost of Yankee Doodle*, which had opened only three days earlier, and continues:

> The project now is to get myself going again and out of the hole so that I can afford to give these children of mine all that is coming to them. That is the main object of the farm. Well, we shall see what we shall see both of how I can go about this and to what extent I can realize it.

For the first time we feel a reduction in Sidney's fire and vitality. He still has the stolid grit to continue in the face of failure, but the depression seems to have bitten deep enough to require more fight to overcome it—"the project now is to get myself going again." Even in the 1931 entry the sheer enormity of the program he outlines for himself suggests not a waning of talent but its renewal. What seems to be missing now is Clare. In 1931, as he recommenced his career, as it were, he was without Clare and filled with dread that he could not work in the theater without her.

In fact he managed. Before the productions of *Alien Corn* and *Yellow Jack*, he had a tremendous success in 1932 with an adaptation of the French *Prenez Garde à la Peinture*, by Rene Cauchois, which Sidney called *The Late Christopher Bean*. Two years later he had another hit in his adaptation of Sinclair Lewis's *Dodsworth*. But neither play had the impact of *They Knew What They Wanted* and *The Silver Cord*, his major hits of the previous decade. The California comedy was on the cutting edge, carving out new things in form and substance in the drama and pointing to desirable changes in American culture. *The Silver Cord* was the most trenchant Freudian drama of the time and a chilling critique of the cult of momism in this country. But the two successes of the thirties left no impression other than that of charming adult audiences in the theater. The ability to create such entertainments is no small talent. But it fails to keep a finger on the American pulse, one of Sidney's professed aims, nor does it show any attempt to make more malleable the theatrical form.

Yellow Jack, one of the plays on which he counted to lay Clare's ghost, did attempt innovation in its use of the multiple-set stage. It was a *succès d'estime* but a failure at the box office. Its technique came to be used extensively in the American post–World War II theater, but apparently that use did not derive from *Yellow Jack*. *Alien Corn* succeeded mainly because of Katharine Cornell's personal popularity.

Sidney made two other interesting attempts in the thirties. One, an adaptation of Humphrey Cobb's novel *Paths of Glory*, tried, like *Yellow Jack*, for technical experimentation, but it, too, was a failure at the box office. In *The Ghost of Yankee Doodle* Sidney wrote an ambitious multifaceted play, which was obviously meant to be an important drama on American life, but that too flopped critically and financially.

After Clare left, Sidney, while remaining a successful and admired American dramatist, ceased to be at the forefront of the American theater. The reasons may have had only a little to do with Clare. But Sidney, at the beginning of the decade, thought that perhaps he could not manage writing for the theater without Clare, and possibly her spirit, like Caesar's ghost with Brutus, which mocked him until his death.

On other fronts Sidney did important work in the theater. He led the Dramatists' Guild for a strenuous two years. He also joined forces with Robert E. Sherwood, Elmer Rice, S. N. Behrman, and Maxwell Anderson to form the Playwrights' Company, a development which almost destroyed the Theatre Guild. Sidney had made up with the guild, and the group produced *The Ghost of Yankee Doodle*, but he nevertheless entered the new producing company, for here the dramatists would have control over their own productions.

Sidney did not live long enough to produce any play with the Playwrights' Company. He had finished *Madam, Will You Walk?* and was preparing to take it on the road where, with the play before an audience, he ordinarily made many changes. After his death the Playwrights tried the drama out of town, where Polly refused Sherwood permission to change one word of the text. The play never came to New York. In 1953 it opened the new off–Broadway group called the Phoenix Theatre. Starring Jessica Tandy and Hume Cronin, it received respectful reviews.

As the drama of the 1920s recedes ever more into the past except

Sidney Howard around 1938, about the time of the formation of the Playwrights' Company. (Courtesy of the New York Public Library.)

in the minds of a few theater historians, Sidney Howard's name fades into ever greater obscurity. For in that pivotal decade he made his greatest impact on American drama. Ironically enough, his name springs into the light of people's memory when one mentions *Gone with the Wind*. Sidney wrote the original script for the film. Even though a number of other writers worked on the movie, his name appears on the screen as the script writer, and in that capacity he won a posthumous Academy Award. Each of the many times that film is revived, viewers will still see Sidney Howard's name and some will even remember it.

On August 23rd, 1939, Sidney, as was his custom, wrote all the morning, and in the afternoon went out to work on his farm in Tyringham. In the barn he cranked up the tractor, which a workman had left in gear. The tractor leaped forward and crushed him to death inside the wall (*New York Times*, August 24th, 1939, 1).

On August 26th he was buried in Tyringham. *The New York Times* reported:

NOTABLES AT RITES
OF SIDNEY HOWARD

Visitors and Residents of
Tyringham, Mass., Overflow
Little White Church

EPISCOPAL SERVICE HELD

Neighbors Decorate Pulpit—
Spalding and Thompson Play
Bach Compositions

Attending, among many others, were Ernest Angell, Roger Burlingame, Leonard Bacon, Harold Freedman, Guthrie McClintic, Margalo Gillmore, S. N. Behrman, and John P. Marquand (August 27th, 1939).

Far and wide the world registered shock, horror, and grief. Perhaps Brooks Atkinson's remarks of August 27th, 1939, may speak for all:

> It is hard to realize that Sidney Howard is dead. Since he was more energetic than most men, it was easy to assume that his energy would endure indefinitely. Forty-eight is an age of abundance for a man of his fire and strength: and there were many more years of work in his head, heart and hands. The manner of his death makes it incomprehensible. He was crushed by a tractor he was cranking on his farm in Tyringham Valley in the Berkshires. Death in the fullness of life; death by the most unlikely chance; death by a frivolous stroke of fortune. It has no intelligible relation to the capacious life he was living at home, in the community and in the theatre. To have come safely through the aviation service in the war and all the natural hazards of a busy life in the cities and yet to die by caprice in the summer hills is to make death seem wholly unnatural. It is a bitter thing for his relatives and friends to accept....
>
> We have lost one of the few men on whom the theatre can lean and at a time when we can ill afford it. More tragic than that is the loss of a man of superior character—intellectually dynamic and honest. As his responsibilities broadened he lived up to them. He was a man of action who never shirked a job or backed away from a fight. The theatre was lucky to have had so much of him for so many years and the theatre is better for the thrust, drive and keenness of his work. Playgoers in America and England will join his relatives and friends in mourning the death of a man who was wholly alive to the last tragic moment of an honorable career.

Bibliography

Abbott, George. *Mister Abbott*. New York: Random House, 1963.
Agate, James. *First Nights, Volume I*. New York: Benjamin Blom, 1971.
Aherne, Bolan. *A Proper Job*. New York: Houghton Mifflin, 1969.
Barnes, Eric Wollencott. *The Man Who Lived Twice: The Biography of Edward Sheldon*. New York: Charles Scribner's Sons, 1956.
Bolin, John Seelye. "Samuel Hume: Artist and Exponent of American Art Theatre." Dissertation, University of Michigan, 1970.
Brown, Jared. *The Fabulous Lunts*. New York: Atheneum, 1986.
Bryer, Jackson R., ed. *The Theatre We Worked For: The Letters of Eugene O'Neill to Kenneth Macgowan*. New Haven: Yale University Press, 1982.
Clark, Barrett. *Intimate Portraits*. Port Washington, NY: Kennikat Press, 1951, 6.
Craig, Edward. *Gordon Craig: The Story of His Life*. New York: Harper & Row Limelight Editions, 1985.
De Azartis, Lorenzo. *Casanova*. Translated by Sidney Howard. New York.: Brentano's, 1924.
Deutsch, Helen, and Stella Hanau. *The Provincetown: A Story of the Theatre*. New York: Russell & Russell, [1931] 1972.
Eames, Emma. *Some Memories and Reflections*. New York: Appleton, 1927.
Flory, Julia Cone. *The Cleveland Playhouse: How It Began*. Cleveland: The Press of Western University, 1965.
"George Pierce Baker, a Memorial." New York: Dramatists Play Service, 1939.
Gillmore, Margalo, *Four Flights Up*. Boston: Houghton Mifflin, 1964.
Gould, Eleanor Cody, transcriber. *Charles Jehlinger in Rehearsal*. New York: American Academy of Dramatic Arts, 1968.
Hapgood, Hutchins. *A Victorian in the Modern World*. Seattle: University of Washington Press, 1939.
Hopkins, Arthur. *To a Lonely Boy*. Garden City, NY: Doubleday, Doran, 1937
Kinne, Wisner Payne. *George Pierce Baker and the American Theatre*. Cambridge: Harvard University Press, 1969.
Langner, Lawrence. *The Magic Curtain*. New York: Dutton, 1951.
Le Gallienne, Eva. *At 33*, New York: Longmans, Greer, 1934.<None>
_____. *With a Quiet Heart*. New York: Viking, 1953.

Leverenz, David. *Manhood and the American Renaissance*. Ithaca: Cornell University Press, 1989.
Marcaccio, Michael D. *The Hapgoods: The Earnest Brothers*. Charlottesville: University Press of Virginia, 1977.
Martin, George. *The Damrosch Dynasty: America's First Family of Music*. Boston: Houghton Mifflin, 1983.
McClintic, Guthrie. *Me and Kit*. Boston: Little, Brown, 1955.
Morley, Sheridan. *Gladys Cooper: A Biography*. Boston: Houghton Mifflin, 1983.
Murphy, Brenda. *American Realism and American Drama, 1880–1940*. Cambridge: Cambridge University Press, 1987.
O'Neill, Eugene. *Desire under the Elms*. New York: Wiley Publishing, 1976.
Pickford, Mary. *Sunshine and Shadow*. London: Heineman, 1956.
Ruff, Loren K. *Edward Sheldon*. Boston: Twayne, 1982.
Sergeant, Elizabeth Shepley. *Shadow Shapes, the Journal of a Wounded Woman*. Boston: Houghton Mifflin, 1920.
Sheaffer, Louis. *O'Neill, Son and Artist*. New York: Paragon House, 1990 [1973]
Sheehy, Helen. *Eva Le Gallienne: a Biography*. New York: Alfred A. Knopf, Inc., 1996.
Sprinchorn, Evert, Seaberg Quinn Jr., and Kenneth Peterson, eds. *August Strindberg, the Chamber Plays*, "Introduction." NY: E. F. Dutton, 1963.
Strauss, Gerald H. "John Drinkwater" from *Modern British Dramatists, Part I: A–L, 1900–1945*. Detroit: Gale Research, 1982.
Strindberg, August. "Motherlove," from *Plays from the Cynical Life*. Washington: University of Washington Press, 1994.
Valency, Maurice. *The Flower and the Castle*. New York: Macmillan, 1963.
Webster, Margaret. *The Same Only Different*. New York: Knopf, 1969, 287.

Plays by Sidney Howard discussed or mentioned in this volume:

Bewitched (with Edward B. Sheldon), typescript in Theatre Collection, Houghton Library, Harvard.
Casanova (translation of *Casanova* by Lorenzo De Azartis), New York: Brentano's, 1924
Half Gods, New York: Charles Scribner's Sons, 1930
The Last Night of Don Juan (translated from the original, by Edmond Rostand), typescript in Sidney Howard Collection in the Bancroft Library, University of California, Berkeley
Lucky Sam McCarver, New York: Charles Scribner's Sons, 1926
Madam, Will You Walk? New York: Dramatists' Play Service, 1955
Michael Auclair, Lexington, MA: Lexington Historical Society, 1924
Ned McCobb's Daughter, New York: Charles Scribner's Sons, 1926
Salvation, 1927, typescript in Sidney Howard Collection in the Bancroft Library, University of California, Berkeley
Sancho Panza (adaptation of the original, by Melchior Lengyel), typescript in Sidney Howard Collection in the Bancroft Library, University of California, Berkeley
The Silver Cord, New York: Samuel French, 1926
S.S. Tenacity (translation of "Le Paquebot Tenacity" by Charles Vildrac), in S. Marion Tucker, ed., *Modern Continental Plays*, New York: Harper and Bros.
Swords, New York: George H. Doran, 1921
They Knew What They Wanted, New York: Doubleday, Page and Co. 1925
Three Flights Up, Book of short stories: New York: Scribner's, 1924

Index

Abbott, George 74
Aglavaine and Sélysette (Maeterlinck) 104–105
Aherne, Brian 183, 212–213, 217, 226, 229, 234, 237–240, 242–243, 252–253, 255, 274
Anderson, John 161
Anglin, Margaret 91
"The Art of Acting" (Macgowan) 33–34
Atkinson, Brooks 169, 199, 240, 281

Bacon, Leonard 204–205
Baker, George Pierce 73–75, 96, 163–164
Bewitched (Howard/Sheldon) 56
Broun, Heywood 19
Brown, John Mason 167, 183, 261

Casanova (de Azertis) 145–146
Clark, Barrett 86–87, 161
Coleman, Jennifer 12, 41, 53–54, 71, 157–158, 234–236, 238; custody issues, 243–246, 265–269
Corbin, John 31, 37, 40
Cornell, Katherine 51
The Cranbrook Masque 78
Cromwell, John 155–156, 168–169

Damrosch, Polly 262–265
Desire Under the Elms (O'Neill) 60–62, 63, 152

Eames, Clare 9, 63, 77, 82, 87, 100–101; acting methods 32–33, 35, 106, 200–201; in *Aglavaine and Sélysette* 104–105; and Aherne 183, 212–213, 217, 226, 229, 234, 237–240, 242–243, 252–253, 255, 274; ambitions of 16–17, 44; Atkinson on 169, 199, 240; Broun on 19; Brown on 167; in *Candida* 51–52, 63; on *Casanova* 146; childhood 10–11; custody issues 243–246, 265–269; Corbin on 31, 37, 40; death of 271–275; divorce proceedings 234–241, 243–248, 265–269; domestic concerns 110, 112–118; early training and performances 13–15, 18; and Elsie Sergeant 102–103, 107; and Emilie Hapgood 109–110, 128–129, 112; Ervine on 240; in the Experimental Theatre 24–26, 29; in *Fashion* 35, 43; in *The First Fifty Years* 106–107; Gabriel on 38; Goodrich on 41, 43; Hackett on 99; Hammond on 50, 52; health concerns 66–67, 174–175; in *Hedda Gabler* 39–41, 46; in Hollywood 119–128, 147–148; Hornblow on 19–20, 22; Howard inheritance issues 130–135; Howard on 35–37, 39; intimacy issues 136–141, 264–265; Jennifer born 53–54; in *Juarez and*

Maximilian 196–198; as Lady Macbeth 36–38; Langner on 171; leaves Theatre Guild 193–195, 198; Le Gallienne on 41; in *The Little Angel* 50; in *Little Eyolf* 167–169; Lockridge on 240–241; *Lucky Sam* 155–158; MacGowan on 33; in *Man of Destiny* 167; marital difficulties 203–206, 211–233; in *Mary Stuart* 20–22; miscellaneous correspondence 44–50; 209–210; Morgan on 252; in *Ned McCobb's Daughter*, 199–200; plagiarism issues 154–155, 270–271; Rathbun on 199–200; romantic letters to Sidney, 111–112, 118, 202–203, 205; in *Rosita*, 124–125; in *S.S. Tenacity* 253–256; in *Sacred Flame* 240–241, 250–251; on *Sancho Panza* 110; *Scythia* incident 142–144; Sergeant on 32–33; *Silver Cord* 176–180, 184, 186, 191, 270–271; in *The Spook Sonata* 29, 31; on "Such Women" 146; *Swords* 91–100; with Theatre Guild 151, 169, 176; Walsh on 37–38; in *Wild Duck* 53; Wilson on 20–21; Woolcott on 22, 99, 104; Young on 32, 34–35, 50, 52, 53, 63, 169
Eames, Emma 10, 11, 12
English 47, 73–74, 163–164
Ervine, St. John 240
The Experimental Theatre 24–26, 31, 163

Fashion (Mowatt) 35
The First Fifty Years (Myers) 106–107

Gabriel, Gilbert W 38
Gillmore, Margalo 9, 15–16; 193
The Greenwich Village Players 18–19

Hackett, Francis 97, 99
Half Gods (Howard) 258–262
Hammond, Percy 50, 59
Hapgood, Emilie 108–110, 128–129
Hornblow, Arthur 19–20, 22, 51, 107
Howard, Helen 67–70, 88, 102, 112, 130–135, 184–186

Howard, Jean 67–68, 71, 109; inheritance issues 130–135
Howard, John 67, 70, 130
Howard, Sidney 63, 64, 100; ambitions of 79–81; on Baker 74–75; *Bewitched* 56–57; brother dies 81–82; *Casanova* 145–146; censorship issues 152–153; childhood 66–69; on Clare's death 271–273; on Clare's performances 35–37, 39, 43, 50, 51, 52, 106; on class 89–90; custody issues 243–246, 265–269; and Damrosch 262–265, 270, 276; death of 280–281; diary entries 276–279; divorce proceedings 234–241, 243–248, 265–269; domestic concerns 110, 112–118; education 70–75, 77; and the Experimental Theatre 26–29; *Half Gods* 258–262; and Hapgood 108–110, 128–129; in Hollywood 249–250, 256–257, 270; Howard inheritance issues 130–135; intimacy issues 136–141, 264–265; on Jennifer's birth 53–54, 71; as journalist 55, 85–86, 88–89, 114; legacy of 1; 280–281; *Lucky Sam* 155–167; MacGowan on 33; marital difficulties 203–206, 211–233; maternal relationship 68–70, 88, 102, 112, 184–186; methods of 60; miscellaneous correspondence 44–50; 209–210; *Ned McCobb's Daughter* 176, 180–183; and New Stagecraft 76–79, 85, 163; plagiarism issues 154–155, 270–271; post-war adjustments 85–87; *S.S. Tenacity* 103–104; *Sancho Panza* 108–110, 128–129; *Scythia* incident 142–144; and Sergeant 82–84, 85, 102–103; *Silver Cord* 176–180, 182, 183, 184, 186–192, 207–208; as soldier *Swords* 91–100; 65–66, 69, 81 on theater 163–166; with Theatre Guild 176–181; *They Knew What They Wanted* 58, 142, 152–154, 162
Hume, Samuel J. 75–78, 85, 154

Jehlinger, Charles 14–15, 105, 106, 164

Jones, Robert Edmund 23, 39–40, 48–49, 76, 157, 163
Juarez and Maximilian (Werfel) 196–198

Krutch, Joseph Wood 59–60, 188, 261

Langner, Lawrence 57, 171, 183
Le Gallienne, Eva 17, 40–41, 105, 172–173
Lexington (Howard) 154
Little Eyolf (Ibsen) 167–169
Lockridge, Richard 240–241
Lucky Sam McCarver (Howard) 155–167

Macgowan, Kenneth 23, 24, 33–34, 52, 103–104, 107
"The Man of Destiny" (Shaw) 167
Mantle, Burns 187–188
Moeller, Philip 196–198
Morgan, Charles 251
Morris, Mary 39, 78

Ned McCobb's Daughter (Howard) 176, 180, 181, 182–83, 199–200
The New Stagecraft 24, 75–76, 78, 79

O'Neill, Eugene 23, 29, 30, 61–62, 74, 163

Pemberton, Brock 92, 95, 96–97
Pickford, Mary 120, 126
A Proper Job (Aherne) 239
The Provincetown Players 24–25

Rathbun, Stephen 199–200

"Robert Edmond Jones: Poetic Artist of the New Stagecraft" (Black) 39

S.S. Tenacity (Howard) 103–104, 253–256
Sacred Flame (Maugham) 240–241
The Same, Only Different (Webster) 142
Sancho Panza (Lengyal) 108–110, 128–129
Sergeant, Elizabeth 32, 82–84, 85, 102–103, 107
The Silver Cord (Howard) 176–180, 182, 183, 184–192; in London 207–208; 270–271
The Spook Sonata (Strindberg) 29, 31–32, 35
"Such Women as Ellen Steele" (Howard) 146
Swords (Howard) 87, 91–100

The Theatre Guild 29, 57–58, 151, 169–171, 176–180; 193, 198
They Knew What They Wanted (Howard) 58, 142, 152–154, 162; compared to *Desire Under the Elms* 60–61; reviewed 59–60; in revival 1, 2; sold to Theatre Guild 29, 57

Walsh, Robert Gilbert 37–38
Watts, Richard, Jr. 162
Webster, Margaret 142
"Who Is the Best American Actress?" (Goodrich) 41–43
Wilson, Edmund 20–21
Woolcott, Alexander 22, 99, 104

Young, Stark 31–32, 34–35, 45, 50, 51, 53, 63, 104, 107, 146, 169, 188